FREE eGUIDE!

Enter this code at primagames.com/code to unlock your FREE eGuide:

8ENR-2PTW-U9FQ-SKV3

Mobile Friendly

Access your eGuide on any web-enabled device.

Searchable & Sortable

Quickly find the strategies you need.

Added Value

Strategy where, when, and how you want it.

Check Out Our Complete eGuide Library at primagames.com!

THE LEGEND OF
ZELDA™
Tri Force Heroes

CONTENTS

BECOMING A HERO — 3

Gameplay Mechanics — 4

HYTOPIA'S FAB AND DRAB — 8

The Fab — 8

The Drab — 10

ACCESSORIZE — 23

Tools of The Trade — 23

Link's Wardrobe — 25

Materials — 34

CLOTHING QUEST — 38

World 1: The Woodlands — 40

Level 1: Deku Forest — 40

Level 2: Buzz Blob Cave — 46

Level 3: Moblin Base — 50

evel 4: Forest Temple — 55

rld 2: Riverside — 60

l 1: Secret Fortress — 60

2: Abyss of Agony — 65

Cove of Transition — 70

ater Temple — 74

olcano — 80

g Trail — 80

ine — 85

mes — 89

— 92

rn — 96

— 96

— 100

— 104

— 109

World 5: Fortress — 114

Level 1: Sealed Gateway — 114

Level 2: Bomb Storage — 118

Level 3: Training Ground — 123

Level 4: The Lady's Lair — 128

World 6: The Dunes — 133

Level 1: Infinity Dunes — 133

Level 2: Stone Corridors — 137

Level 3: Gibdo Mausoleum — 142

Level 4: Desert Temple — 145

World 7: The Ruins — 150

Level 1: Illusory Mansion — 150

Level 2: Palace Noir — 155

Level 3: Lone Labyrinth — 160

Level 4: Grim Temple — 165

World 8: Sky Realm — 170

Level 1: Floating Garden — 170

Level 2: Deception Castle — 175

Level 3: Dragon Citadel — 180

Level 4: Sky Temple — 185

ODDS AND ENDS — 192

Challenges — 192

Levels — 197

Outfits — 219

Materials — 231

Coliseum — 238

BECOMING A FASHION HERO

Tri Force Heroes is a surprisingly challenging game, and if you want a better chance of overcoming its myriad obstacles, you're going to want to read this section of the guide.

Here you'll find a breakdown of all of the buttons in the game and what they do. We also go into detail about a multitude of the game's mechanics, so you can start the game off with a bit of an advantage.

CONTROLS

Circle Pad: Used to move Link around the game.

A Button: Pressing the A Button will pick up any objects that are able to be picked up, as well as your Doppels and your teammates. Press the A Button again to throw whatever you picked up. While in water, pressing the A Button will cause Link to shoot forward. This makes swimming a much faster experience, but you'll also burn through your energy gauge by using this ability.

B Button: Press the B Button to slash your sword. Hold the B Button to perform Link's signature spin attack.

X Button: Once you've spoken to the Photo Bro, you can press the X Button to take a picture while you're in a level. You can then upload that picture to the Miiverse to share with *Tri Force Heroes* players around the world.

Y Button: Pressing the Y Button will use whatever Sub-Weapon you have equipped. Holding the button will often allow you to hold your Sub-Weapon before firing it/unleashing it. This has a number of uses that completely depend on what Sub-Weapon you're using.

R Button and L Button: Pressing either the R Button or the L Button will make Link run in a straight line until you release the button, slash your sword, or hit a wall or enemy.

START & SELECT Buttons: Press the Start Button or Select Button to pause the game in both multiplayer and single-player.

Touchscreen: In single-player, tap a Doppel on the bottom screen to have Link take control of him. In multiplayer, clicking and holding your stylus on another player will move the camera over them, so you can get a good look at what they're up to and where they're at. This is perfect for strategizing during particularly tough puzzles.

Gameplay Mechanics

You'll find a breakdown of several of the game's mechanics in this section.

Single-Player

To start a single-player game, you'll need to enter the door on the right side of the castle foyer; if you've gone down the stairs, you've gone too far. It will be marked with a symbol of a single "person" in front of it, letting you know that this is for one player only.

Once you're inside, talk to the old man. He'll offer you two Doppels for your control. You can pick them up and throw them into each other's hands to make Totems. If you throw either or both of them onto a Triforce gateway, they'll automatically re-arrange so that they are each standing on a piece of the symbol.

Take note: You'll need to have the green Link selected in order to leave the single-player lobby. If you try and leave as either the red or blue Links, the guard will stop you, telling you that Doppels are not allowed to roam free outside of this room, except when in the Drablands.

Switching Characters

While playing in single-player, to replace the two other players you won't have, you'll be given two Doppels. You'll need to control the two Doppels and your Link to complete puzzles. The way to do this is by touching the box of the Link you want to control on the bottom screen.

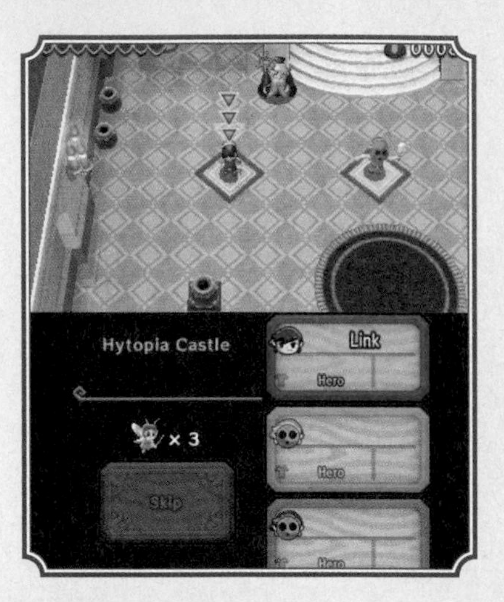

Try to keep track of where each Link is while you play. You'll sometimes have to make some quick switches to different Links, and knowing where each Link is will make those situations a lot easier.

Multiplayer

Naturally, multiplayer works differently than single-player. While the levels are all the same, how you tackle them is a very different experience. You can't take control of other Links when playing with other players, so you'll have to count on communication and planning to complete some of the game's tougher, more time-restricted puzzles.

Another key difference is that all three players can choose an Outfit before the level starts. This can allow for some pretty interesting Outfit combinations and strategies. We cover a lot of combinations and strategies in the "Clothing Quest" section of the guide.

To reach the multiplayer lobby, enter the door in the center of the castle foyer, which is marked with three "person" symbols, indicating that this room is for three players.

Once inside, head to the top-left corner of the room and talk to the old man. He'll present you with three options: Local Play, Online Play and Download Play. Select "Local Play" if you're in the same room as your friends and they also have a copy of the game. Select "Online Play" if your friends are in their respective homes, or if you want to play with anyone else online. Select "Download Play" if you're in a room with your friends, but they don't actually own their own copies of the game. From there, the old man will ask you to create a team or join one. If you host, you'll need the other players to select "Join a team", but if your friend is hosting, you'll need to be the one to select "Join a team".

Once you're in a room, you'll need to talk to the old man to disconnect from the room and to leave the multiplayer lobby. If you try to walk out while playing in multiplayer, the guard will stop you in your tracks.

Communicating in Multiplayer

If you're playing with friends who aren't with you in person, you can tap the various callouts on the bottom screen to try and communicate with your teammates. The more you tap them, the bigger they get, so don't be afraid to really lay into them.

Lucky Lobby Ball

One final note about the multiplayer lobby: You can try using the R Button to ram various spots of the walls in this room. If you hit the right spot (and it changes every time), the Lucky Lobby Ball will fall from the ceiling. Hitting the ball will play various songs from different Zelda titles. If you keep hitting the ball and keep it from touching the ground, the music will continue and you'll rack up Rupees. Once the ball finally touches the ground, you'll be told how many hits you got on the Lucky Lobby Ball and how many Rupees you earned. The more you hit the ball, the more Rupees you rack up!

Coliseum

On the far-right side of the foyer, down the stairs and into the dimly-lit lobby, you'll find the Coliseum, the place heroes go to test their strength and skills.

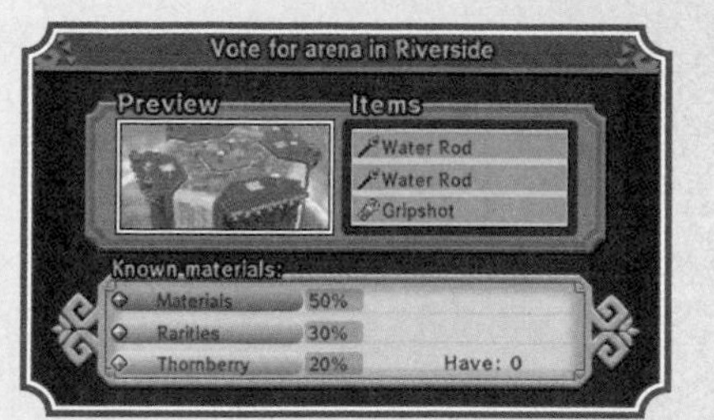

You can fight against one or two of your friends here for glory, Rupees, and some Coliseum-only Materials. There are a total of eight zones to fight in inside the Coliseum, each one representing a world from the Drablands, and each with Sub-Weapons and elements distinct to that world.

Your goal in the Coliseum is to reduce your opponents' Heart Containers down to zero, all while keeping yours as full as possible. Your sword, Bows, Bombs, Fire Gloves, and the Magic Hammer are all used to damage your opponent, while other Sub-Weapons allow you to stun them or get you closer to them. You can also throw your opponent off the edge of a platform to deal them damage.

While you fight in any zone, if you're only playing against one other player, you'll have to avoid a Wallmaster that will chase you or your opponent around the room. It will wiggle its fingers, then slap its hand down to the ground, crushing any Link underneath it. Getting crushed by the Wallmaster is an instant KO, meaning you lose a life. During the last 30 seconds of a match, the Wallmaster will begin pursuing any player, not just the first-place player.

You'll need to win in the Coliseum to have a chance at each zone's rare, golden Material. You only have a 20% chance of getting each Material, so make sure to win on each stage A LOT.

Challenges

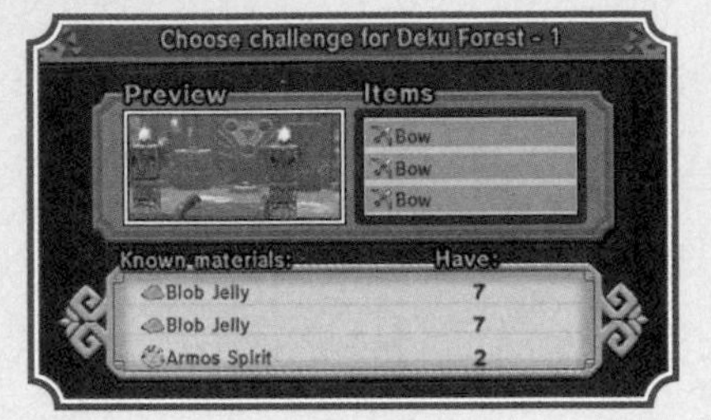

Once you've played through all four levels in a world, you'll unlock twelve additional challenges for that world—three for each level. These challenges vary from having less health to playing the level again (but this time in the dark), to having to carry an orb all the way through to the level's end. Each one will offer different Materials as rewards, some of which can only be obtained by completing challenges.

You can keep track of the challenges you've completed and how many more you need to complete for each level by looking at the map on the upper-right corner of the single-player and multiplayer lobbies.

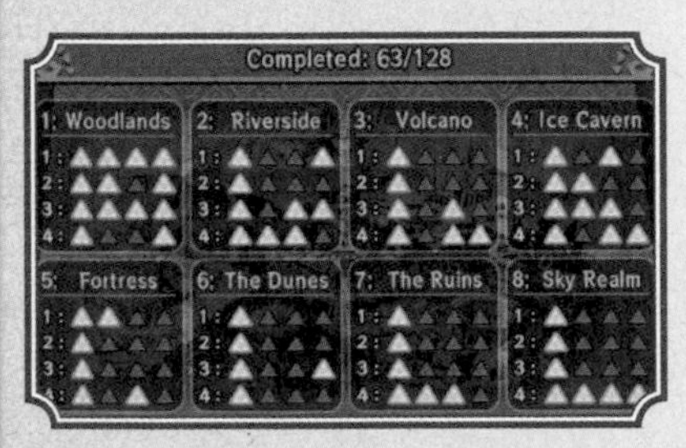

The Triforce gateways indicate how many challenges you've completed, while the darkened symbols show what remains to be completed. Use this map to keep track of your progress and use it to beat all 128 challenges and levels in the game!

Sub-Weapons

Every level in the game has Sub-Weapons for you and your co-Links to use. These items are fixed and are used specifically to deal with the challenges that are thrown your way during the level. When you complete the level, the Sub-Weapons are taken away from you and you'll start the next level without them, free to pick up any new Sub-Weapons this new level offers you.

You can see what Sub-Weapons each level is going to have by taking a look at the Level Selection screen. Each level you highlight will give you details on Materials and which Sub-Weapons you'll have access to. This will help you pick an appropriate Outfit for the level and help you track down Materials you are looking for.

Each Sub-Weapon does something different, and the way to use your Sub-Weapons is to press or hold the Y Button. Experiment with the different Sub-Weapons to get a feel for how they work. There are always tricks you can find with each Sub-Weapon, so make sure to try out all sorts of techniques.

Outfits

Outfits are the bread and butter of *Tri Force Heroes*. Sure, you can get through the game without using any Outfits, but you'll be missing out on half the fun of the game!

Each Outfit has a different and usually beneficial effect. Some of them have general effects that will benefit you and your teammates no matter the circumstances, like the Legendary Dress making Hearts drop more frequently, or the Sword Suit making anyone who wears it do twice the amount of damage per sword swing. Some Outfits, however, are specific to certain circumstances. The Duneswalker Duds keep you from sinking into the quicksand that almost exclusively appears in world 6. The Boomeranger will increase the size of your Boomerang, provided you have access to one in the level you're playing. You'll need to look at the Sub-Weapons and the level you've chosen, then gauge what the best Outfit would be to help you get through as easily as possible.

The way to make Outfits is by gathering Materials, which only appear at the end of each level (Which includes completing challenges; though some Materials can only be earned by buying them in town or winning in the Coliseum). Each Outfit requires a fixed number of Materials and Rupees to create, and most Outfits will only appear as you complete worlds in the Drablands. Once you have the required items and Rupees, speak with Madame Couture in town to have her craft it for you.

Once you've made an Outfit, you'll need to select it during the Level Selection screen, after you've picked which level you're going to take on. You can use any Outfit for any level without penalty or restriction, but as we said before, some Outfits work on certain levels better than others. Make sure you read the "Clothing Quest" section of this guide for suggestions, and take your time to consider the pros and cons of each Outfit in your wardrobe.

The Town

The Town is the hub you'll need to visit frequently between levels. This is the place you'll find Madame Couture's boutique for all of your Outfit needs; the Street Merchant, who sells Materials (some of which can only be purchased from him); the Photo Bro, who will give you a camera to take pictures during a level, which can then be uploaded to the Miiverse (press the X Button to snap a photo during the level); and the Daily Riches Shop mini-game, which will give you the chance to open a treasure chest daily with the possibility of finding a Material of the shop owner's choosing.

Another thing to note about the Daily Riches shop: Any time you pick the wrong box, you'll be given a Material called a "Freebie". Keep this in mind, because you'll need ten of them to craft an Outfit that will only appear in Madame Couture's boutique after you lose the Daily Riches mini-game five times.

Make sure to pop in to Town regularly to check out new Outfits, to look for new Street Merchant Materials, and to play the Daily Riches mini-game.

Important Items

There are a few items of importance that you'll need to know about if you're new to the Zelda series.

RUPEES

Rupees are the gems that pop out of enemies, destructible objects, and treasure chests. You'll need these in order to make Outfits and purchase Materials from the Street Merchant. Outfits cost quite a few Rupees, so make sure to grab any Rupees you lay your eyes on.

HEARTS

Hearts are essential to keep you alive in any Zelda game, but it's especially true for *Tri Force Heroes*. Picking up a Heart will refill one whole Heart Container. (You can see your Heart Containers on the top-left corner of the top screen.)

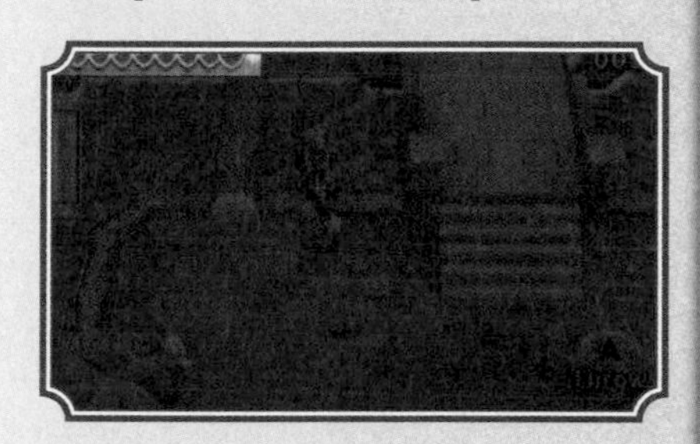

While playing multiplayer, your Heart Containers are shared, so any damage any Link takes is shared between all three Links. That's why picking up Hearts as often as possible is the key to staying alive. Even though your Heart Containers aren't shared with anyone in single-player, the levels are challenging enough that you'll find yourself burning through your Heart Containers faster than you could've imagined. Make sure not to let a Heart slip by whenever you have a chance to grab one.

TREASURE CHESTS

You will find treasure chests scattered around each level of the game. Opening a chest will yield Hearts or Rupees. Always make a point to open treasure chests when you see them, because they will often have multiple Hearts or large quantities of Rupees.

Hytopia's Fab and Drab

This is the chapter to take a look at all of the characters and enemies you'll find during your trip through *Tri Force Heroes.*

The Fab

King Tuft

The King of Hytopia's daughter was cursed by The Lady and all of her inglorious fashion! It is the king that seeks three stylish heroes to defeat The Lady and break the curse on his land.

Princess Styla

Princess Styla's beautiful looks and impeccable sense of style have been cursed by The Lady. Now Princess Styla is doomed to wear gaudy tights for the rest of her life. That is, unless some stylish heroes can break The Lady's curse first!

Madame Couture

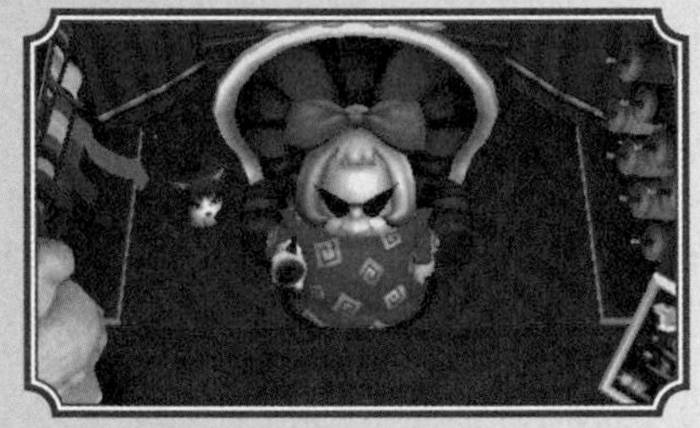

The fashionista and expert designer of Hytopia. Madame Couture will help you defeat The Lady by designing outfits imbued with magical powers. If you want to break Princess Styla's curse, you're going to need to get yourself a new wardrobe and Madame Couture is just the woman to help you.

Street Merchant

A Material salesman who is profiting off of these troubled times. He'll sell you Materials, but at a high price. Just because the kingdom's cursed, doesn't mean EVERYONE needs to be miserable, right?

Photo Bro

While most Hytopians are in fear of The Lady and her curse, the Photo Bro seeks to capture every moment of it. It's only when we look back that we truly understand how great our experiences were, even when they involve a fashionable witch, her army of monsters, and a terrible curse. Ah yes, the memories...

Faux Hero

When the king called for stylish heroes, the Faux-Hero answered the call dutifully and without fear! And then he was promptly rejected and left to sulk out in front of the castle. Many have courage, but only a few have the style necessary to save the kingdom. Better luck next time, huh pal?

Owner of the Daily Riches

Every kingdom in peril needs an entertaining diversion for all its citizens to unload their burdens, and the owner of the Daily Riches is just the fellow to provide such a distraction. Visitors can come and play his treasure chest mini-game to earn Materials, and they can do so completely for free! What a charitable guy!

Sir Combsly

Devoted to his king, Sir Combsly spends his time filtering out the fab from the drab. He's on the front lines in the hunt for the three stylish heroes who have been spoken of in legend. He won't let any but the true heroes of style step beyond the castle's foyer.

Doppel Master

The one who empowers the Doppels to be at Link's beck and call, the Doppel Master is the maestro of all things Doppel.

The Drab

The Soldiers

There are an awful lot of Soldiers in this game and several of them share the same characteristics, but different armor. We'll break down what you can expect when you run into one of these guys, but we'll keep the descriptions here, instead of listing them under their pictures.

Most Soldiers are experts at blocking your attacks with either their swords or shields. A few exceptions to this are the Bomb Soldiers, Spear Throwing Soldiers, and Ball & Chain Soldiers. If you can get in close to them, you can give them a good smacking with your sword, but the challenge, specifically with Ball & Chain Soldiers, is actually reaching them.

The best way to deal with the attack-deflecting Soldiers is to steal their shields with a Gripshot, stun them with the Gust Jar or, if you're playing multiplayer, have one of your friends distract them while you move in behind them.

Another good technique for dealing with any Soldiers holding a sword or a shield is to position a Doppel behind them, then draw their attention with one of your Links. As soon as they come running, switch to the Doppel behind them and slash them in the back. They'll immediately change their focus to their new attacker, which is when you switch Links and slash their backs again. Repeat this process until they are defeated.

GREEN SWORD SOLDIER

BLUE SWORD SOLDIER

SPEAR THROWING SOLDIER

SILVER BALL & CHAIN SOLDIER

GOLD BALL & CHAIN SOLDIER

BOMB SOLDIER

SKY SWORD SOLDIER

SKY SHIELD SOLDIER

SKY SPEAR SOLDIER

SKY BOMB SOLDIER

SKY BALL & CHAIN SOLDIER

SKY FIRE CHAIN SOLDIER

Humanoid-Type Enemies

AERALFOS

These obnoxious flying enemies are some of the most challenging in the game. They'll flap about in the air, sending down small tornadoes as projectiles at you. Eventually they'll swoop in on you and begin a three-hit combo. This is your chance to strike! You'll need to hit them before they swing a third time, then back off. If you have access to a Magic Hammer and the Hammerwear in a level with these flapping foes, you can smash them in a single hit when they start their combo. Otherwise, you'll have to take your time and hit them as they fly down and begin their combo.

SUPER AERALFOS

Despite its name, the Super Aeralfos isn't too different from the Aeralfos, with exceptions of its color and its ability to unleash a pretty mean fire attack on unsuspecting Links. Other than those two things, you can use the same strategies on a Super Aeralfos as you can a normal one.

SPEAR THROWING MOBLIN

These fellas are a bit of a pain. They like to keep a good distance away from you and yours while they unleash a volley of spears at you. The spears themselves are easy enough to dodge, IF you're paying attention. But sometimes you'll be in a fight with three or four other enemies and this guy will start throwing spears at you from the top of the screen, out of your field of vision. Once you've cleared out those enemies and then made a beeline to the Moblin, it's easy-peasy, but before then you might feel like you're the world's most famous juggler who has been asked to juggle two chainsaws, three torches, and an elephant. Yes, they can be that irritating.

ICE WIZZROBE

Wizzrobes are irritating enemies in pretty much every Zelda game, but surprisingly, they're pretty easy to deal with in this game. For the uninitiated, Wizzrobes are wizards that will disappear and reappear on other points of the map. When they reappear, they'll unleash a wave of energy and, in this game, that energy is a freezing ice wave. Once they've shot out an ice wave, they'll linger for a good, long while before teleporting again and repeating the entire process. The ice beam is incredibly easy to dodge and Ice Wizzrobes almost only show up when there are no other enemies BUT Ice Wizzrobes. You won't have to juggle a bunch of different enemies while trying to deal with these icy nuisances. The only real catch to these enemies is that they'll appear at different heights, meaning you'll need to make a Totem of the appropriate height to reach them.

STALFOS

Now these enemies will really give you a headache. Stalfos are jumping, bone-throwing skeletons that will dodge most attacks you throw their way. The only real ways to damage them are by backing them into a corner and then unleashing a maelstrom of sword swipes; by stunning them with the Gust Jar, Gripshot, or Boomerang (though they tend to dodge the Boomerang as much as the sword); or by turning their brittle bones into dust with the Magic Hammer.

GIBDO

Gibdo is pretty much just a mummified Stalfos. It'll attack more relentlessly than Stalfos and it can take more damage, but if you use the Gripshot or Fire Gloves to remove its bandages, it will quite literally become Stalfos.

REDEAD

These are the scariest enemies in the game, bar none! They'll walk around an area slowly, dig into the ground, and then pop back out and let out a blood-curdling scream that will freeze any Link near them dead in his tracks. The ReDead will then charge toward the Link, wrap around him, and begin draining his Heart Containers until it is knocked off or until Link is knocked out. Creepy… These enemies only show up in groups, which can make for a true nightmare as you try to dodge all of their screams. Your best bet is to take them out one at a time and stay a good bit away from them whenever they dig into the ground. If you're in single-player and a ReDead freezes you, you'll need to immediately switch to a different Link. If you're in multiplayer, you'll need one of your teammates to immediately hit the ReDead with a Sub-Weapon to stun it—sword slashes just won't do.

HINOX

These big, lumbering, one-eyed gorillas will toss Bombs at you whenever they get the chance. They're not too terribly difficult, however. Just pick up their Bombs, slap a big "Return to Sender" sticker on them, and then, well, return to sender! They can take a lot of damage, but they don't do much besides throw Bombs at you.

Monster-Type Enemies

BLOB

Blobs are painfully easy to defeat. They'll just sort of waddle around an area. If they touch you, they'll damage you, but that's their only real defense mechanism.

BUZZ BLOB

Buzz Blobs have the same behavior as normal Blobs, but their defense mechanism is that they are electrified. If you hit them with your sword, expect a nice jolt of electricity. Instead of using the direct approach, hit them with a Sub-Weapon to attack them from a distance or to stun them. You can safely attack them with your sword when they are stunned.

TEKTITE

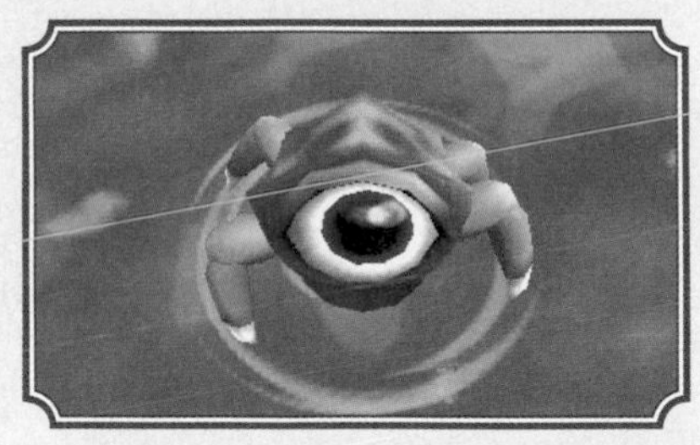

The one-eyed, hopping pondskimmers won't do much to attack you, except jump onto you occasionally. They're as happy on water as they are on land. Just give them a few sword slashes and they'll be good and done.

TOTEM DEKU

Totem Dekus are really tall Deku Scrubs that spit Deku Nuts at you from a distance. If you approach them, they'll dive down into the ground to keep you from damaging them. You'll need to create a Totem at the same height as the Deku, and then use a Sub-Weapon to stun them or damage them at a distance, the cheeky little plants that they are.

RAT

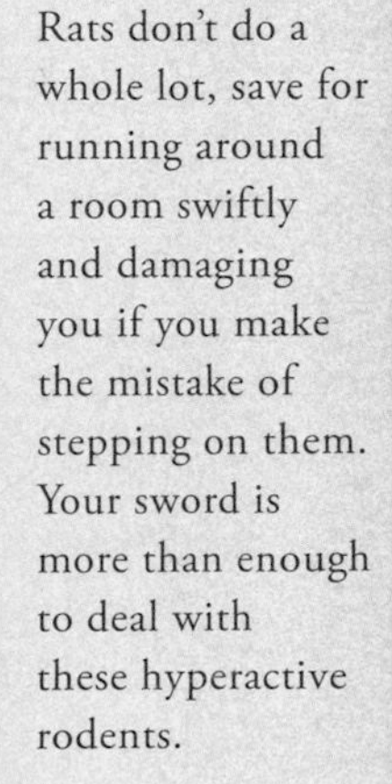

Rats don't do a whole lot, save for running around a room swiftly and damaging you if you make the mistake of stepping on them. Your sword is more than enough to deal with these hyperactive rodents.

ROPE

These slithering reptiles are a bit like Rats, in that they just sort of roam around a room, waiting for unsuspecting individuals to walk into their field of view. If you do end up in front of them, that's where the key difference between them and Rats becomes all too apparent. They'll lunge straight toward you as soon as they lay their thin, cold eyes on you. Let us tell you, they can really move if they're looking to take a bite out of a Link. You can easily avoid them by moving out of their path, but if you're not paying attention, they'll definitely get a nibble or two out of you.

SKULLROPE

Skullropes are just the Rope's more gothic older brother. Like their name suggests, they have skulls over their heads, but these slithering reptiles have a few extra tricks up their sleeves. (Or scales? Wherever they hide things is where you'll find the tricks.) Instead of just milling about and hitting you if you're clumsy enough to walk into them, Skullropes like to divebomb their prey. They'll leap into the air and come down on top of inattentive Links. This is made much worse if you're in multiplayer and you've made a Totem. The Skullrope will hit every Link on the way down for a whopping three full Heart Containers! Don't ignore these fiends whenever you see them in a level; that skull definitely isn't just for show.

KEESE

These pesky, winged rodents also have a good deal in common with Rats and Ropes. They'll perch or just sort of flap about until you approach them. That's when the fun happens. They'll start flapping their way toward you persistently until they get to take a nibble of Link. What makes these enemies a nuisance is that they usually like to hang out when you're on a small, moving platform or a narrow pathway. Their favorite pastime is knocking Links into the unholy abyss in any level, so be alert whenever you lay eyes on one of these flappy bloodsuckers.

FIRE KEESE

Fire Keese are Keese that are on fire. The name truly says it all! The difference with Fire Keese is that they'll light any Link on fire that comes into direct contact with them, or if a Link hits one with his sword. You'll need to put out its flames with the Gust Jar, stun it, or defeat it at a distance with another Sub-Weapon.

ICE KEESE

Ice Keese are almost identical to Fire Keese, except that they freeze you if you hit them with your sword or let them touch you. You'll need to stun them with a Sub-Weapon or use one to defeat them at a distance if you want to avoid becoming a Linksicle.

CHASUPA

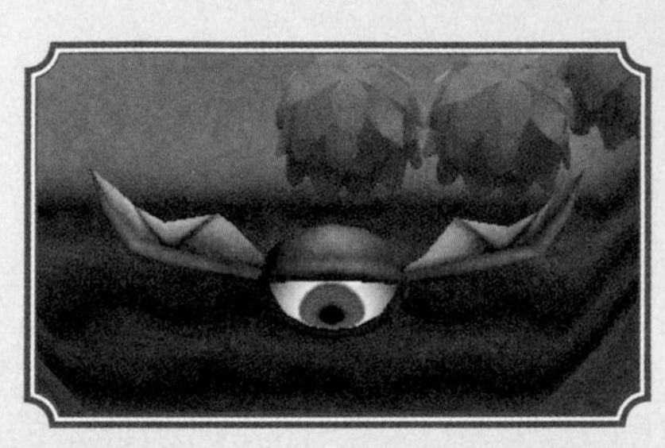

Chasupas are just creepy, one-eyed Keese. They move a bit more erratically than Keese do, but they're still defeated just as easily. Give them a few swats with your sword and they'll be defeated with no problems at all.

TERRORPIN

These terrible turtles will deflect any attack with your sword, no matter how determined you are. Instead, you'll need to flip them either by blowing up a Bomb near them or slamming your Magic Hammer next to them. This will flip them on their back momentarily, and once that happens, they'll be as helpless as a turtle. On its back. Because it literally will be. You know what we're saying!

HARDHAT BEETLE (BLUE)

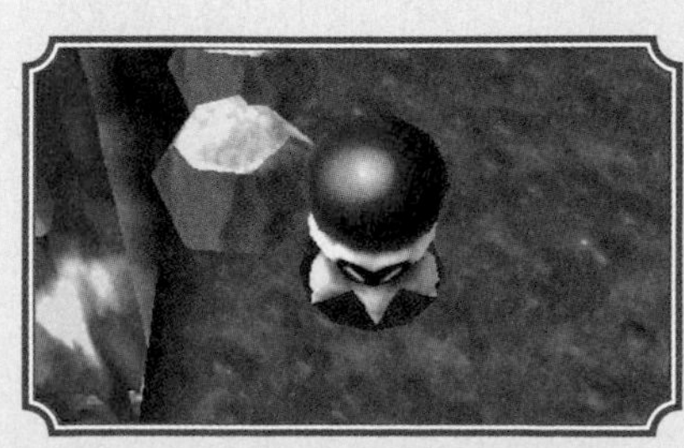

Blue Hardhat Beetles are like the bouncy cousins of the Terrorpin. They'll slowly inch toward you and they'll deflect any sword attacks. The key differences are that you don't need to flip them and when they deflect your attacks or if they touch you, they'll bounce you backwards.

They specialize in bouncing you off of platforms and into other enemies. Lucky for you, even though they bounce you back when you hit them with your sword, you're still doing damage to them, so keep up the assault! Just make sure to keep track of where you're at, to avoid being bounced into anything unsavory.

HARDHAT BEETLE (RED)

The red versions of the Hardhat Beetles are the same as the blue ones, but they are also on fire. You'll need to stun them or put out their flames with a Sub-Weapon to be able to hit them, but they're pretty much the same as their blue counterparts once the fire is gone.

KODONGO

Kodongos are speedy little dinos that love to breathe fire in straight lines. They're just as comfortable in lava as they are out of it, so when you encounter them, don't be surprised if you see them camping out inside a pool of liquid, hot magma. Once they're in your reach, just hit them with your sword and you're good to go.

WATER TEKTITE

Water Tektites share very little with their one-eyed older brothers. Sure, they can stand on water, but that's pretty much all they have in common. That's also pretty much all they do in general. They'll skate around the water and you'll take damage if they touch you, but a single slash from your sword will do away with them.

GYORM

Gyorms are shell-dwelling crustaceans who love to hide when trouble comes a-knocking. You'll need to get a good distance away from them, and then Gripshot them to pull them out of their highly protective shells.

KEELEON

Keeleons love to fly in the air and spit Bombs at you. They're pesky during intense fights, but they aren't particularly challenging themselves. Making a Totem or using the Water Rod below them will allow you get on their level and give them a good thrashing. Just keep an eye on those Bombs!

FIRE KEELEON

Fire Keeleons can really give you a hard time. They'll fly in the air like their Bomb-spewing cousins, but instead of spitting Bombs at you, they'll spit fire at you. And, of course, if you touch the fire, you'll go racing around the room until it goes out. You'll want to either steer completely clear of these foes until you've cleared every other enemy off the field, or you'll want to challenge them immediately. You'll need to put out these char-broiled foes' fire with a Gust Jar before you can hit them directly.

WATER OCTOROK

Water Octoroks are an awful lot like Totem Dekus, but instead of being tall and plant-like, they're short and live in the water. You can use a Water Rod to pull them out of the water at any point, but if you don't have one handy, you'll need to stun them with another Sub-Weapon when they pop their heads up out of the water. Just watch out for the rocks they like to spit at their enemies.

CROW

Crows like to wait for you to come by before they swoop in and attack relentlessly. Just think of them as over-confident Keese. You'll need to try and take them out as soon as possible to keep them from badgering you incessantly. Other than their swooping tactics, they don't have much in the way of offensive capabilities.

VULTURE

Like the Crows, the Vulture is nearly identical to its avian brethren. Vultures tend to be more erratic and persistent than its cousins, but not much else is different.

LEEVER

A classic Zelda enemy, the Leever shows up in sandy areas where it can burrow into the ground and pop up in other areas of the map. They'll spin around rapidly, but other than that, there isn't much to them. Reaching them while they whiz around the room can be a pain, but unless they touch you directly, they have no offensive capabilities.

Just stun them or give them a proper beating with your sword to stop these dizzying pests from bouncing around the room.

KARAT CRAB

Karat Crabs are sort of like sand Ropes, but they are far more persistent. If you're lined up with them, whether to the north, south, east, or west, they'll charge at you and they won't stop until you get out of their range. They also like to hide under sand and bump into unsuspecting Links.

HOKKUBOKKU

Not only are their names weird, the way they fight is too. Their bodies are made up of ball-like segments. When you hit one of them, they go bouncing all over the room at high speed, making them incredibly difficult to dodge. You'll need to knock each one of its segments out from under its head, then hit its head directly in order to damage it. A handful of hits and Hokkubokku will be finished.

DEADROCK

Now these are some pesky enemies. Any time you hit a Deadrock, it will turn to stone, making it completely invulnerable to any follow-up attacks. Well, it would if you didn't have a Magic Hammer handy. Whenever it turns to stone, turn that stone into rubble with your Hammer.

HELMASAUR

Helmasaurs are bothersome little pests to say the least. Their helmets make them impossible to damage from the front, so your only options are to attack from the back or remove their helmets. You can remove their helmets with the Gripshot, so long as you're pointed directly at their heads. Once the helmet is off, they'll be little more than Rats.

LIFE LIKE

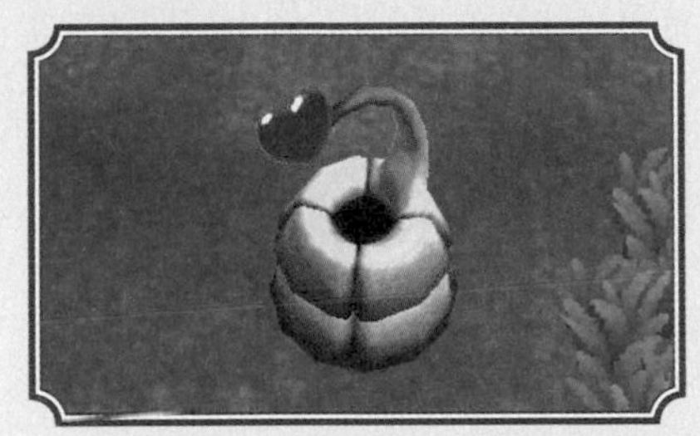

These spongy anglers are about as devastating as a ReDead if you don't have friends with quick reflexes. Every so often, you'll see a lone Heart sitting on the ground. You'll think to yourself, "Well, I do have an empty Heart Container, so why don't I grab this lone Heart and fill it up?" That's the moment the Life Like has you! It'll pop out of the ground and begin draining your life away, unless you switch Links or have a teammate hit it. Life Likes are tricky, while simultaneously simple. They need to reach you to eat you, and a well-placed Bomb in their center will defeat them instantly. But the second you find yourself inside their squishy, spongy maws is when you're in for a world of trouble.

MORTH

Morths aren't very common in this game. They mostly hang out in sandy areas and they don't actually have the capacity to deal damage to you. What they do have is the ability to slow you down, which, if you're on quicksand or facing a lot of enemies, can be a pretty hefty burden. If you're in multiplayer, have a friend hit them off of you. If you're in single-player, swap to another Link. Just don't let them linger.

SKULLFISH

Skullfish are water-based enemies that like to throw themselves onto land if it means dealing you damage. If they're in the water, they'll torment you relentlessly. If you're feeling safe on a platform, expect them to launch themselves at you. You can use a Water Rod to pull them out of the water, or hit them with your sword when they finally decide to lunge at you.

SANDFISH

Sandfish are exactly the same as Skullfish, except they swim around in quicksand. The strategies are the same—pull them up with a Water Rod or wait for them to lunge at you to defeat them.

MINI FREEZARD

Mini Freezards don't do much but obscure your path—that is, until you hit them. One swing of your sword and the Mini Freezards will go bouncing around a room wildly. If they come into contact with you, you'll be frozen solid! You can bounce them away from you with another sword slash, but you'll have to make sure your timing is spot on.

FREEZARD

Freezards don't move; they just stay in one place, breathing ice breath that will freeze any Links who get caught in it. A simple fireball from your Fire Gloves will make short work of them.

Ghosts and Spectral Enemies

GHINI

Ghinis don't do much except fly around and pester you. If they come into contact with you, they'll deal damage, but that's the extent of their damage capabilities. When you hit them with your sword, they'll disappear and reappear somewhere else in the area, making them a bit tricky to defeat.

POE (WHITE)

Poes are like slow Ghinis that don't teleport. They'll fly around a room, but they're easy to pin down. Two sword slashes and they'll be dealt with, no problem.

POE (RED, BLUE, OR GREEN)

Colored Poes are a bit more challenging to deal with. You can only hit each type of colored Poe with a Link that matches its color (Red Link hits a red Poe, blue Link hits a blue Poe, and Green Link hits a green Poe). Generally when these foes show up, it means trouble. You'll almost exclusively deal with colored Poes under pretty challenging circumstances, so take their appearance as a warning of things to come.

LANTERN POE

You can't actually damage a Lantern Poe directly. They'll light the area around them in dark rooms. The way to defeat them is by lighting all the torches in the room they are in. Once you do, they'll just sort of pop and disappear.

PRANKSTER POE

Never has there been a more irritating enemy in the whole of the Zelda-verse! These Link-faced jerks attack by picking up Links and throwing them into the nearest pit. When you hit them, they'll immediately appear behind you. If you're not quick enough to hit them, you can try to run, but they won't stop chasing you until they have you. They're not hard to defeat, but once you're in their arms, it's almost a guarantee that you're going to be thrown off of your platform. Infuriating!

KEY BANDIT POE

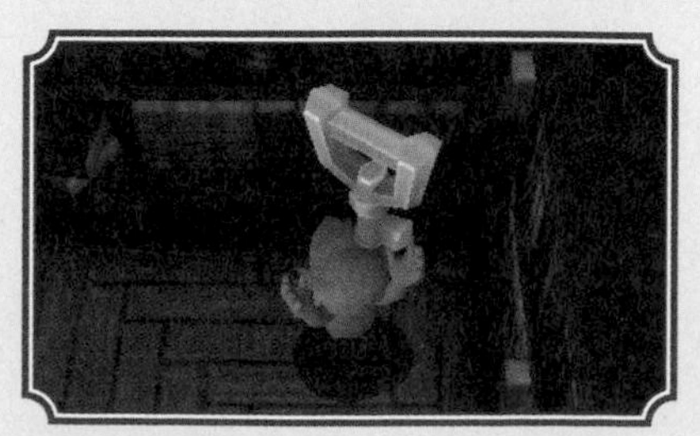

Key Bandit Poes love keys. In fact, they will do everything in their power to get their hands on their beloved keys whenever they lose them. Just know that if these guys are around, grabbing a key means you'll be attacked relentlessly until they either have their key back or you defeat them.

Trap Systems and Harmless Enemies

MINI-MARGO

The traps are pretty simple. You're not likely to get hit by them if you observe the trails that they follow along the ground. To defeat them, you need only throw a Bomb into their center.

BEAMOS

Beamos use their singular eye to search around the room for any Links that they can zap. Unlike their appearances in previous Zelda titles, if you make a Totem and get on their level, you can hit them with your sword or your Sub Weapons and defeat them. You'll need to watch out after you've defeated them. They'll begin rolling toward you and flashing, ready and waiting to explode. Just keep track of that rotating eye to avoid getting zapped!

TOTEM ARMOS

Totem Armos aren't really enemies so much as they are mounts for you and other enemies to ride. They'll hop around the room, stomping anyone who is unlucky enough to get under foot. While being controlled by an enemy, the Totem Armos will jump high into the air and smash down to the ground whenever they are near a Link. Once their rider has been defeated, the Totem Armos will spin around violently towards you and then explode.

WALLMASTER

Wallmasters only show up in challenges and the Coliseum and there's a good reason for that: They are terrible and powerful. They'll float over a Link momentarily, wiggle their fingers, and then swat down to the ground. If they manage to hit a Link, they'll KO him instantly. You can hit a Wallmaster while it's on the ground, but it will just come back after being knocked out, giving you only the most temporary of respite. Keep your eyes on the Wallmaster's fingers to avoid getting crushed!

SQUIDDY

Squiddy is harmless. Hitting Squiddy will force it to drop Rupees and Hearts. The more you hit it, the more it will drop, but it will also pick up speed with every hit. If you manage to hit it enough times without letting it sit on the ground for more than a second, Squiddy will explode into a big pile of Rupees and Hearts. Now get out there and give ol' Squiddy a good thrashing! Really, when you think about it, you're the monster in Squiddy's eyes.

Mini-Bosses

ELECTRIC BLOB KING

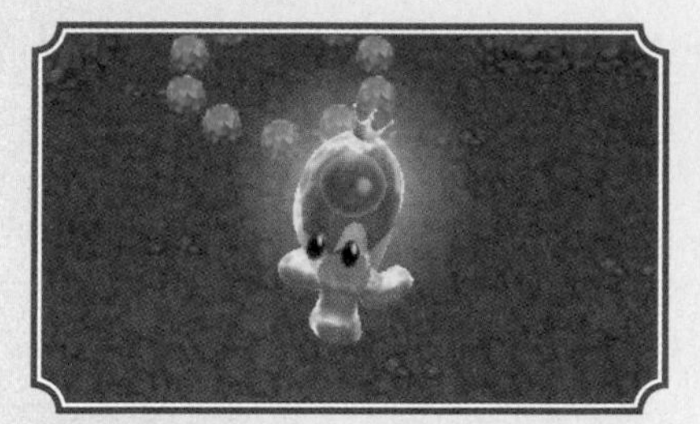

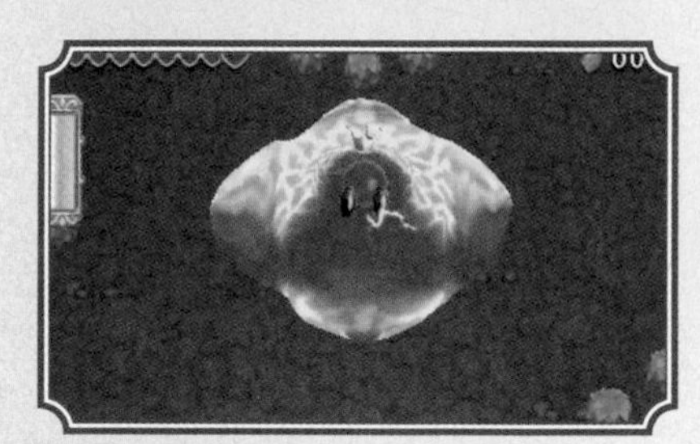

The Electric Blob King is the leader of the Buzz Blobs and really tries to prove it. It has the ability to shoot out massive amounts of electricity from its tendrils, and hitting it with your sword will only leave your hair standing on end.

ELECTRIC BLOB QUEEN

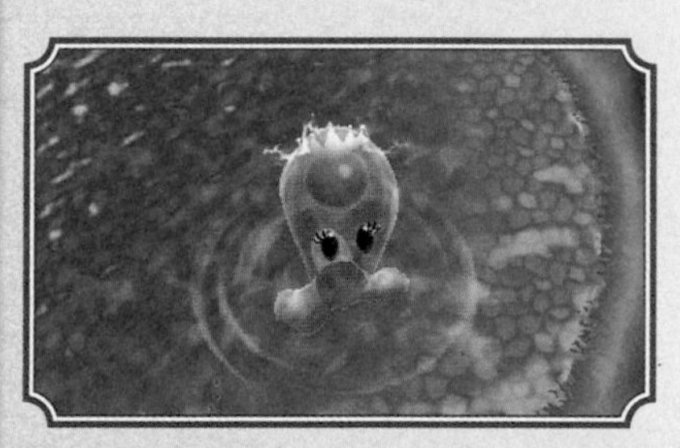

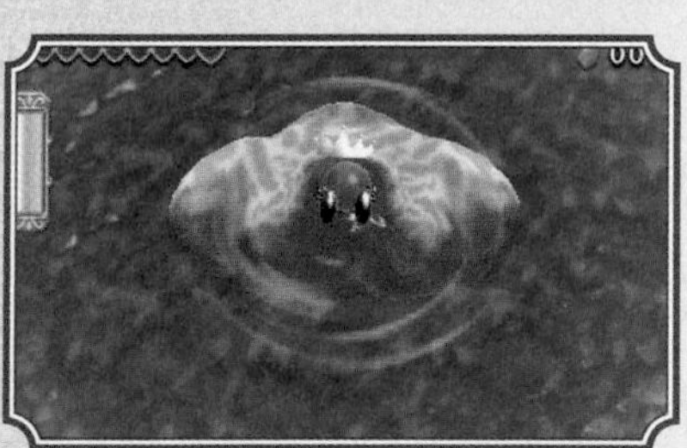

The Electric Blob Queen is very similar to its kingly counterpart. The key difference is the fact that it's standing in a pool of water. Whenever it shoots out electricity, it electrifies the whole pool. You'll have to be clever if you want to defeat it.

LI'L HINOX

The youngest of the Hinox Brothers, Li'l Hinox actually happens to be the most pesky of the bunch. The Hinox Brothers love tossing Bombs furiously, but where Li'l Hinox differs is the size of the Bombs it likes tossing. Instead of the normal, small Bombs, Li'l Hinox will throw a massive, megaton Bomb. Just don't stand too close, or you'll get a face full of fire!

HINOX THE ELDER

Hinox the Elder isn't much different from a normal Hinox. The key differences are that it throws Bombs from a minecart and it throws them much faster than your normal Hinox.

HINOX THE ELDEST

Hinox the Eldest is just like its younger brother, Hinox the Elder. You'll face Hinox the Eldest while riding in a minecart. It loves throwing Bombs—perhaps you should follow suit?

FREEZLORD

As its name implies, Freezlord is a giant Freezard, ice breathing, sliding, and all. It doesn't stray too far from the center of the room, but if you step into the icy pool of water surrounding it, prepare to catch hypothermia!

VULTURE VIZIER

This fight is painful. It's surprising that Vulture Vizier is just a mini-boss when you're actually fighting it! You'll have to fight this beast while balancing on an all-too-delicate platform, one that will gladly dump you into the abyss below it if you fail to keep it balanced. This one takes patience, that's for sure.

GRIM REPOE

The king of Poes here in the flesh. Or rather, here in the white bed sheet. Grim Repoe can disappear and stay invisible for as long as it wants, but don't worry! You can see its scythe no matter where it goes. It sure does hate those torches, huh?

GIGALEON

A giant Keeleon, Gigaleon is a flying battle platform, ready and willing to spew long-lasting fire below itself until all three Links are good and charred. The problem with Gigaleon is that it never leaves the air. If only there was a way to level the playing field!

Bosses

MARGOMA

Margoma is the big boss of all the Mini-Margos. It will shuffle around the room until it gets within reach of a Link. When it does, it will lunge forward in hopes of turning that Link into roadkill.

MOLDORM

A classic Zelda boss, Moldorm's sole purpose is to push you off of any platform it can find. Now that it has three Links to push, it'll have to adjust its focus and you'll have to observe when that shift in focus happens.

ARRGHUS

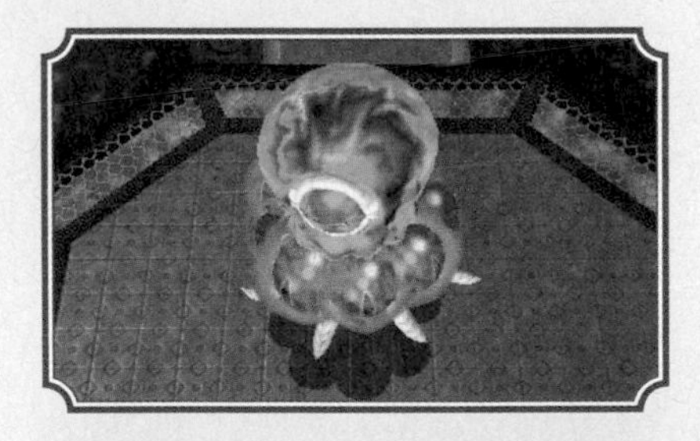

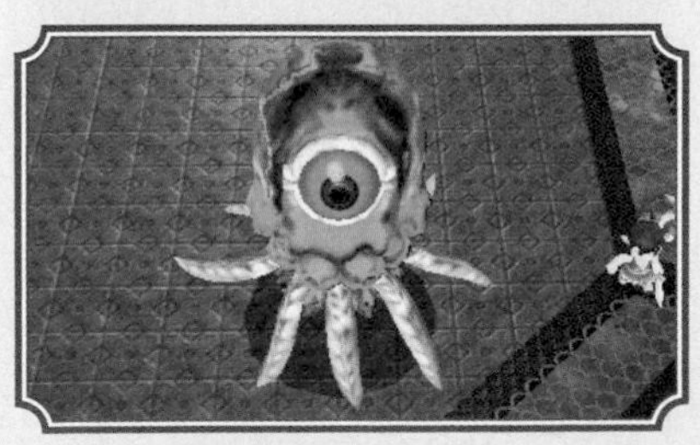

You think your vision is good? Well Arrghus has 20/20/20/20/20/20/20/20/20 vision! This eyeball-based cephalopod uses its eyes to protect its main eye from any attacks. You'll need to be clever in order to damage this ocular enemy.

BLIZZAGIA

Blizzagia is an ice snake that loves hiding in caves, then popping out and snapping its enemies up in its jaws. You'll need to be quick to avoid its attacks, but the real challenge is figuring out how to damage the brute.

THE LADY'S PET (MARGOMA)

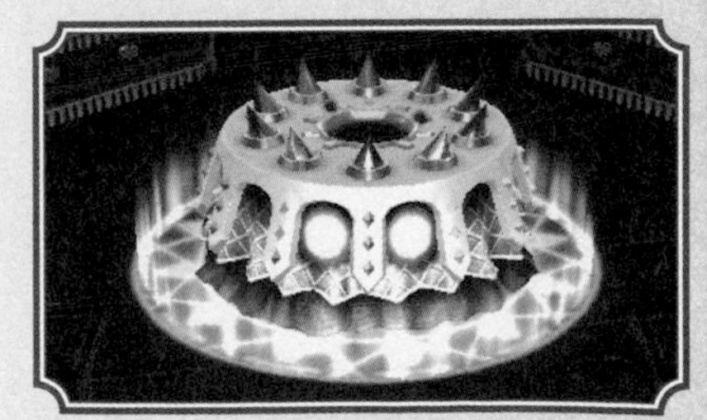

A faster, more mobile, more fashionable version of Margoma, under direct control of The Lady. You'll have less open land to work with this time around, so make sure to be careful.

THE LADY'S PET (MOLDORM)

A more erratic and stylish version of Moldorm. This time, it'll start out just bouncing around the platform, so you'll have to be careful and quick to avoid taking damage.

THE LADY'S PET (ARRGHUS)

The Lady's Pet Arrghus doesn't have as many eyes as it did during the first fight, but the eyes it does have are definitely more of a pain than the ones it had during your last encounter. You'll need to use your surroundings and your head to overcome Arrghus this time.

STALCHAMPION

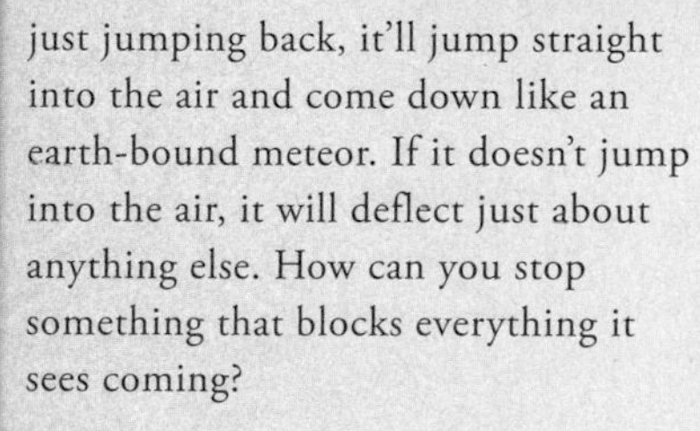

Stalchampion takes Stalfos tactics to a whole new level. It'll jump out of the way of your attacks, but instead of just jumping back, it'll jump straight into the air and come down like an earth-bound meteor. If it doesn't jump into the air, it will deflect just about anything else. How can you stop something that blocks everything it sees coming?

PRISMANTUS

This glorified triangle can be a pretty mean foe if you're not careful and quick. You'll need to hit each of its colored orbs at the ends of its appendages to get its eye open and stun it. There isn't much to this fight mechanically, but its erratic movements and fast speed allow it to turn any unaware Links to powder within no time at all.

THE LADY

The Lady herself. The queen of sheen, the last bastion of true fashion, the sleek sheik. Whatever you call her, The Lady is the source of all of Hytopia's troubles and she needs to be brought to justice for her crimes against humanity, stylish though she may be! The battle with her is a true test of everything you know about making Totems and working as a team, whether with real players or Doppels. This fight comes in multiple phases and will push you pretty hard. Stay strong! She may be so classy it hurts, but that doesn't mean you can't deal a little hurt of your own!

ACCESSORIZE

In this chapter, you will find descriptions for all of the Sub-Weapons, Outfits, and Materials in the game, which happen to be all of Link's tools of the trade in the game. This section isn't about where to find these items, but about what they are, what they look like, and what Madame Couture thinks about them. Enjoy!

TOOLS OF THE TRADE

Here, you'll find all of Link's tools in the order they appear in the game (provided you're going through each of the worlds numerically, instead of hopping around all willy-nilly).

HERO'S SWORD

Link's trusty sword—where would he be without it? No true adventure can begin and no would-be hero could ever call themselves an adventurer without one. Its simplicity makes for ease of use, but its sharpness is the bane of all foes everywhere. Most Sub-Weapons in the game will help Link overcome puzzles, some will help defeat enemies, but none will be as useful to Link as this sword, his loyal friend.

BOW

The Bow is likely the most practical of all of Link's tools (aside from the Hero's Sword, of course). The Bow not only damages enemies, but it's one of the most essential and used Sub-Weapons for solving puzzles. It's the only other weapon in the game that we'd say is a safe bet to use instead of the sword, but the good news is you won't have to make that decision! Combine the Bow with the Kokiri Clothes and you've got yourself a wooden, pointed, enemy-shooting machine.

BOMBS

Another Zelda staple, the Bombs can be placed, thrown, air blasted, and exploded, all with great effect. They are excellent for defeating foes that tend to block attacks or for defeating enemies that are hiding in locations unreachable by your Links. Throw on the Big Bomb Outfit and you can raise some real chaos. Every Bomb, whether of your own creation or not, that your Link touches while wearing the Big Bomb Outfit will turn into a massive, monster enemy exploder that'll shred friend or foe alike.

WATER ROD

Magic rods have been around the Zelda series for some time, but they've never been used in quite as interesting of a way as the Water Rod. Instead of just blasting enemies with water, the Water Rod creates vertical platforms of pure H_2O. A lot of areas in *Tri Force Heroes* require all three Links to stack to reach a higher platform or a flying enemy, but the Water Rod circumvents that whole system altogether. Just create a water platform on the ground and BOOM! You're looking a flying enemy right in the eyes, instead of trying desperately to reach it from below. You can also create the water platforms directly underneath enemies to lift them into the air and stun them temporarily. This Sub-Weapon gives new meaning to the age-old idiom "You're all washed up".

GRIPSHOT

The Gripshot is exactly how you remember it from all of its previous Zelda roles. Point this grabby grappling hook at a peg, another Link, or a chain-link fence and you'll be dragged across the room toward it. Use it on enemies to stun them at a distance, then move in and give them the ol' one-two slasher with your sword. The Gripshot's utility is pretty limited, but when you get to used it, my oh my is it a good time.

BOOMERANG

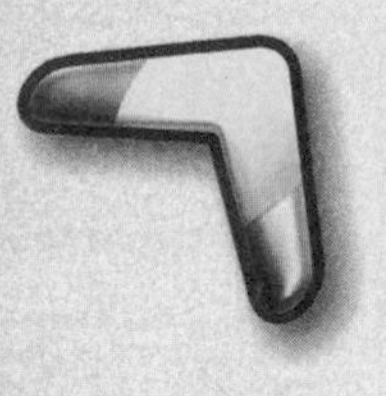

Is there a single item in the Zelda series that is more renowned, more beloved, and more used than the Boomerang? We think not! Series veterans will know this Sub-Weapon all too well and will know exactly how to use it. If you are new to the franchise or haven't been around in a while, let us give you a refresher. The Boomerang can be thrown to hit switches, grab other Links, and pick up Rupees and Hearts, as well as for stunning enemies. Once you've tossed it, you can expect it (like all good boomerangs) to come right back to you. That means you can throw the Boomerang and then, if you miss whatever you were trying to hit, you can move to adjust the Boomerang's return path. This will in turn hit enemies or grab whatever you're trying to get your hands on, provided you move in the right direction. Get some practice with it and you'll be a pro in no time!

GUST JAR

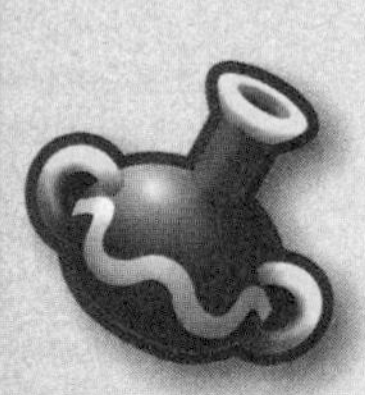

The Gust Jar is perfect for putting out fires and blasting your friends across otherwise uncrossable gaps. It's also an excellent tool for stunning enemies, as it can stun multiple enemies at the same time. It can be a bit tricky to get the hang of, but once you've got it down it's an invaluable tool for solving puzzles and defeating enemies.

FIRE GLOVES

The Fire Gloves are likely the most technical of Link's Sub-Weapons. They specialize in two things: Lighting torches and melting ice. And while it specializes in those things, that's far from the limits of the Fire Gloves. You can use them to swiftly defeat ice-based enemies and light dark rooms. You can hold the Y Button to create and hold a fireball, which a Bow or Boomerang Link can fire an arrow or throw a Boomerang through to light them on fire. The fireballs can also melt platforms and bounce around corners. Yes, the Fire Gloves truly offer the most utility of any other Sub-Weapon in the game.

MAGIC HAMMER

Likely the most direct of Link's tools, the Magic Hammer does one thing and it does it very well: It smashes things. Smash enemies into the ground, smash destructible objects, smash down pegs, smash smiling spring pads—you name it, the Magic Hammer can probably smash it. Add into the mix the Hammerwear Outfit and you're now a terrible smashing machine that cannot and will not be stopped.

Link's Wardrobe

This section gives you a good look at each of Link's various Outfits. You won't get a ton of detail here, but you can find plenty of information on crafting each Outfit in the "Odds and Ends" section near the end of the guide.

Hero's Tunic

Madame Couture Says

"So you want to be a hero, do you? Then you simply can't go on without a Hero's Tunic in your sad little closet."

Kinda Cursed Tights

Madame Couture Says

"A curse or a blessing? Either way, they certainly are cutting edge, aren't they, dahling?"

The Lady's Ensemble

Madame Couture Says

"The Lady's Ensemble is something special. Paired with a hero, it can save our dahling princess from her curse!"

Tri Suit

Madame Couture Says

"The Tri Suit is tres special. If three heroes wear this at the same time... You'll have to wait and see!"

Timeless Tunic

Madame Couture Says

"The Timeless Tunic is a fan favorite! Vintage at its finest, my dahling. Ooh! I'm feeling tres nostalgic now!"

Bear Minimum Outfit

Madame Couture Says

"Dahling, you're a walking fashion disaster!"

Kokiri Clothes

Madame Couture Says

"The Kokiri Clothes are to die for! They let you shoot three arrows at once. I'm quite gifted, no?"

Big Bomb Outfit

Madame Couture Says

"The Big Bomb Outfit turns normal Bombs into Big Bombs. The name says it all, really."

Legendary Dress

Madame Couture Says

"The Legendary Dress makes those darling little hearts appear more often. No need to thank me, dahling!"

Lucky Loungewear

Madame Couture Says

"The Lucky Loungewear improves luck on the battlefield. You'll occasionally evade attacks without even trying!"

Zora Costume

Madame Couture Says

"The Zora Costume lets you swim much faster. They say cold water halts aging. Perhaps I should ... oh, nothing."

Torrent Robe

Madame Couture Says

"The Torrent Robe has piqued your interest, has it not? It improves your Water Rod. Quite handy!"

Jack of Hearts

Madame Couture Says

"The Jack of Hearts gives you an extra Heart Container to play with. Do with it what you will, my pet!"

Goron Garb

Madame Couture Says

"The Goron Garb lets you swim in lava. Is that not what fashionless young heroes do in their spare time?"

Boomeranger

Madame Couture Says

"The Boomeranger improves le Boomerang. If you're into that sort of thing, my pet."

Energy Gear

Madame Couture Says

"The Energy Gear increases your energy gauge by 50%. It's the caffeine-killer!"

Cozy Parka

Madame Couture Says

"The Cozy Parka comes with antislip boots. There's nothing stylish about a broken leg, oui hee hee."

Hammerwear

Madame Couture Says

"Hammerwear is ideal for lovers of Magic Hammers. It's popular with turtle enthusiasts, oddly enough…"

Tingle Tights

Madame Couture Says

"The Tingle Tights are for those brimming with confidence. They save you from falling up to three times!"

Cacto Clothes

Madame Couture Says

"The Cacto Clothes are like a rose… gorgeous but YOUCH! They hurt foes who dare to touch your wear."

Sword Suit

Madame Couture Says

"The Sword Suit allows your sword to shoot stylish beams. It's quite extraordinary."

Rupee Regalia

Madame Couture Says

"The Rupee Regalia makes it easier to find Rupees. That means you can buy more clothes, oui hee hee!"

Queen of Hearts

Madame Couture Says

"The Queen of Hearts gives you three extra Heart Containers. I never cease to amaze, do I?"

Cheetah Costume

Madame Couture Says

"The Cheetah Costume lets you move a lot faster than normal. And it looks positively fierce! Rawr, dahling!"

Dunewalker Duds

Madame Couture Says

"The Dunewalker Duds have been in vogue for ages, dahling. They prevent you from sinking in quicksand!"

Gust Garb

Madame Couture Says

"The Gust Garb comes highly recommended. It's bold and breezy, and it powers up your Gust Jar too!"

Ninja Gi

Madame Couture Says

"The Ninja Gi is an import. You'll look dashing... and also do triple damage WHILE dashing!"

Light Armor

Madame Couture Says

"The Light Armor is a must when heading somewhere dark. Banish those unflattering lighting conditions!"

Fire Blazer

Madame Couture Says

"The Fire Blazer gives your Fire Gloves a little extra oomph! It's my hottest design, dahling."

Serpent's Toga

Madame Couture Says

"The Serpent's Toga makes you a chiseled, invincible statue. The effect fades upon moving... Such is fashion!"

Showstopper

Madame Couture Says

"The Showstopper attracts stares from everyone, including enemies. It's impossible to look away..."

Robowear

Madame Couture Says

"Robowear is fashion of the future! It also improves your Gripshot. The future is here, and it's tres fab!"

Sword Master Suit

Madame Couture Says

"The Sword Master Suit is the mark of a truly gifted sword wielder. Wearing it is considered an honor, my pet!"

Spin Attack Attire

Madame Couture Says

"The Spin Attack Attire is fierce, my dahling. It lets you do a fancy Great Spin Attack. Divine!"

Cheer Outfit

Madame Couture Says

"The Cheer Outfit increases the energy gauges of your teammates. All for one and such and such."

Dapper Spinner

Madame Couture Says

"The Dapper Spinner ensemble lets you Spin Attack much faster! And you'll look like ... HIM. *le swoon*"

MATERIALS

This section will show you each of the Materials and what they look like. You'll also get their in-game descriptions to round this section off. If you want to know more about how to find the Materials, hop over to the "Odds and Ends" section of the guide.

LADY'S GLASSES

DESCRIPTION
Sleek glasses to grace the nose of a sophisticated lady.

LADY'S COLLAR

DESCRIPTION
A high-quality collar to adorn the neck of a stylish lady.

LADY'S PARASOL

DESCRIPTION
A fabled item, untouched by grubby hands of drab mortals.

FRILLY FABRIC

DESCRIPTION
A Street Merchant exclusive. It's supposedly handmade.

FRIENDLY TOKEN

DESCRIPTION
More friends is better than none. So go get some, son!

FREEBIE

DESCRIPTION
This will undoubtedly come in handy one day. Don't lose it!

BLOB JELLY

DESCRIPTION
Blobs drop this. It's best not to question what it is...

ARMOS SPIRIT

DESCRIPTION
When an Armos falls, its spirit remains for three days.

TEKTITE SHELL

DESCRIPTION
This is a good-luck charm! I mean...probably. Maybe?

SWEET SHROOM

DESCRIPTION
Somewhat poisonous, but it smells like a sweet dream.

BLIN BLING

DESCRIPTION
Only Blin Blings manage to amass this kind of glitz.

GOHMA'S EYE

DESCRIPTION
Pure gold/emerald. Beauty is in the eye of the Gohma.

MYSTERY JADE

DESCRIPTION
Nobody knows where this comes from. Mysterious!

SUPPLE LEAF

DESCRIPTION
A jiggly leaf brimming with collagen. So soft and elastic.

FRESH KELP

DESCRIPTION
Grown far from the sea, so it's low on minerals.

ZORA SCALE

DESCRIPTION
Scales that grow as a Zora grows. This one's enormous!

HYTOPIAN SILK

DESCRIPTION
Spun from the cocoons of rather dapper silkworms.

AQUA CROWN

DESCRIPTION
When an impure soul dons this, it evaporates. Harsh!

OCTOROK SUCKER

DESCRIPTION
A Drablands delicacy! Eat it raw or cook it to perfection.

FAIRY DUST

DESCRIPTION
Cute dust that fairies sneeze. It has a million uses.

RAINBOW CORAL

DESCRIPTION
So beautiful, folks travel from faraway lands to nab one.

THORNBERRY

DESCRIPTION
Too spiky to eat, but it makes a fine fabric.

GORON ORE

DESCRIPTION
Named for its Goron-like sturdiness. And musk.

MONSTER GUTS

DESCRIPTION
Madame Couture's favorite! It's loaded with iron!

DEMON FOSSIL

DESCRIPTION
Cheap knockoffs abound, but this one's the real deal.

RUGGED HORN

DESCRIPTION
Would look cool in a piercing or hanging above a doorway.

KODONGO TAIL

DESCRIPTION
Don't worry—Kodongos can regrow their tails over time.

KEESE WING

DESCRIPTION
Use it to brew an invigorating tea, or grind for a purple dye.

STAR FRAGMENT

DESCRIPTION
Prized as a gift from the sky, this rock is out of this world!

DIVINE WHISKERS

DESCRIPTION
From the maw of a sacred beast, grown over a millennia.

FLUFFY FUZZ

DESCRIPTION
So soft, you'll want to rub your face all over it.

TINY SNOWFLAKE

DESCRIPTION
Fragile and delicate. These only form at -25 degrees.

SERPENT FANGS

DESCRIPTION
Razor-sharp fangs that can pierce through anything.

CRIMSON SHELL

DESCRIPTION
A mysterious shell that never misses a foe when thrown.

FREEZARD WATER

DESCRIPTION
Formerly a Freezard. Now the purest of pure water.

CHILL STONE

DESCRIPTION
Guaranteed to keep its cool at all times. Can you dig it?

ICE ROSE

DESCRIPTION
This rare flower only blooms in the coldest conditions.

BEASTIE PATCH

DESCRIPTION
A bandage for beasts. Helps wounds heal faster.

STIFF PUFF

DESCRIPTION
It looks puffy, but it's actually rock solid. Go figure!

SILVER THREAD

DESCRIPTION
Spun from glinting gossamer. Antibacterial and deodorizing.

ROYAL RING

DESCRIPTION
A ring with a royal legacy. Unfit for "commoner" fingers.

ANTIQUE COIN

DESCRIPTION
Everyone loves gold! Keep this somewhere safe.

FANCY FABRIC

DESCRIPTION
A master artisan slaved over this for decades. Pretty, yes?

EXQUISITE LACE

DESCRIPTION
Such detail! Sadly, they don't make 'em like this anymore.

VIBRANT BROOCH

DESCRIPTION
Such vibrant colors! Sure to make strangers jealous.

BRITTLE PAPYRUS

DESCRIPTION
Love letters written on this supposedly always work.

PALM CONE

DESCRIPTION
Taken from trees that can go for centuries without water.

ANCIENT FIN

DESCRIPTION
Smells heavenly when baked. Cook too long and it hardens.

VINTAGE LINEN

DESCRIPTION
How to make this is a family secret. Enough said!

GIBDO BANDAGE

DESCRIPTION
Gibdos like to clean, like cats. They aren't as cute, though.

STAL SKULL

DESCRIPTION
Did you know Stalbone can be used as a white dye?

SANDY RIBBON

DESCRIPTION
A magic ribbon that can rouse a sandstorm when shaken.

CRYSTAL SKULL

DESCRIPTION
The secrets this thing must hold! Probably diseases too.

GOLDEN INSECT

DESCRIPTION
Some of these things are worth more than actual gold.

CARRUMPKIN

DESCRIPTION
This carrot loved autumn so much, it became a pumpkin.

MYSTERY EXTRACT

DESCRIPTION
Nobody knows what this is... That's probably for the best.

SPIDER SILK LACE

DESCRIPTION
Made from unbreakable and totally creepy spider thread.

POE SOUL

DESCRIPTION
A Poe hides its soul not in its body, but elsewhere.

TWISTED TWIG

DESCRIPTION
A highly prized talisman said to ensure marital bliss.

LAVA DROP

DESCRIPTION
A fire spirit's tear, perhaps? Carrying one is good luck.

SANCTUARY MASK

DESCRIPTION
A mask used to ward off evil. It's seemingly ineffective...

GOLD DUST

DESCRIPTION
Looks like sand, but it's sooo much more. CHA-CHING!

CUCCO FEATHERS

DESCRIPTION
Cuccos are always losing and regrowing feathers. Weirdos.

CARMINE PEARL

DESCRIPTION
A red jewel from the sky. Often called a "sun seed".

SKY DRAGON TAIL

DESCRIPTION
An Aeralfos tail. It's pliable, strong, and oh-so rare.

PRETTY PLUME

DESCRIPTION
A feather that charms man and beast alike. Women too.

MOCK FAIRY

DESCRIPTION
Threatened fairies conjure these up as decoys.

AURORA STONE

DESCRIPTION
A large stone with a hefty helping of aurora aura.

STEEL MASK

DESCRIPTION
A speck of this steel makes swords way stronger.

FABLED BUTTERFLY

DESCRIPTION
An ethereal butterfly, only visible to the very valorous.

Clothing Quest

The kingdom of Hytopia is under the curse of a wicked witch known only as "The Lady". The kingdom's princess, known far and wide for her impeccable fashion sense, is the victim of The Lady's greatest curse. Her father, King Tuft, has been feverishly looking for three legendary and stylish heroes to help break the curse, which is where *Tri Force Heroes* begins.

There are a few things you need to know before you truly set off on your adventure. Read on to learn a few important details about the game.

Magical Materials

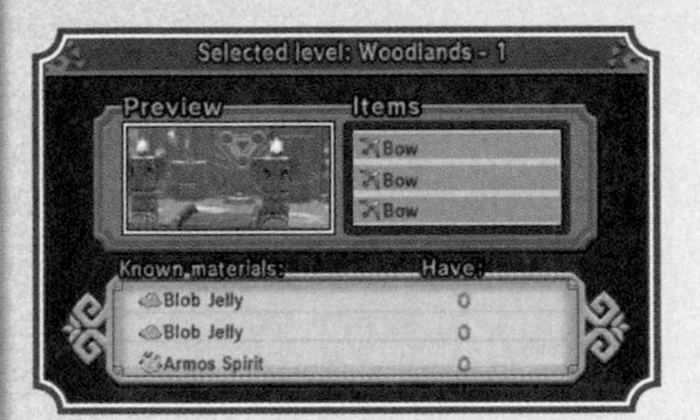

At the Level Selection screen you'll see information for what Materials can be found and what Sub-Weapons are available. Materials allow you to make Outfits that can be used during levels. You won't have enough Materials to make any Outfits right now and you'll start your first level with only two Outfits: The Hero's Tunic, which does nothing but keep you looking like a true hero, and the Bear Minimum Outfit, which removes a Heart Container when it is worn and makes the player wearing it take double damage.

Never Say Die!

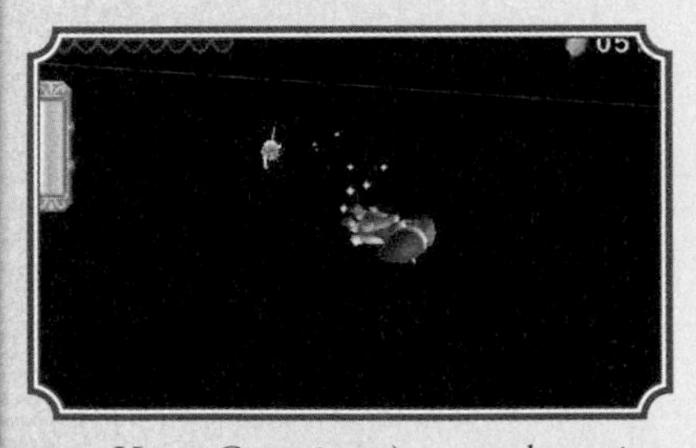

One last thing before heading off into the Drablands: For any level, with friends or Doppels, you can die (empty all of your Heart Containers) up to three times. When you die, a Fairy will come out and revive you with full health at the start of whatever room you died in. If this happens more than three times, you'll be booted back to the lobby and forced to start the level all over again.

While in single-player, neither of your Doppels will take damage while not in your control. But in multiplayer, anyone can take damage and your health is shared, so be extra careful! Heart Containers can empty incredibly fast if you and your two friends get in a tricky situation.

And So Our Story Begins...

Your Link can be seen reading the notice board in town, though we're not the only ones who see him. A young green-haired boy, catches Link reading the sign and races down to meet him. It turns out that the boy works for Hytopia's resident fashion designer, Madame Couture. The boy suggests that you take a trip over to Madame Couture's, just north of your current location, to get a much-needed makeover. But we're rebels here, and we're going to ignore that request.

Instead, head north and cross the bridge. You'll be stopped by the guard at the entrance of Hytopia castle. He'll give you a quick once-over to see if you have what it takes to be one of the legendary stylish heroes that legend tells will save Hytopia from the witch's curse. He'll let you pass to go speak with Hytopia's resident witch-hunting commander, Sir Combsly, inside the castle foyer. Sir Combsly will explain Hytopia's predicament in a bit more detail and request that Link take up arms against the wicked witch. Accept his request (not that he really gives you a choice) and Sir Combsly will ask you to name yourself and he will give you your first Material: Hytopian Silk. This Material can, and must, be used to create the Hero's Tunic. Sir Combsly won't let you step foot into the Drablands without it!

What's in a Name?

Remember that other players online will be able to see the name you give yourself, so take care not to put anything offensive or embarrassing. You're a legendary stylish hero, so make sure to name yourself accordingly.

Now head out of the castle, cross the bridge, head down the stairs and then hang another left at the fountain to reach Madame Couture's boutique.

Consider Madame Couture your new best friend, because she's going to be the most helpful person in aiding you in your quest to defeat The Lady. She's in the business of making magical Outfits that grant their wearers new abilities and powers. As your quest carries you through the Drablands, you'll discover more Materials. Bring these Materials back to Madame Couture regularly and she'll turn them into Outfits.

Have Madame Couture make you the Hero's Tunic, then return to Sir Combsly. He'll grant you access to the Drablands by allowing you enter either the multiplayer or single-player lobbies. If you're playing with friends, head through the door above Sir Combsly. (The door is marked with three "person" symbols to indicate that it is a three-player room.)

In order to play multiplayer, you'll need two other players to join you. The main quest is either for one player or three. If you're hankering for some multiplayer, but only have one other player with you, you can head down the stairs on the right side of the room and enter the Coliseum. You'll be able to battle one or two other Links for Coliseum-exclusive Materials, Rupees, and bragging rights. But we're getting side-tracked.

In the multiplayer lobby, you'll need to speak with the old man in the top-left corner of the room. One of you will need to select "Host a Room" while the other two players select "Join a Room". Once all three players are in, the Triforce gateway at the north end of the room will light up and you'll be good to go! Have each player step on a piece of the Triforce gateway and you'll be moved to the Level Selection screen (Unless you're playing an online game, which will require you to choose the area you want to play in before you join a room). You'll only have access to one world at this point, but you're free to choose any level you want in that world.

If you're playing single-player, you'll need to head through the door north-east of Sir Combsly. (It will be marked with a single "person" symbol to show you that this is for one player.) Getting single-player started up is almost identical to starting multiplayer. Talk to the Doppel Master in the top-left corner of the room. Since you don't have two other Links to join you in your quest, the Doppel Master will lend you wooden dolls called Doppels. Link is able to transfer his spirit to either of the dolls at any time in order to take control of them. You can take control of the Doppels by tapping their image on the touchscreen. Once you're ready, you can pick up or control each Doppel and move them onto a piece of the Triforce gateway.

Once all three of you are on the Triforce gateway, you'll be moved to the Area Selection screen.

Now that you're ready, select your level and let's get this witch hunt underway! We'll be starting with 1-1 Deku Forest.

WORLD 1: THE WOODLANDS

Level 1: Deku Forest

Challenges

Fewer Heart Containers

Clear within the time limit

Guard the orb

Sub-Weapons

 Bow

 Bow

 Bow

Materials

 Blob Jelly

 Blob Jelly

 Armos Spirit

Recommended Outfits

 Kokiri Clothes

This level is about as simple as it gets in *Tri Force Heroes.* It is an excellent way to get the hang of the game's mechanics and working with Doppels or your teammates.

You won't have access to any Outfits besides the Bear Minimum and Hero's Tunic at the start, so go ahead and choose the Hero's Tunic for your first time through this level. When you are able to get more Outfits, the best one for this stage is the Kokiri Clothes, which we'll talk about later.

Unbearable

Bear Minimum reduces your total Heart Containers by 1 and makes whoever is wearing the Outfit take double damage.

ROOM 1

You start on an elevated plateau. In the area just north of you, you'll find three Bows sitting on pedestals. In order to exit the room, you need to have each Link pick up a Bow.

Once you pick up all three Bows, a Triforce gateway will appear at the north end of this room. Having all three Links each stand on a piece of that Triforce gateway will send you to the next area. There is more you'll have to do before you can exit the room, but always remember that the Triforce gateway is your key out of every room in the main quest of *Tri Force Heroes*.

With all three Links equipped with Bows, head north. You can find Rupees in the water on the west side of the room inside the creek and on a ledge on the east side of the room. You'll also see blue Rupees on top of the two totem poles in front of the bridge leading to the north half of the room. Blue Rupees are worth a whopping five Rupees each. Remember, every little bit counts! To get the blue Rupees you'll need to stack all three Links and have the Link in the middle of the stack throw the Link on top or over each of the totem poles.

Getting Paid

You can cut the tall grass and bushes, cut or throw the pots, and throw the rocks sitting around each level to find Hearts and Rupees.

Link Stacking

Stacking in this game is called making a Totem. We'll be referring to stacking as making a Totem from this point forward.

After crossing the bridge you'll reach a closed gate and three switches on three separate platforms. You'll need to make a Totem with all three Links and then have the middle Link throw the top Link on top of the tallest platform first. Now have the bottom Link throw the remaining Link onto the second highest platform. All three Links need to stand on the switches at the same time to open the gate.

Once the gate is open, head in and have all three Links each stand on a piece of the Triforce symbol to be teleported to the next room.

ROOM 2

There aren't any puzzles to solve in this room. You'll need to defeat eight Blobs in order to make the Triforce gateway appear. Make a Totem and throw your Links up to each tier of the room to reach all eight Blobs.

Make sure to grab the treasure chests on the north side of the room before moving on to the next room.

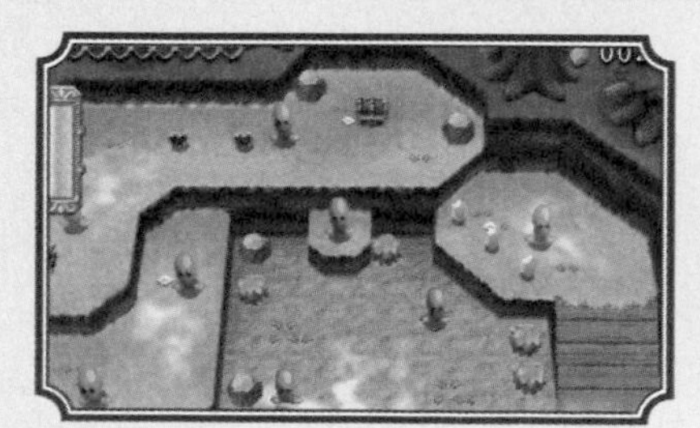

ROOM 3

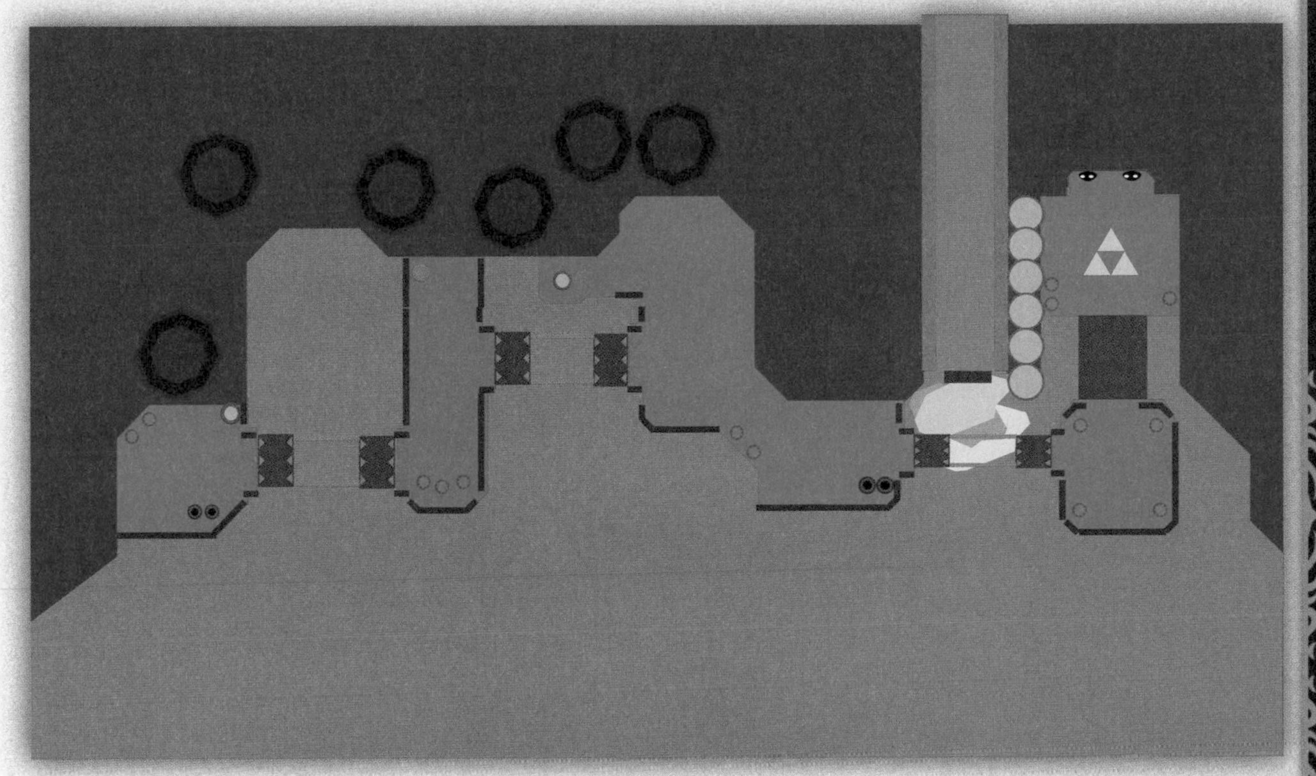

This room can be a bit tricky. Start by making a two-Link Totem, then switch to your remaining Link and hit the orb switch above you. This makes the platform to your right begin moving to the left and right, allowing you to cross the gap. You can make a Totem if you're playing alone to get all of the Links onto the platform together.

Once across, throw one of the Links up to the elevated area on the north side of this plateau to destroy the grass and rock. Once you're done, make a three-Link Totem and point it to the orb switch in the top-right corner of the screen. Fire an arrow from your Bow to hit it. This will activate another platform, which will travel back and forth over the gap. Cross using the platform to reach the next plateau.

A Blob and a treasure chest can be found on the lower-right side of the plateau, while another Blob and treasure chest can be found on the plateau's north side. You'll need to throw your Links up to reach the treasure chest, but a simple two-Link Totem will allow you to shoot the Blob, if you're feeling particularly malicious.

Now head to the bottom-right and you'll find another platform, but this time it's already moving. Make a three-Link Totem, walk onto the platform, and face north. Shoot the switch in the waterfall to raise the bridge leading to the Triforce gateway. Getting the timing right can be a bit of a challenge without the Kokiri Clothes, but a couple of tries should be enough to hit the switch.

Before you cross the bridge you'll encounter a Squiddy. Hitting this creature will yield Hearts and Rupees. The more you hit it, the more Hearts and Rupees it will drop until it explodes in a shower of health and cash. You'll have a hard time getting the Squiddy to explode without being able to bounce it off of a wall in most stages, but you can hit him north up the bridge, which will give you plenty of space to work with. A Squiddy is always worth trying to defeat.

Jam Session

If you don't have a wall to bounce the Squiddy off of, you can try hitting it up and down or left and right, if you have the space for it. When playing multiplayer, you can try positioning your teammates across from you to play some Squiddy tennis. In single-player, however, you'll have to do everything by yourself, which is quite the challenge.

Once you've finished with the Squiddy, head up the bridge and onto the Triforce gateway to move on to the next room.

ROOM 4

This room requires excellent coordination from your teammates if you're playing multiplayer, but single-player only requires the right amount of Links in a Totem to win. You'll be dealing with four different stacked Totem Dekus. You'll need to make a Totem of Links equal to the number of the Totem Deku's roots plus its head. If a Totem Deku has one brown, round root, you'll need two Links to reach it.

Don't stand still during this battle to avoid the Deku Nuts the Totem Dekus fire. You'll need to stand just outside of the dark green grass patches around each Totem Deku to keep them from hiding in the ground. Hit each Totem Deku with one arrow apiece to defeat them and open the path to the Triforce gateway.

Have each Link stand on the Triforce gateway to enter the final room of this level.

ROOM 5

Room 5 marks the end of every level in *Tri Force Heroes*. At the end of this room are three large treasure chests. You'll only ever be able to open one chest per level, and what you find inside can be one of two items: Two chests contain a common Material and one of them will contain a rarer Material.

Choose your treasure to finish the level and be sent to the results screen. You'll earn thirty Rupees for each Fairy you kept by avoiding death throughout that level, so be extra careful if you want to rack up some sweet cash. If you're playing multiplayer, you and your friends don't split Rupees—you all get the same amount, so there's no need to fight over them. All for one and for all, as they say!

Questing for Outfits

Before you move on to the next level, there are a few things you need to know about Outfits and how to make them. The Materials listed on each level at the Level Selection screen are the Materials you have a chance of obtaining in room 5 of every level in the game. You're guaranteed to get at least one of the listed Materials, so you'll never walk away empty-handed (unless you wait too long to open a chest). The Materials can then be taken to Madame Couture's back in town and transformed into Outfits, provided you have the necessary Materials and Rupees to have Madame Couture make them.

Most Outfits have unique benefits or disadvantages that can make the game harder or easier depending on your choices. For instance, the Kokiri Clothes allow you to fire three arrows from your Bow at a time, instead of the usual one. This makes hitting enemies and solving some puzzles a lot easier. You do not need Outfits to beat the game, but they will make the game significantly easier, especially in the later levels. Make a point to head to Madame Couture's and see what Outfits she has to offer regularly. If the levels you have access to have the Materials she needs for an Outfit, make a point to gather them up and get that Outfit made ASAP!

Don't Miss Out!

If you're playing multiplayer, don't wait to select your treasure chest at the end of each level! If you wait too long, you'll run out of time and end up finishing the level empty-handed.

Questing for Outfits

If you're willing to put in the time, you can head back into level 1 to try and get Blob Jelly and Armos Spirit Materials. If you have one of each and some pocket Rupees, you'll be able to make the Kokiri Clothes we keep gushing about. They'll not only serve you well for the rest of this world, they'll be an excellent tool for several levels throughout the game.

WALKTHROUGH

Level 2: Buzz Blob Cave

Challenges

Pop all balloons

Clear within in the time limit

Clear using only Bombs

Sub-Weapons

 Bow

 Bow

 Bow

Materials

 Blob Jelly

 Blob Jelly

 Tektite Shell

Recommended Outfits

 Kokiri Clothes

Most of this level is pretty Bow heavy, so wearing the Kokiri Clothes will provide excellent assistance in taking out enemies and solving puzzles.

ROOM 1

Each Link starts the room in a different location at the start of this level. Make sure that each Link grabs a Bow from the pedestal directly ahead of him. This will reveal the Triforce gateway, but you still have more to do to be able to reach it.

Once each Link is in the center of the room, clear out the Blobs, make a three-Link Totem, and head to the northeast corner of the room near the gate. Have the bottom Link throw the middle and top Links onto the lower ledge to the right of the gate, then have the bottom Link of that Totem throw the top Link on top of the ledge immediately north of the ledge you are currently on.

The Link that is on the highest ledge needs to shoot his Bow at the balloon with the key icon on it, positioned directly in front of the gate.

What a surprise! The key balloon had (you guessed it) a key in it! Grab the key and walk into the lock on the gate to unlock it, then head through to the Triforce gateway.

ROOM 2

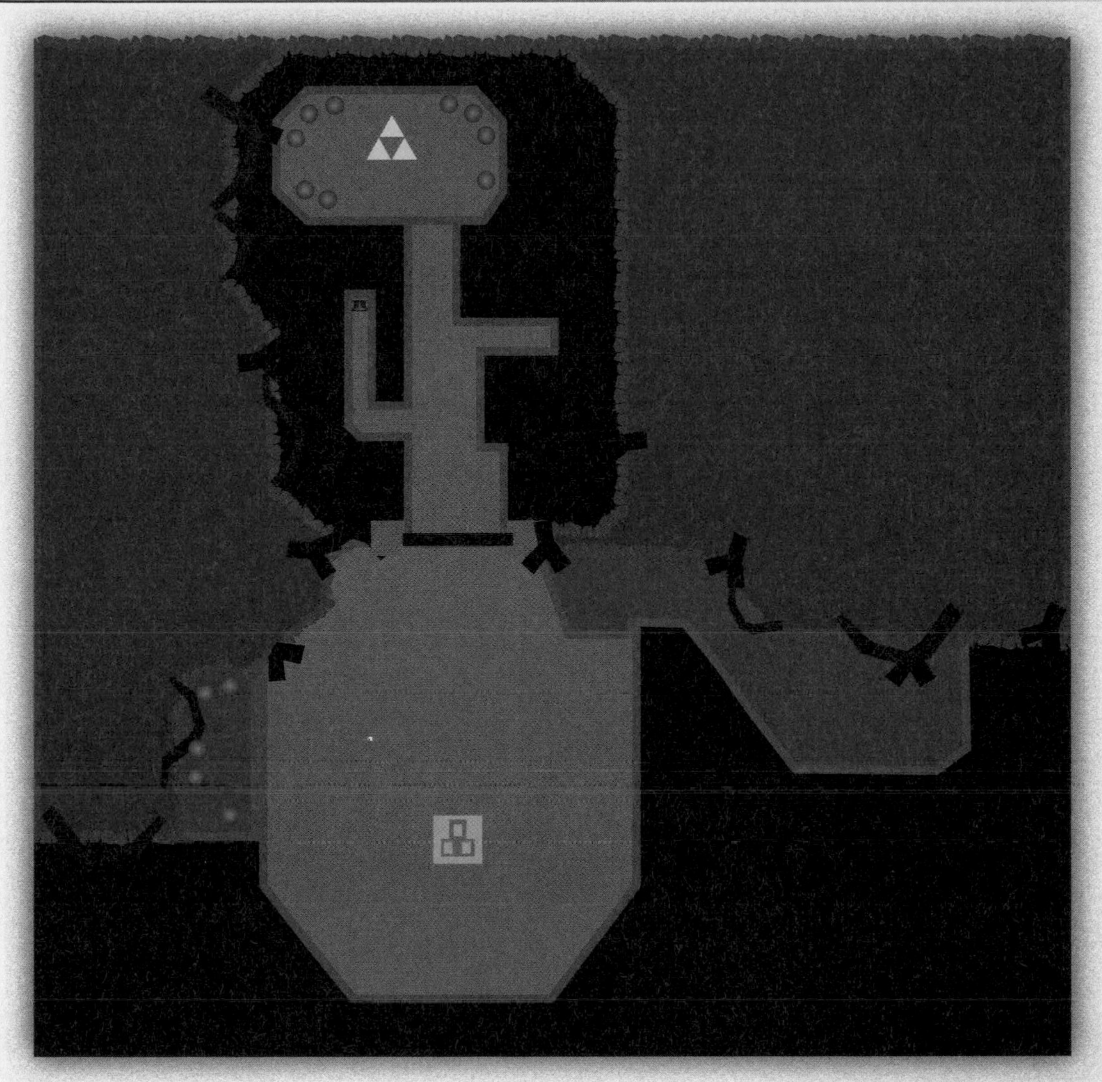

Head northwest along the path and drop down with all three Links to the lower level of this room. In the room's center is a three-man switch. You'll need all three Links standing on it to activate it. You can trigger it with all three Links standing on it or while in a Totem.

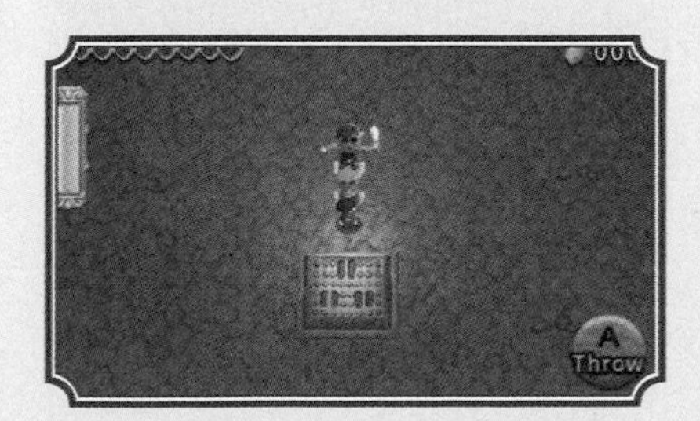

Once the switch is pressed, seven Blobs and a Buzz Blob will appear. The Blobs can be knocked out with your sword, but the Buzz Blob must be defeated at a distance. If you touch the jolting Buzz Blob with your sword you'll be electrocuted and lose a Heart.

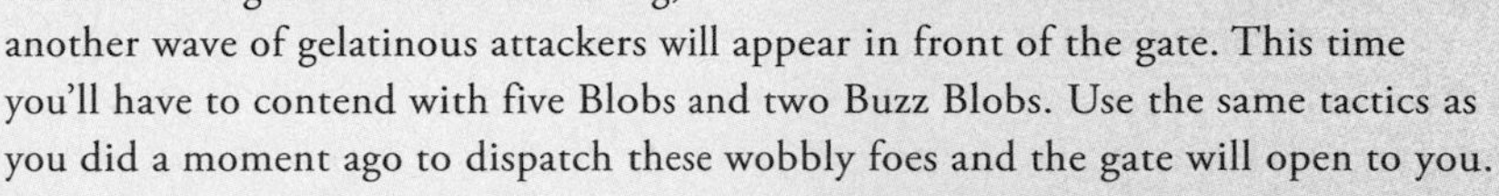

After finishing off the Buzz Blob ring, another wave of gelatinous attackers will appear in front of the gate. This time you'll have to contend with five Blobs and two Buzz Blobs. Use the same tactics as you did a moment ago to dispatch these wobbly foes and the gate will open to you.

Head through the gate on the north side of the room. You can nab a treasure chest by taking the first left onto an even narrower path. After you grab the treasure, head to the north end of the room to find the Triforce gateway.

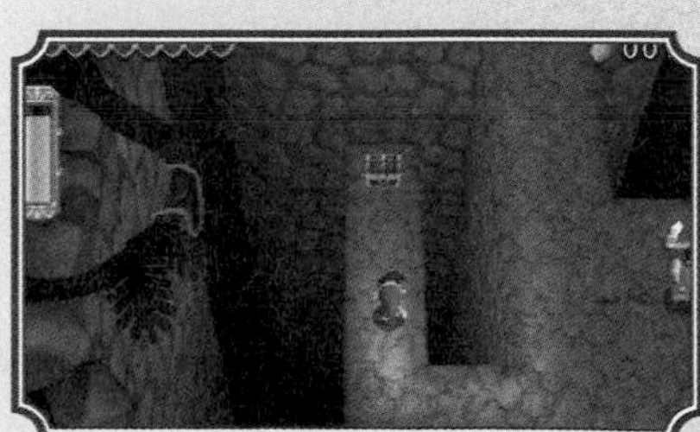

ROOM 3

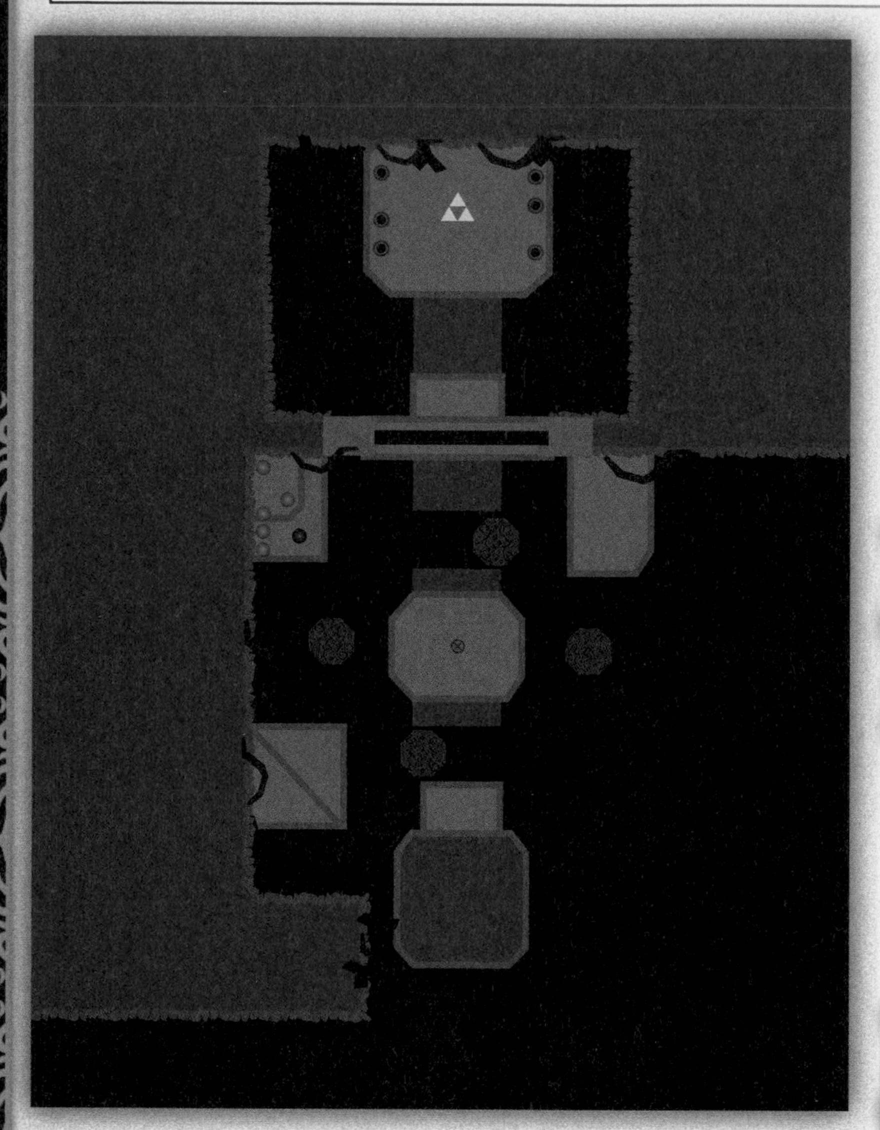

You'll need to hit two more switches on the east and north sides of the room to open the gate. Both switches require you to make a three-Link Totem in order to reach them, and the east switch is guarded by a Buzz Blob.

Hidden Treasure!

You can also find a treasure chest on the west side of the room. Make sure to grab it before moving on!

Once you hit all three switches, the gate will open and you'll be able to reach the Triforce gateway and another Squiddy.

Smack that Squiddy!

The Squiddy in this room is perfect for exploding like a gooey piñata. Just hit it toward the wall behind the Triforce gateway until it starts bouncing off the wall. If you position yourself well you'll pretty much be able to stand still and smack the Squiddy until it detonates into a pile of Rupees and Hearts. Stay on your toes! The Squiddy can easily start to slide out of range of your sword and it'll move faster with every hit!

In the center of this room is a set of moving platforms that circle a plateau. You'll find a two Totem Dekus and a rather shy switch on the center plateau. You'll need to make Totem tall enough to reach the Totem Dekus, then stand back and shoot them in order to defeat them. In order to hit the shy switch, you'll need to use the same strategy: Step back, aim at the switch and, when you're far enough away from it to get it to open, fire!

ROOM 4

BOSS FIGHT: ELECTRIC BLOB KING

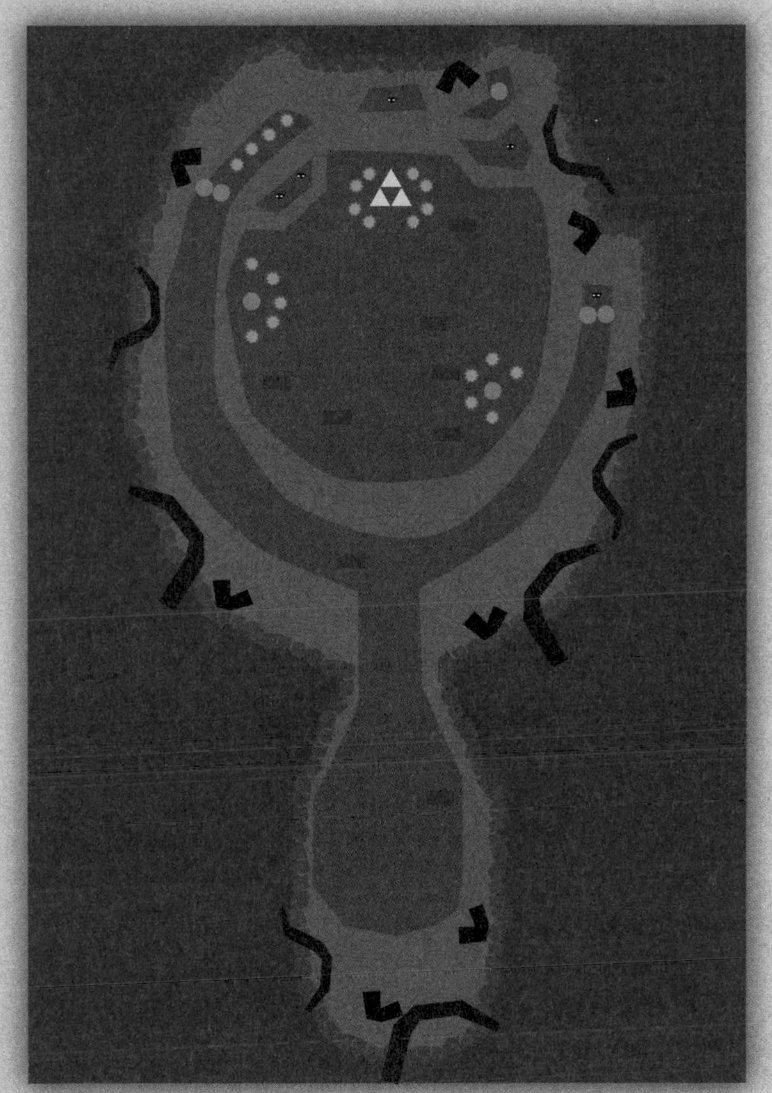

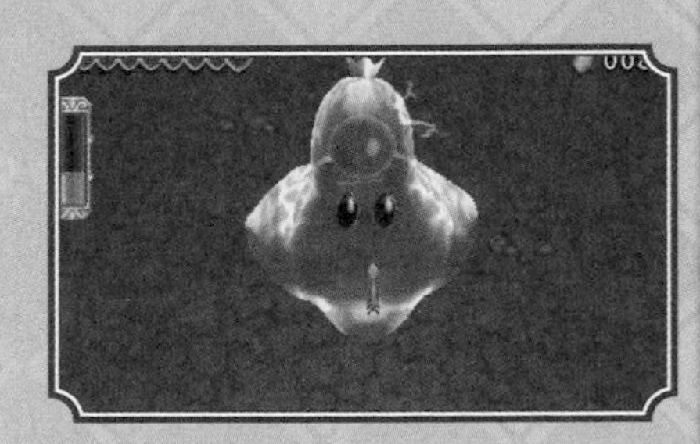

Your goal is to hit the red ball inside Electric Blob King with your Bow. This starts out pretty simply: Aim your Bow at the red ball and fire. After three hits, Electric Blob King will stand a bit taller, forcing the red ball out of your range. Make a two-Link Totem, aim at the red ball, and fire. After three hits Electric Blob King will stand even taller, meaning you need to meet its tall-man challenge and stack 'em high! Make a three-Link Totem, aim for the red ball once again, and turn this royal Blob into paste! Four more hits and Electric Blob King will be nothing more than a puddle after it explodes into a delicious pile of Rupees. Grab the Rupees quick, as they don't stick around for more than a few seconds.

In Case of Emergency

If your health is low, you can make a three-Link Totem and throw the top Link onto the ledges that adorn the outer areas of the room. You'll find rocks to destroy and a couple of Hearts to refill your Heart Containers.

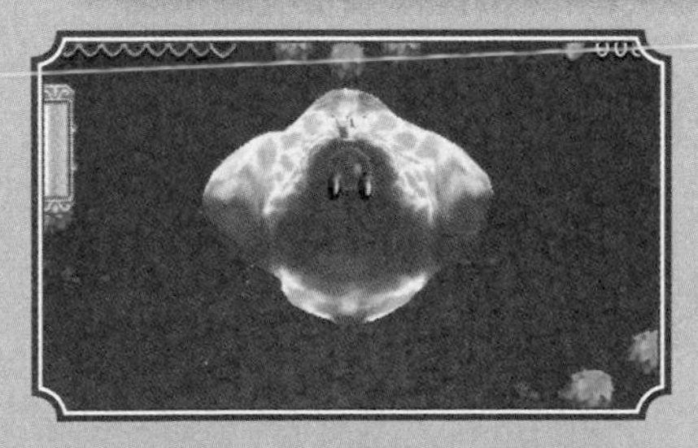

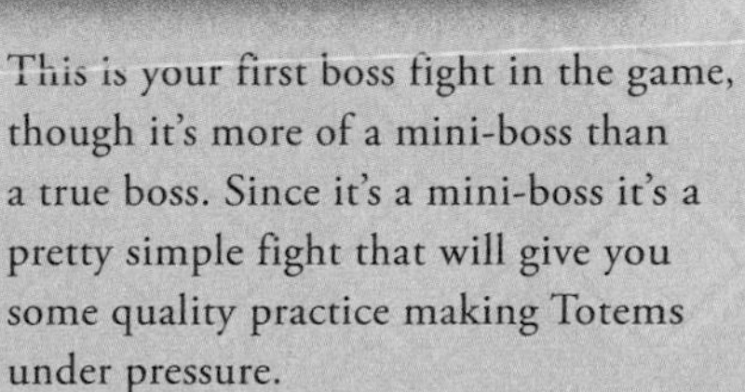

This is your first boss fight in the game, though it's more of a mini-boss than a true boss. Since it's a mini-boss it's a pretty simple fight that will give you some quality practice making Totems under pressure.

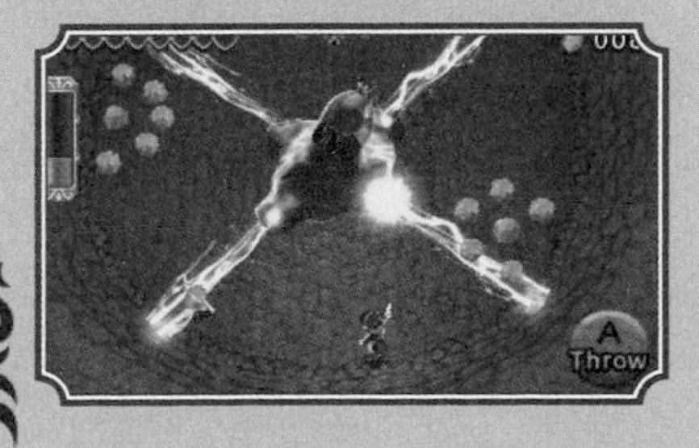

You'll need to watch out for when Electric Blob King starts making a charging sound. This means it's going to fire electricity in straight lines out of its squishy little nubs and begin to move either clockwise or counterclockwise. Just follow the electric blasts in the direction they're heading until they disappear to avoid damage.

Questing for Outfits

If you're up for it, you can replay the first level of the Woodlands, the Deku Forest, to get another Armos Spirit and replay Buzz Blob Cave to get a Tektite Shell. With both items in hand and a pocket full of Rupees, you can head over to Madame Couture's and make the Big Bomb Outfit, which is useful in the next level. This dynamite Outfit will increase the size of your Bombs, as well as the size of their explosion and the damage they do, making enemies and obstacles crumble in an instant.

Just make sure to be extra careful when wearing the Big Bomb Outfit: You'll do double damage to anything that gets caught in the blast, including you and your teammates.

Level 3: Moblin Base

Challenges

Pop all balloons

Defeat all foes without a sword

Transport the orb quickly

Recommended Outfits

 Big Bomb Outfit

 Kokiri Clothes

There are two Bows and a Bomb Sub-Weapon in this level, which is why we suggest using both the Kokiri Clothes and Big Bomb Outfit. You only need one Big Bomb Outfit, as the Outfit's effects will only work on the one wearing the outfit. If you're playing multiplayer, choose one player to wear the Big Bomb Outfit and have the other two pick the Kokiri Clothes. If you're playing single-player, you'll want to bring the Kokiri Clothes instead of the Big Bomb Outfit: They'll help you solve a challenging puzzle near the end of the level a lot easier.

Sub-Weapons

 Bow

 Bow

 Bombs

Materials

 Armos Spirit

 Armos Spirit

 Sweet Shroom

ROOM 1

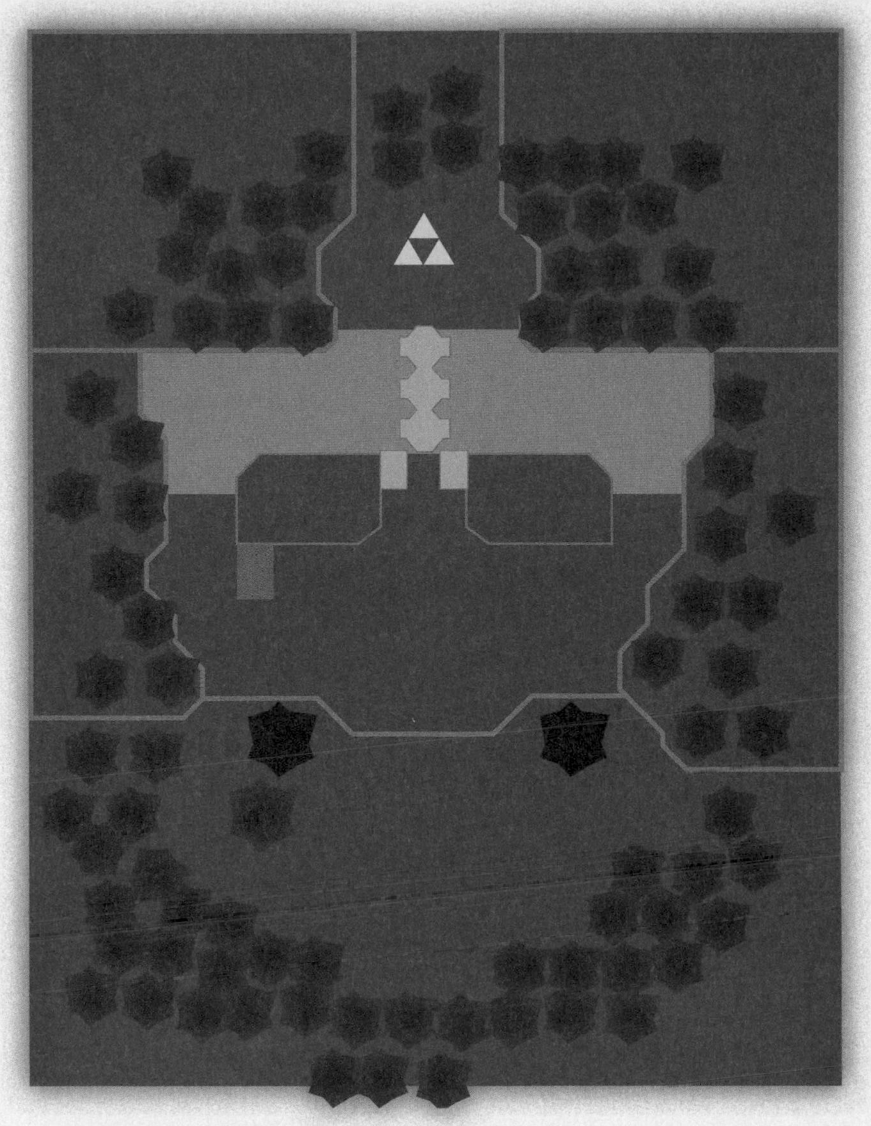

At the start of the level, you can head to either the northeast or northwest corners of the area to find giant leaves that will carry you to this level's Sub-Weapons. Have each Link grab a Sub-Weapon, keeping in mind that only the Links wearing Kokiri Clothes should pick up Bows, while the Big Bomb Outfit-wearing Link should grab the Bombs.

Just northwest of where you grabbed your Sub-Weapons, you'll find four cracked blocks. Use your Bombs to destroy the blocks, then have all three Links meet on top of this plateau.

There are two orb switches, one on either side of the giant statues in the center of the river. You'll need a two-Link Totem with a Bow user on top to hit these orbs. First pick up one of the Bow-using Links and throw him across the gap to the right of the statues. Have that Link line up with and face the switch on his side, taking extra care to have him stand on the platform directly in front of the switch. Now, as the Bomb-using Link, pick up the remaining Bow Link and point him at the first switch.

As soon as you have the top Link fire his Bow, turn and immediately throw him over to the Link across the gap. Have either Link make a two-Link Totem, face the second switch, and fire. If you timed it right, the statues will lower and you'll be clear to head to the north side of the room.

ROOM 2

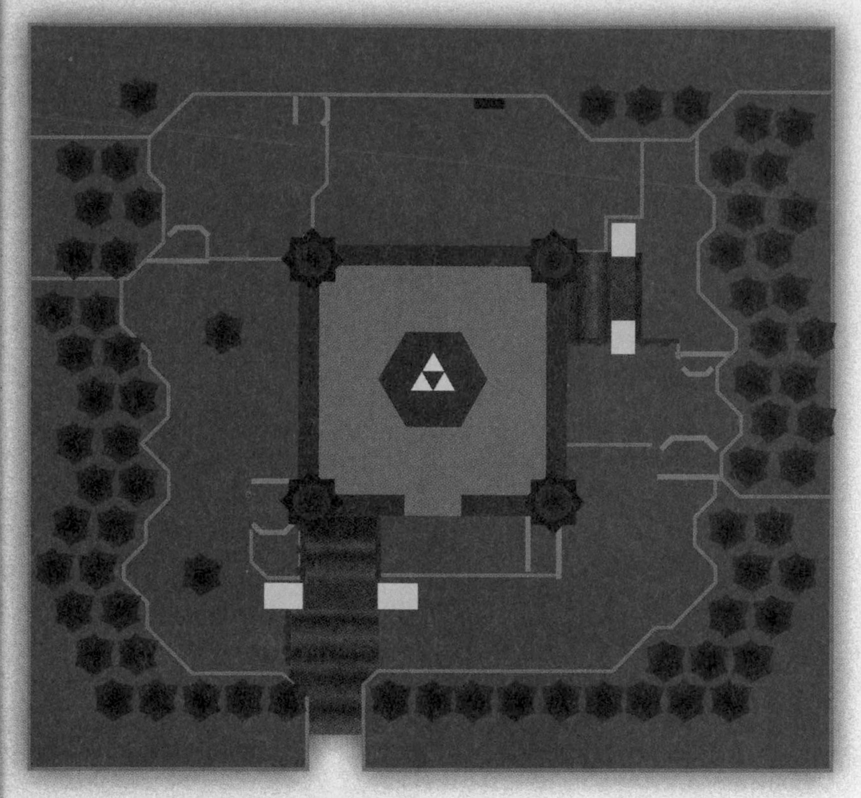

This room just requires you to defeat all the enemies in it in order to progress. You'll find three Totem Dekus on the east side of the room.

On the north end you'll find a couple of cracked walls that conceal treasure chests, a Buzz Blob, and a new enemy type: The Life Like. Life Likes are one of the most devastating enemies in the game when playing multiplayer, and a complete pain in single-player. The best way to defeat these glorified leeches is by using your Bombs. If you can land a Bomb inside a Life Like's mouth, it'll blow up like a squishy Dodongo. If your Bomb Link is too far away, just use your Bow and keep your distance. If this monster cheese puff gets its grubby little sucker on you, it'll start eating you, draining your health in the process. If you're on multiplayer and your teammates aren't around, you're in a whole lot of trouble. If you're in single-player you can just swap to one of your Doppels to stop being damaged, but that doesn't stop this guy from being a real pain. Take care whenever you see a Life Like or a Heart sitting on the ground inexplicably.

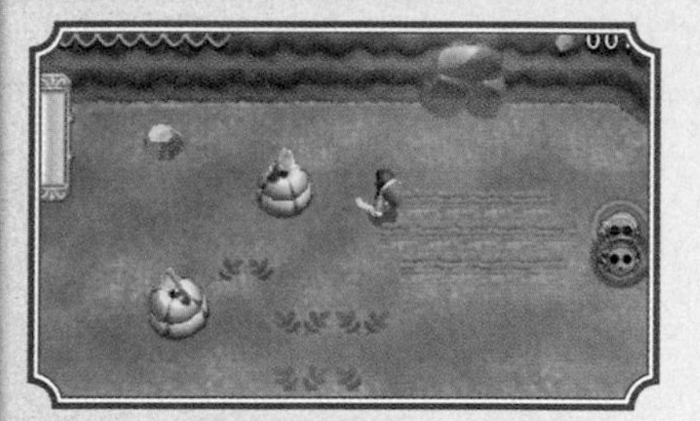

After defeating the Life Likes, head to the west side of the room and clear out the Buzz Blobs to reveal the Triforce gateway at the center of the map. The gates surrounding the fortress-like structure at the room's center will open, allowing you to reach the Triforce gateway and another Squiddy.

ROOM 3

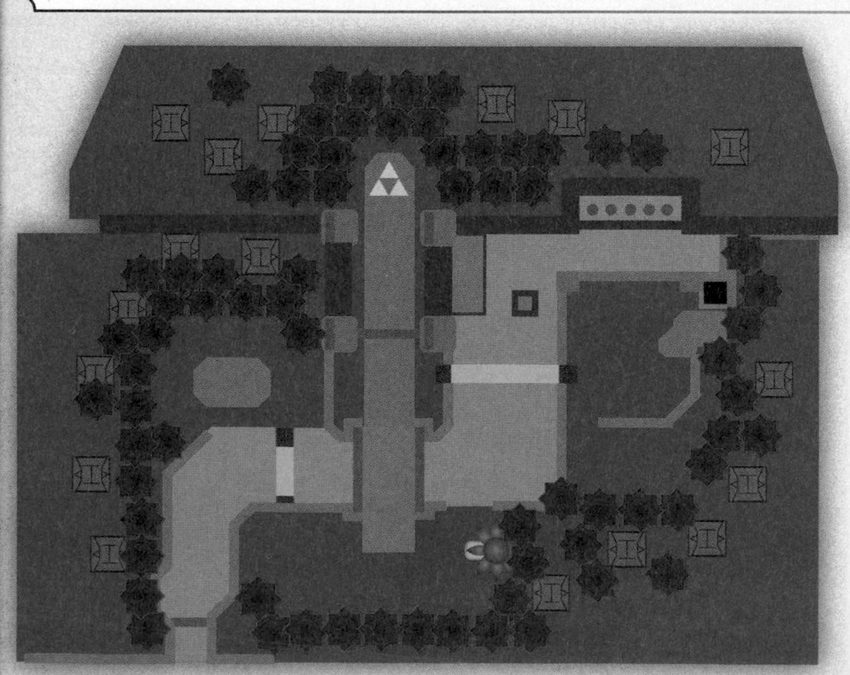

You'll find two Blobs right as you enter the room. Take them out and head across the log to the south side of the room.

At the end of the log you'll run into a Buzz Blob and a Heart conspicuously sitting in the center of some tall grass. Defeat the Buzz Blob and then quickly approach the Heart, stopping just short of picking it up, then walk away. If you did it right another Life Like will pop up out of the ground. It was trying to bait you into its spongy maw with a Heart! Defeat the Life Like in the same fashion you dispatched the last two, then head right.

You'll find another Totem Deku on the right side of this plateau. Defeat it, then cross the bridge.

On the other side of the log is a gate with a lock on it and a new enemy—the Spear-Throwing Moblin. These guys are cowards: If you keep marching toward this cowardly swine, they'll back away from you and try to throw spears. The spears are pretty easy to dodge and the Moblins don't move particularly fast. You can use your Bow to take them out at a distance or turn them into bacon strips with your sword.

Take out the second Moblin on the log bridge to your right, then cross that very bridge.

Remember when we mentioned a challenging puzzle near the end of this level? Well, here you go! There is a large gate blocking five orb switches and an orb switch under a grate to the right of the gate. Have your Bomb Link throw a Bomb on top of the grate to hit the switch.

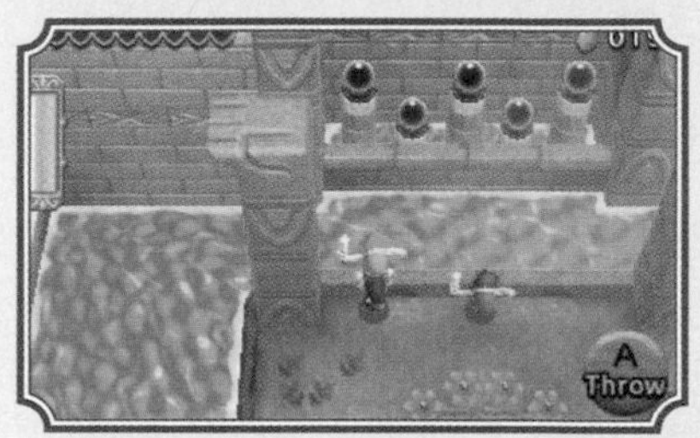

Once the switch has been hit, the gate will open to reveal the switches. This puzzle is pretty simple if you have the Kokiri Clothes on at least one of the Bow Links. In single-player, have the two Bow Links make a Totem, with the Link wearing the Kokiri Clothes (if you have them) on top. If you have the Kokiri Clothes, you'll want to aim at the center switch. If you don't, start with the far left or far right switch. Fire at each of the higher switches, throw the Link off the top of the Totem, and use the bottom Link to hit the lower switches.

A Multiplayer Method

Have the Bomb Link lift whatever Link has the Kokiri Clothes and the Bow. Have the second Bow Link stand in front of the orb switch to the right or left of the center orb switch. At the same time, have the Totem Bow Link fire at the center switch; if you're using the Kokiri Clothes, it should hit all three. The lower Link should quickly take care of the two lower switches.

If you did it fast enough a key will appear across the river to your left. Now make a three-Link Totem, approach the edge of the river, just in front of the platform sitting in the middle of the river, and have the bottom Link throw the top two Links onto that river platform. Have the bottom Link of the smaller Totem throw the top Link to the platform with the key on it. Good work! The hardest parts are done.

Take the key and throw it to the Link on the river platform, then have that Link throw it to the Link back on dry land. March the key to the lock on the gate in the center of the room, open it, and stand on the Triforce gateway to head to the next room.

ROOM 4

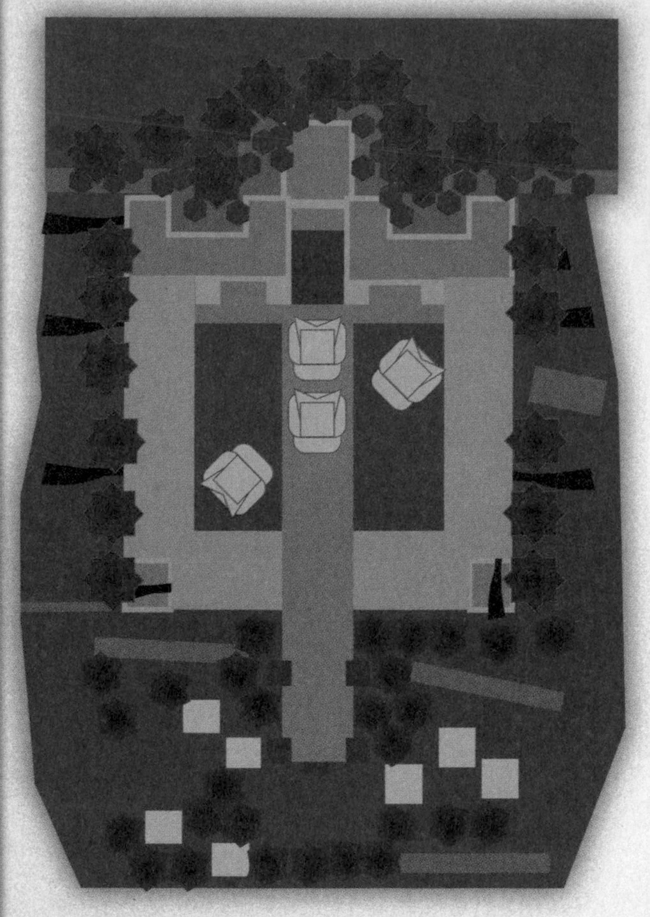

This is another combat-heavy room that requires you to defeat every enemy in it to get the Triforce gateway to appear. On the east and west sides of the room are towers that house Moblins. Ignore them for now; if you keep your distance from them you won't have to worry about their attacks.

The enemies you have to watch out for are the Totem Armos-riding Moblins. These enemies work like Totem Dekus in that you need to make a Totem to defeat them. What makes them different is that they will march toward you while throwing spears, and when you defeat the pilot of the statue, the statue will spin toward you, exploding after a few seconds.

You can make this fight a lot easier by trying to take out any of the Moblins without Totem Armos before taking on the ones that have them. Just don't linger in front of the towers for too long and you'll be fine.

In Case of Emergency

If things aren't going well, you can throw one or two of your Links onto the ledges on the east and west sides of the room. You'll find plenty of Hearts on either side that will get you back into shape.

Once you've cleared the first set of enemies on the ground, another set will appear, including more statue riders. Defeat them and a final wave will appear. Take them out, then make a three-Link Totem and head toward one of the towers. There are a few ways you can deal with this: If you're playing single-player, you can just throw your top Link onto each tower, switch to him, and defeat the Moblins. Doppels don't take damage (unless they fall off of a cliff) and they can also be used as a throwable weapon if they land on an enemy. Switch to that Link and dice up the porkers to open the door to the Triforce gateway.

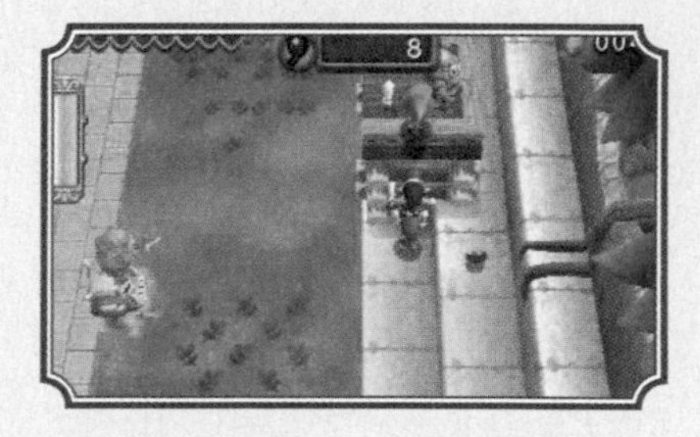

You can either throw the top Link onto the towers (which is risky and can easily get that Link knocked back to the ground), or you can put the Bomb Link on top of the Totem and have him throw Bombs onto each tower to make short work of the enemies.

No matter what method you choose, when all of the Moblins have been eliminated, the door will open and the level will be complete. Head to room 5 and claim your prize.

OPEN FOR BUSINESS!

The Street Merchant will open up shop to the left of Madame Couture's boutique. The Street Merchant has new Materials for sale every day, but the one to look out for is the Frilly Fabric. The only way to obtain the Frilly Fabric is by purchasing it from the Street Merchant and you need three of them if you want to purchase the newly unlocked Cheer Outfit from Madame Couture. Make sure to save up some Rupees and purchase these Materials whenever possible!

Questing for Outfits

If you're willing to take the time, you can gather a Tektite Shell from level 2 and a Sweet Shroom from level 3 to have Madame Couture make you the Legendary Dress. This dress will increase the likelihood of Hearts dropping for the player wearing it. That means you can have a Link cutting down bushes, smashing pots, and breaking rocks to find Hearts, so long as they are wearing this Outfit. It'll help keep you alive in many of the challenging levels to come, so it's definitely worth the effort to make it.

Level 4: Forest Temple

Challenges

Adventure in the dark

Clear within the time limit

Fewer Heart Containers

Sub-Weapons

 Bow

 Bombs

 Bombs

Materials

 Tektite Shell

 Tektite Shell

 Blin Bling

Recommended Outfits

 Big Bomb Outfit

 Kokiri Clothes

Big Bomb Outfits are a near must for this level. You'll be encountering enemies that can only be killed by Bombs, so you'll get a lot out of using that particular Outfit. If you're playing multiplayer, you can have the other Link wear what that player wants to wear. It's not vital to have Kokiri Clothes this time around, but it doesn't hurt if your third player doesn't have anything else to wear.

ROOM 1

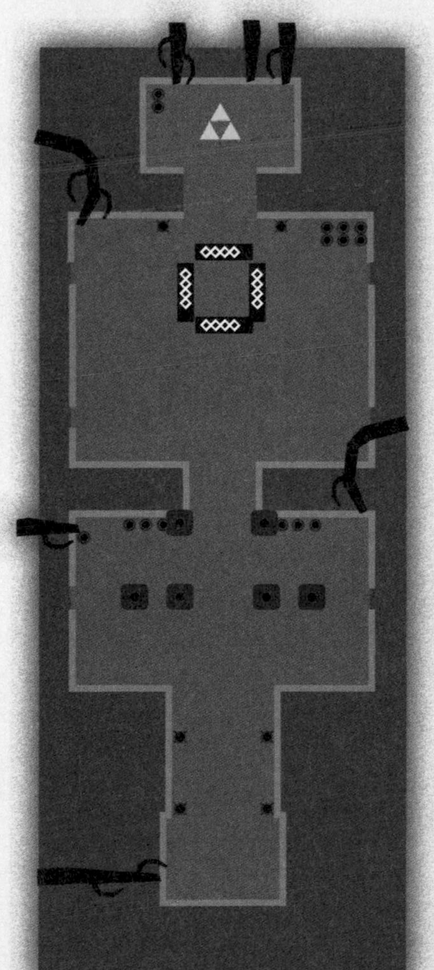

The Sub-Weapons for this level are directly in front the level's starting point. Have your Big Bomb Link pick up the Bombs and then distribute the other items to your remaining two Links.

In the center of this area is a row of four torches, one of which is unlit. Have the Bow-wielding Link head to the right side of the far-right torch, then have him face left and fire an arrow. The arrow will catch on fire and light the unlit torch.

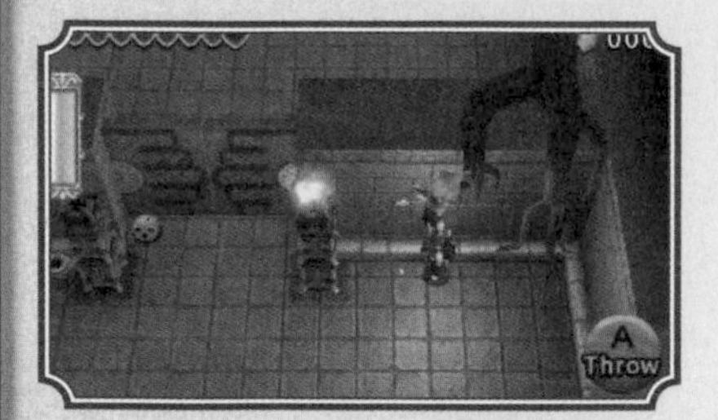

Now clear out the pots to the right of the tall torch on the right side of the gate. Make a three-Link Totem on the right side of the torch, face left, and fire another arrow. This will light the second and final unlit torch, which will open the gate to the next room.

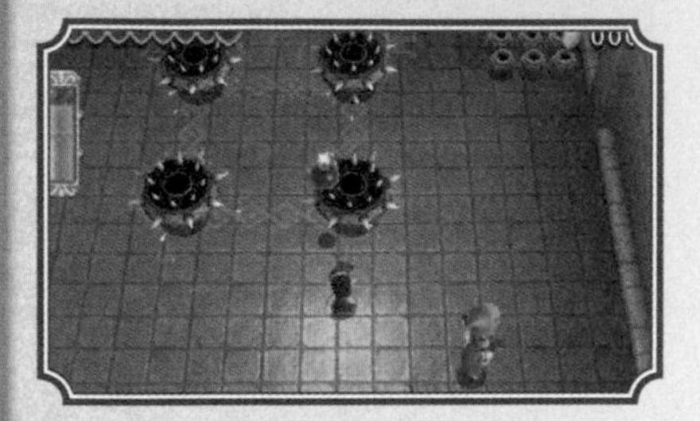

You'll meet a new type of enemy once you're in the next area—a bladed, spinning Mini-Margo. In order to defeat it, you'll need to throw a Bomb into its center. It only takes one to take it out, but you'll have to time it right if you want to hit the bullseye. Spinning Mini-Margos almost always follow along paths shown on the ground below them, so predicting their movements is quite easy. Whenever ever a Mini-Margo reaches a corner on its path, it will come to a brief stop. That's your chance to strike!

Once all four of the traps have been destroyed, a key to the locked gate on the north side of the room will drop. Open the gate to gain access to the Triforce gateway. Before you go, make sure to explode the Squiddy to get Hearts and Rupees.

ROOM 2

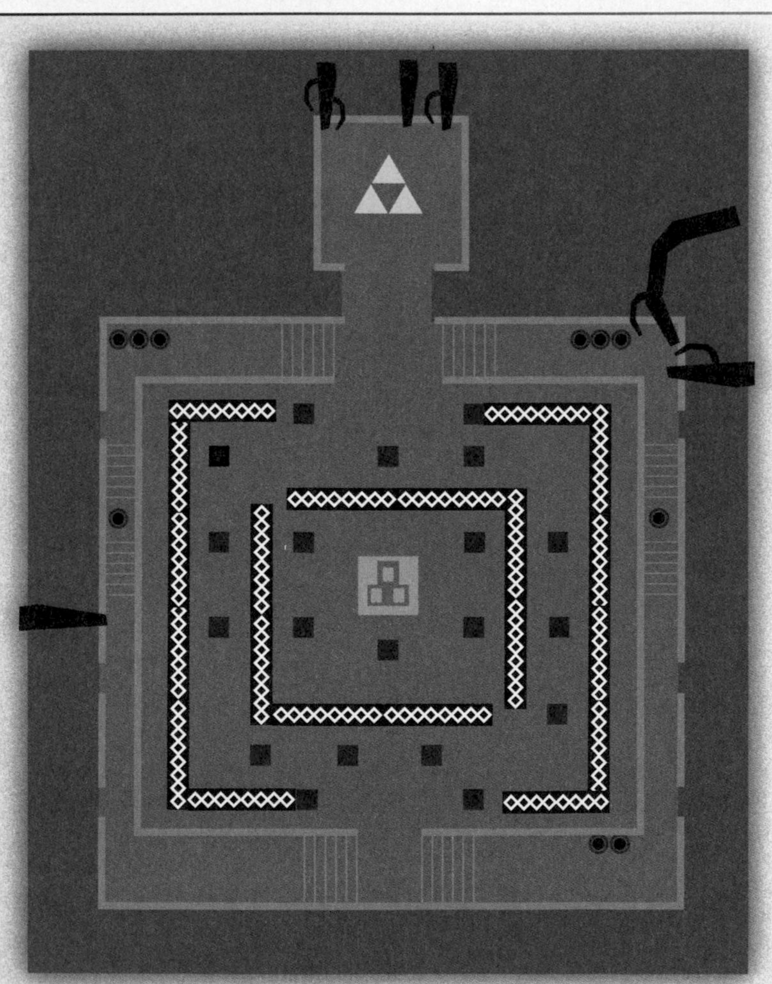

This room starts out empty, with nothing but a three-man switch in the center. Before you activate the switch, have one of your Bomb Links destroy the cracked blocks on the northeast and northwest corners of the room. This will make things a little easier once you hit the switch.

Now have all three Links stand on the three-man switch in the center of the room and prepare for battle! Pillars will rise from the floor and spinning Mini-Margos and Tektites will appear in the room. The pillars give the one-eyed Tektites something to stand on, meaning you'll have to make a two-Link Totem to hit them—or rather, you would if you didn't destroy those cracked blocks. Now the Tektites will jump on the pillars near you and eventually land where the cracked blocks used to be, giving you the chance to defeat them without having to create a Totem to do so.

Watch out for the spinning Mini-Margos that follow along the electric path on the floor. Once you've dealt with the Tektites, destroy the Mini-Margos. Remember, they stop whenever they reach corners and they'll also stop briefly when they reach the end of their path.

In Case of Emergency

If you're having any trouble with this room, you can break the pots on the east and west sides of the room to potentially find some Hearts.

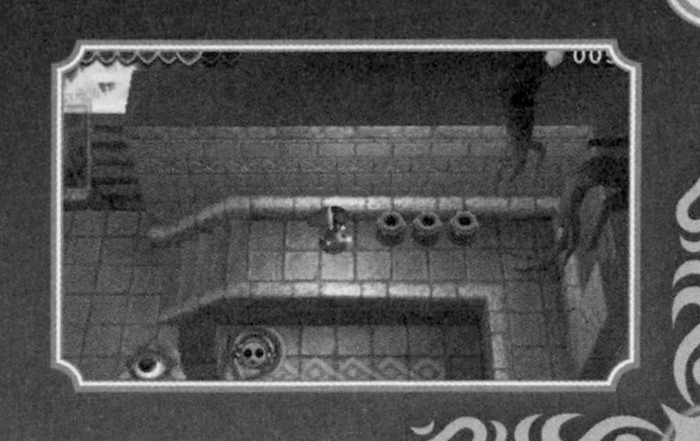

Once you've defeated the Mini-Margos and Tektites, the north door will open and you'll be free to move on to room 3.

ROOM 3

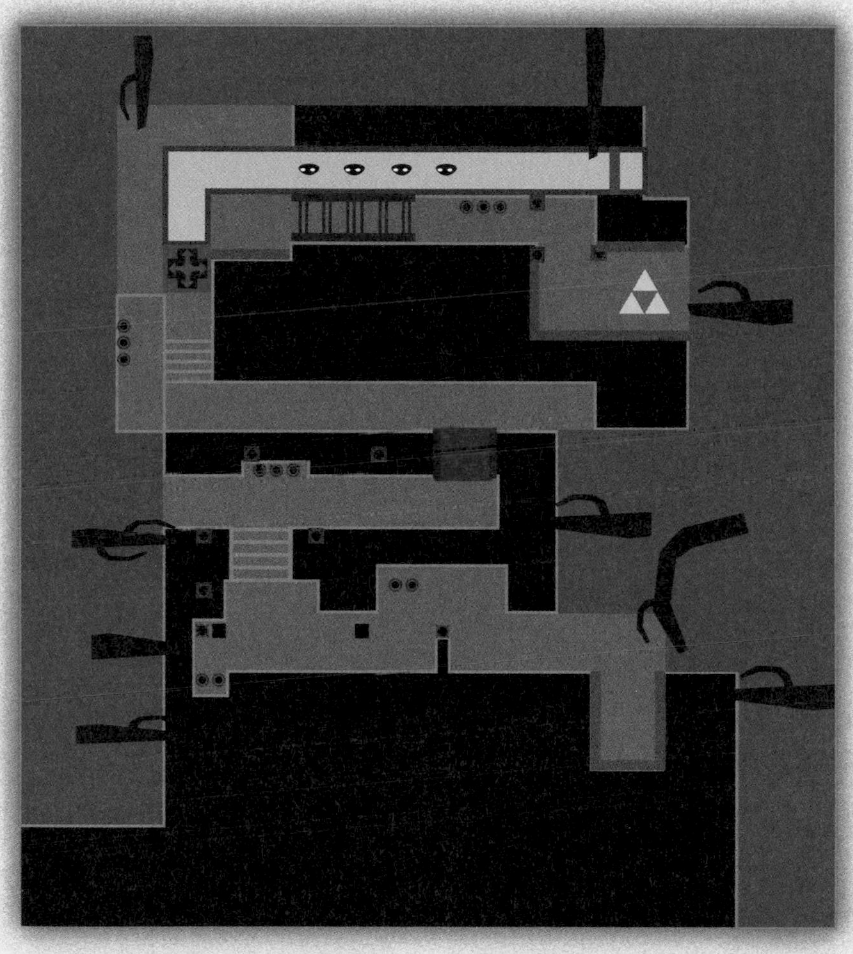

Now here's a tricky room! On the path directly ahead of you you'll see arrows firing out of the wall. You'll need to squeeze in between shots and make your way to the west side of the room. Getting in between the arrows isn't terribly hard if you're only trying to get in front of one of the three firing arrows. As soon as the bottom arrow fires, follow behind it and slowly and carefully move your way up.

After a short walk you'll reach a safe part of the path. You can stand and take a breather or keep moving to the end of the path. Once you're at the end of the path you'll see two cracked blocks. Use your Bombs to destroy the one on the left first, then destroy the one on the right. This will allow the top arrow from the arrow trap to reach the unlit torch to your left while on fire, lighting the first of three torches.

Your next step is to position your Bow-wielding Link below the newly-lit torch where the pots are. (Just make sure to destroy the pots first.) Line up the Bow Link with the flaming torch and have him fire. The arrow will start on fire and light the two remaining torches. Once the torches are lit, a set of stairs will rise from the depths to allow you to ascend to the path north of you. (Sounds pretty intense, huh?)

You'll have to deal with another arrow trap here, but this time there are only two of them, so they are much easier to avoid. Wait for the arrows to fire, then follow behind them until you reach another flight of stairs.

Wouldn't you know it? Another arrow trap! Don't worry, you're getting close! Wait for the arrows to fire on this new trap and follow behind them until you reach another set of stairs, some pots, and a giant steel box.

Make sure to check the pots for Hearts to refill any empty Heart Containers, then head up to the giant box. If you're playing multiplayer, you'll need all three Links to be pushing this box at the same time. If you're in single-player, however, just one Link will do the trick.

Push the box along the pinkish path on the ground. Another arrow trap waits for you at the east end of this long path, but don't worry. Now's your chance for revenge! Push the box to the east toward the arrow traps to create a safe path for you and your Links to get through.

Once you reach the end of the path, you'll be right next to the Triforce gateway, but a Mini-Margo will be bouncing over it chaotically and without a path to follow. Use expert timing to land a Bomb in this wild one. Once it's defeated you're free to move on to room 4.

ROOM 4

BOSS FIGHT: MARGOMA

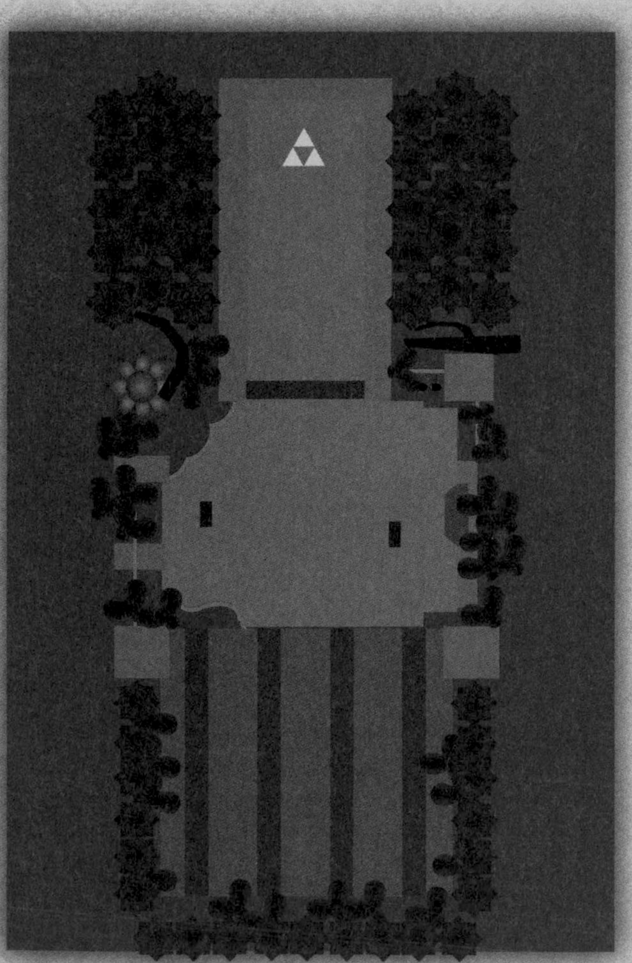

Each Link will start out in different parts of this room. Have them all slide down into the lower level of the room. Welcome to your first true boss fight.

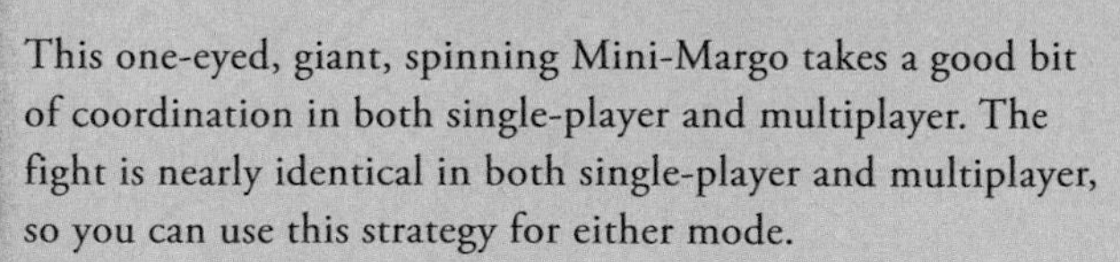

This one-eyed, giant, spinning Mini-Margo takes a good bit of coordination in both single-player and multiplayer. The fight is nearly identical in both single-player and multiplayer, so you can use this strategy for either mode.

Margoma has a very simple moveset: It spins towards you until it hits something. That's all. If you stay on the ramps on the east and west sides of the room, it won't be able to hit you at all. Defeating it is an entirely different story.

On the east and west sides of the room, near the ramps, you'll see cracked boxes. DO NOT DESTROY THEM. These are excellent barriers between you and Margoma. You can hide behind them and remain safe, at least until it charges at you.

In order to damage Margoma, you'll need to get to its eye, but those spikes surrounding it are pretty nasty. So what do you do? You need to get it to charge into something. When Margoma stops in place and begins spinning its blades rapidly, that means it's about to charge at you. Get close to a wall, behind the cracked boxes, or up the ramp. When Margoma slams into one of those things, the hole in its center will open up, giving you a chance to throw a Bomb in it. Make a two-Link Totem and throw a Bomb in there.

After successfully landing a Bomb inside Margoma, its eye will pop out, it'll retract its spikes, and it will get dizzy. This is your chance. To reach Margoma's eye, walk your two-Link Totem over to Margoma and throw the top Link onto Margoma. Now have that top Link slash away. After a short time the hole will close back up and it'll begin to shake. That's your cue to get off of Margoma ASAP.

Repeat these steps two or three times and Margoma will grow, meaning you need to as well. The rules are still the same, but you now need to make a three-Link Totem to throw Bombs into the open hatch and to get on top of it. Repeat this two or three more times and Margoma's eye will bounce out of the Mini-Margo and begin to bounce around the room. Chase it down and slash it until it explodes.

Congratulations! You just defeated your first boss! With that level completed, you'll unlock new worlds and the ability to do level challenges for all of world 1's levels.

THE KING'S SUMMONS

Beating the first world in the Drablands has given the people of Hytopia hope, especially King Tuft! Head out of the lobby and Sir Combsly will inform you that the King wishes to speak to Link. Head up the stairs on the left side of the castle foyer to reach the king. King Tuft will better explain the curse The Lady has placed on the kingdom and he will also explain level challenges.

Once you're done speaking with him, make sure to speak with Madame Couture and check out her new supply of Outfits. She'll go into detail about The Lady's Glasses Material you found at the end of the Forest Temple and also explain how to break Princess Styla's curse!

Once you're done, feel free to head back to the lobby and move on to your next world.

A Real Challenger

You may have noticed the challenges listed at the start of each level in this guide. Well, up until this point you haven't been able to do them. Now that you completed each level in world 1, you can try your hand at three individual challenges per stage for added gameplay and different Materials. These variations of world 1's levels truly live up to their name of "Challenge", meaning you'll have to stretch yourself and your teammates pretty far to get through them. Some of them you won't even be ready to complete until you get better outfits. Regardless, you can head over to the "Odds and Ends" section of the guide at the back of the book to get some tips and tricks on how to complete each challenge type.

WALKTHROUGH

WORLD 2: RIVERSIDE

Level 1: Secret Fortress

Challenges

Pop all balloons

Clear with halved energy

Evade the Wallmaster

Sub-Weapons

 Water Rod

 Water Rod

 Water Rod

Materials

 Fresh Kelp

 Fresh Kelp

 Zora Scale

Recommended Outfits

 Big Bomb Outfit

 Legendary Dress

This level introduces you to the Water Rod, a Sub-Weapon that creates climbable pillars of water that allow you to ascend to new heights without having to make a Totem. This allows for a lot of new and interesting puzzle-solving techniques. (And using the Water Rod to annoy your friends is a great time too.)

You won't have either of the Outfits that work exceptionally well on this level (the Zora Costume and the Torrent Robe), but one Outfit that will help terrifically on a challenging puzzle near the end of the level is the Big Bomb Outfit. If you're playing multiplayer, have one player wear the Big Bomb Outfit and have the remaining two players wear the Legendary Dress. (You can also wear the Lucky Loungewear, if you took the time to make it.)

ROOM 1

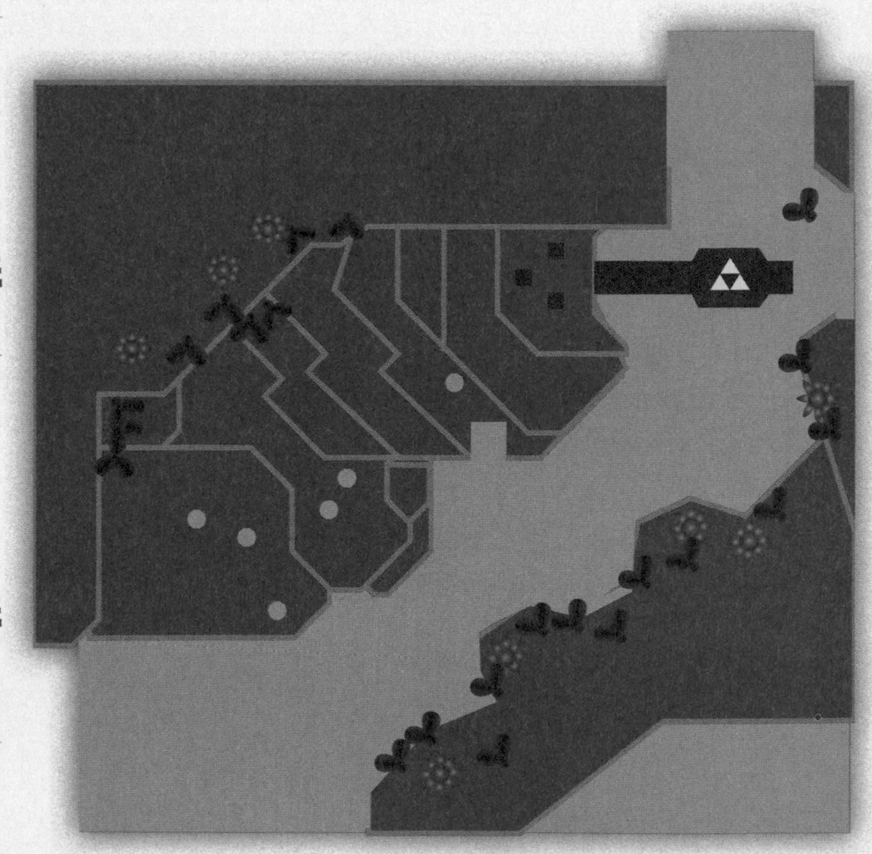

You'll start this level at the base of a set of cliffs. Make a three-Link Totem and throw the top two Links onto the ledge to your right. You'll find a Water Rod on this first ledge. Grab it and use it to get the Link on the lower level up to where your other two Links are.

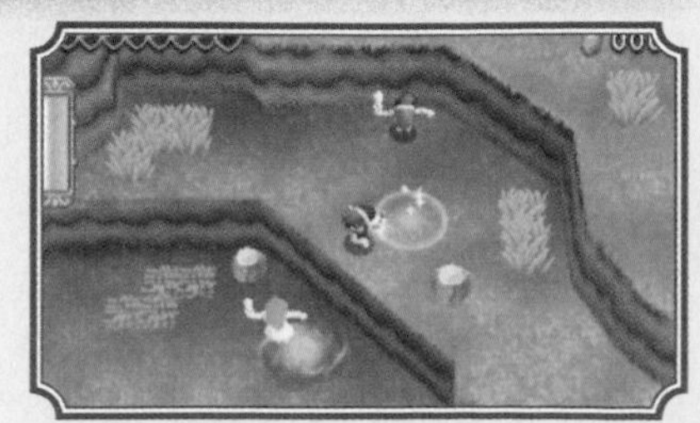

Make a three-Link Totem with the Water Rod Link at the top, then use that Link's Water Rod to create a platform to the next cliff. On the north and south ends of the cliff you have moved to, you'll find two more Water Rods. Grab them with your Sub-Weaponless Links, make a three-Link Totem, and use the Water Rod to scale the cliffs to your right. Just make sure to avoid the Blobs on your way up.

Once at the top of the cliff, you'll find three short towers, each with a switch on top, and two of which have Spear Throwing Moblins on top. Use the Water Rod with each Link and position them on each of the three switches. This will cause a bridge to extend from the east, giving you access to the Triforce gateway.

ROOM 2

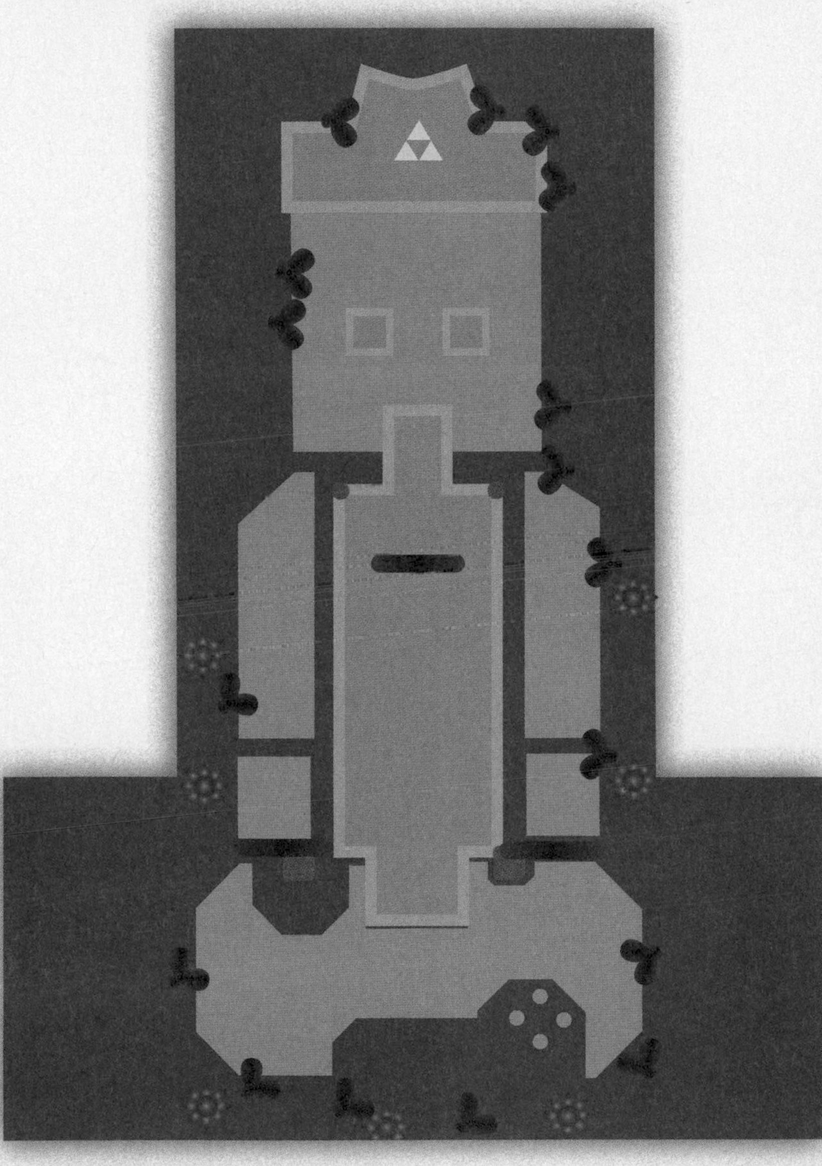

There are two orb switches, one on the left and one on the right side of the gate, just north of your starting position. To reach them, grab a Link to make a two-Link Totem, then use the Water Rod to create a bridge of water pillars to the orb switch on the right. Throw the top Link onto the platform the orb switch is on, then swim back to the shore you started on. These switches aren't timed, so you can have Link standing next to the right switch and hit it at any time.

Now make a two-Link Totem with the remaining Link and use the Water Rod to create a bridge of water pillars leading to the left side of the gate. There's a Moblin patrolling the plateau the orb switch is on, so take care not to get knocked back into the water by it. Once the coast is clear, create a water pillar just below the orb switch and then throw the top Link onto the switch's platform. Have that Link hit his switch and the gate will open for you.

Things get a little tricky in this room. There are three switches for the three Links. All three Links must stand on their switches at the same time to activate them. Problem is, there are flame rods covering two of them. In order to keep the fire at bay momentarily, you need to create a water pillar in front of the flame rod's source. This will buy you a few seconds to stand on the switch. If you're playing single-player, you can create a water pillar to stop the fire, position your Link on the switch, and then switch Links. Doppels can't take damage unless they fall off of a cliff, so you don't have to worry about them taking damage while they keep the switch pressed.

If you're playing multiplayer, you'll need to coordinate with your teammates in order to hit the two switches under the flame rods. Count down from three, have two of the Links create water pillars in front of the flame rods, and then step on the switches while the third Link stands on the safe switch. If you time it right you'll open the northern gate leading out of this room.

Two more flame rods will try to impede your quest in this next area. To make matters worse, they spin in a circle. Don't worry, however—these ones can be easily thwarted. Wait for the flame rod on the left to pass you, then quickly create a water pillar to the plateau on the north end of the room. You'll want to have one Link pass at a time if you're playing single-player. The timing here is very tight and you'll likely need to jump into the water, wait for the flame rod to pass, and then hop back on your water pillar.

You'll find another Squiddy and the Triforce gateway out of this room on the other end of this room.

ROOM 3

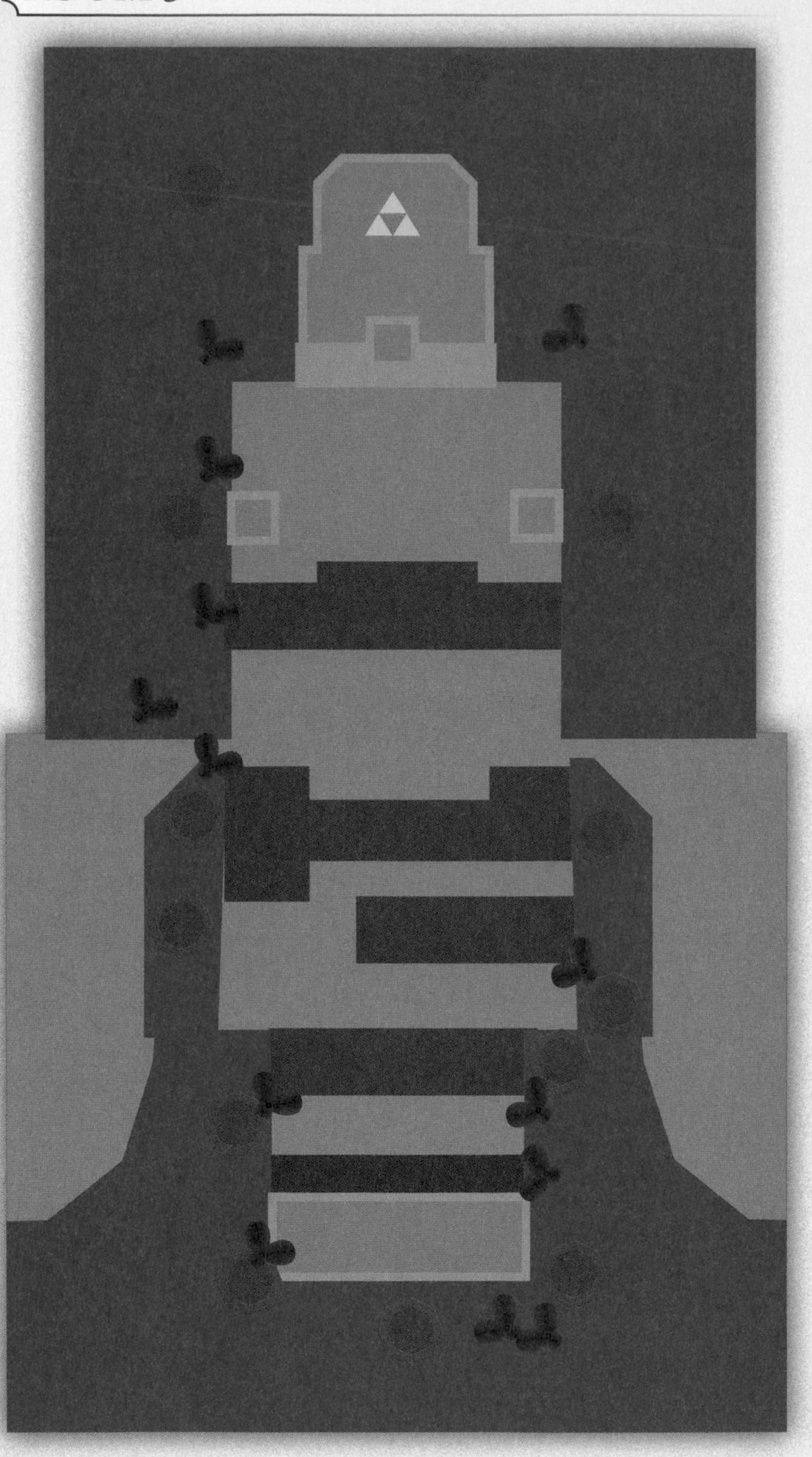

The first half of this room simply requires you to create water pillars to reach the grated platforms sitting above the river. Spear Throwing Moblins will try and knock you into the water every chance they get, so take care to defeat them as quickly as possible while you make your way north.

After crossing three of the grated platforms, you'll come to a waterfall and some Tektites. The Tektites are easily defeated or ignored, depending on how determined they are to get to you. Create a water bridge north to the wood platform above the waterfall. This is where things get tricky.

A gate is blocking your path on the north end of this area and you'll need to open it to progress. To do that you'll need to hit the orb switches on the left and right sides of the room. These aren't timed switches, so you don't have to worry about rushing. Simply create a water pillar, grab a Bomb from the Bomb Plant, hop onto your water pillar, and throw the Bomb next to the orbs. You don't need to create a water pillar to get the Bombs up next to the orbs, but it definitely makes it easier.

Once you've done that, the gate will open. Unfortunately, this is where things get tough. Two giant cracked blocks impede the way to the Triforce gateway and you need to destroy them with the Bombs on the wood platform you're standing on. Before you attempt this, create a water bridge to the northeast and northwest corners of the room to defeat the pesky Crows circling the area. (They'll gladly make this area more difficult for you than it needs to be.)

This is the reason we suggested the Big Bomb Outfit: This puzzle is very challenging in single-player and requires some excellent teamwork in multiplayer. In order to reach the cracked blocks in single-player, create a water pillar as close to the cracked blocks as possible while still being able to reach it with a Bomb. Your job is to create two platforms, grab a Bomb, get on top of
the second platform, and then throw the Bomb at the cracked blocks. If you don't have the Big Bomb Outfit, you'll likely have to throw two Bombs up near the cracked blocks.

The timing is very tight, so you need to be as quick as possible.

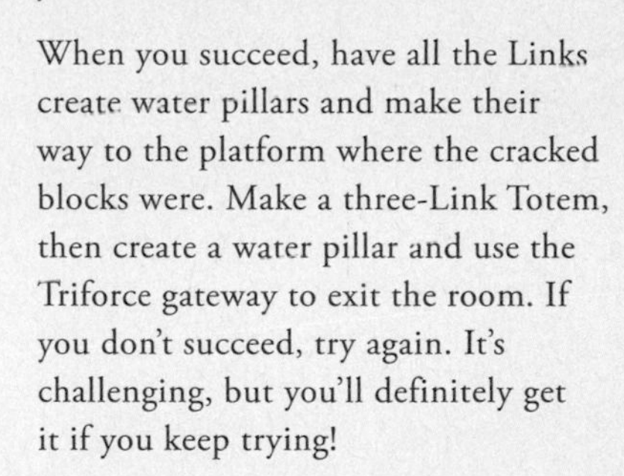

Things work a bit differently in multiplayer. You'll need to have one Link pick up a Bomb, while another Link creates a water bridge to the cracked blocks. This is much easier than the single-player method, but it requires accuracy and speed with the Water Rod to avoid having the Bomb blow up in your teammate's hands.

When you succeed, have all the Links create water pillars and make their way to the platform where the cracked blocks were. Make a three-Link Totem, then create a water pillar and use the Triforce gateway to exit the room. If you don't succeed, try again. It's challenging, but you'll definitely get it if you keep trying!

ROOM 4

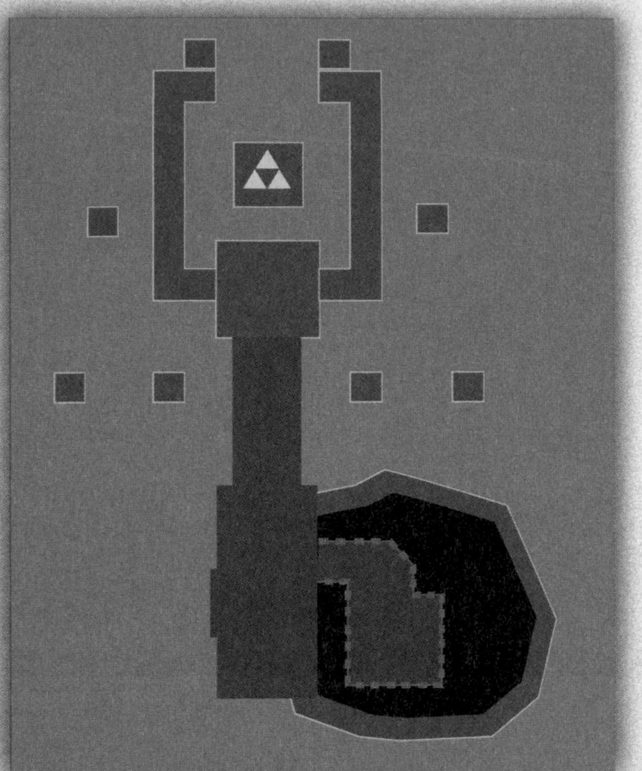

The last room of this level requires you to defeat all the enemies in it to reveal the Triforce gateway. There are several Spear Throwing Moblins standing on isolated platforms and a couple of new enemies called Keeleons. These flying pests will likely cause you more trouble than the Moblins could ever hope to, so taking them out should be your priority. They'll fly above your reach and spit Bombs at you. You can take them out in a handful of ways, one of which is to use the Water Rod on the platform you're standing on and hop on it to reach the same height as the Keeleon. This allows you to hit them directly with your sword. You also can make a three-Link Totem to reach them. Finally, you can pick up their Bombs, wait until the Bombs are flashing (signaling that they are about to explode), and then throw them toward the Keeleon. If you're wearing the Big Bomb Outfit, you'll take the Keeleon out with ease, but you'll need to make sure you're far away from the explosion to avoid taking damage.

White Water Rapids

Take extra care not to fall in the water in this room. The current is incredibly fast and will take you off to the waterfall in an instant. If you do fall in, try your best to swim in front of one of the platforms. They'll stop you from falling over the waterfall, which will allow another Link to use the Water Rod to get you back up.

Once you've defeated all the enemies in the area, a platform with the Triforce gateway will rise in the center of the room, meaning you completed this level!

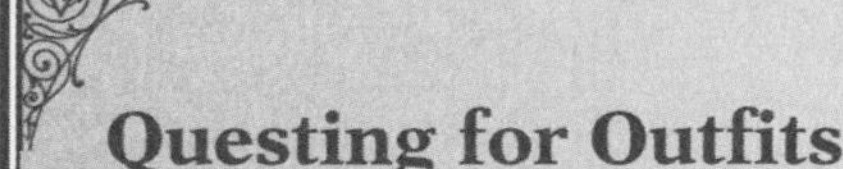

Questing for Outfits

Before moving on to the next level, you should replay the Secret Fortress until you have a Fresh Kelp and a Zora Scale Material. This will allow you to make the Zora Costume, which lets you swim much faster than without it. It'll make the rest of the levels in this world a lot easier.

Level 2: Abyss of Agony

Challenges

Halved attack and defense

Guard the orb

Clear within the time limit

Sub-Weapons

 Bow

 Water Rod

 Water Rod

Materials

 Fresh Kelp

 Fresh Kelp

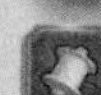 Hytopian Silk

Recommended Outfits

 Zora Costume

 Kokiri Clothes

This level lives up to its namesake with challenging puzzles. The Zora Costume will help a bit here if you have it, but whatever Link is designated to use the Bow should definitely wear the Kokiri Clothes.

ROOM 1

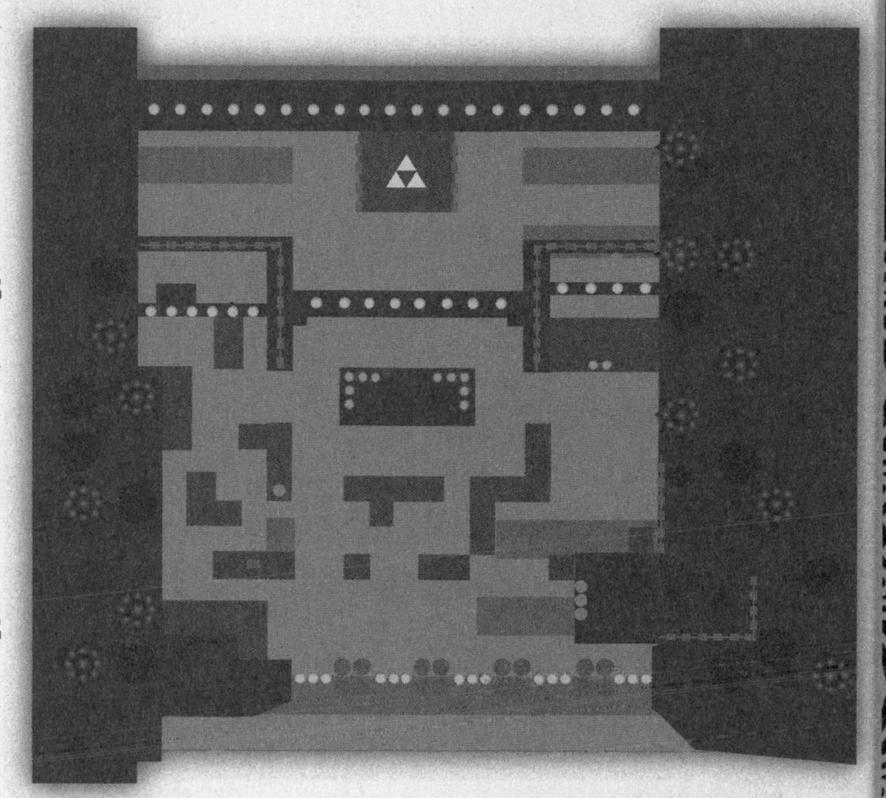

In order to get the Triforce gateway to appear, grab each of the Sub-Weapons off of the pedestals in the center of the room. Make sure to give the Bow to the Kokiri Clothes-wearing Link. In order to reach the Triforce gateway, you're going to have to jump through some hoops. Namely, you have to avoid the water as much as possible.

The water has fast currents running through just about all of it. If you fall in, you'll be dragged along on a wild ride and likely taken back to the island in the center of the room. Use the Water Rod to traverse through the water safely.

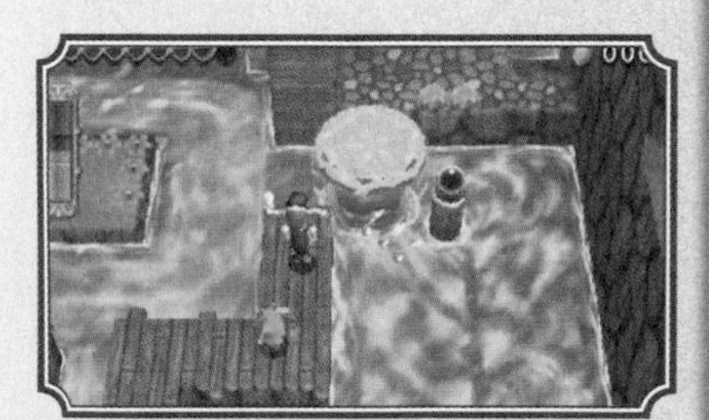

On the east side of the room is your first of three orb switches. Make a two-Link Totem with a Water Rod Link on top. Use that Link to create a platform to reach the east side of the room, then have your Bow Link line up with the orb switch and fire.

This will lower a gate just north of you, giving you access to another orb switch. Use the Water Rod to cross to the platform above you, make a two-Link Totem with the Bow Link on top, and have that Link shoot an arrow at the orb switch.

Make a two-Link Totem with the Water Rod Link on top and head to the west side of the room, taking care to avoid the spikey, exploding mines in the water. You'll find another orb switch to the left of the platform you started the level on. Create water pillars, throw your top Link safely to the other end of the platform, and then hit the switch.

This will open another gate, but this time to the northwest. Three more mines are floating in the water above the gate and you'll have to deal with a pesky Water Octorok. You can use the Water Rod to pull the Water Octorok out of the water and slash it with your sword to defeat it, but you'll need to be careful not to pull the mines up with you.

Make another two-Link Totem with your Water Rod Link on top and create a path up to the orb. Throw your top Link into the water at the top of the waterfall and have him swim up to the orb and hit it; just make sure to avoid the two mines in front of the orb. This will unlock the gate at the center of the room, giving you access to the Triforce gateway.

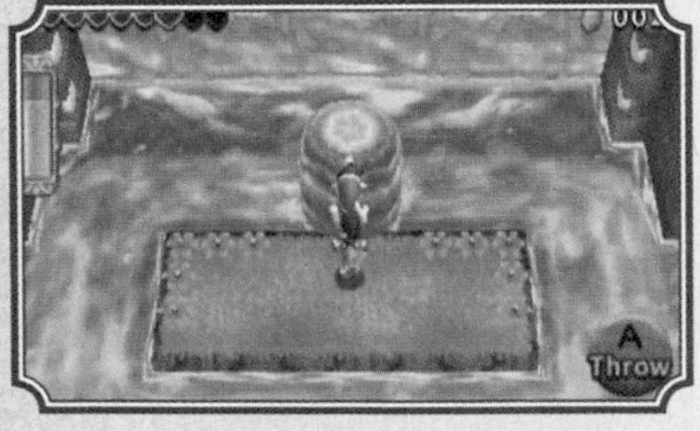

Head back to the platform in the middle of the room and make a three-Link Totem with a Water Rod Link on top. Create a water bridge up to the waterfall, then create another platform on top of it. You should be able to walk onto it with no problem. But if you're not close enough or if you accidentally touch some of the water above the waterfall, your Totem will fall apart, so take extra care. At the top of the room is the Triforce gateway. Get all three Links on it to move on to the next room.

ROOM 2

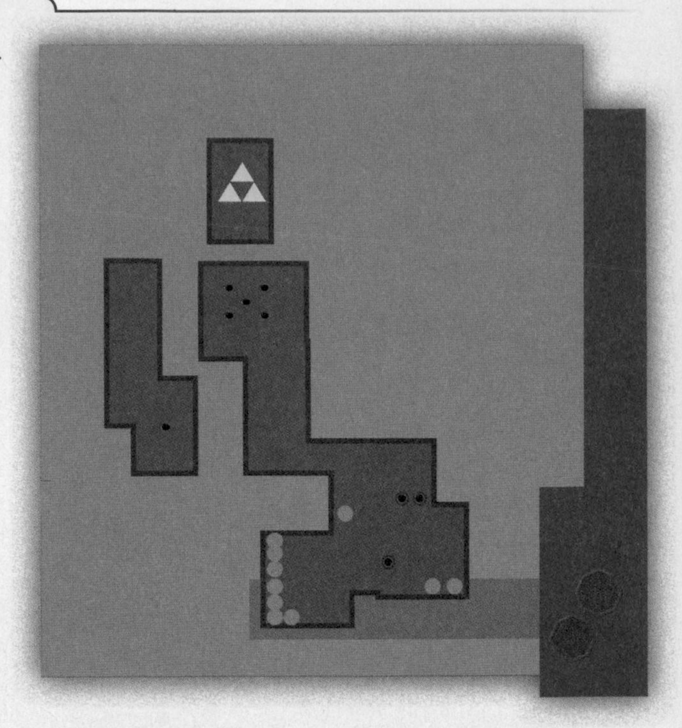

Start by scaling the ledges on your right, taking care to avoid falling into any water along the way. The currents are just as strong in this room as they were in the last, but this time you'll either fall back to the bottom of the room or lose health by being thrown off of a cliff. Climb until you reach the waterfall at the top of the cliff, then carefully jump down onto the lower platform to your left.

When all three Links jump down into this area, four Water Octoroks and a Keeleon will appear. Use the Water Rod to pull the Water Octoroks out of the water and to also put yourself at the same height as the Keeleon. Defeat all five enemies and a second wave of enemies will appear—this time two Buzz Blobs and two more Water Octoroks. Use the Bow Link to defeat the electrified Buzz Blobs, then use a Water Rod Link to defeat the Octoroks.

Once the room is clear, the Triforce gateway will light up. Carefully create a water pillar against the ledge the Triforce gateway is sitting on, then head to the next room.

ROOM 3

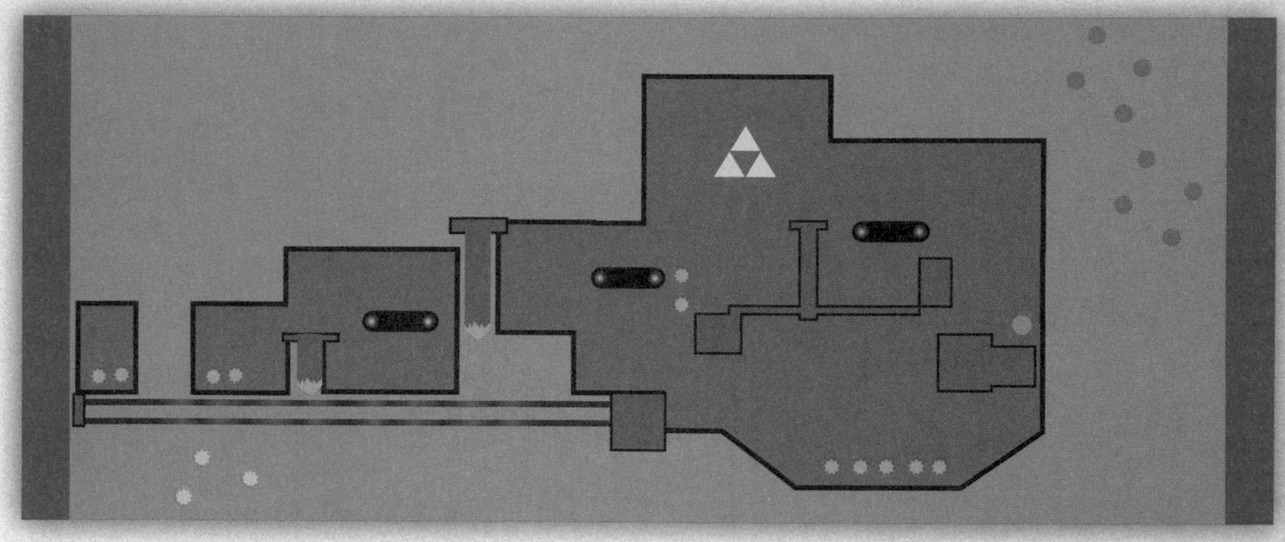

This room is quite a challenge on both single-player and multiplayer. You'll need to position your Doppels properly or have your teammates on the same page as you—this is a troll-free zone!

At the start of the area you'll find a Squiddy and a stone pillar. Smack the Squiddy against a wall and break it for its sweet, sweet treasures, then head west. Make a three-Link Totem with a Water Rod Link on top and scale the cliffs on the west side of the area. At the top of the cliffs is a wheel that is powered by water, which you happen to have control over. Designate a Water Rod Link to stand by the right side of the water wheel while the other two Links are positioned on the platform just below the wheel. Make sure to not be in a Totem and watch out for the pesky Crows that are flying around in front of the platform.

Lightning Fast!

If you're fast enough and up for a challenge, you can use the Water Rod Link that is controlling the wheel to hop onto the platform while it's moving. Have that Water Rod Link aim diagonally right toward the right side of the wheel, make a water pillar, and then immediately head toward the platform. This will save you a trip to pick him up later, but it is risky, so be careful if you try it out.

Position the Bow Link so that he is facing north, then have the Link that stayed behind use his Water Rod on the right side of the water wheel. This will propel the platform west. There is an orb switch just left of the water wheel that you'll need to have your Bow Link shoot while the platform moves, so be ready!

Once you've shot the orb switch, a gate will open to the left. The platform will come to a stop in front of another water wheel. Have the Water Rod Link on the platform move over, and use his Water Rod on the left side of the wheel to send the platform back to the other Water Rod Link. Once the second Water Rod Link is on the platform, have the first Water Rod Link hit the right side of the wheel to bring the second Water Rod Link back.

Leave the Bow Link and Water Rod Link on the platform and have the Link controlling the water wheel hit the right side again once the two Links stop near him. Have the Bow Link face south and prepare to shoot another orb switch.

Shooting the second orb switch will open another gate higher up on the cliffs. This will give you a clear route up near the top of the cliffs. Use the Water Rod Link on the platform to create a water pillar up to the ledge above, and then move both Links up there. Make a two-Link Totem with the Water Rod Link on top, then create a water pillar over the rushing water to reach the right side of the two platforms.

Next, have the wheel-controlling Link use his Water Rod to make a platform on the left side of the ledge he is currently standing on. Make a three-Link Totem with a Water Rod Link on top and create a platform against the ledge on the northeast corner of the ledge you're currently standing on.

Scale the mountain using the Water Rod until you reach another water wheel. Designate one of the Water Rod Links to control this wheel and make a two-Link totem with the remaining Links. Have the two-Link Totem carefully walk onto the wooden platform ahead; any mistakes here and you'll fall back down to the beginning of the room.

Use the Water Rod to move the platform to the other side of the ravine, then have the two-Link Totem hop off. There is another orb switch on the other side of the ravine. Hit it and it will activate the giant stone pillar you saw at the beginning of the room. This is actually an elevator that you can use to have your other Links cross the ravine.

Hidden Treasure!

You'll find a treasure chest on a platform just below the orb switch. Move very slowly when trying to fall onto the platform, or you'll fall to the ground below.

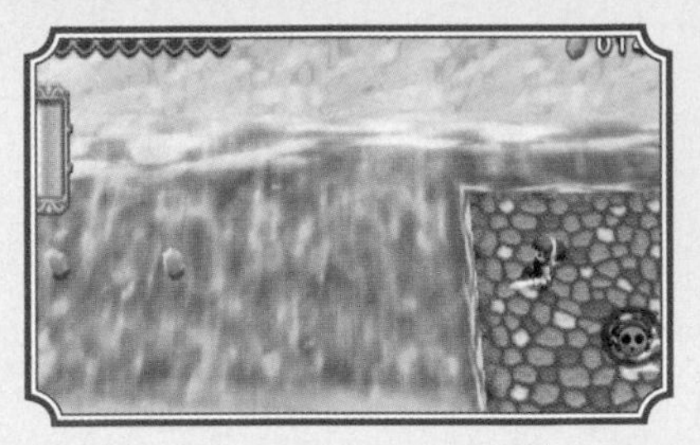

Once all of the Links are on the other side of the ravine, make a three-Link Totem with a Water Rod Link on the top and scale the cliffs on the north side of the ledge you're currently on. At the top of the ledge you'll find the Triforce gateway and, if you're feeling brave, you can use a Water Rod Link to travel over the water to the left of the Triforce gateway to obtain some Rupees. Just make sure to pay close attention to your energy gauge.

ROOM 4

BOSS FIGHT: ELECTRIC BLOB QUEEN

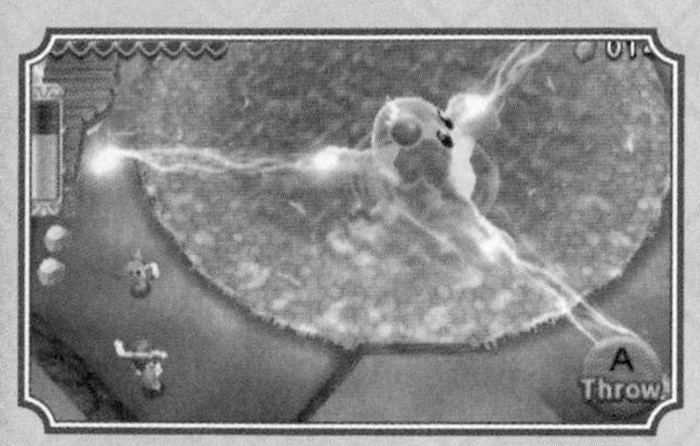

You can use the platforms along the walls to shoot her after she grows the first time. You'll be completely safe up here and, if you're using the Kokiri Clothes, you'll be able to shoot the red ball with relative ease. The second time she grows, you only need to make a two-Link Totem while on one of the platforms to reach her.

Once you hit the red ball in her head four times, she'll submerge underwater. The only way to get her out is to have one of your Water Rod Links create a water pillar underneath her. At this point, she'll grow a little taller, meaning you need to have one of your Water Rod Links pick up the Bow Link in order to shoot the red ball again. Shoot it four more times and she'll submerge again. Pull her up with another water pillar and she'll grow taller yet again. Make a three-Link Totem with the Bow Link on top and fire away. Four more shots will liquefy this shocking blob.

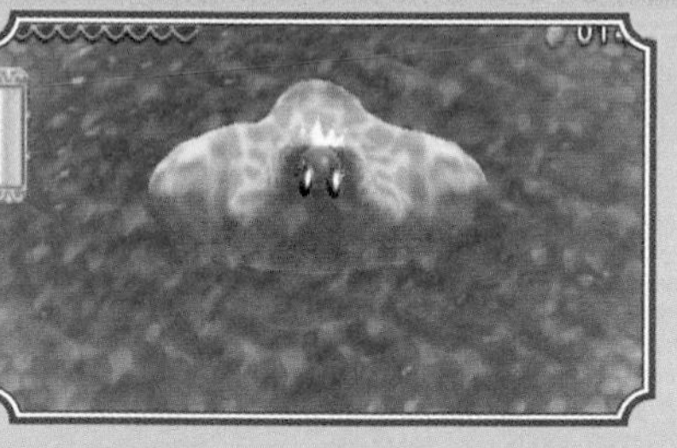

This fight is very similar to the Electric Blob King fight in world 1. You need to use your Bow-wielding Link to shoot the red ball inside the Blob Queen's head. After taking so much damage, she will dive under the water and you'll need to use a Water Rod Link to pull her back up.

The biggest change during this fight is her ability to electrify the water when she does her electric blast attack. She'll not only shock the entire pool of water.

Hidden Treasure!

You may have noticed Rupees underneath the northern platform of this room. To reach them, all you need to do is use a Water Rod Link to create a water pillar and then head up and over the edge of the platform Triforce gateway is on. Link will ride the current under the platform and nab up the Rupees with no trouble at all.

Level 3: Cove of Transition

Challenges

Halved attack and defense

Evade the Wallmaster

Clear within the time limit

Sub-Weapons

 Gripshot

 Gripshot

 Gripshot

Materials

 Zora Scale

 Zora Scale

 Aqua Crown

Recommended Outfits

 Zora Costume

There is a whole lot of water and a whole lot of swimming in this level. If you took the time to get the Zora Costume, make sure to wear it for this stage—it'll help you quite a bit!

ROOM 1

Each Link will start on a different plateau with a Gripshot ahead of them in this room. Grab the Gripshot, head right, and shoot it at one of the pegs across the ravine.

The Gripshot can pull Link across distances whenever it is shot at pegs like these. You can also use it to pull items to Link and it will stun enemies if they are hit with it. It's a pretty handy gadget, if we do say so ourselves.

Once each Link has crossed the first ravine, have each of them walk onto the wooden platform on the right side of the plateau and then use the Gripshot on the pegs to pull each of them over.

Make a three-Link Totem and head to the north end of the plateau. Throw the top two Links onto the wooden platform to your right. Switch to the Link at the bottom of the Totem and drop down onto the lower wooden platform, and then onto the plateau below.

Position the Links parallel to the lone Link, but don't stand too close to the left edge of the plateau. There is another feature to the Gripshot that we haven't mentioned yet. In addition to hooking onto pegs, the Gripshot can hook onto other Links. Have the lone Link Gripshot the other Links to get him across the ravine.

Have the Link on the wooden platform drop down onto the plateau below, then position him so that the other Links can Gripshot across the ravine, using him as their anchor point. Once all three Links are across, have them step on the Triforce gateway and move on to the next room.

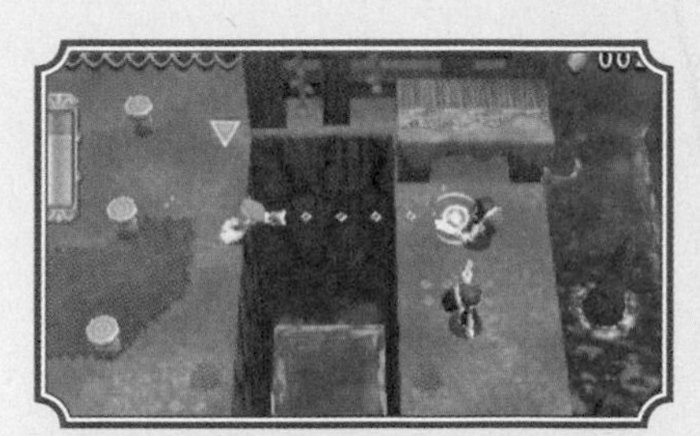

Follow the plateau east until you reach a break in it. Throw two Links over the break, then use the Gripshot on those Links to pull the remaining Link across.

Head to the north end of the plateau and make a three-Link Totem. Face the Totem to the right and line it up with the peg on the wooden platform. Have the top Link Gripshot the peg to pull him across the ravine.

ROOM 2

This is another combat room, but with a twist: The water level of the room fluctuates up and down while you're fighting, making hitting your enemies a challenge. You'll only have to face Tektites and their smaller, pond-skimmer-like cousins the Water Tektites during this fight, so there isn't too much to worry about. Whenever the water level rises, rush over to land. These enemies may not be tough out of the water, but they'll give you a good thrashing while you're in it.

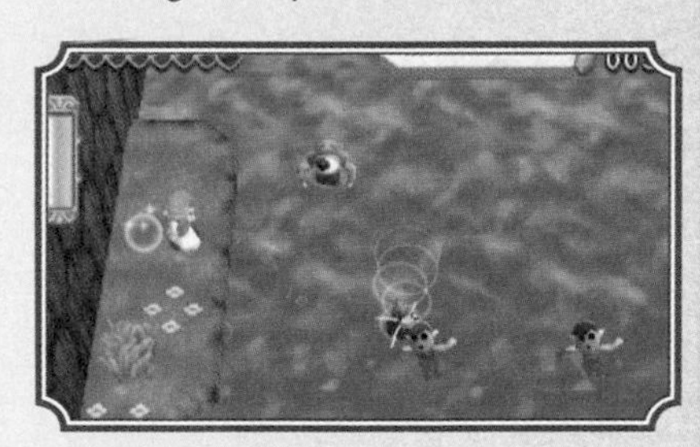

Once you defeat all of the enemies, the Triforce gateway will light up, giving you access to the next room.

ROOM 3

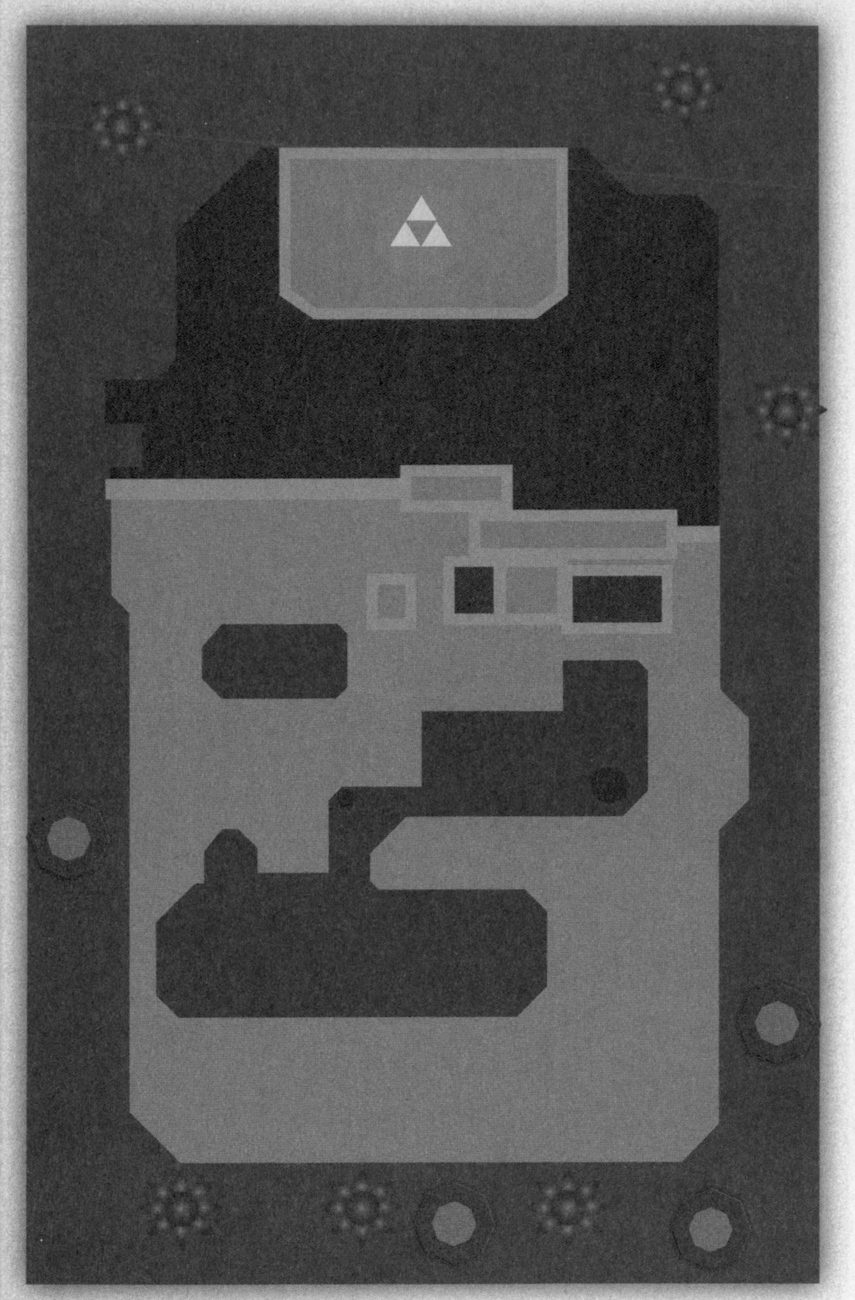

Now you'll need to switch to another Link and have him stand on the gray platform north of you.

Gripshot that Link with the Link on the raft to pull yourself forward, then face right again and Gripshot onto the pegs to the right. Now make a three-Link Totem and have the middle Link throw the top Link onto the pressure switch on top of the wall you are up against.

Hitting this switch will raise the water level, allowing you to head to the north side of the room. Swim north and you'll find the Triforce gateway and another Squiddy. You know what must be done. Once the Squiddy is no more, stand on the Triforce gateway to move on to the next room.

There is a raft almost directly above where you start in this room. Walk over to the raft with just one Link and Gripshot onto the pegs north of your position. This will drag the raft along the water toward the pegs. Next, Gripshot onto the pegs to your right.

ROOM 4

In order to complete this room, you'll need to defeat all the enemies in it—but that's easier said than done. You'll face a new enemy called a Gyorm. While a Gyorm is hiding in its shell, it is invincible. So you just need to pull it out of the shell, right? Yes, but with a caveat: If you pull a Gyorm out of its shell while standing near it, it'll immediately race back into its shell before you can even swing. What should you do then? Stand farther back, of course! Stand as far away from the shell as you can while still being in range with your Gripshot. When you pull out the Gyorm, it'll still race to its shell, but it will hesitate before climbing back in, giving you a chance to strike. Instead of chasing the Gyorm directly, race back to its shell after pulling it out and then start swinging. If you're far enough away when you Gripshot it, you'll be able to take these slippery punks out before they can re-enter their shells. Clear a couple waves of Gyorms and you're home free.

A Multiplayer Method

You can also double-team the Gyorms by having one of your friends stand by the shell while you Gripshot the Gyorm out, or vice versa.

Questing for Outfits

Before heading off to the final stage of the Riverside world, try gathering a Fresh Kelp and a Hytopian Silk from level 2 (the Abyss of Agony) and an Aqua Crown from level 3 (the Cove of Transition). When you get all three Materials, you can take them, along with a small pile of Rupees, to Madame Couture to make the Torrent Robe, an Outfit that makes your Water Rod platforms significantly bigger.

Level 4: Water Temple

Challenges

Fewer Heart Containers

Clear with halved energy

Transport the orb quickly

Sub-Weapons

 Water Rod

 Gripshot

 Gripshot

Materials

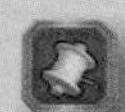 Hytopian Silk

 Hytopian Silk

 Octorok Sucker

Recommended Outfits

 Zora Costume

 Torrent Robe

If you took the time to make the Torrent Robe, make sure to have it equipped on the Link that is going to be using the Water Rod. This level will be made a good deal easier with that Outfit—plus, making giant water pillars is a blast! If you're in multiplayer, have the other players wear Zora Costumes to make traversing the water a breeze.

Hearing the name "Water Temple" may cause groans for some, but in this game those groans are misplaced. That doesn't mean that this temple isn't going to give you a run for your money, though. Get ready for some challenging puzzles and a challenging boss!

ROOM 1

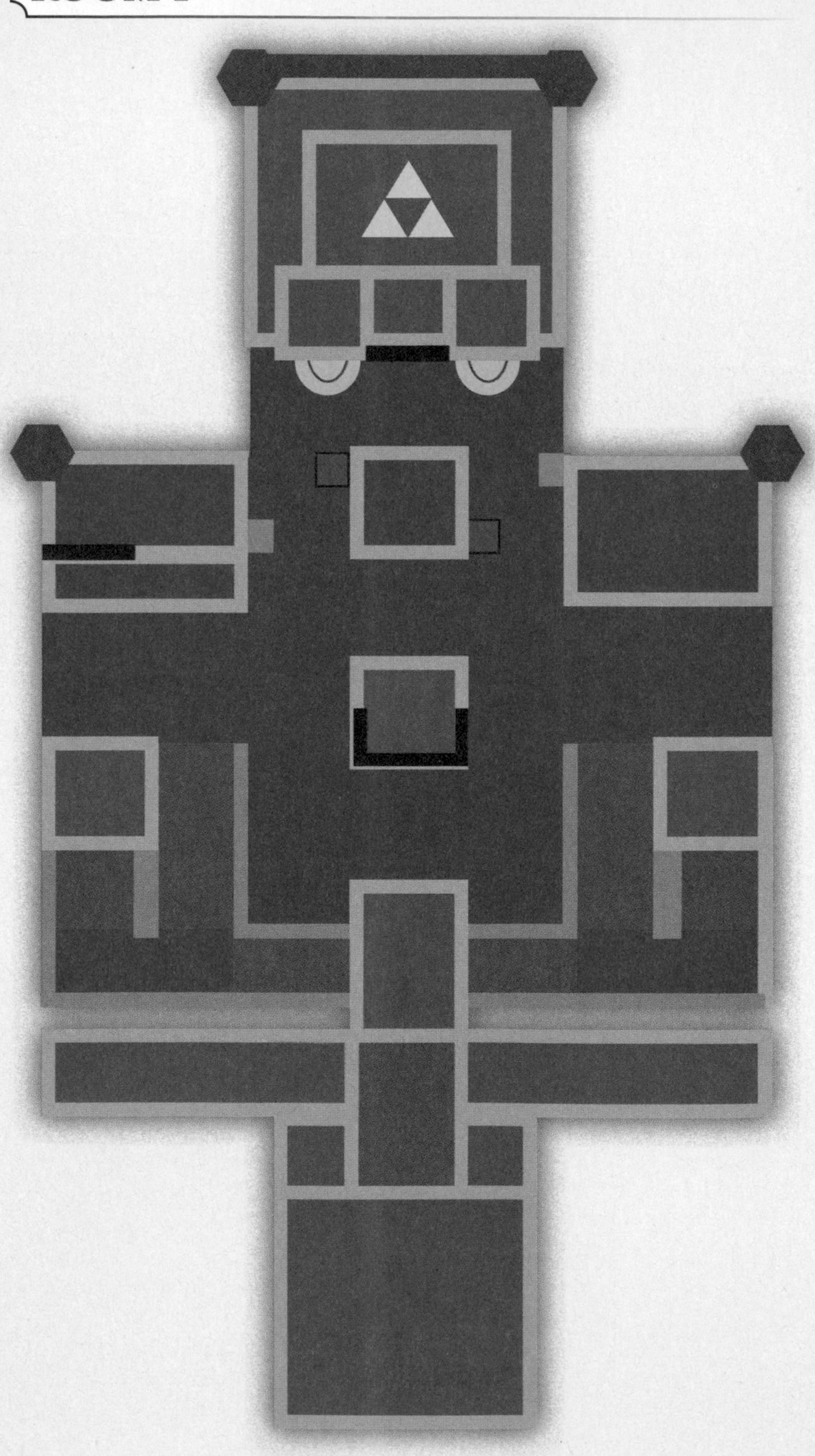

On the left and right sides of the room are Gripshots ripe for the taking. You'll need two Links to each grab one and then use them to travel onto the islands north of where the Gripshots were placed. The eastern island can be reached with just one Link. Have the Link over there shoot the fence on the island and he'll be pulled over to it with ease. Have that Link wait patiently on that island while you and the other Link work on getting onto the western island.

The western island requires two people to get the remaining Gripshot Link in position. What's the position? Be patient my friend! We'll tell you why we're doing this shortly. We promise! Have the remaining Gripshot Link and the Sub-Weapon-less Link swim to the lower ledge of the western island.

Have the Sub-Weapon-less Link throw the Gripshot Link onto the upper area of the island, then have both Gripshot Links stand on the small, protruding platforms sticking out of the ends of their respective islands. Your goal is to hit the two orb switches at roughly the same time, and to do that both Gripshot Links need to be standing on the protruding platform facing toward the center of the room.

If you're playing multiplayer, count down from three and then have both Gripshot Links fire their Gripshots at the same time. If you're in single-player, fire one Gripshot at one of the orb switches, then immediately switch to the other Gripshot Link and fire at the remaining orb. If you timed it right, a platform will rise in between the two orb switches.

Now have one of the Gripshot Links head onto the platform and shoot at the crank on the north side of the room, aiming specifically at the handle on its left side.

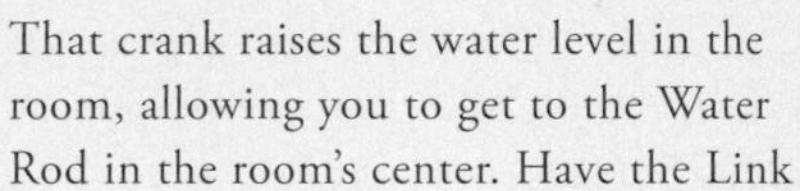

That crank raises the water level in the room, allowing you to get to the Water Rod in the room's center. Have the Link wearing the Torrent Robe pick the Water Rod up. Once the last Sub-Weapon has been obtained, the Triforce gateway will appear on the north side of the room. Use the Water Rod Link to create a water bridge to the room's north side to reach the Triforce gateway.

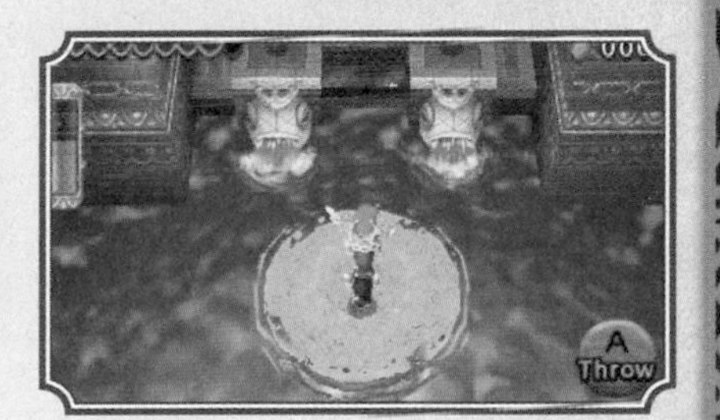

ROOM 2

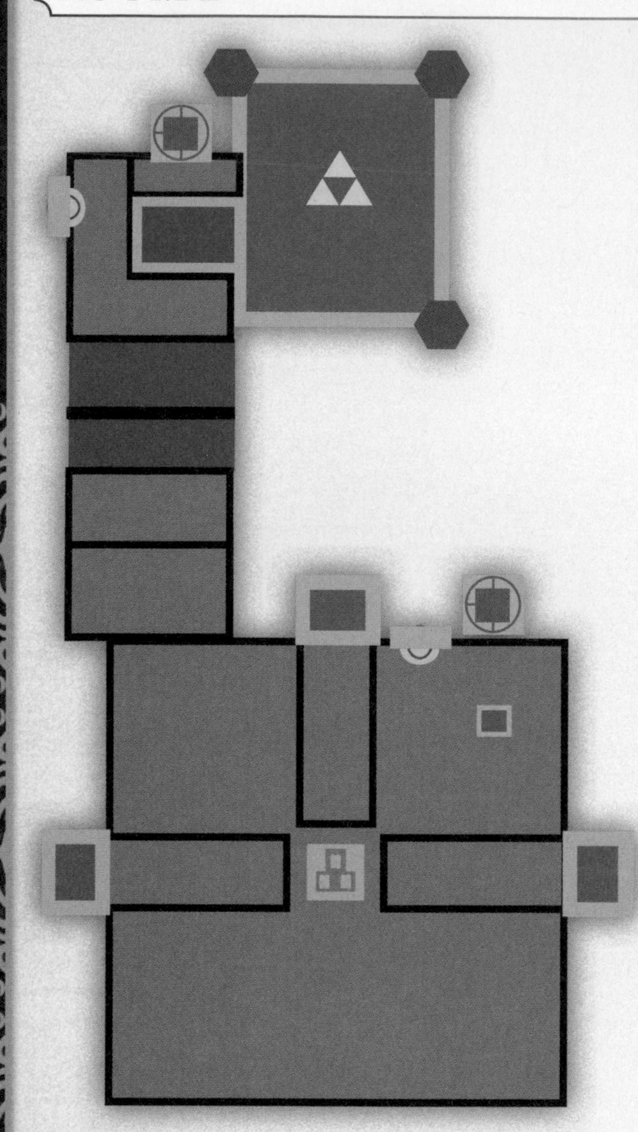

This is another combat room, very similar to the one in the last level, but this room has significantly less land to stand on. You'll only be given two tiny squares on the north side of the room to stand on, and they are incredibly easy to get knocked off of. Have all three Links stand on the three-man switch in the center of the room to start the battle.

You'll face off with Tektites, Water Tektites, and a new enemy called a Skullfish. These nasty-looking aquatic beasts own the waters and will gladly throw themselves on land to flop around and attack you. You'd normally be able to avoid them if you had more land to work with, but you're very likely going to get hit by them during this fight. Your best bet is to attack them like crazy to keep them from jumping back in the water.

You can end this room very quickly by rushing with your Water Rod Link and a Gripshot Link to the platform in the top-right corner of the room. Quickly have the Water Rod Link create a water pillar, then have the Gripshot Link shoot at the crank ahead. This will lower the water level and make all of the enemies pretty effortless to defeat.

Defeating all of the enemies in the room will open the gate in the room's northwest corner. Once that happens, swim under the fence and stand on the grated platform ahead. Have the Water Rod Link create a water pillar to get all three Links onto the landing above.

Once on the platform, have the two Gripshot Links make a Totem while the Water Rod Link stands on the south edge of the platform. Have the Water Rod Link face north, create a water pillar, and then pick up the two-Link Totem to make it a three-Link Totem.

Aim at the handle on the left side of the crank ahead and fire the Gripshot. The water level will rise again and you'll be given access to the Triforce gateway and everyone's favorite Rupee-giving octopode, Squiddy! Smack Squiddy like it's a national holiday and then head to the next room.

ROOM 3

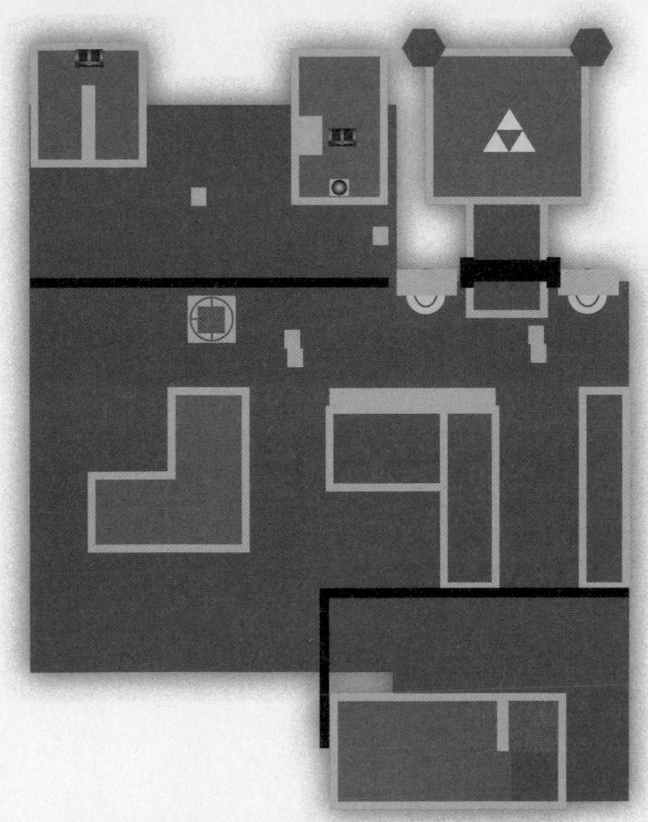

On the fence directly ahead of your starting point is a piece of fence that seems to be framed. Shoot this square with your Gripshot Links and you'll flip to the other side of the fence. Have the Water Rod Link pull the Water Octorok with a water pillar and then defeat it. Have your Gripshot Links stand on the two pressure switches on the other side of the fence to open the gate.

With the gate open, your Water Rod Link can swim through to the other side. Head west and have the Water Rod Link create a platform up to the raised island on the west side of the room. Now have a Gripshot Link pull the crank at the end of the island to raise the water level.

On the northwest corner of the room, just right of the crank, you'll find another one of those flipping fence segments. Have the Water Rod Link create a platform in front of the segment, then have a Gripshot Link shoot it.

You can find a treasure chest in both corners of the area. Have your Gripshot Link pull the raft with the peg embedded in the platform on the right side of the room. Use the fence to pull the raft south, then use the peg on the far right to pull it to the right corner of this area.

Your goal is to pull the raft in this area out of this area, but to do that you'll need to get the second Gripshot Link behind the fence too. Once you have the second Gripshot Link, have him climb on the raft and pick up the first Link. Throw the first Link onto the platform and have him stand on the pressure switch. That will open the gate. Have the Link that just hit the switch open the treasure chest. Inside is a key that you'll need to bring to a locked gate to the right of your current location. Have that Link hang on to the key and jump on the raft.

You'll need to lower the water by pulling the crank again. As the water level is raised, you can just swim onto that platform in front of the crank. Have the Water Rod Link and the Gripshot Link that isn't holding the key head over to that platform. Have the Water Rod Link create a water pillar, move your Gripshot Link on top of it, and then pull the crank to lower the water level.

Have the Gripshot Link swim back to the raft and shoot his Gripshot at the peg south of the raft. Now turn to the right and Gripshot the peg ahead. This will pull you in front of the locked door, allowing you to open it and reach the Triforce gateway. Use the Water Rod Link to create a platform up to the Triforce gateway and move all the Links onto it.

ROOM 4

BOSS FIGHT: ARRGHUS

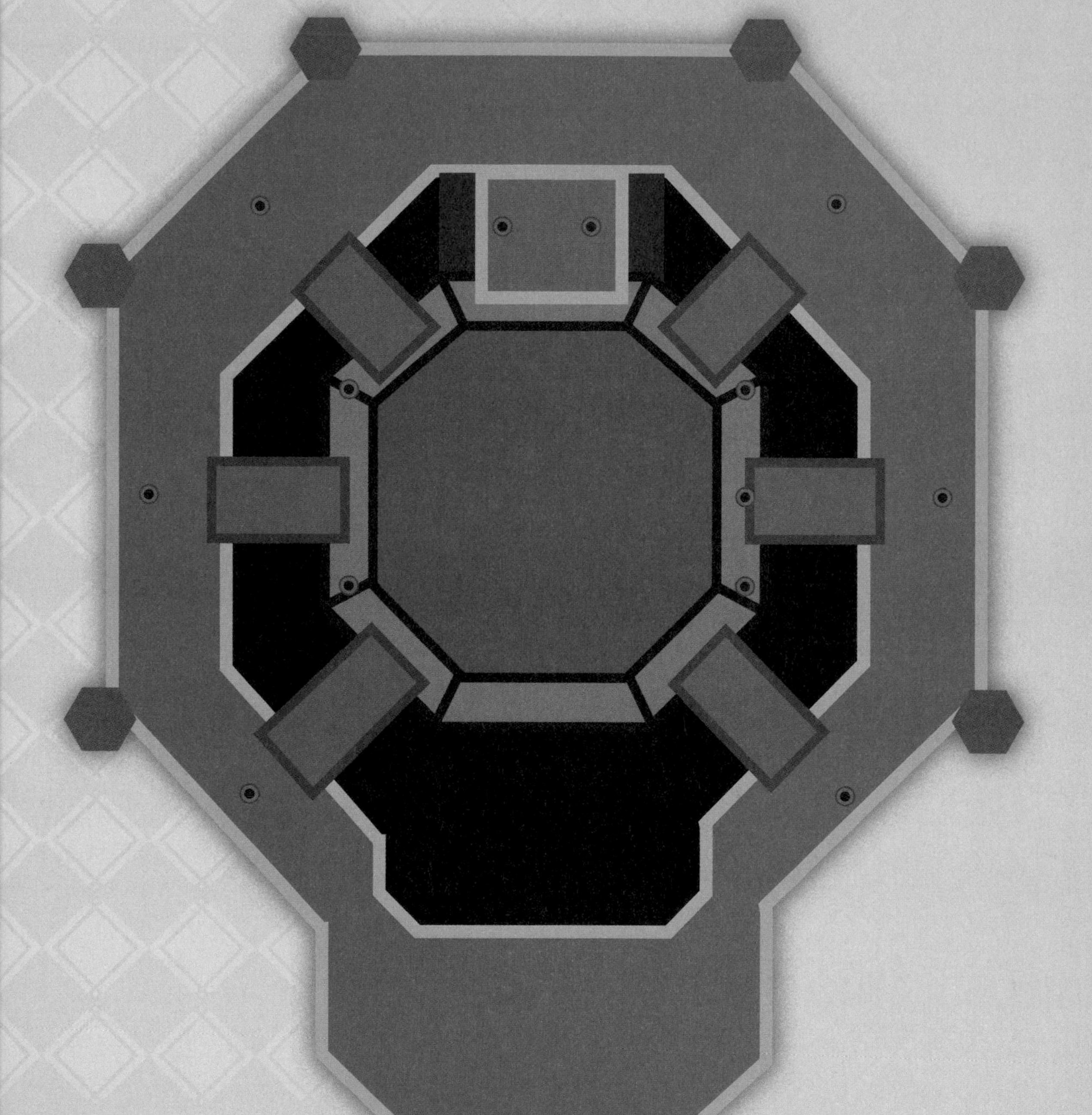

This room is an octagonal shape with platforms jutting out of a deep pool of water. Pots line the walls, potentially holding Hearts—remember that for later. For now, get ready to face the Riverside boss!

This eight-eyed squid monster is going to test your ability to swap between Links and coordinate with your friends. It has three phases, the first of which has it sitting in the center of that pool and shooting its eyeballs at you. Position all three Links on different platforms, preferably in a triangle pattern.

The two Gripshot Links should try to shoot at Arrghus's eyes to pull them close and then give them a good slashing. It takes two slashes per eye to destroy them, but they'll likely slide away before you can destroy them the first time you pull them to you. This is where your Water Rod Link comes in.

The eyes will dive underwater and begin circling Arrghus, moving closer and closer to its owner before reattaching. Have the Water Rod Link pull the eyes out of the water as they pass him and then give them another slash to destroy them.

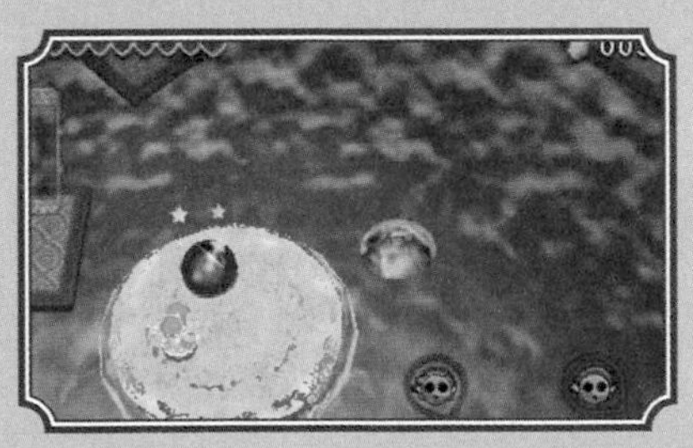

Repeat this process while avoiding Arrghus's eye attacks to complete this phase. Once you've destroyed all the eyes, Arrghus will lower the water level and retract the platforms you're standing on.

In Case of Emergency

You can have a Link step back onto the ring surrounding the wall of this room as you get to the last two eyes. This will prevent him from falling into the lower level of the room, allowing him to break the pots and get Hearts as he sees fit.

In this phase, Arrghus will circle the room and shoot its eyeballs at you. When this happens you can either Gripshot the eyeballs and attack them or put up a water pillar with the Water Rod to stun them and make them free for you to attack. Trying to attack them directly without doing either of the above will result in you taking damage, so make sure to stun them first. If you keep destroying eyes until Arrghus runs out, you'll start its third phase.

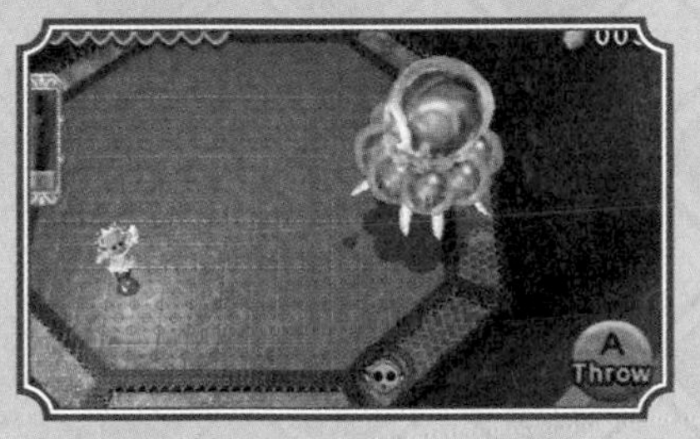

For this phase, Arrghus will open its own eye and move around the room faster. Its main attack creates eight dark rings, which spin across the floor. If you hear a charging sound, move away from Arrghus immediately. Getting hit by this attack will not only make you lose Hearts, it will also temporarily disable the Sub-Weapon of the Link that was hit.

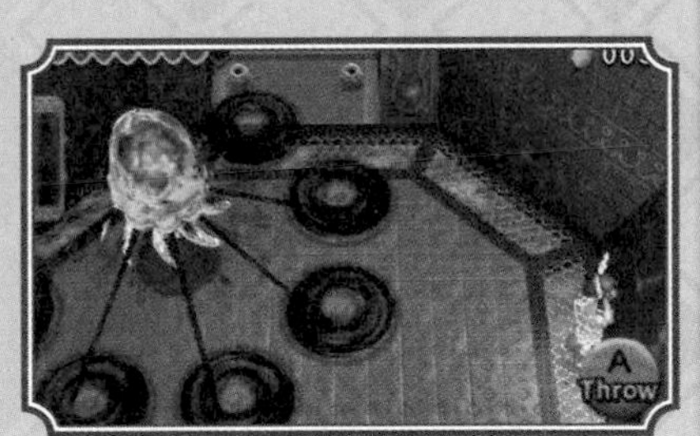

In order to damage Arrghus in this phase, you'll need to make a three-Link Totem with a Gripshot Link on top. Every time you're in line with its eye and its eye is opened, shoot the Gripshot into it and Arrghus will fall to the ground stunned. This is your chance to strike! Attack it while it's down to damage it directly. After a handful of strikes, Arrghus will get back up and begin floating around the room again.

Continue to Gripshot Arrghus's eye and slash it while it's down in order to defeat it. After being knocked down three times and slashed to ribbons, this eight-armed, nine-eyed freak will be finished!

WORLD 3: VOLCANO

Level 1: Blazing Trail

Challenges

Pop all balloons

Evade the Wallmaster

Transport the orb quickly

Sub-Weapons

 Boomerang

 Boomerang

 Boomerang

Materials

 Goron Ore

 Goron Ore

 Monster Guts

Recommended Outfits

 Legendary Dress

 Goron Garb

This level is one of the more challenging levels in the game. There's lava, Fire Keese, and flaming boulders that rain down from the sky; the Blazing Trail will try anything and everything to burn your Hearts away. Cautious play and the Legendary Dress will be excellent boons to you here. You can come back with the Goron Garb later to nab up some previously unreachable treasures as well, so keep that in mind on any subsequent playthroughs.

You'll be using a Zelda staple for most of this level: The Boomerang. This curved stun stick works the same way as it does in other titles, but this time you can use it to pick up your teammates or Doppels. Throw the Boomerang at an enemy and it will be stunned or defeated. Throw it at a teammate and you'll pick them up and bring them back to you, automatically creating a two-Link Totem in the process. Most of this level requires you to think outside the box with how you can use the Boomerang, so be open to experimentation and you'll go far.

ROOM 1

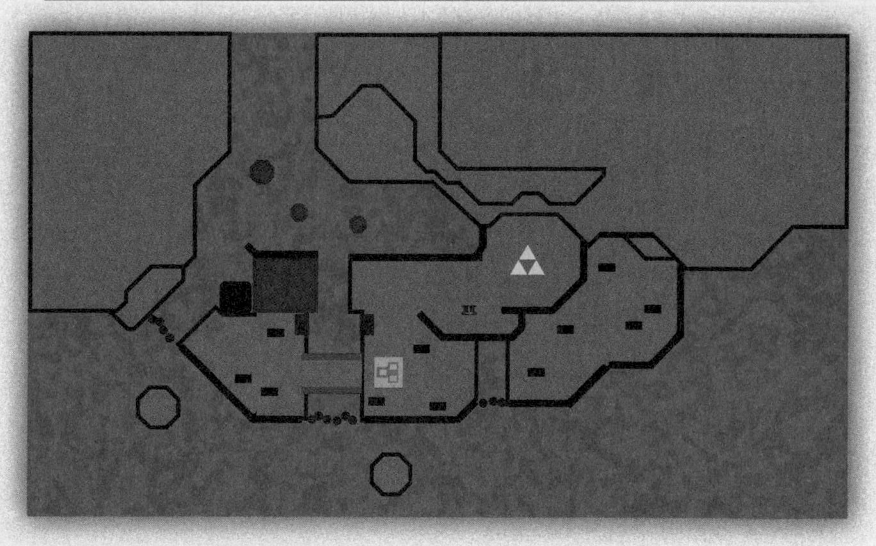

From the start, head west until you reach a lava creek. Make a three-Link Totem and throw the top two Links to the other side of the creek—this is where you'll find the Boomerangs. Use the Boomerang to grab the lone Link, then stand on the three-man pressure switch to raise a bridge. Make sure to have each Link grab a Boomerang to reveal the Triforce gateway at the top of the map.

You'll run into a new enemy called a Hardhat Beetle on the other side of the bridge. These enemies are incredibly easy to defeat, or they would be if they were in a level that wasn't engulfed in lava. Hitting a Hardhat Beetle, or being touched by it, will bounce you backwards. Not much of a defense mechanism, except when there is lava behind you. These bouncy bugs specialize in bouncing you into lava or off of cliffs, so take extreme care not to attack them whenever you have one of those two hazards behind you.

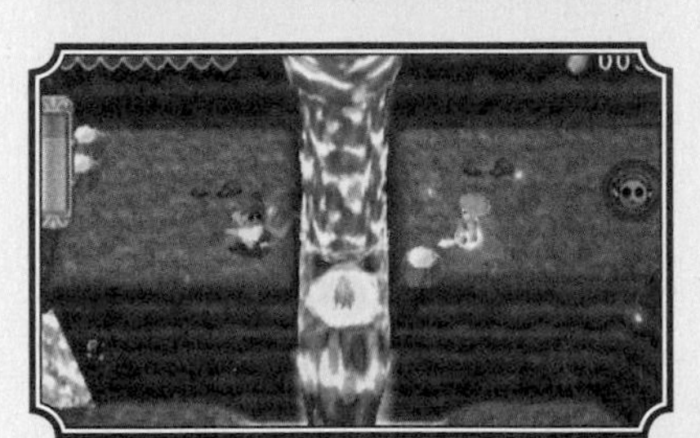

After defeating the Hardhat Beetle, stand on the brown lava rock slab north of you. A lava fountain will shoot the platform up to the next level, allowing you to reach new heights. If you're playing single-player, you should only send up one Link for now. There's another Hardhat Beetle waiting to knock you off of the platform if you let it. Having more than one Link on the platform when the Hardhat Beetle approaches could spell disaster.

Once all three Links are on the next level, make a two-Link Totem and approach the lava creek ahead. Wait a minute before throwing any of the Links over. Two lava fountains will spew out of this creek at fixed intervals, so waiting for them to lower before throwing your Links is a wise plan. Once both Links are over, defeat the Hardhat Beetle and grab the lone Link from the other side of the creek.

Hidden Treasure!

You can throw a Link onto the ledge to the left of the Triforce gateway to find some Rupees. We suggest you wait until you have the Goron Garb to try and obtain these Rupees, because it is all too easy to fall in. If you must try, then send two Links up and have them use their Boomerangs to grab the Rupees off of the small platforms. Have them throw each other over the gap in the ledge and onto the small platform in the middle of the lava lake.

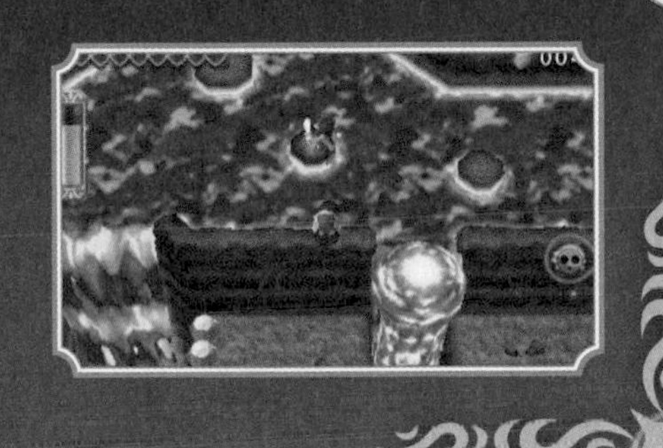

ROOM 2

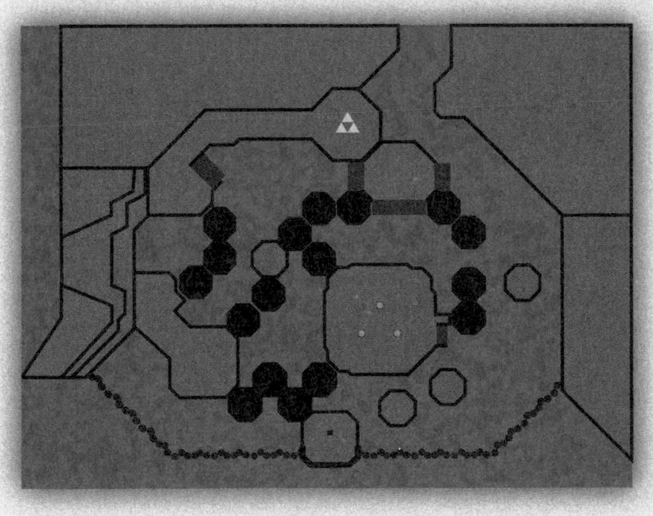

You start on the west side of this lava-filled room. If you head north along the wall, you'll reach a ring of fire surrounding the Triforce gateway. Your goal is to shut that bad boy down so you can advance to the next room, but doing that is easier said than done.

The dark brown rock slabs sitting on the lava can only support your weight for a few seconds before sinking. That means anything you do while on those platforms you'll have to do quick. This room can get very tricky on your first try, but we'll make sure to make it as painless as possible.

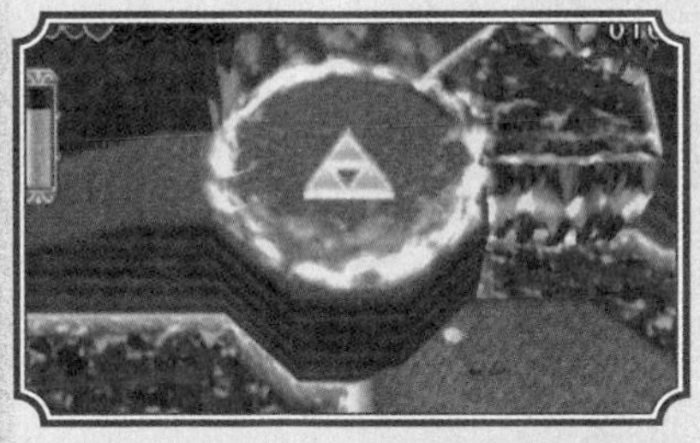

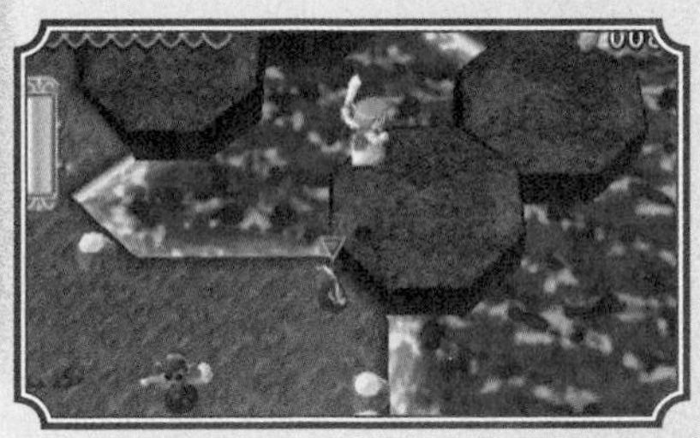

There are three sets of brown, sinking platforms near where you start in this room. Your goal is to get everyone to the center of the room, but two of the three sets of brown lava rock slabs require you to throw your Links onto them, leaving one Link behind. To solve this, throw two of your Links onto the middle path of brown lava rock slabs and have them move up until they reach a stable dirt platform, two platforms up the path.

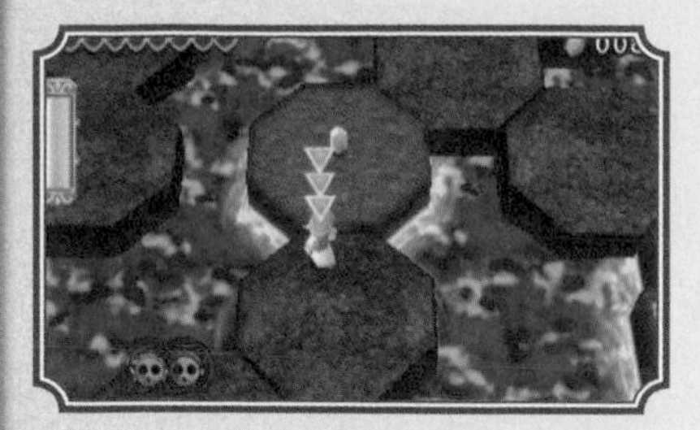

Have those two Links wait on the stable platform, then have the remaining Link move up the northern-most path of brown lava rock slabs.

You'll need to be quick with this next part. Move the lone Link onto the brown lava rock slab parallel to the platform your other Links are on, then immediately switch or have one of your other two Links throw a Boomerang at the lone Link to pull him over. If you were quick enough, all three Links should be together, unburnt by the fiery lava below.

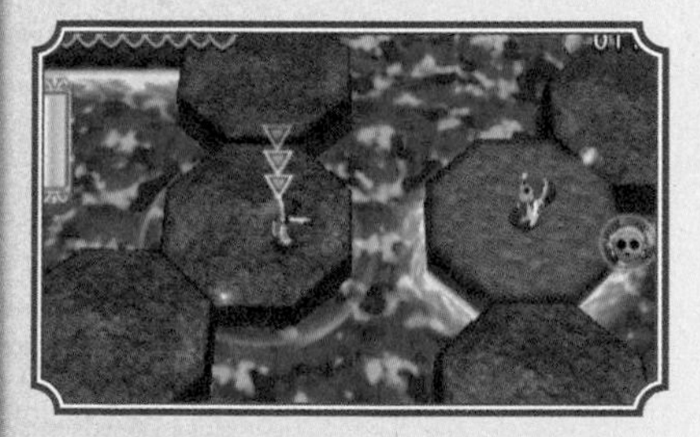

Now make a three-Link Totem and follow the path of platforms north as it rounds to the other side of the room.

Walk your Totem until you reach a gap in the path on the east side of the room, then throw your top two Links to the other side of the gap.

Have those two Links continue on the path until they are on the island in the center of the map, surrounded by flames. Then switch back to the lone Link quickly and move him to the island in the middle of the brown lava rock slab path you are on.

Now have one of the two Links on the island head to the island's northwest corner and wait there.

You'll need to do this next part quickly, so stay on your toes! Have the lone Link stand on the platform on the left side of the island he is currently on, then quickly switch to the Link on the northwest side of the island in the center of the room and Boomerang the lone Link.

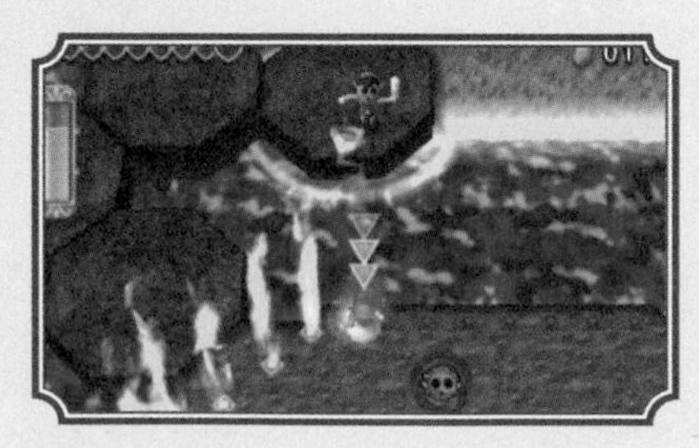

With all three Links now on the center island, the worst is over! Sort of. Have all three Links stand on the pressure switches in the center of the island and get ready for a fight! As soon as you hit all three switches, the flame wall extends around the center island and enemies fill the area. You'll have to deal with three Fire Keese and two brutish Hinox before you escape this scorching prison. DO NOT attack the Fire Keese with your sword! A single touch from these flaming, flying rodents will set you on fire and send you racing around the room. Instead, hit them with your Boomerang to defeat them at a distance. The Hinox will gladly lob Bombs at you with reckless abandon. To prevent this, hit them with the Boomerang to stun them, then swing away! It takes several hits with your sword to defeat these lumbering behemoths, but if you continue to stun them with your Boomerang every time they come to, you can keep them in a perpetual standstill, making them a piece of cake!

Once you've defeated all five enemies, the flame wall will drop, as will the ring of fire surrounding the Triforce gateway on the north side of the room. Proceed back to the starting area, then head onto the northern brown lava rock slab path to reach the Triforce gateway and leave the room.

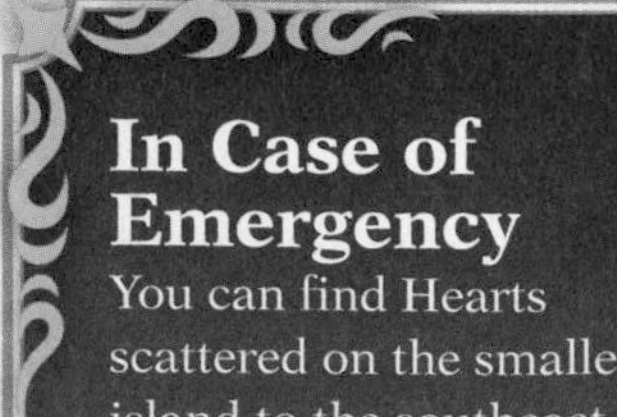

In Case of Emergency

You can find Hearts scattered on the smaller island to the southeast of the center island. Use your Boomerang to pull them through the flame wall and get yourself up to fighting fit.

ROOM 3

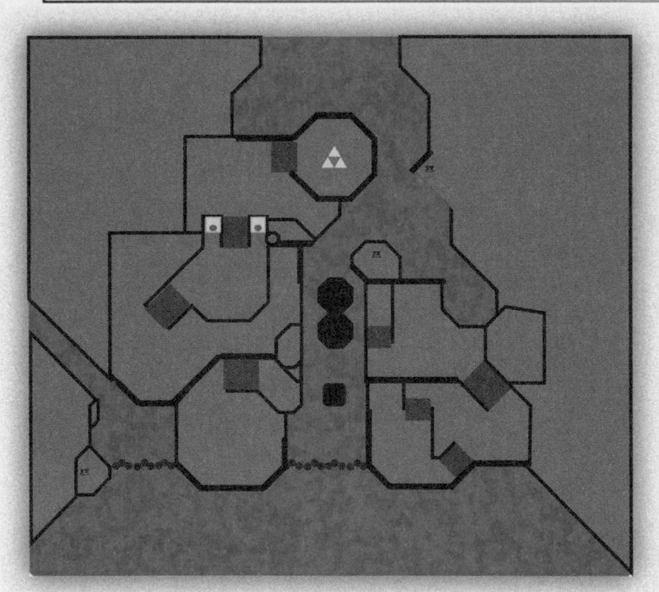

This room doesn't have any terribly devious puzzles, but boy is it challenging! Flaming rocks rain down from on high, delivering divine judgment on unobservant Links. In single-player, you'll have a much easier time, because there is only ever one Link to damage at a time, but multiplayer is a completely different story. Regardless of how many players are playing, tread lightly, walk slowly, and pay close attention to the shadows that appear on the ground. These are indicators that a flaming rock is about to smash into that location. You'll take damage if you're under it when it does.

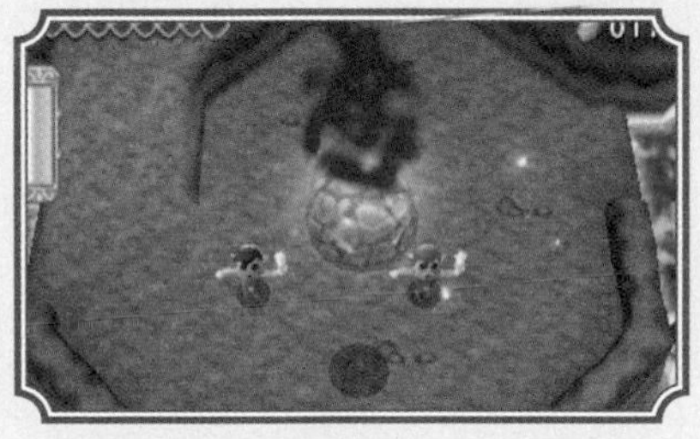

Head north up the ramp directly ahead of you. At the top of the ramp is a lava waterfall and a brown lava rock slab that moves up and down on a lava fountain. Make a three-Link Totem and throw your top two Links onto the platform, then have the bottom of the now two-Link Totem throw the top Link to the other side of the waterfall.

Next, have the Link on the middle platform turn around and Boomerang the Link on the left side of the lava waterfall to pull him onto the platform. Throw that Link to the right side of the lava waterfall, then have one of the two other Links Boomerang the Link off of the brown lava rock slab.

Head up the eastern path, following the wall north. Take out the Fire Keese with your Boomerangs and don't slash the blue Hardhat Beetle while you have lava behind you, or you'll risk being knocked in.

Proceed west and you'll find the top of the lava waterfall you crossed earlier. You can nab some Hearts sitting on the edge of the waterfall if your health isn't looking too great. This next part can be a little tricky and will require some quick movement, so get ready!

Have two of the Links line up at the top of the ramp, then throw the third Link onto the brown lava rock slabs in the center of the lava river. That Link is going to have to pace back and forth from one platform, to the next, and then back again to avoid having the platforms sink.

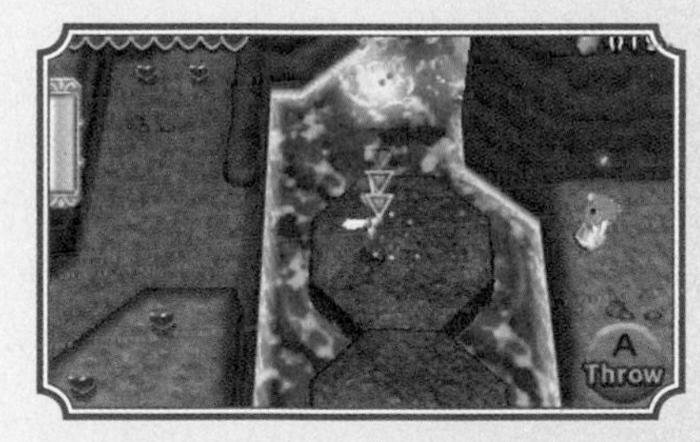

Have the Link on the brown lava rock slabs Boomerang the other two Links, one at a time, then throw them to the left side of the lava river. Once the two Links are safely on the other side, have one of them Boomerang the remaining Link onto the other side of the river as well.

Take out two more Fire Keese, then head up the northern ramp to reach another wall of fire. Make a Totem that is three Links tall and quickly hit the orb switches on the left and right side of the fire wall. This will drop the fire wall and give you access to the Triforce gateway at the top of the mountain.

ROOM 4

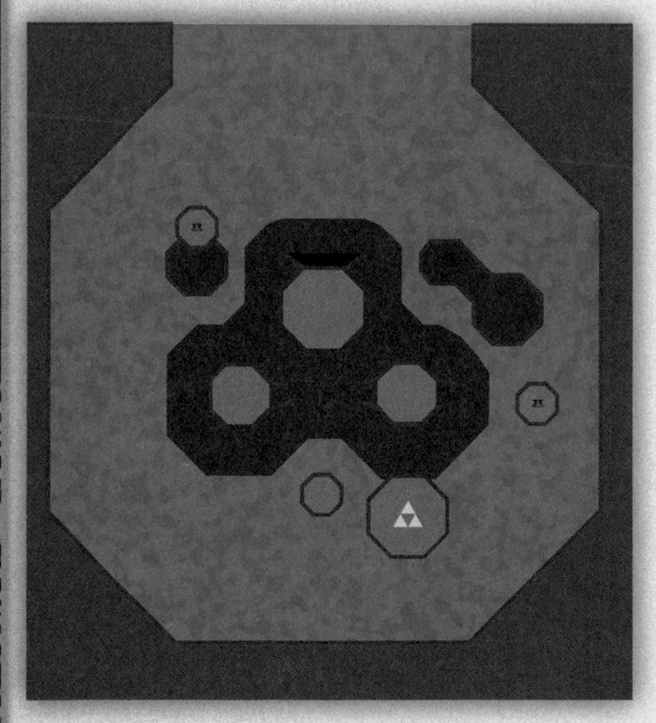

As scary as this room looks, it's actually quite simple if you play cautiously. The lava will rise and lower periodically and monsters will appear continuously until you've defeated them all. You'll have to deal with Fire Keese and fire-breathing Kodongos. Deal with the Fire Keese in the same way you've been defeating them up to this point. The Kodongos can become a problem if they're allowed to breathe fire, but they only shoot in a straight line. If you stand above or below where they're facing, they'll miss you outright.

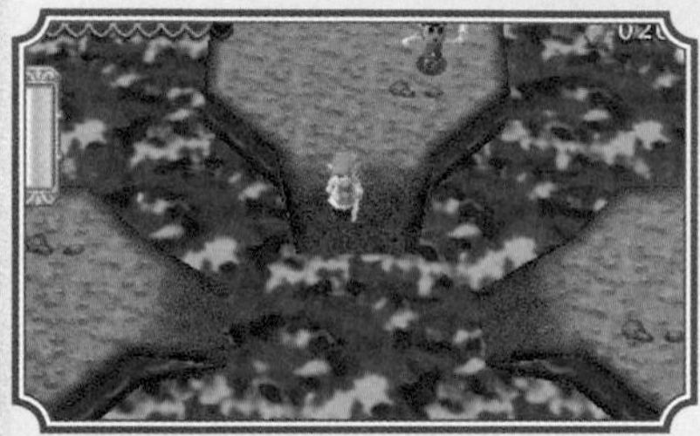

Don't push your luck by staying on the dark brown lava rock for too long. At any point you can safely walk back onto the lighter platforms and wait safely for the lava to rise and fall again, so there's no reason to risk taking damage when the lava rises. You can lose a lot of health here easily, so being patient and cautious is absolutely in your favor.

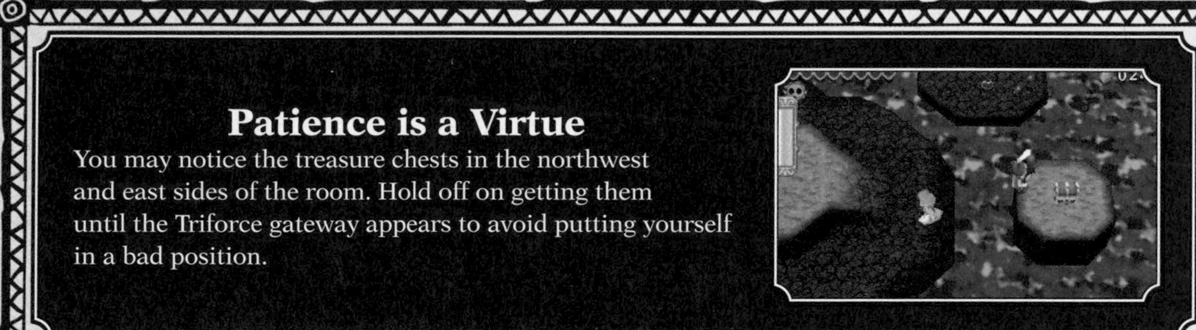

Patience is a Virtue

You may notice the treasure chests in the northwest and east sides of the room. Hold off on getting them until the Triforce gateway appears to avoid putting yourself in a bad position.

Once you've defeated all of the enemies in the room, the lava level will lower permanently and the Triforce gateway will appear on the southeast corner of the room. Make a three-Link Totem and throw the top two Links onto the platform with the Triforce gateway. Have the remaining Link stand on the platform directly north of the Triforce gateway, then have one of the other two Links Boomerang him over.

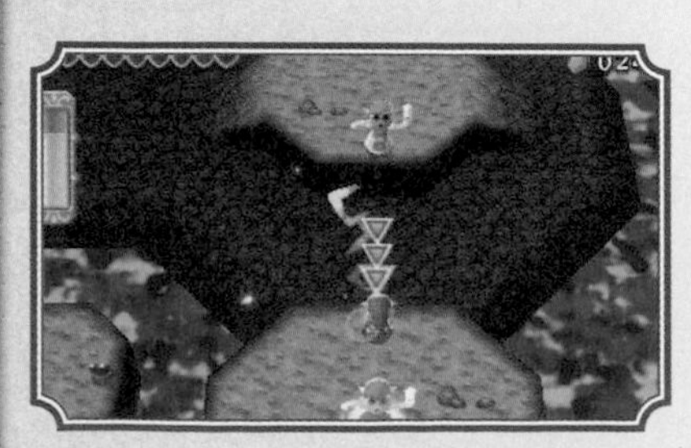

Questing for Outfits

Take the time to gather a Goron Ore and Monster Guts from level 1, Blazing Trail. With those parts in hand you'll be able to make the Goron Garb, an Outfit that is completely fireproof. Lava burning your hindquarters? Fire got your Links sprinting for the nearest water supply? Not anymore! Put on the Goron Garb and you'll swim through lava like a Zora through water.

Level 2: Hinox Mine

Challenges

Clear within the time limit

Pop all balloons

Don't pop any balloons

Sub-Weapons

Bow

Boomerang

Boomerang

Materials

Goron Ore

Goron Ore

Demon Fossil

Recommended Outfits

Big Bomb Outfit

Kokiri Clothes

The Big Bomb Outfit will help you tremendously in this stage, so make sure to choose it above anything else. There is a lot of Bomb throwing that happens in this level and the Big Bomb Outfit's Big Bombs will make it so much easier and quicker. The Kokiri Clothes can be worn by whichever Link decides to fire the Bow to make some of the puzzles easier and quicker.

Most of this level is spent on a minecart, so there aren't a lot of puzzles to deal with. The combat can get pretty intense, however, so stay alert!

ROOM 1

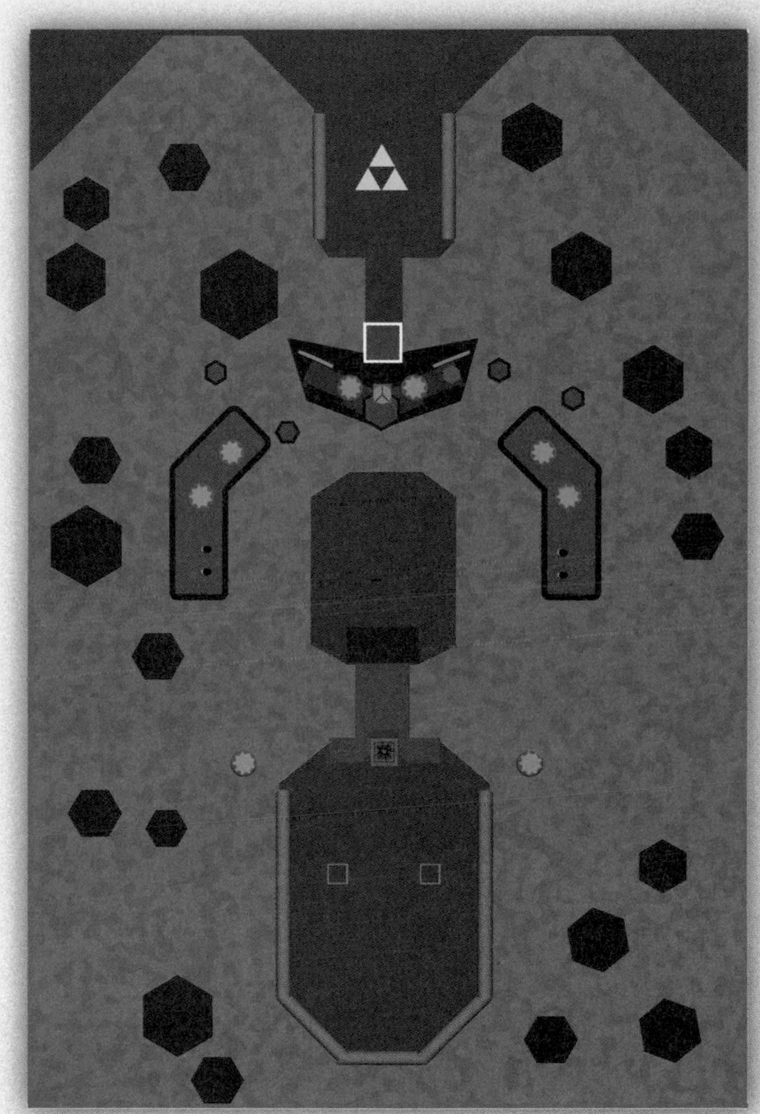

This level's Sub-Weapons will be right in front of you from the start. If you have a Link wearing the Kokiri Clothes, make sure they grab the Bow, then divide the Boomerangs amongst the remaining Links. Whatever you do, don't pick up the Bow with the Big Bomb Outfit Link.

Head farther north and you'll come to a cracked block and a Bomb Flower on either side. Use your Boomerang Links to grab either Bomb and throw it at the cracked block. Do this once more to destroy the block entirely.

Now hit the orb switch lodged into the wall of the platform ahead to make a staircase rise.

Head up the stairs to the end of the path and you'll find more Bomb Flowers and orb switches. This is where either the Kokiri Clothes or the Big Bomb Outfit will come in handy. If you're using the Big Bomb Outfit, make a two-Link Totem with the Links not wearing the Big Bomb Outfit, then use the Big Bomb Outfit Link to Boomerang a Bomb from one of the Bomb Flowers on the left or right side of the room. Immediately throw the Bomb as close as you can to the center of the orb switch platform, then grab the two-Link Totem, making it a three-Link Totem. Aim for the center orb switch and throw your Boomerang or fire your Bow. If you timed it right, or if your Bomb-throwing aim was spot on, all three switches should be activated at roughly the same time and an elevator will come down to pick you up.

If you're wearing the Kokiri Clothes, you can make a two-Link Totem with the Boomerang Links and position them near the edge of the platform you're currently on. Switch to your Kokiri Clothes Link, get as close to the edge of the platform as you can while centering yourself with the gray platform in between the two Bomb Flowers, and then fire your Bow. The two side arrows should hit the two Bomb Flowers, triggering the left and right orb switches. Immediately pick up the two-Link Totem and hit the upper switch to cause the elevator to come down.

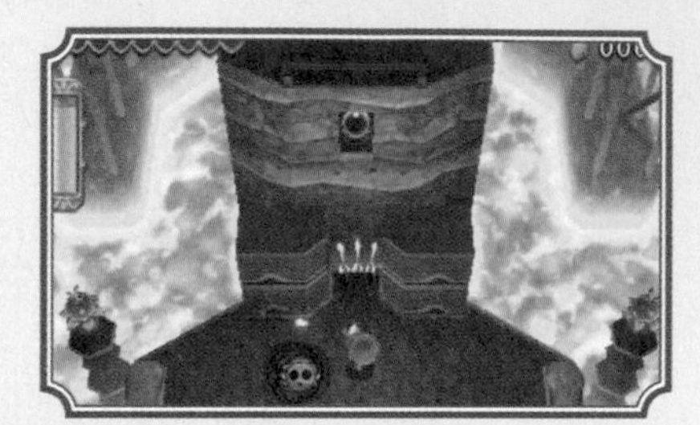

Keep your three-Link Totem, hop on the elevator, and head to the Triforce gateway at the top of the room.

ROOM 2

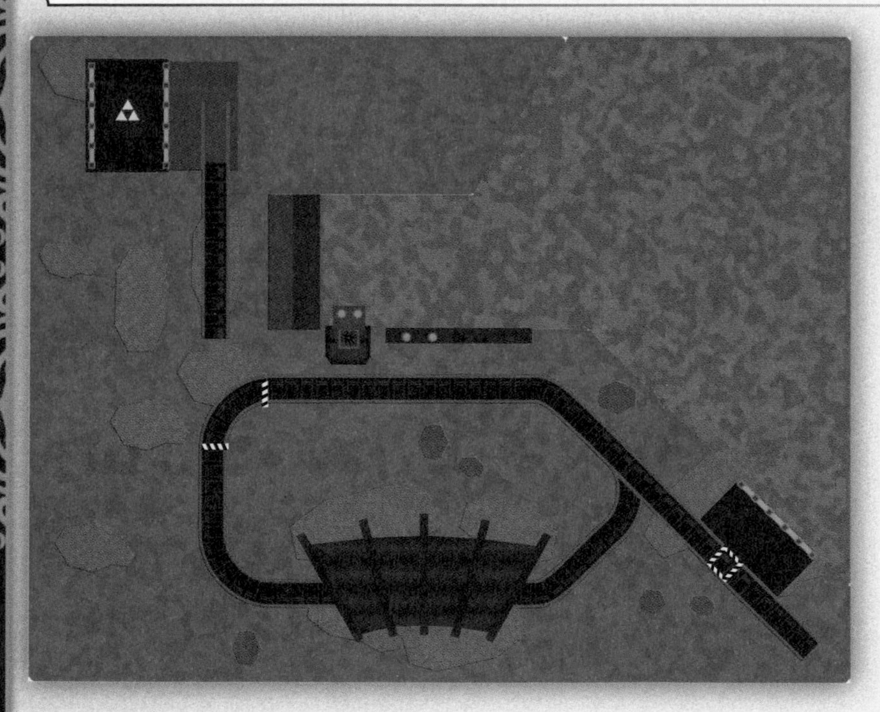

Hop down the hole in the grated platform you start this room in to land on a minecart. Face your Big Bomb Outfit Link toward the north side of the room at all times. You'll see two red Rupees lining the north wall. Immediately after that are a couple of Bomb Flowers and a giant cracked block. Use your Boomerang to grab a Bomb, then throw it onto the platform with the cracked block. If you have the Big Bomb Outfit Link throw the Bomb, the cracked block will blow up with one Bomb, but it will take two Bombs otherwise.

Once the block is destroyed, an orb switch will be revealed. You won't be able to hit it this time around the track, but that's okay, because you have some preparing to do. Make a three-Link Totem with the Bow Link on the top and face the north wall at all times. When you pass the Bomb Flowers again, shoot as many arrows as you can at the orb switch. If you did it right, the track will switch and you'll be taken to the Triforce gateway. Don't forget to smack Squiddy on your way out!

ROOM 3

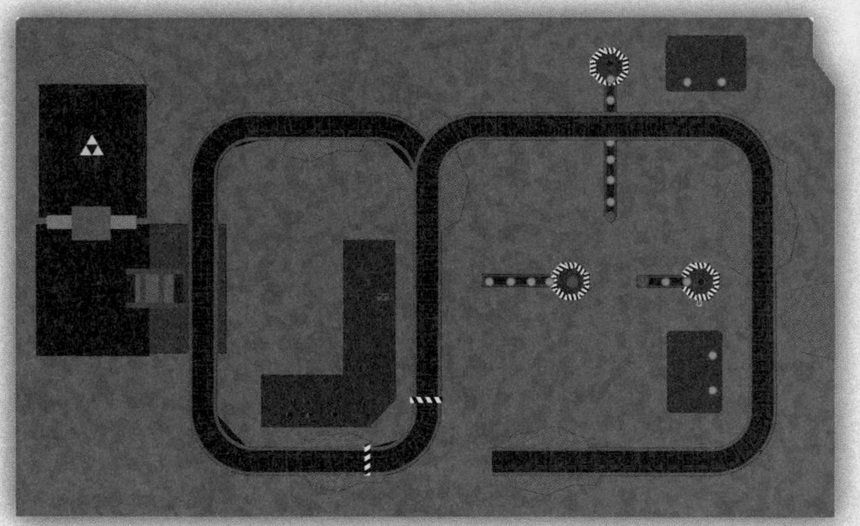

If you have the Kokiri Clothes for this area it's going to pay dividends. If not, the same strategies work, but you'll have to have more precise aiming.

Hop into the minecart will all three Links and switch to the Bow Link. As soon as you step into the minecart, have the Bow Link face the cart's right side and DON'T MOVE HIM. This area has two tracks and you need to hit a switch to transfer the minecart to the second track. Keep your Bow aimed and ready. When the cart moves around the second turn, your Bow Link will be facing left. Shortly after that turn you'll find a switch with a blue handle. You need to shoot that switch to transfer to a separate track.

There are three orb switches in this next area: one north, one east, and one west. You are supposed to use your Boomerang on some Bomb Flowers and throw them on the platforms with the east and north switches, but if you have the Kokiri Clothes, you can fire your Bow toward those two switches and hit them reliably.

To hit the east orb switch, fire diagonally to the right as you reach the bottom-left corner of the track. This may take a couple tries without the Kokiri Clothes, but keep at it and you'll get it eventually.

You can reach the northern switch by firing your Bow off the right side of your platform just before it reaches the top-left corner of the track.

To hit the west orb switch, you'll need to make a three-Link Totem with the Bow Link on top and fire at the switch as you roll down the west side of the track.

If you're struggling to hit the north and east orb switches, you can use the Boomerang to nab up one of the Bomb Flowers just before both switches, then throw a Bomb onto the platforms with the switches. You'll still need to use the Bow and a three-Link Totem to hit the western switch, however.

Once you've hit all three switches, you'll need to hit the blue-handled switch again to change the track back to its original position. The track will take you back to the start of the area, where a gate that concealed the Triforce gateway is now open.

ROOM 4

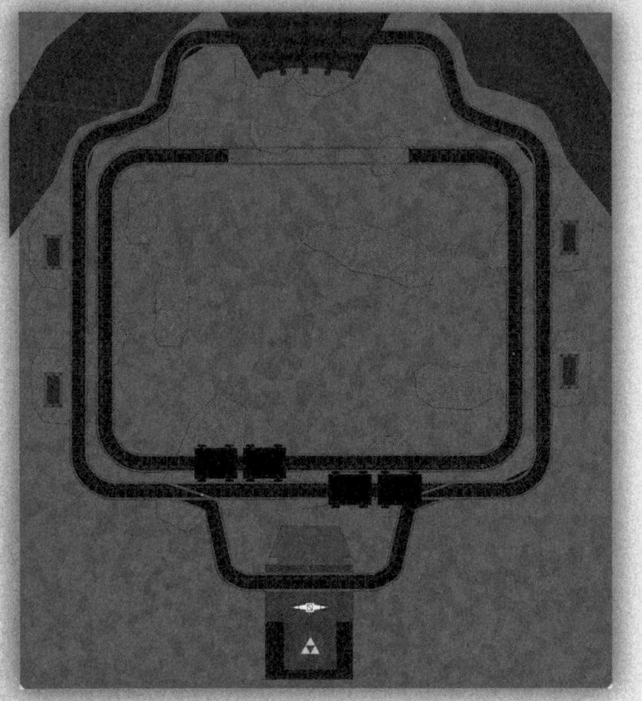

This room has two minecarts linked together on a track ahead of you. Before you step on the cart, you'll need to do some preparation. Once you step on the cart you'll have to do battle with two of the Hinox Brothers. If you remember the Hinox from the last level, you'll know all too well that they love throwing Bombs. If you have a Big Bomb Outfit Link with you it's really going to pay off here.

If you're playing single-player, make a two-Link Totem with the Links not wearing the Big Bomb Outfit. (If you didn't bring the Big Bomb Outfit, put the Bow Link and a Boomerang Link in a Totem, leaving one Boomerang Link for the fight.) When the Links are stacked, throw them as close to the left or right edge as possible. You can also put a Link on the back corner of each side of the cart. You'll be throwing a lot of Bombs during this fight, so you want to keep your Doppels as far out of the way as possible.

If you're playing multiplayer, have each Link stand as far apart as possible. That means you'll have one Link near the left edge of the cart, one Link on the right edge, and one Link standing in the middle. Designate zones for each Link in which that Link must stay in during the fight. As we said earlier, you'll be throwing a lot of Bombs and it's all too easy to throw your own teammates into the lava by mistake.

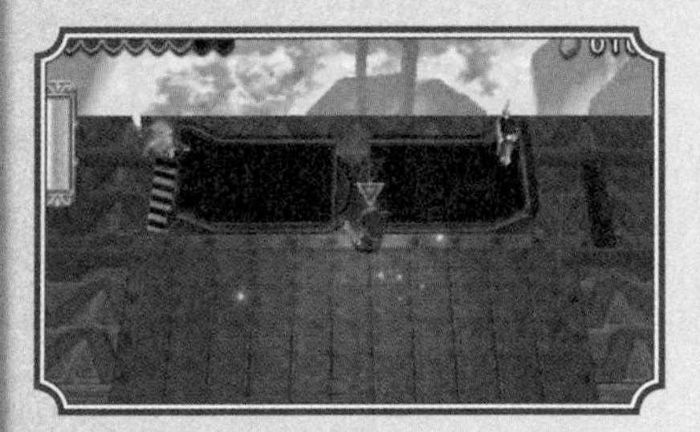

When all three Links are on the minecart, it will begin to move and the first Hinox Brother will appear. Hinox the Eldest will begin throwing Bombs onto your cart, which you'll want to take care to remove as quickly as possible. Pick them up and throw them right back at Hinox the Eldest. If you have the Big Bomb Outfit, every Bomb you pick up will turn into a giant Bomb that does double damage, making this fight much easier than without the Big Bomb Outfit.

If you're in multiplayer, make sure to stay in your designated spot and only grab Bombs from your side. If you're in single-player, stick to one side of the cart until you miss a few Bombs that start flashing, then head to the other side of the cart and repeat.

After doing enough damage to Hinox the Eldest, its brother, Hinox the Elder will join the fight. The fight is the same, but with twice as many Bombs. Use the same strategies you've used and focus on taking out one of the Hinox Brothers as soon as possible to decrease the flow of Bombs.

Once you've taken out both Hinox Brothers, you'll be taken back to the room's start where a Triforce gateway has appeared.

In Case of Emergency

If the Hinox Brothers are getting the best of you, use your Boomerang to grab some of the Hearts that litter the outside of the track.

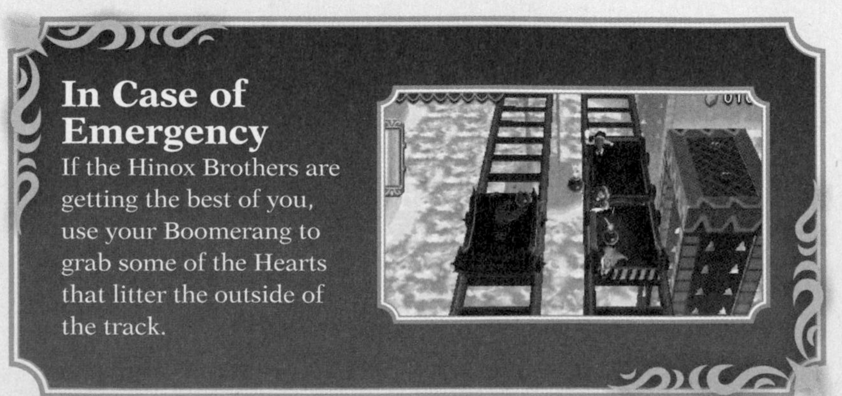

Level 3: Den of Flames

Challenges

Fewer Heart Containers

Avoid the volcanic rocks

Clear within the time limit

Sub-Weapons

 Boomerang

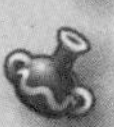 Gust Jar

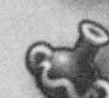 Gust Jar

Materials

 Monster Guts

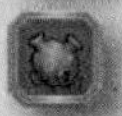 Monster Guts

 Rugged Horn

Recommended Outfits

 Goron Garb

You'll get to use a new Sub-Weapon called a Gust Jar for this level. This Sub-Weapon sends out blasts of wind that can be used to propel your friends across gaps, push swinging platforms, or put out fires.

The Goron Garb is incredibly helpful on this stage. There is plenty of fire, lava, fire enemies, and flame rods to more than justify the Goron Garb's usage. If you don't have it, we suggest you use the Legendary Dress to keep your health up—you'll need it.

ROOM 1

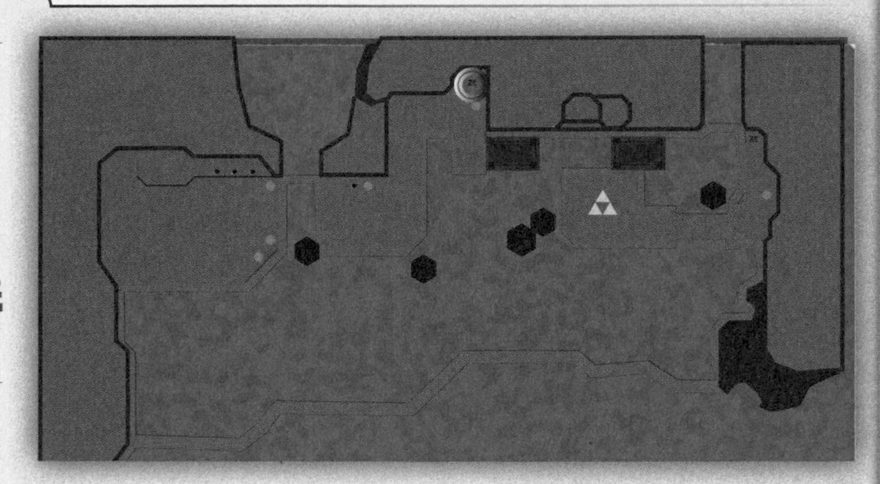

You'll find two Gust Jars and a Boomerang to your right as you start this level. It doesn't matter who grabs what. (But if you're playing multiplayer, you should probably grab the Gust Jar before your friends do—it's a real good time.)

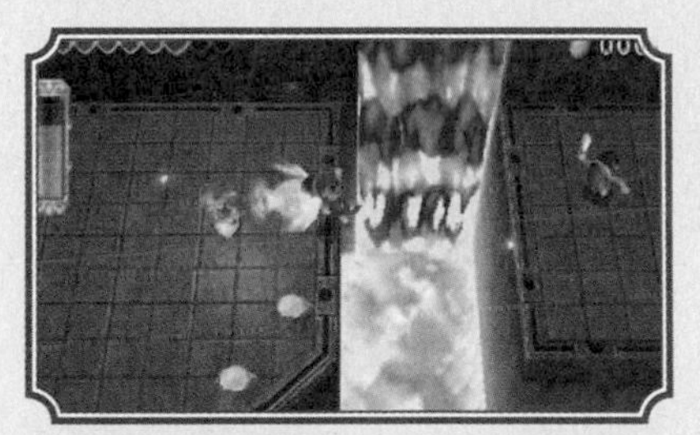

Have all three Links head to the right end of the platform, then use the Gust Jar to blow two of the Links over to the other side of the gap. Have the Boomerang Link grab the lone Link from the left side of the gap, then follow the path to the right.

Near the end of the path, you'll find a treasure chest engulfed in flames. Make a three-Link Totem with the Gust Jar Link on top, then use the Gust Jar to put out the flames.

Just south of that is a steel platform. A swinging platform will reach that steel platform, then swing back the other way. Naturally, wait for the platform to swing to your side, then walk all of your Links onto it.

You can use the Gust Jar to cause the swinging platform to swing higher and faster. Just point the Gust Jar in the opposite direction from where the swing is swinging, then fire. This will allow you to reach extra Rupees and treasure chests.

Get off of the swing when it swings to the platform the Triforce gateway is on. Before you step onto the Triforce gateway, however, you can make a three-Link Totem and throw the top Link on top of the platform on the bottom right corner of the Triforce platform. Make sure the Link you throw up is a Gust Jar Link. You can find a few treasures up here that make the trip worth the effort.

ROOM 2

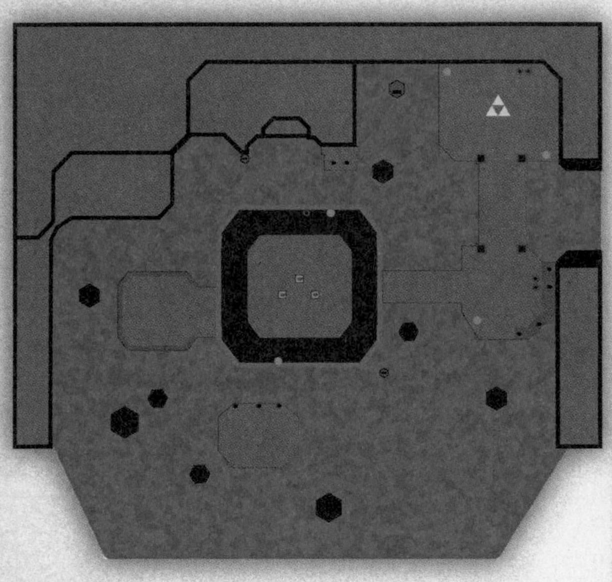

This is another combat room, but this time you'll be facing flaming, red Hardhat Beetles. Like Fire Keese, if you hit these enemies with your sword, you'll catch fire and begin racing around the room like, well, someone on fire. Instead, you can use your Gust Jar to blow out the Hardhat Beetles' flames to make them normal ol' Hardhat Beetles. You can also use the Gust Jar to blow the Beetles off the edge of the platform if you want to take them out quickly.

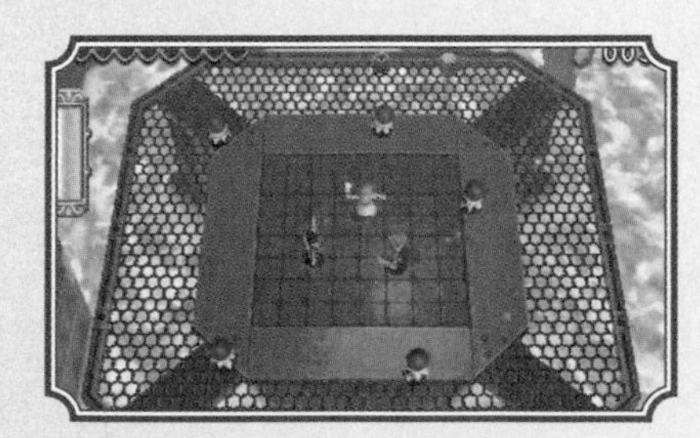

Once you take out the Hardhat Beetles, a bridge will extend to the right side of the platform you're on. Head over the bridge and follow the path to reach the Triforce gateway.

ROOM 3

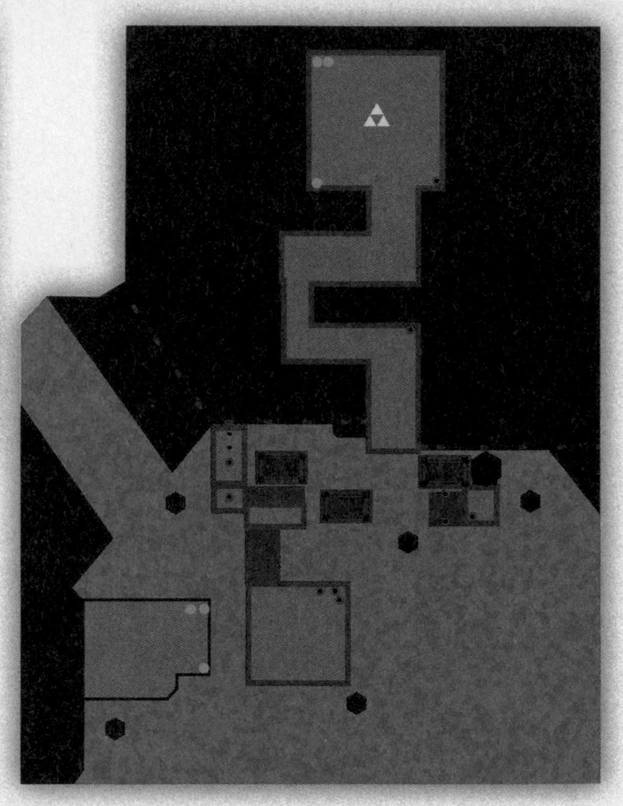

This area really benefits from the Goron Garb, as the room is loaded with flame rods. Approach the right side of the platform you started on and use the Gust Jar to blow two of the Links to the other side. If you don't have the Goron Garb, you'll need to time your shots in multiplayer to avoid launching your teammates directly into the flame rods. if you're playing single-player, you don't have to worry about it, since Doppels won't take damage from the flames. Use the Boomerang Link to pull the lone Link over, then head north with all three Links.

You'll find another swinging platform here, which you can move faster and higher with the Gust Jar. If you want to reach the pots on the platform to your left, you'll need to propel the swing higher with the Gust Jar, then move all three of your Links onto the platform. Make a two-Link Totem and throw the top Link onto the platform the highest pot is sitting on.

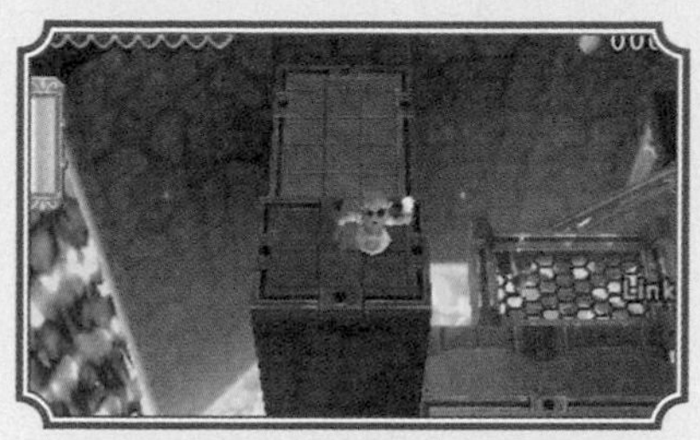

Get back on the swing and wait for it to swing to all the way to the right. A second swing is supposed to meet your swing in the middle, but the timing is off, as is your swing's height. You can use the Gust Jar to delay the swing from swinging back to the left and push it higher.

Once you're on the second swing, ride it until it takes you to the platform on your right. Step on the brown lava rock slab just above and wait for the lava fountain to launch the platform up. Another swinging platform will swing near the brown slab of lava rock you're currently on. When it reaches the lava rock slab, transfer onto the swing.

Use the Gust Jar to push the swing higher, then get off when it reaches the platform at the end of its path. Follow this path north, defeat the red Hardhat Beetles, and then continue on. There are three flame rods on this path, all moving at different speeds. If you have Goron Garb, this section will be no problem. If you don't, you're going to need to wait for an opening to get past the first two rods without getting hit.

At the end of this path is a Triforce gateway and a Squiddy. Smash that Squiddy into delicious jelly, Rupees, and Hearts, then move on to the next room.

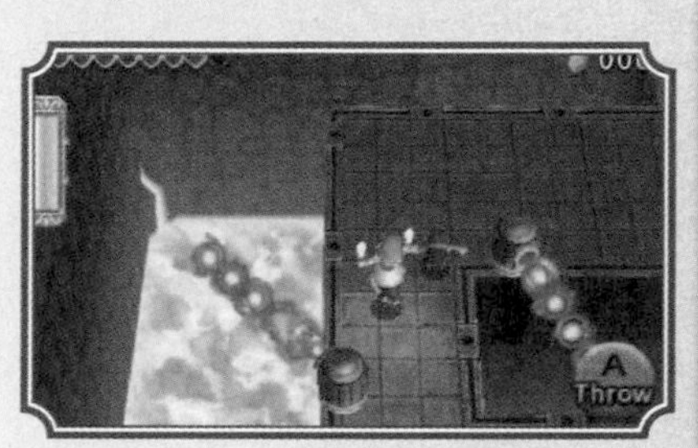

ROOM 4

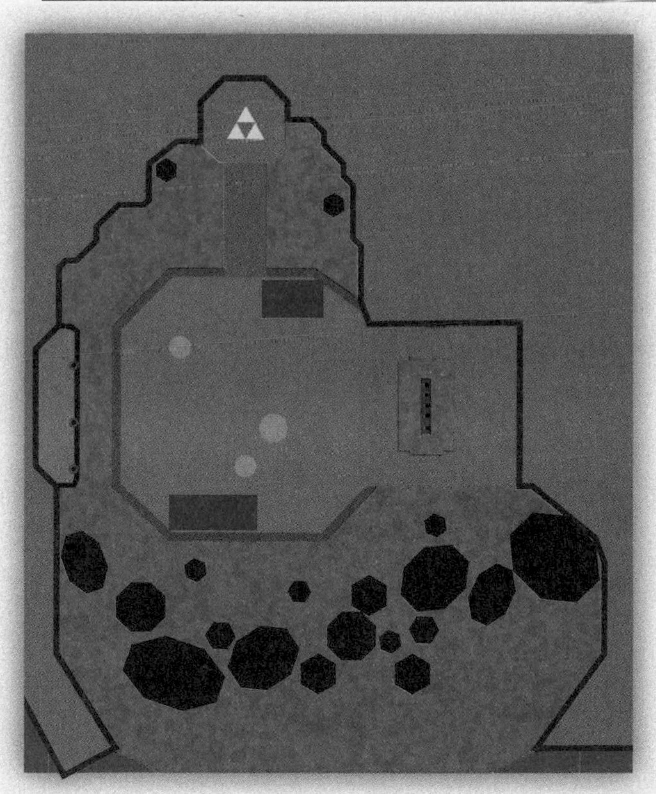

In order to complete this room, you'll need to defeat all of the enemies in it. You'll have to deal with red Hardhat Beetles and Fire Keeleons. Fire Keeleons are nearly identical to their Bomb-spewing counterparts, but instead of Bombs, they shoot arcing fireballs, and they themselves are also on fire. To reach them, you'll need to make a three-Link Totem with a Gust Jar Link on top, and then use the Gust Jar to put out their fire. Once the fire is gone, swing away!

Once you clear out the first wave of Fire Keeleons, two more appear, as do four red Hardhat Beetles. Defeat them and a staircase will rise in the north part of the room, giving you access to the Triforce gateway.

Level 4: Fire Temple

Challenges

Clear within the time limit

Evade the Wallmaster

Only Bombs—no swords

Sub-Weapons

 Bow

 Boomerang

 Gust Jar

Materials

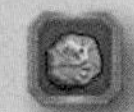 Demon Fossil

 Demon Fossil

 Kodongo Tail

Recommended Outfits

 Goron Garb

 Big Bomb Outfit

 Kokiri Clothes

This level is significantly easier to tackle with the Goron Garb. If all three players in multiplayer have it, then you should absolutely use it. There is a lot of fire and lava to contend with here, and wearing the Goron Garb will make it almost funny. If you don't have the Goron Garb, use the Big Bomb Outfit. If you don't have that, the Kokiri Clothes will work for a few puzzles. But Goron Garb is definitely what you want to go for during this level.

ROOM 1

You'll start with the Sub-Weapons ahead of you: a Bow, a Boomerang, and a Gust Jar are at your disposal. Any Link can pick any item, but if you have Kokiri Clothes on a Link, make sure to have that Link grab the Bow. The Big Bomb Outfit would work well with the Boomerang in this level too, but it's not necessary.

To cross the gap on the north side of your starting platform you'll need to use the Gust Jar. Line up the Links without the Gust Jar on the gray steel strip on the north side of the platform, then use the Gust Jar to blast them over to the other side. If you're playing single-player, you'll want to do this with one Link at a time. Once a Link has crossed the gap, switch to him immediately and then move him off of the dark brown lava rock slabs and onto stable ground. Then repeat this procedure with the second Link. Once two of the Links are on the other side of the lava, have the Boomerang Link come over and grab the Gust Jar Link.

Your Goron Garb will pay off in this section of the room. There are two flame rods spinning over two of three pressure switches. You'll need to have all three switches pressed at the same time, which can be a little difficult with the flame rods around.

If you have the Goron Garb, however, the flames will just pass right through you without issue. Just stand on the switches at the same time and POW! No problems. If you don't have the Goron Garb and you're playing single-player, just throw your Doppels on the switches the flame rods swing over. They won't take damage unless they are under your control.

If you're playing multiplayer, you'll need to coordinate with your teammates to hit the switches at the right time.

When all three switches are pressed, a gate will open just north of your position. Head north and deal with the two Hardhat Beetles. This next section is pretty challenging for single-player. At the ends of the brown lava rock slabs are three orb switches. You'll need to hit all three within roughly five seconds. If you're in multiplayer, you can just have you and your two friends each hit a switch with your Sub-Weapons. Single-player requires a bit more finesse.

This puzzle is best solved by your Bow Link, while the other two Links stay on solid ground. You'll need to be quick and accurate to hit all three switches in time, so don't dawdle! Start by shooting either the left or right switch. Then immediately move to the middle switch and shoot it. Finally aim diagonally to the remaining switch and fire. This might take a few tries, but you'll get it eventually.

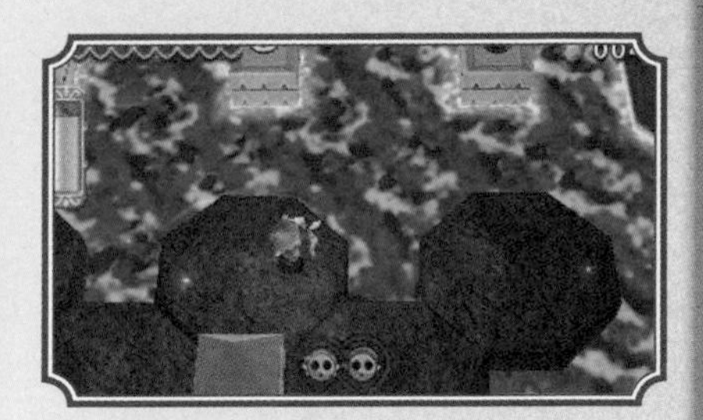

Once all three switches are hit, a staircase will appear, giving you access to the Triforce gateway.

ROOM 2

You'll have to battle some minecart-riding Hinox again, but instead of battling them in a minecart, you have a large platform to roam around on. If you have a Big Bomb Outfit, this is the place where it comes in handy. If not, it's okay; this is a much simpler fight since you're not facing the true Hinox Brothers this time around.

The fight will start in the same way it did last time. One Hinox throws Bombs, which will be followed up with two more Hinox to take the place of the first one. They'll shower your platform with Bombs, but you just need to walk on any of the four corner platforms and throw the Bombs back as the Hinox drive by.

Once the Hinox are defeated, a staircase will appear on the north side of the platform. Climb the stairs to reach the Triforce gateway.

ROOM 3

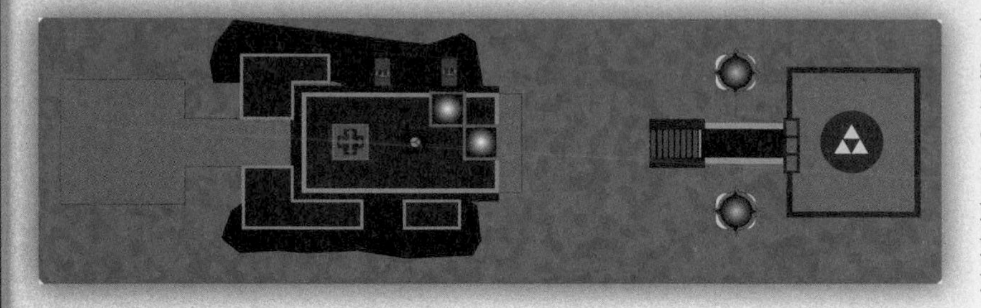

You'll need to move a giant block onto grates that lava shoots through. Getting hit by the lava is pretty easy. With the Goron Garb you can actually stand on top of the lava if you wanted to and you wouldn't take damage. It won't help you much, but it's definitely something you can do.

Head east and push the block off of the red-hot grate. You can position the block in front of the tower just northeast of the first grate, then throw two of your Links up onto the block to reach the treasure. Once you're done, keep pushing the block east toward the next red-hot grate. Throw two Links on top of the box, wait for the lava fountain to lift the block, and then throw a Link onto the northern tower.

Move the block to the red-hot grate just south of where it currently is, throw your Bow Link on top of it, have him face west, and then shoot the the orb switch on top of the tower in the center of the platform.

This will lower a bridge from the east side of the room. Move over it and carefully defeat the Hardhat Beetles to reach the Triforce gateway and... Oh my! Is that...? It is! Another Squiddy! Take care of business, then move on to the next room.

ROOM 4

BOSS FIGHT: MOLDORM

Each Link will start out on a different platform in this room. Move them all into the center and you'll face the Volcano world's boss and a Zelda staple, Moldorm.

This boss can be tricky if you don't know what's going on, but we'll give you all the info you need to take it out with ease.

Moldorm will project light from its eyes in the color of the Link it's going to attack. Then it will slowly make its way over there, leaving its backside exposed to the other Links. An orb on its tail marks its weak point, but its tail must be fully extended before the orb will appear.

If you're playing single-player, put each Link on a corner of the platform and wait for Moldorm to try and attack. When you see Moldorm's eyes change color, switch to a Link that isn't targeted, and preferably the one positioned behind Moldorm. Then rush to its tail orb and strike. If the orb hasn't appeared, stay near its tail and wait it out.

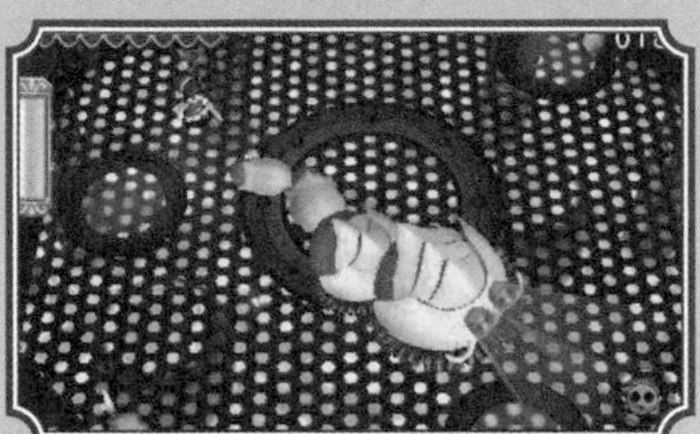

If you're playing multiplayer, you'll need to have the Link being chased keep the Moldorm busy while the other two Links make a Totem and attack the tail.

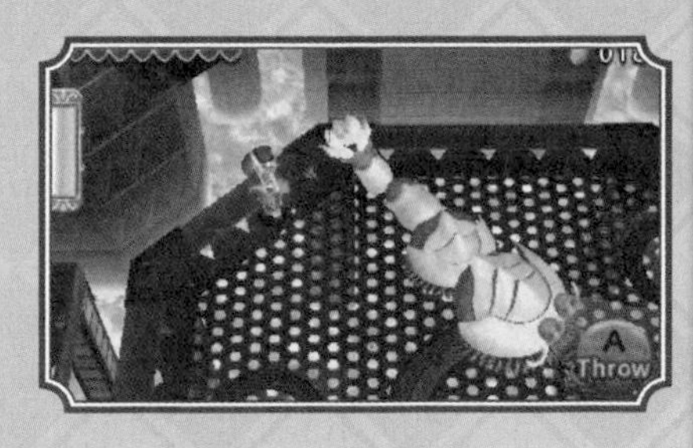

On Moldorm's final phase, it'll go completely nuts, bouncing around the platform erratically. Make a three-Link Totem, get behind it, and smack its tail one more time to finish it off.

The best time to try and strike Moldorm is immediately after its eyes change color and its tail orb pops out. If you wait too long, Moldorm will reach your Doppel and change its focus to your currently controlled Link. If you're not quick to hit Moldorm, it might even knock your Doppel into the lava below, dealing damage to you.

Hit Moldorm a few times and it'll raise its tail orb off the ground. You'll need a two-Link Totem to be able to reach the Moldorm, which limits how frequently you can attack it. If Moldorm's eyes change to the color of one of your Links in the Totem, immediately switch to the lone Link and approach the Moldorm. As soon as it taps the Totem, it will go after your lone Link. Quickly move your lone Link back to the edge of the platform and switch to your Totem. Smack Moldorm's tail and then repeat this process until Moldorm raises its tail again.

Questing for Outfits

If you're willing to take the time, you can purchase the Boomeranger Outfit from Madame Couture's. It won't make any of the puzzles substantially easier, but it will make anything involving a Boomerang more convenient. You'll need a handful of Rupees, a Goron Ore from Volcano level 2, a Rugged Horn from Volcano level 3, and a Demon Fossil from Volcano level 4.

World 4: Ice Cavern

Level 1: Frozen Plateau

Challenges

Don't get hit by snowballs

Pop all balloons

Guard the orb

Sub-Weapons

 Fire Gloves

 Fire Gloves

 Fire Gloves

Materials

 Fluffy Fuzz

 Fluffy Fuzz

 Tiny Snowflake

Recommended Outfits

 Legendary Dress

You won't have access to any Outfits that will directly help you with this stage (namely, the Cozy Parka), so bring the Legendary Dress or any other generally helpful Outfit that you might have made at this point.

This stage isn't particularly long or difficult. It's mostly to get you used to walking around on ice and dealing with the ice enemies. You'll be able to get an Outfit that will help tremendously with these stages after you complete level 2, but for now we're just going do what we can with what we've got.

ROOM 1

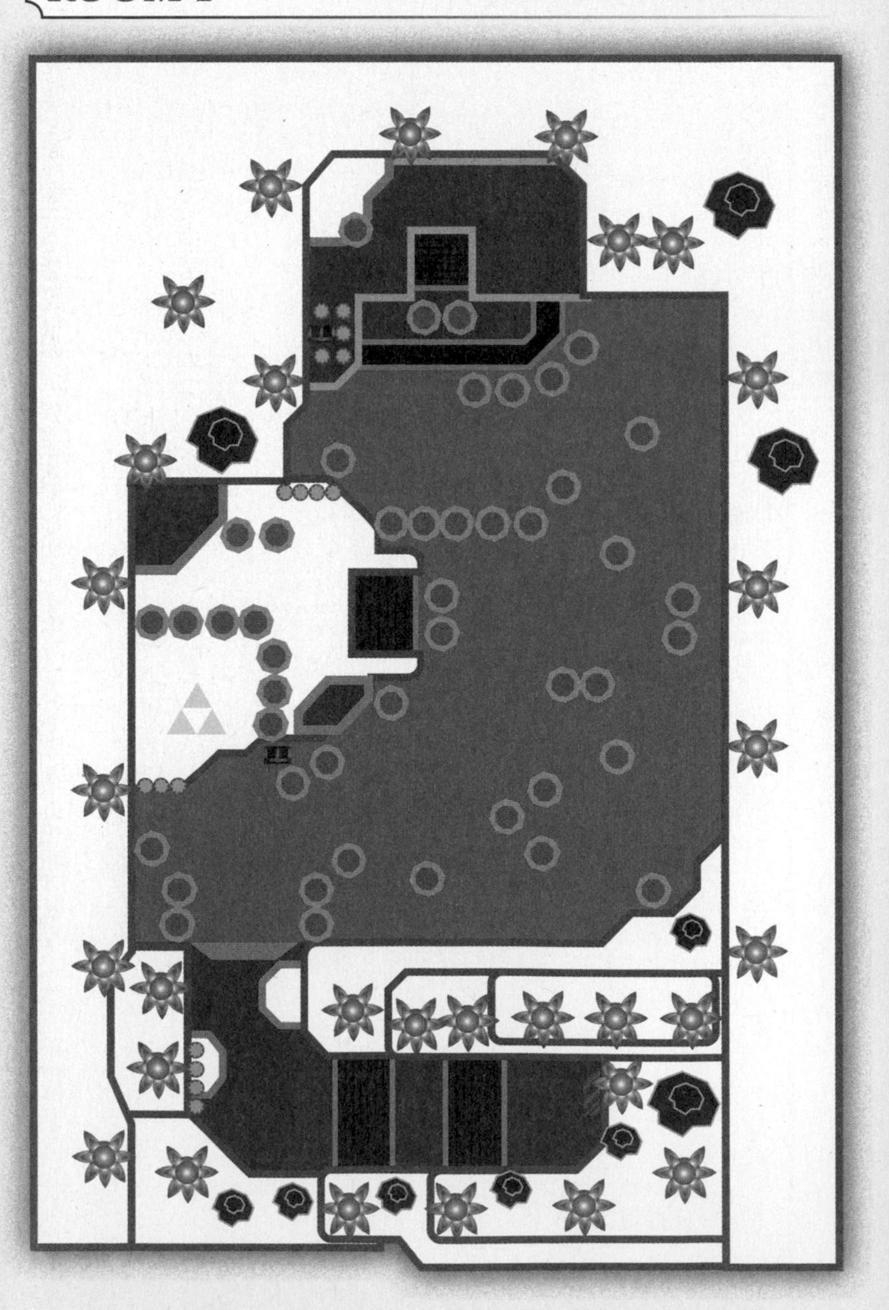

Make a three-Link Totem, head left, and then proceed up onto the ice. The ice is quite slippery, making it hard to move around accurately. Try not to go full throttle while walking on the ice by holding a direction for too long, or you'll slide much farther, making it hard to stop or change directions.

You'll also need to watch out for the small ice creatures that litter the ice. They're called Mini-Freezards and if they hit you directly they'll freeze you solid. You can hit them with your sword, but they'll bounce wildly, making their movements hard to predict. That means you'll be at a much higher risk of being frozen by them. Your best move is to just try to navigate around them.

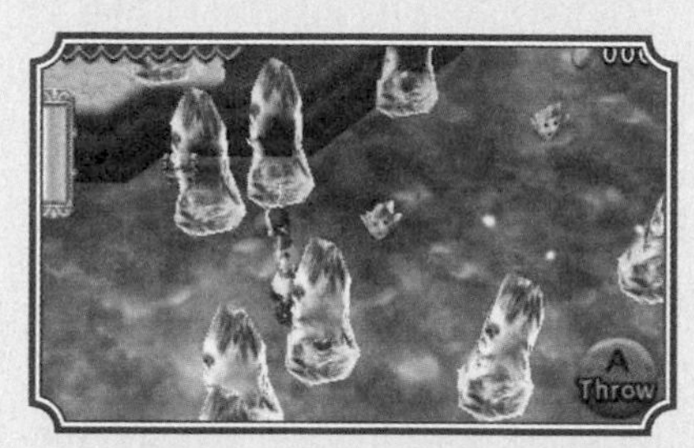

There is only one way you can go at this point, so follow the path east until it turns west in the northern part of the room. Once you reach a set of stairs in the northwest corner of the room, you'll know you're in the right place.

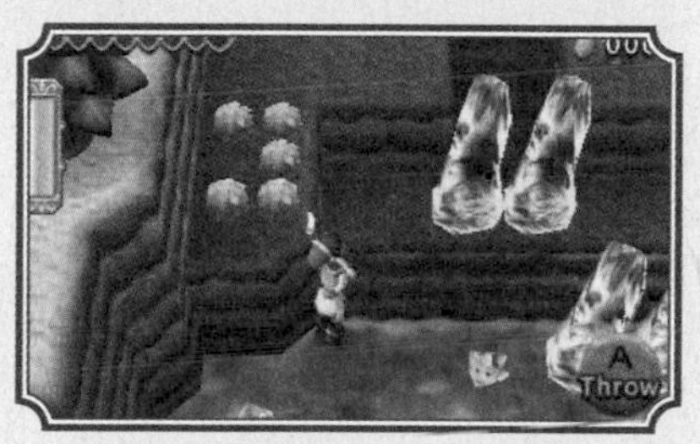

Throw your two top Links onto the ledge above you and have them grab the Sub-Weapons off the pedestals on the right side of the platform. These are the Fire Gloves, and they give you the power to shoot fireballs out of your hands like some sort of Super Mario Brother. You can use them to melt the icicles littered around the room and they also do a wonderful job of defeating ice-based enemies, like those pesky Mini-Freezards, provided you can hit them.

Melt the icicles blocking the stairs to get the Sub-Weaponless Link up to his own set of Fire Gloves, then head to the center of the room. There are two more icicles blocking the stairs leading up to the Triforce gateway. Melt them and you'll be able to leave the room.

We suggest you take the time to explore the room a little before you go. There are plenty of Rupees to find frozen inside the icicles.

ROOM 2

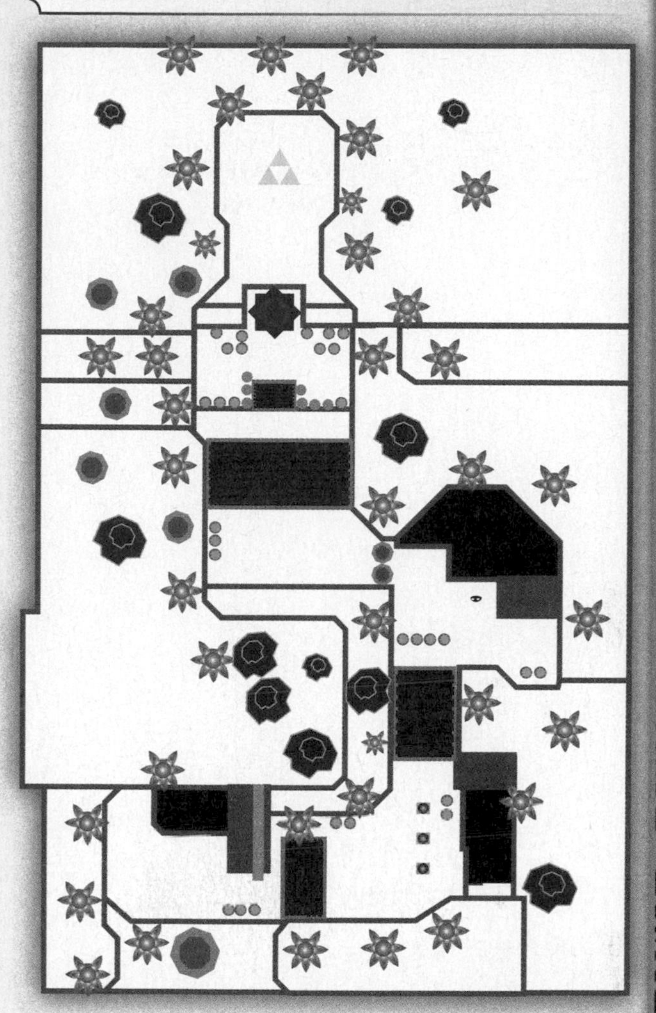

At the start of this room, you'll see a torch surrounded by spikes and an ice statue breathing ice breath. The statue is a Freezard and it's easily dispatched by a single Fire Glove fireball, but you need to be able to reach it before you can melt it down.

Line up with the torch and throw a fireball at it to light it. This will move the gate that is blocking the Freezard from your attacks. Once the gate retracts, throw a fireball at the Freezard and head up the stairs.

You'll find three pressure switches at the top of the stairs. Step on all three and a gate to your right will retract. Your goal is to light the torch at the end of that spike path to open the northern gate. To do that, throw a fireball at the angled corner of the right wall and the fireball will bounce toward the torch with ease.

Once the gate is open, head up the stairs. Three more Freezards gladly greet you with great tidings of terrible frozen breath. In order to destroy them, you need to head to the pit on the right side of the area, point yourself at the angled wall straight across the pit, and throw a fireball. The fireball will bounce majestically across the spikes and into one of the Freezards. You only need to hit one of the icy enemies to get the others.

Walk into the space no longer occupied by Freezard breath and melt the two remaining Freezards. Melt the two icicles blocking the western path, then continue on.

You'll run into a handful of Keese on the other side of the icicles. One in particular will give you trouble, and that's the frosty Ice Keese. Like their fiery counterparts can harm you with fire, if you hit Ice Keese or if they touch you, you'll be frozen solid. You'll need to hit the Ice Keese with a fireball to defeat it safely.

Once the Keese have been dealt with, head up the stairs until you reach another Freezard. Make a two-Link Totem and throw a fireball up at the Freezard to melt it away.

Wait! Before you think about stepping on that leaf platform, you'll need to make a three-Link Totem and throw a Link onto both the left and right ledges behind the Freezards. Melt both Freezards on the right and both on the left before stepping on that leaf platform.

Once the Freezard menace has been formally thwarted, hop onto the leaf platform to reach the Triforce gateway.

ROOM 3

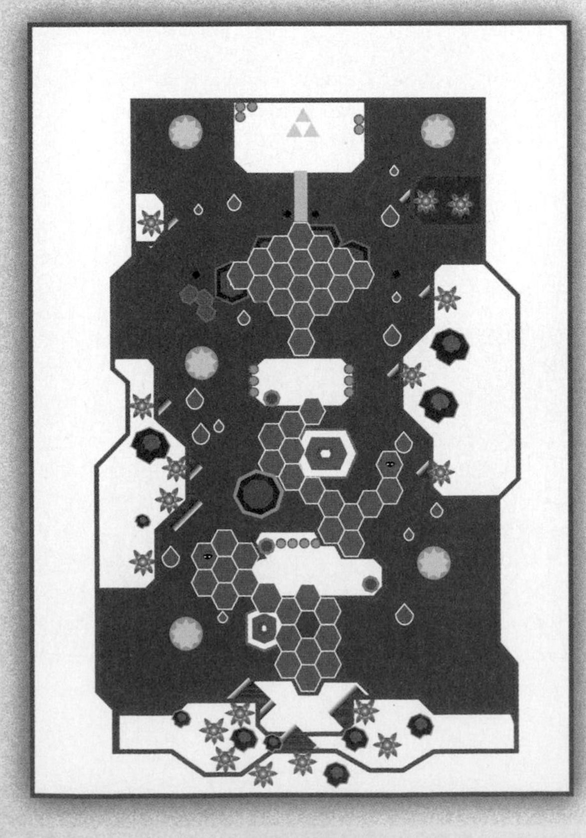

The ice sheets in this room work very similarly to the lava rock platforms back in the Volcano world. If you stand on them for too long, they'll crack and then break, dumping you into the great beyond below. That's why it's in your best interest not to linger too long on any single ice sheet, lest you fall to your doom.

You'll also need to look out for the Freezards littering the area. Don't waste time on any of them if you don't need to. The ice will more than likely break before you can land a clean fireball on the Freezard.

One more thing to keep in mind: DON'T. THROW. FIREBALLS! These are thin sheets of ice we're working with here. A single fireball will melt it in a mere second, which will at best limit your ability to move around in the level, and at worst send you plummeting to your doom. If you're on the ice sheets, don't throw a fireball unless you're positive it won't land on an ice sheet.

Head north onto the next landing and… Wait a minute! Is that a Squiddy!? Trounce that Squiddy like it's your last day in Hytopia!! Ahem. Sorry about that. Moving on. Continue north until you reach another landing. The path will branch before you reach the landing. Head right to get a red Rupee and head left to continue with the level. You'll need to try and wait out the Freezard blocking your path to the landing, however. The best way to do this without breaking any ice sheets is to move back and forth between the two ice sheets in front of the Freezard's breath. When the Freezard stops breathing, carefully move past it and set your feet on solid ground once again.

You'll run into two more Ice Keese on this landing. You can freely use your Fire Gloves to take them out. Once they're out of the way, make a three-Link Totem and continue on to the north.

You'll run into a Keeleon hanging out over the ice sheets. You do not want that Keeleon over those ice sheets! It will spew out Bombs that will shatter the ice sheets, and it can shatter several of them with a couple of Bombs. Immediately run over to it with your Link Totem and smack it into Keeleon heaven.

You'll need to light two torches, one on the left side of the ice sheets and one on the right. You don't need to disband your Totem in order to hit both, so keep the team together!

Once both torches are lit, a bridge will connect to the north side of the ice sheets. Cross the bridge to reach the Triforce gateway.

ROOM 4

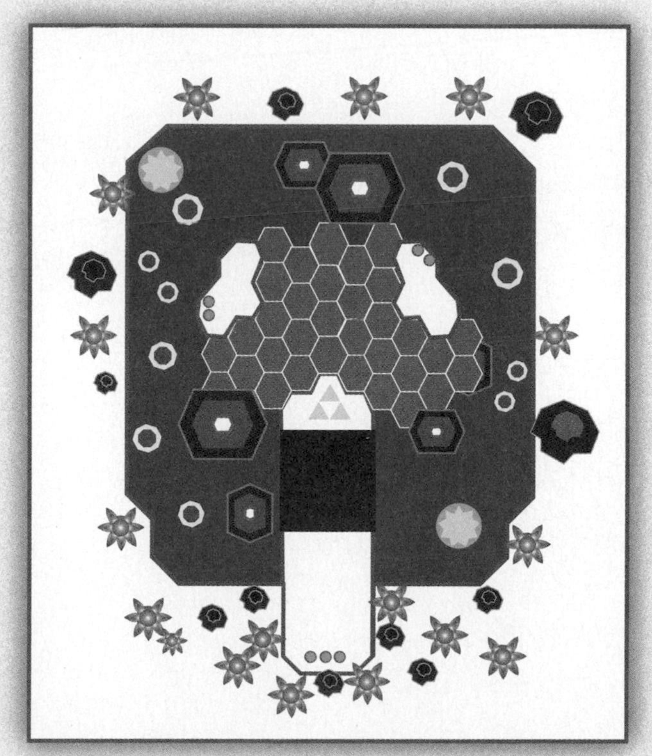

To wrap up this level, you'll have to defeat five of a new type of enemy: The Ice Wizzrobe. These chilled wizards can, and will, teleport around the room after they shoot a few icy blasts of magic. If you're hit by the ice wave, you'll be frozen solid.

Now, we know we told you not to use the Fire Gloves while walking on the ice sheets, but we're going to take that back. (For now.) If you're very careful you can defeat the Ice Wizzrobes with a single fireball per Wizzrobe. Don't run around the room like crazy. Just take your time, pick one Wizzrobe off at a time with a fireball, and everything should be pretty simple.

If the Wizzrobes aren't appearing, you'll need to walk out onto the ice a little bit. When they disappear, they won't reappear until you're close by. They're very social creatures!

Once they've been defeated, a Triforce gateway will appear at the base of the ramp you slid down earlier.

Level 2: Snowball Ravine

Challenges

Adventure in the dark

Fewer Heart Containers

Transport the orb quickly

Sub-Weapons

 Boomerang

 Fire Gloves

 Fire Gloves

Materials

 Fluffy Fuzz

 Fluffy Fuzz

 Serpent Fangs

Recommended Outfits

 Legendary Dress

 Boomeranger

Like the last level, you won't have access to any Outfits that would be particularly helpful on this stage. Stick to general Outfits like the Legendary Dress to help you get through.

There isn't a whole lot of combat in this stage, but there is quite a bit of tricky platforming to deal with. You'll need to be patient and pay attention to your surroundings to avoid getting knocked out.

ROOM 1

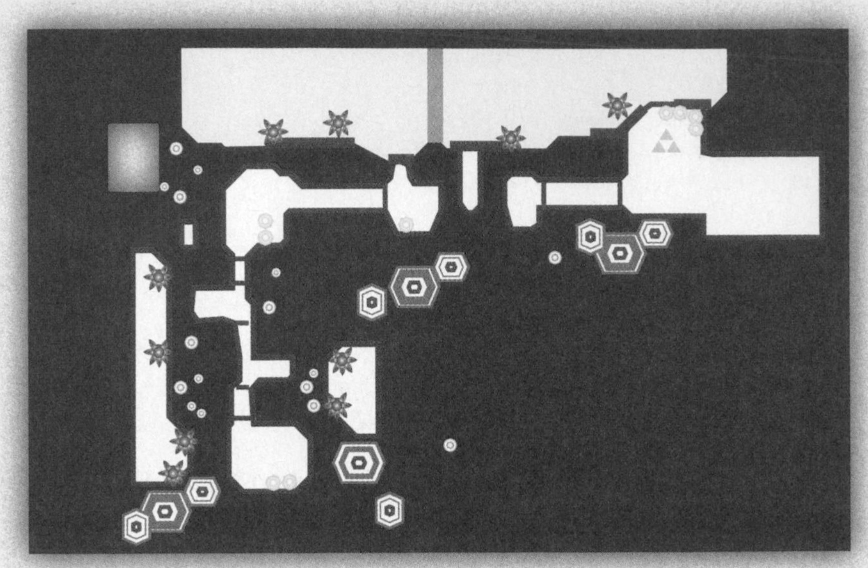

At the start of the level you will see a ramp on the north side of your platform. Wait before heading up it. This place is called "Snowball Ravine" for a reason, and if you wait for a second you'll learn exactly what that reason is.

You'll run into giant snowballs several times throughout this level and they'll almost always be on narrow paths like the one ahead. Once the first snowball passes, head up the ramp until you reach a safe spot with a Boomerang. Grab the Boomerang, then wait for the next snowball to pass before heading up the ramp farther.

Head up the ramp until you reach another safe spot, this time on the left. You can destroy the snow mounds with your sword to give yourself and your teammates or Doppels more space to wait out the next snowball. Grab the Fire Gloves off the pedestal before moving on.

Fire Gloves are quite useful in taking out these monstrous snowballs. If you hold down the Y-Button instead of simply pressing it, Link will hold out a fireball. If you point that fireball at a snowball and walk toward it, the snowball will melt as soon as it makes contact with the flames. This means you don't have to wait any longer. Or rather, you don't have to wait if a boulder isn't coming down the ramp.

After every two snowballs roll down, a giant, angry boulder will be next in line. Naturally, your Fire Gloves aren't going to have any effect on the boulder, leaving you completely at its mercy if you made the mistake of challenging it. Try to keep the count of snowballs in your head as you traverse this level. If you count two snowballs, expect a boulder shortly thereafter. Likewise, if you see a boulder, it means you have two snowballs before you see the next one.

Head up the ramp until you reach the final pair of Fire Gloves. Then, when the coast is clear, head up the ramp to your right. You'll reach a couple of gaps at the top of the ramp. You'll need to make a three-Link Totem with the Boomerang Link on either the middle or top spot. Throw the top two Links onto the center path, taking care to watch out for snowballs and boulders. Make sure to leave the Boomerang Link on the center landing while you throw the other Fire Gloves Link over the right gap. Turn back toward the Link on the left landing and Boomerang him over. Have that Fire Gloves Link throw the Boomerang Link across the right gap, then have the Boomerang Link turn around and grab the Fire Gloves Link with the Boomerang. You should now have all three Links on the right landing. Head up the ramp to find the Triforce gateway.

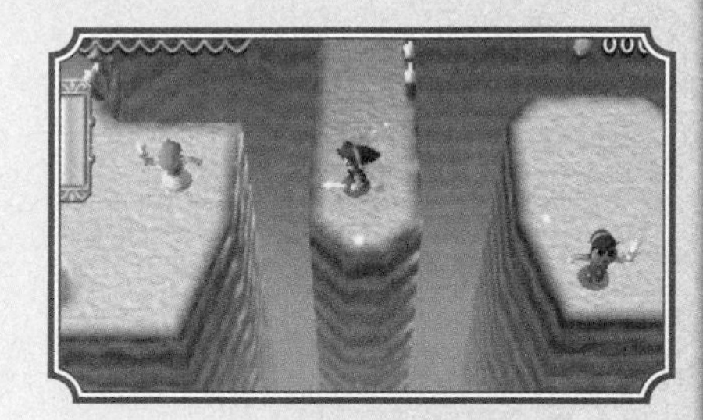

ROOM 2

You'll find a platform on either side of the platform you're standing on. Both sides have puzzles that must be solved with all three Links, so choose a side and throw the Boomerang Link and a Fire Gloves Link over to it. Use the Boomerang Link to pull the remaining Fire Gloves Link over to join the other two and put all three Links together. We're going to start with the right side, but you can do either side first.

There is a cracked block on top of a spire on the right side of this platform. You'll need to pick up the Bomb and throw it toward the block just before the Bomb explodes. The Bomb will explode in the air right next to the block and destroy it. The tricky part of all this is the timing.

You'll need to have a Link pick up the Bomb, then have another Link pick up the Bomb Link and, finally, have the remaining Link lift the other two Links up, making a three-Link Totem. You'll need to immediately face the block, then have the top Link throw the Bomb mere moments before it explodes. The timing is very tight on this, so it might take you a few tries, but once you get it, the block will explode to reveal an unlit torch.

Head north until you reach two torches, one of them unlit. Light the unlit torch with your Fire Gloves and two platforms will rise next to the one ahead of you, which will create a path to the landing north of you. The platforms move erratically, so be careful while walking across them.

You'll find two blue Hardhat Beetles on the other side of the moving platforms. Carefully dispatch them, keeping in mind that they will gladly bounce you off the cliffs and into the depths below. Once you've defeated them, continue north.

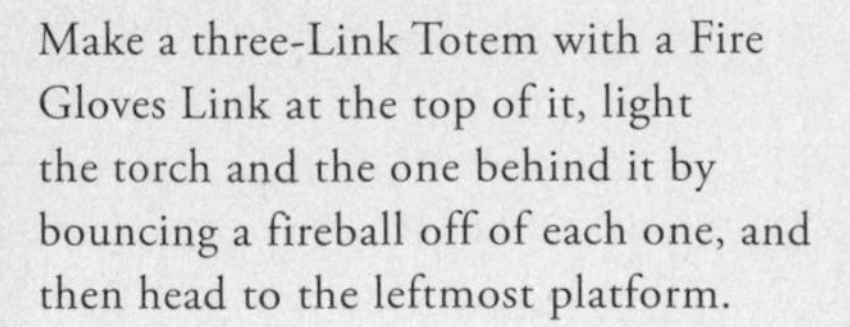

Make a three-Link Totem with a Fire Gloves Link at the top of it, light the torch and the one behind it by bouncing a fireball off of each one, and then head to the leftmost platform.

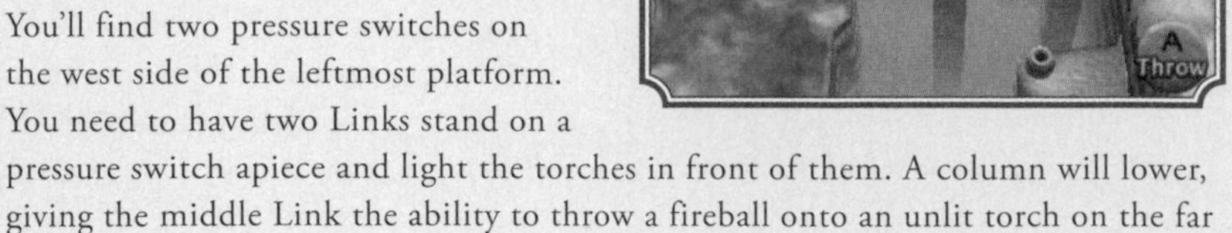

You'll find two pressure switches on the west side of the leftmost platform. You need to have two Links stand on a pressure switch apiece and light the torches in front of them. A column will lower, giving the middle Link the ability to throw a fireball onto an unlit torch on the far left. Have him do just that.

With all the torches in the area lit, platforms will bridge the gaps and grant you access to the Triforce gateway at the northern point of the map.

ROOM 3

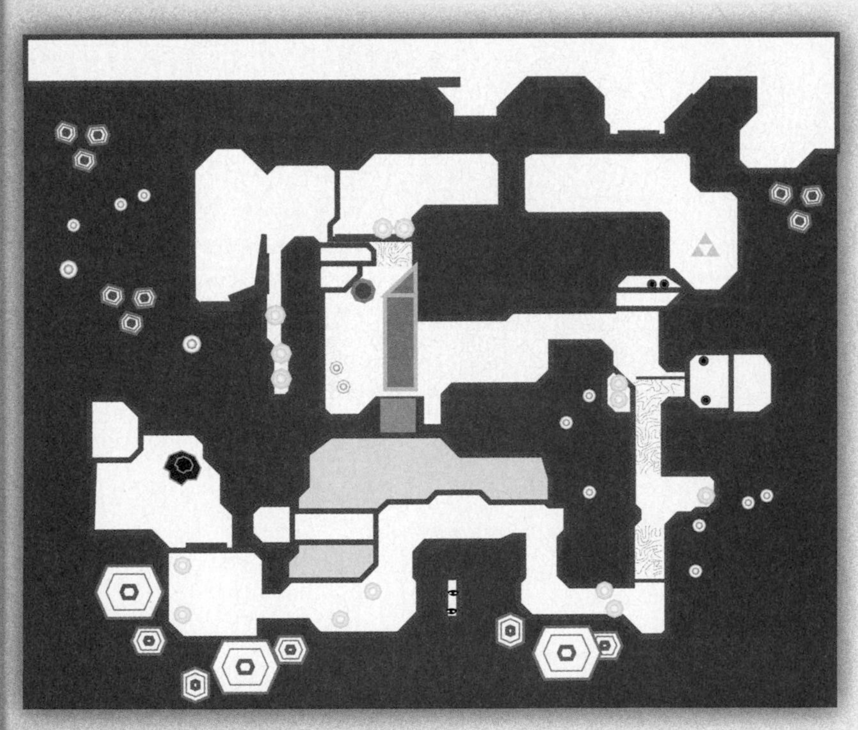

Most of this room is straightforward. There are more snowballs and boulders here and a smattering of enemies. Avoid the snowballs, clear out the enemies, and then continue along the path until you reach a platform with a torch above it.

You can make a two- or three-Link Totem and throw your Links onto the south platform to beat the Squiddy into the great beyond. Once you're done with that noble deed, make a three-Link Totem with a Fire Gloves Link on top, then light the torch. The platform will take you up to the landing above.

The rest of this room is much like the earlier half. Watch out for snowballs, defeat the enemies, and make your way to the end of the path to find the Triforce gateway.

ROOM 4

BOSS FIGHT: FREEZLORD

You'll be surrounded by icicles at the start of this room, two of which contain Hearts. Melt the icicles with your Fire Gloves to get your health back to full, then head north.

When all three Links are near the center of the open area ahead, you'll be face-to-face with the mighty Freezlord!

The Freezlord will stay in place for most of the fight, so you don't have to worry about it chasing you down. For now. Your goal at the moment is to throw fireballs at the overgrown icicle. You can also throw the Boomerang through the lit torches to light the Boomerang on fire and damage the Freezlord (provided the fiery Boomerang hits the Freezlord, of course). You'll see the body parts of the Freezlord flash white if you've damaged it. Hitting its mouth will do nothing unless you land your fireballs or flaming Boomering PRECISELY in its mouth, at which point, Freezlord will be stunned. It's hard to land a hit in its mouth, so we suggest you focus on its back and arms. Keep attacking and you'll begin to break off the Freezlord's body parts one by one.

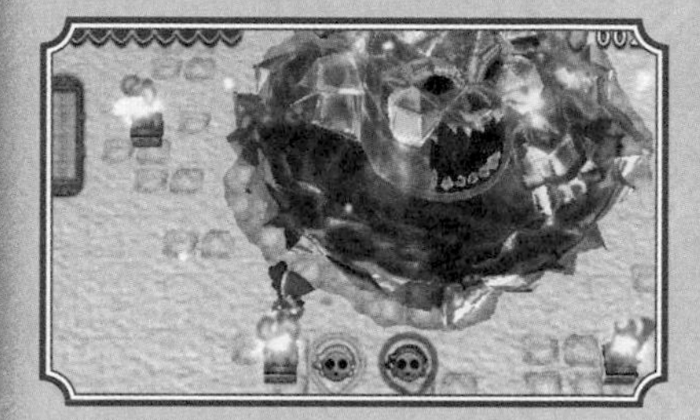

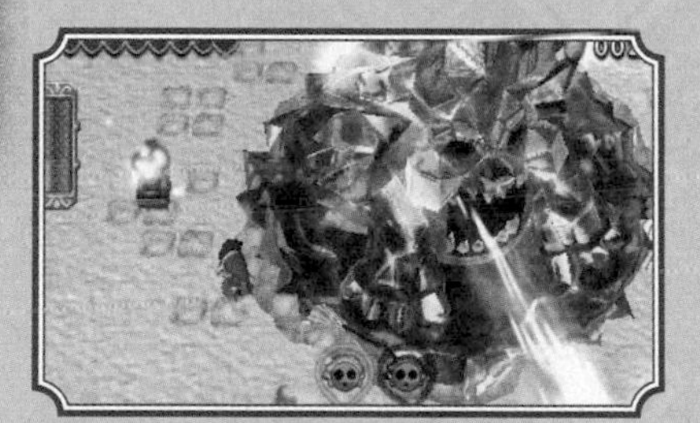

At the start of this fight, Freezlord's main mode of offense and defense is its ice breath. Freezlord will spin in a circle, stop, and then begin breathing ice breath in the opposite direction it spun. (For example, if it spins clockwise, expect its freeze breath to follow you counterclockwise.) Avoid its mouth at all times to stay safely away from its freeze breath. Do not approach the pool around Freezlord if you want to avoid being damaged and frozen!

For every piece of Freezlord you break, it'll spit out balls of ice that will slowly follow you around the room. If they touch you they'll freeze and damage you, so don't hold still if you want to avoid them. You can use the Fire Gloves to destroy them, but don't go out of your way to do it unless they are making things too hard for you.

Once all of Freezlord's parts have been destroyed, the icy pool below it will dry up and the Freezlord will begin to jump into the air and try to smash the nearest Link (or just you if you're playing in single-player). When it slams down it will create an ice pool around it that will freeze any Link standing in it. It will slam down three times, then propel itself backwards with its freeze breath. Continue attacking it with your Fire Gloves and the Freezlord will melt with each hit, making it smaller and smaller as you attack.

If you wait until it has stopped breathing its ice breath, you can hurry up next to it and hold down the Y-Button to hold out a fireball. This will continuously damage the Freezlord, melting it so much faster than attacking with a single thrown fireball at a time.

Keep up the attack! You'll soon defeat the Freezlord and complete the level.

Questing for Outfits

Take the time to get a Fluffy Fuzz and a Serpent Fang from level 2, the Snowball Ravine. You'll be able to take them, and some Rupees, to Madame Couture to make the Cozy Parka. This Outfit works similarly to the Goron Garb, except it specializes in ice protection. While wearing the Cozy Parka, you won't slip on ice at all and you can't be frozen. Definitely worth it for this world.

Level 3: Silver Shrine

Challenges

Win without using a sword

Halved attack and defense

Evade the Wallmaster

Sub-Weapons

 Magic Hammer

 Magic Hammer

 Magic Hammer

Materials

 Tiny Snowflake

 Tiny Snowflake

 Crimson Shell

Recommended Outfits

 Cozy Parka

You'll get to use a new Sub-Weapon in this level: The enemy-pounding, peg-smashing Magic Hammer. This Sub-Weapon is mostly used to smash down spring pads or pegs, but it can also be a pretty effective method of attacking.

If you took the time to get the Cozy Parka from Madame Couture's, equip it. If not, you can stick to general Outfits like the Legendary Dress to get you through the stage.

ROOM 1

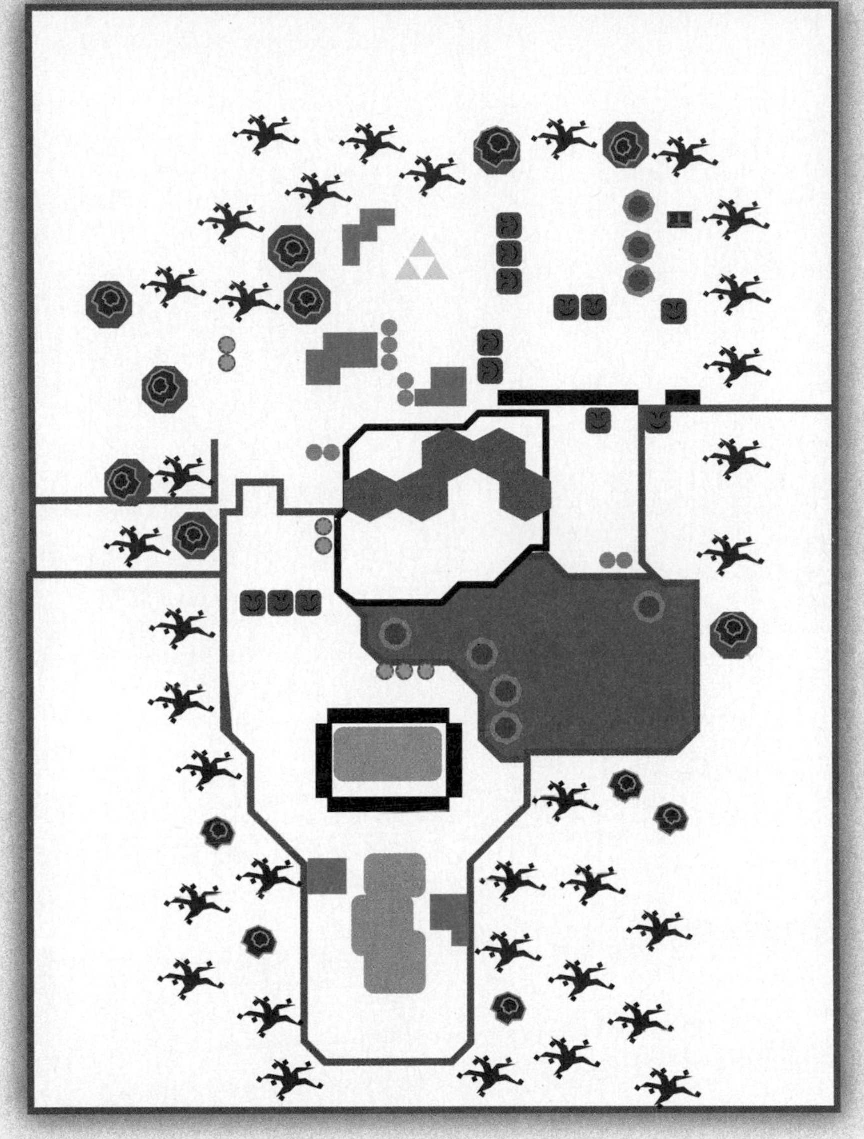

Head north from your starting position to find three Magic Hammer Sub-Weapons surrounded by a fence of pegs. Pick up your Links and throw them over to the Magic Hammers, then have the Hammer Links smash the pegs to let your third Link get his hands on the Sub-Weapon.

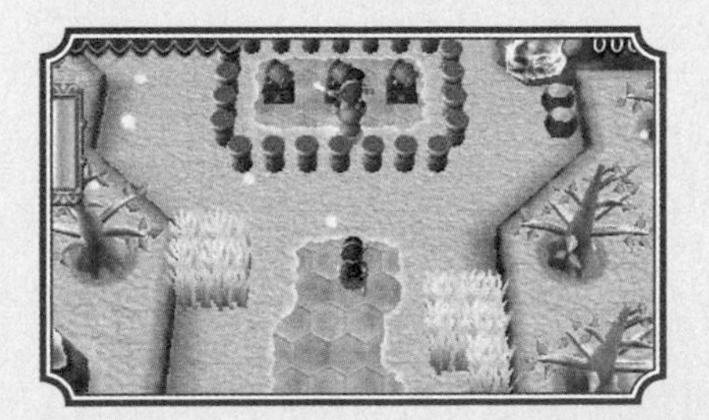

The Magic Hammer can destroy icicles and, as you already saw, flatten pegs. It can also be used to smash down the smiling spring platforms you'll see littered all over the room.

Speaking of which, your next destination is the spring pads in the northwest corner of the room, but if you head east, past the icicles, you'll find a Squiddy. Wring that gelatinous treasure trove free of all of its Rupees, then head to the spring pads.

The spring pads work by smashing them down with the Magic Hammer, then standing on top of them. After a moment, the spring pad will launch you into the air, almost always to a landing above you. Unfortunately, these are only for one person at a time, so either Totem up or have each Link stand on his own spring pad.

Walk across the ice sheets to reach the east side of the room. You'll find two spring pads at two separate heights. Only one of them will launch your Links onto the landing above right now, but not all of your Links can reach it at the moment. Make a three-Link Totem and throw the top two Links onto the upper platform. Have both Links use the spring pad to reach the landing above, then have them make a two-Link Totem. Now have the top Link hammer down the pegs directly above the lower spring pad. Your remaining Link can now rejoin his pals.

This area is worth exploring a bit to find treasure. When you're done, use the northern spring pads, then jump onto the set of spring pads on the left side of the landing to reach the Triforce gateway.

ROOM 2

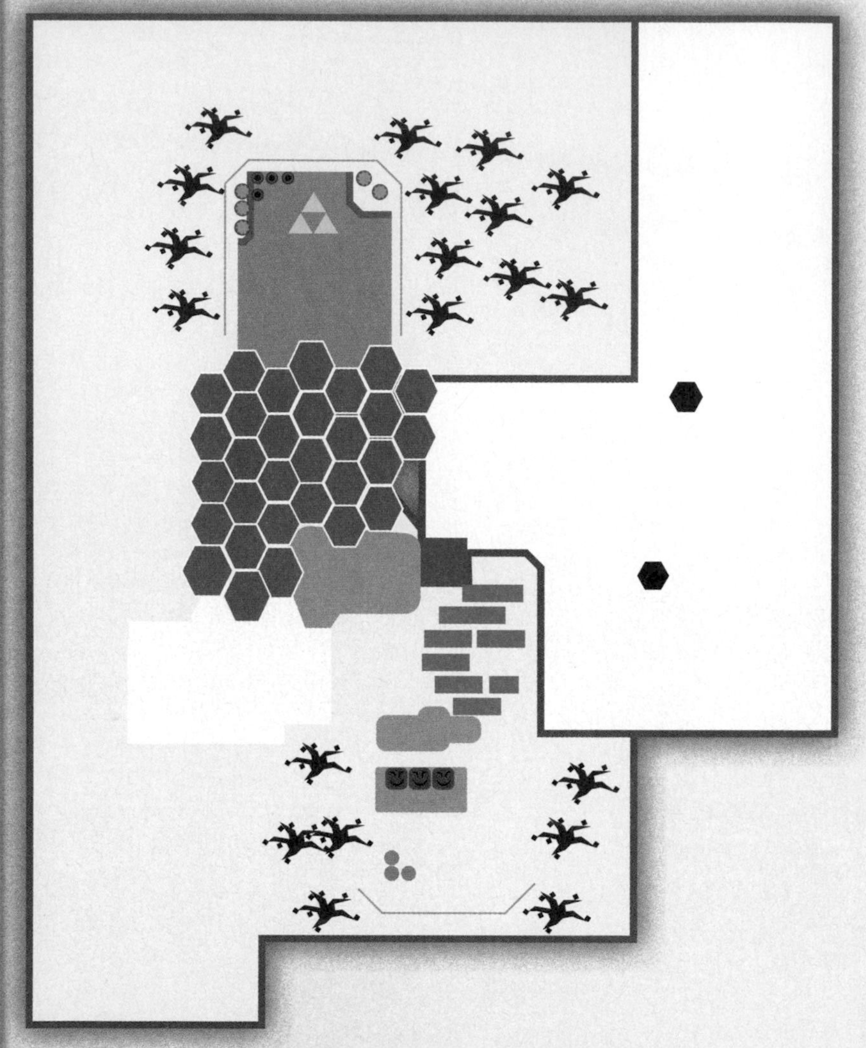

When all seven Terrorpins have been defeated, the platform with the diamond symbol will lower and become an elevator for you and your Doppels or teammates. Eight more Terrorpins will appear on the ice sheets on the north side of the level. Ride the platform to reach them.

You'll need to be very careful while fighting the Terrorpins on the ice sheets. The ice sheets can take a couple of hits with the Hammer and still hold, but any more than that and they'll shatter. To make matters worse, the Hammer's shockwave can hit more than one ice sheet at a time, so if you go crazy with the Hammer, you can run out of ice sheets swiftly. Only swing the Hammer when you absolutely need to in order to avoid taking fall damage.

Once all the Terrorpins have been defeated, a wall to the north will lower, revealing more smiling spring pads. Use them to reach the Triforce gateway out of this room.

Have all the Links use the spring pads at the start of this room. As soon as all three Links are on the next landing, seven Terrorpins, crimson-shelled turtles, will appear. The only way to defeat these enemies is to flip them over by smashing your Magic Hammer down next to them. The Hammer's shockwave will flip them on their backs, leaving their vulnerable bottom half exposed. Slash them with your sword and you'll make short work of them.

ROOM 3

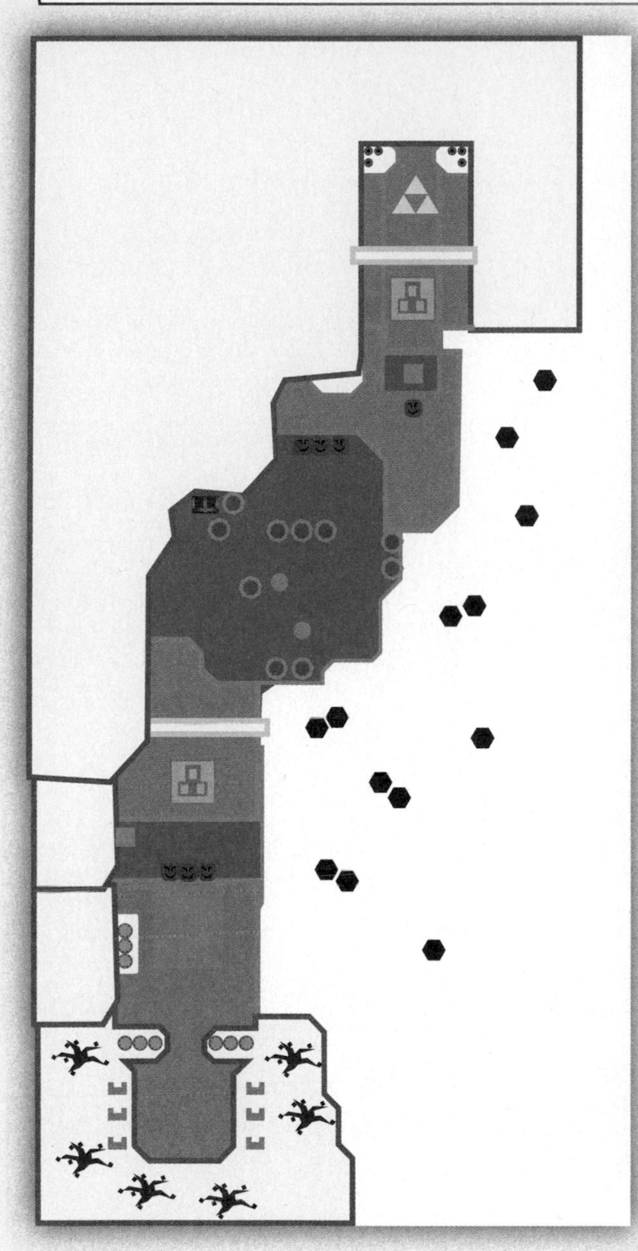

Head north until you reach another set of spring pads, taking out the two Terrorpins on the way. You'll see a moving platform just above the spring pads. You need to time when you smash the spring pad down so that it will launch right as the platform passes. The easiest way to do this is to smash the middle spring pad right as the platform passes it. As the platform comes back, you should launch into the air and land right on it.

Have all three Links stand on the three-man pressure switch to open the gate ahead. The Cozy Parka will make this part of the room a lot simpler. Most of this area's lower level is covered in ice. You'll find a few enemies, but there are plenty of little treasures littering the area in the icicles that are worth grabbing. You can use your Magic Hammer to break the icicles and grab the items, then use the spring pads on the northeast side of the area.

You'll encounter an extra tall spring pad and an orb switch on the landing above. In order to hit both items, you'll need to make a two-Link Totem. If you use your Hammer between both items you'll activate the orb switch and smash the spring pad down. The orb switch causes a platform to appear, giving you something to land on when the spring pad launches.

As soon as you hit the switch and the pad, have your lone Link pick up the two-Link Totem to make a three-Link Totem, then stand on the spring pad. Make a point to smash the spring pad down before hitting the orb switch. It'll make it a lot easier to reach the top than hitting the orb switch first, or hitting them at the same time. Stand on the three-man pressure switch at the top of the room to open a gate and reveal the Triforce gateway.

ROOM 4

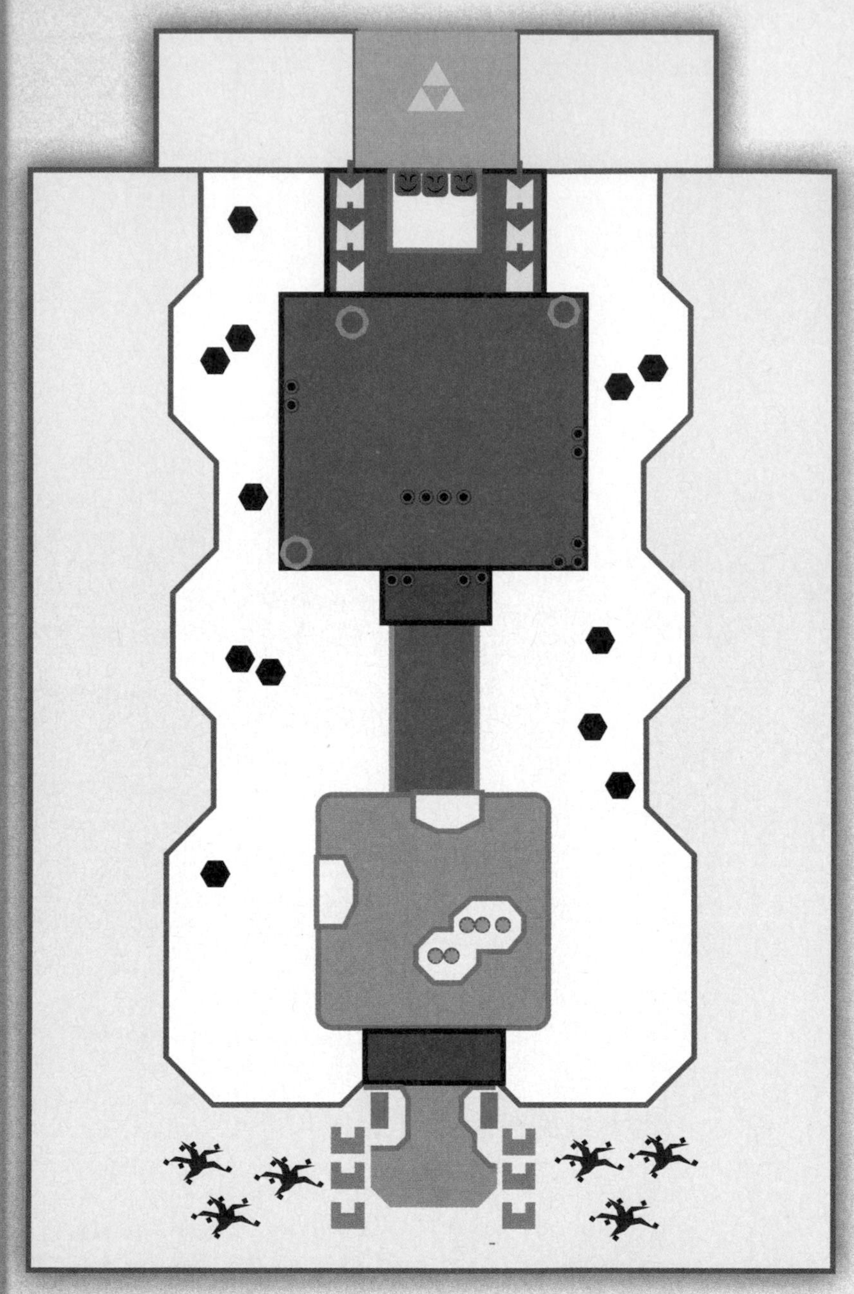

Head north down the ice ramp ahead. Once all three Links are on this lower platform, new enemies called Deadrocks will appear. These speedy lizards will turn into statues any time you hit them. The only way to defeat them is to smash them with your Magic Hammer while they're in their statue form; you can also knock them off of the platform to defeat them if you're feeling particularly malicious. The timing on this is really tight, so the second the Deadrocks become statues you'll need to be on your way to smashing them.

Once you've defeated the Deadrocks, a bridge will extend and give you access to the north side of the room.

Continue north until you reach an ice platform. You'll have to fight three more Deadrocks, which is easier said than done on this slippery ice. You'll have to try even harder to get to the Deadrocks before they switch out of their statue form while you're on this ice. As if this fight wasn't tough enough, hitting the Deadrocks with your sword while they're in statue form will send you flying backwards. If you happen to be anywhere near a ledge, you'll unquestionably fall off of it and take damage. This is where the Cozy Parka helps the most. You won't slip or slide while on the ice, meaning this fight against the Deadrocks is more or less the same as the last one.

Once you've defeated the Deadrocks, the northern wall will lower and you'll be able to reach the Triforce gateway on the north point of the room.

Level 4: Ice Temple

Challenges

Fewer Heart Container

Don't get hit by snowballs

Transport the orb quickly

Sub-Weapons

 Fire Gloves

 Magic Hammer

 Magic Hammer

Materials

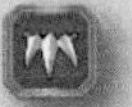 Serpent Fangs

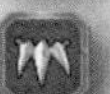 Serpent Fangs

 Freezard Water

Recommended Outfits

 Cozy Parka

The Cozy Parka pays out in full in this level. Right from the beginning of the level, you'll have narrow pathways covered in ice to traverse. Wearing the Cozy Parka? Those pathways are just a merry jaunt to the next area. And what would an Ice Temple be without an ice-based boss to top it off? Wearing the Cozy Parka will limit some of the boss's attacks, so that you can't be frozen. If you haven't made it yet, make a point to do so before continuing on in this level—you'll be glad you did.

ROOM 1

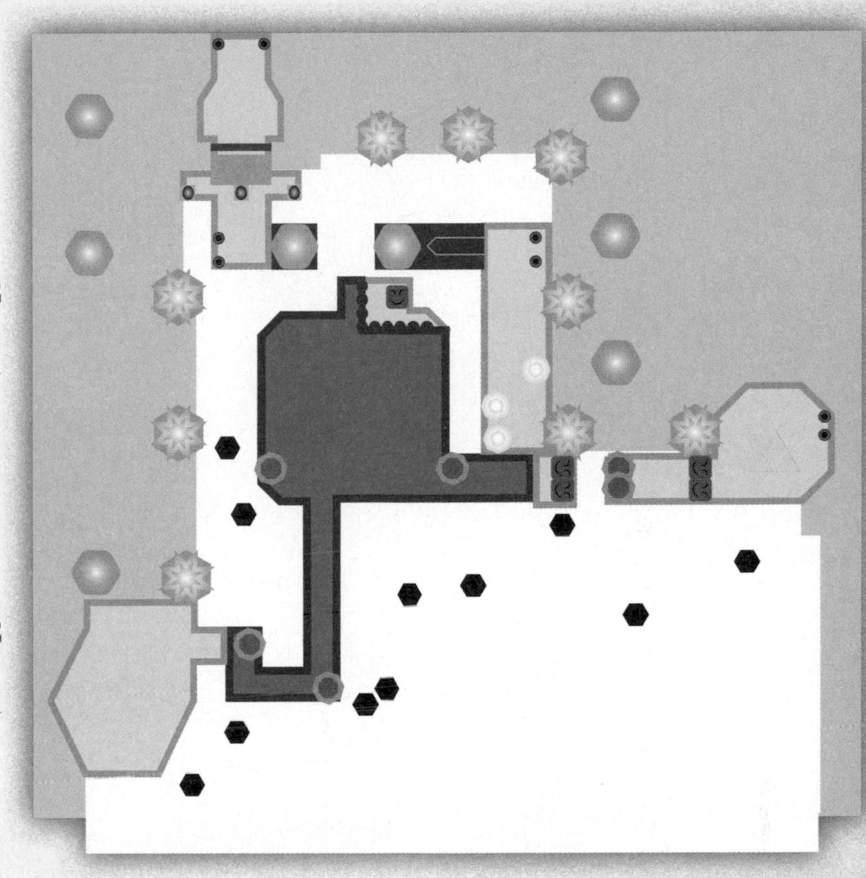

You'll start this level near two Magic Hammers. Pick them up, then destroy the icicle to your right and make your way up the path.

You'll find a group of Terrorpins at the end of the pathway. Defeat them and create a two-Link Totem to smash down the tall pegs in the northeast corner of the room.

We've got good news and we've got bad news. First the bad news: You need to time when you smash down the spring pads in line with the platform above. The good news is that this is a much bigger, more forgiving platform. Wait for the platform to stop on the left side of its route. As soon as it starts moving again, smash the spring pad down, then wait. You should land on the platform perfectly.

You'll find three pressure switches at the end of the moving platform's route. Have all three Links stand on the switches to open the door ahead. You'll find a pair of Fire Gloves behind the door. Now ride the moving platform to the right and get off on the newly-extended bridge.

Follow the path to its south end, then drop down in front of the spring pads below. You'll need to destroy the icicles ahead to get to the other side of the gap. Use your Fire Gloves Link to melt the icicles. Now smash down one of the spring pads and make sure the Fire Gloves Link crosses first.

Make a two-Link Totem with the Fire Gloves Link and a Magic Hammer Link. As the remaining Link, pick up and throw the two-Link Totem onto the spring pads. Smash the spring pads down with your Hammer, pick up the Totem, and wait for the spring pad to launch you up to the Triforce gateway ahead.

ROOM 2

You'll need to defeat five Deadrocks in this room to be able to reach the Triforce gateway. They'll be hanging out on and around ice sheets, which means you'll have to take care not to break them. (The ice sheets we mean, not the Deadrocks. Break those things with a furious vengeance!)

There aren't any tricks to this room. Just defeat the Deadrocks and you'll be free to go on to the next room.

ROOM 3

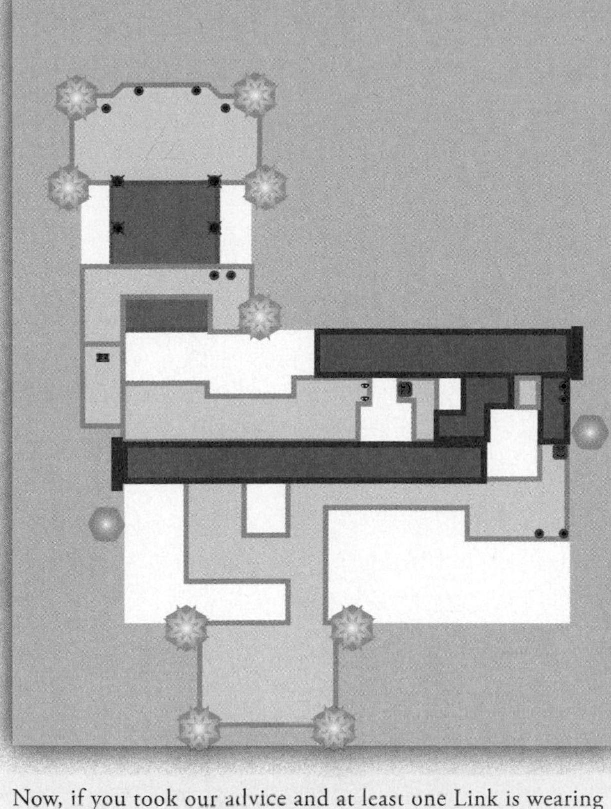

Now, if you took our advice and at least one Link is wearing the Cozy Parka, this room is going to be a lot easier.

Just up ahead and to the left, you'll see a large peg that is blocking giant snowballs. Smash that giant peg, smash the little pegs, and then wait for the snowball to pass each of the ice vents in order to cross safely, staying parallel with the snowball until you reach the spring pad at the east end of the room.

Multiplayer Method

If only one of you has a Cozy Parka in multiplayer, create a three-Link Totem with the Cozy Parka Link on the bottom and have that Link escort everyone to the east. No muss, no fuss!

Wait for a snowball to reach the ice vents ahead before making your way to the spring pad. There are two ice vents next to each other here, so you'll need to take extra care while walking along with the snowballs.

Like the last area, you have to wait for the snowballs to block the ice vents before you can move forward. When you reach the spring pad on the left end of the path, wait for a snowball to appear. Take a look at the wall just above you. See those stripes on it? And the dark stripe in the middle of all those stripes? As soon as the snowball reaches that dark stripe, smash the spring pad down and stand on it. If your timing was on point, you'll land on the other side of the gap right as the snowball passes the vent.

Continue west, then head up the flight of stairs. You'll find two normal Keese and an Ice Keese flying in the gap above the stairs. You can grab a treasure chest to your left by making a Totem and throwing a Link near the chest.

To reach the other side of the room, you'll need to light the torches on the left side of the area. Line up your Fire Gloves Link with the torches and throw a fireball. The fireball should bounce from one torch to the other with ease. Once both torches are lit, a bridge will rise, giving you access to the Triforce gateway and another Squiddy. Head across the bridge, teach Squiddy how to use a sword the hard way, and then hop on the symbol to exit the room.

ROOM 4

BOSS FIGHT: BLIZZAGIA

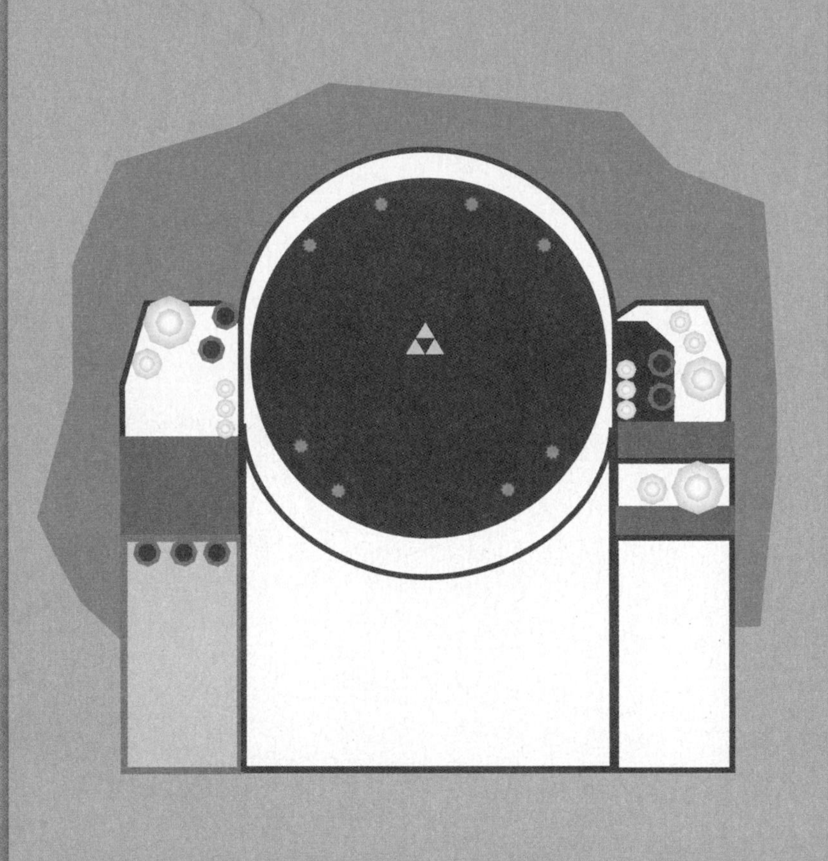

You'll find icicles with Hearts in them littering the path ahead. Make sure to fill up your health, but save the icicles and rocks at the bottom of the slide if you don't need them. As soon as all three Links drop into lowest part of the room, the giant ice snake, Blizzagia, will appear.

Blizzagia will start the battle by hiding in its tunnels. Whenever it pops out, it will breathe heavily, and then its eyes will flash. This is the signal to NOT be in front of the slithering reptile. It will launch itself forward, attempting to bite anyone standing in front of it.

It will linger momentarily after attacking, which is your chance to strike back. You can use your Hammers or Fire Gloves to burn away the ice on its back for Hearts, but if you want to damage the snowy snake, you'll need to hit its head with the Magic Hammer. Stay near the center of the room, instead of near Blizzagia's tunnels, if you want to reach its mask with ease. If you're near its tunnels, it'll shoot out too far for you to reach before it pulls itself back in.

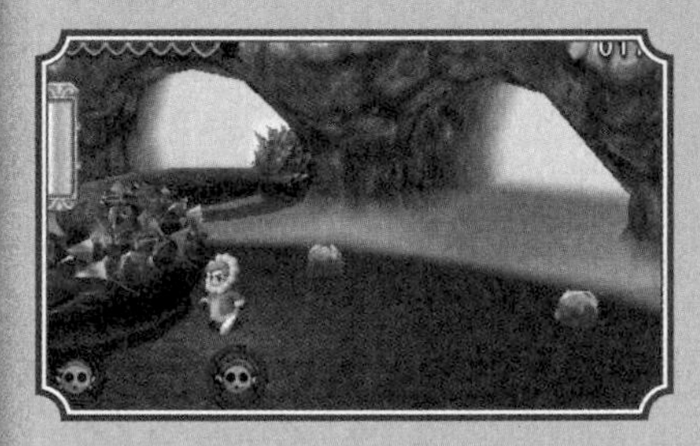

You'll play this game of whack-a-snake for about five or six hits, at which point Blizzagia's mask will crack.

Blizzagia will pop out and completely freeze the ground, making it a slippery mess. If you're wearing the Cozy Parka you have nothing to fear, but all others will have to be very careful with their movements.

After freezing the ground, Blizzagia will stay out of its tunnels, choosing to slither around out in the open instead. You still need to hit its head to progress the fight, but if you hit its unshielded body with the Magic Hammer, it will stop momentarily. During multiplayer, having one person hit Blizzagia's body with the Magic Hammer while the other hits its head is an excellent strategy.

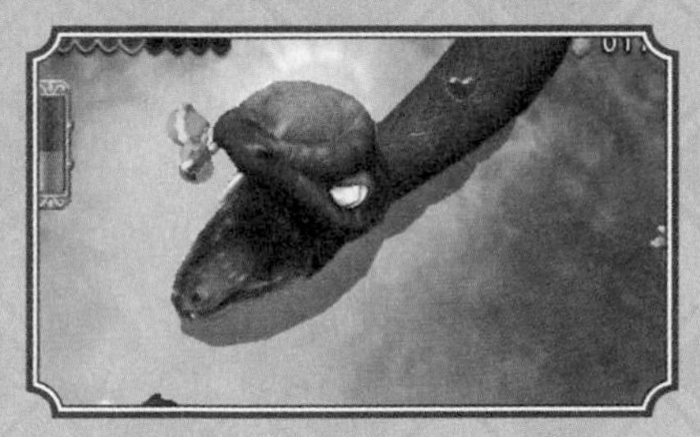

Blizzagia's movements will become a little more erratic. It will travel over its own body, making it elevate its head in the process, but the battle will be more or less the same. You'll need to pay attention to when Blizzagia's eyes flash to avoid getting bitten, however.

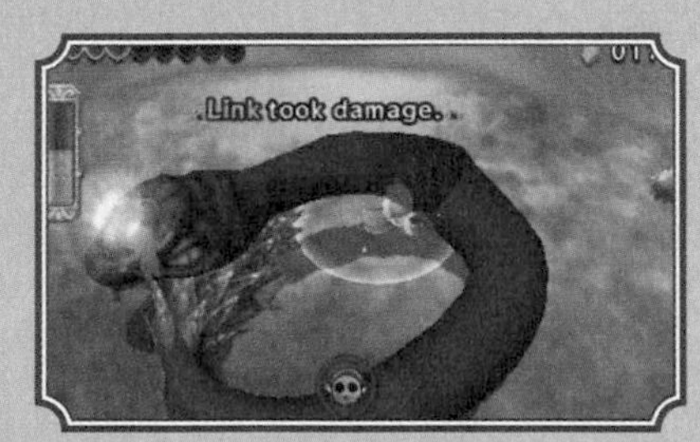

You'll need to watch out for Blizzagia's tail as much as possible. If it hits you, it will cause damage and freeze you—unless you're wearing the Cozy Parka, of course.

If you want to avoid taking a lot of damage and if you want to reach Blizzagia's head as easily as possible, stay near the south side of the room for the rest of the fight. Blizzagia will roam around and snap its mouth with very little warning. Trying to keep up with Blizzagia is either frustrating or deadly, but if you make the serpent come to you, you'll have a much easier time fighting it.

In Case of Emergency

If Blizzagia is getting the better of you, you can make a Totem and throw your Links back up onto the ledge you dropped into the room from, or head to the opposite side of the room to find another ledge. You can destroy the icicles and rocks on either of these ledges for some Hearts if you're running low.

Continue hitting Blizzagia in the head and use the Magic Hammer to stun it momentarily, if needed. After hitting its head several times, Blizzagia will keel over and you'll be left the victor!

After another five or six hits to Blizzagia's head, its mask will finally break and reveal the beast inside. A giant gem adorns the snake's head—a clear weak point. From this point on, you will be able to hit Blizzagia's head with your sword or the Fire Gloves, which means everyone can join in on the battle.

Questing for Outfits

This is a good time to make both the Hammerwear and the Tingle Tights. You can make the Tingle Tights with a Fluffy Fuzz from levels 1 and 2 in world 4, a Tiny Snowflake from levels 1 and 3 in world 4, and Freezard Water from level 4 in world 4. The Hammerwear requires a bit more effort. You'll need a Tiny Snowflake from level 1 and 3 of world 4, a Crimson Shell from level 2 in world 4, Freezard Water from level 4 in world 4, and a Chill Stone, which can only be grabbed from the challenges in levels 2, 3, and 4 of world 4. Both Outfits will serve you well in the levels to come, so taking the time to make them will be well worth the effort.

WORLD 5: FORTRESS

Level 1: Sealed Gateway

Challenges

Don't drop the pot

Evade the Wallmaster

Halved attack and defense

Sub-Weapons

 Boomerang

 Boomerang

 Gust Jar

Materials

 Stiff Puff

 Stiff Puff

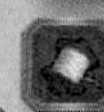 Silver Thread

Recommended Outfits

 Boomeranger

 Legendary Dress

There isn't a lot of puzzle solving in this level, but there sure is an awful lot of combat against obnoxious Soldiers of all types. The Boomeranger Outfit will help you stun the Soldiers, while the Legendary Dress will help you refill the Heart Containers the Soldiers drain.

ROOM 1

Right at the start of this level, you'll be attacked by a green Soldier, while another green Soldier guards the Sub-Weapons on the west side of the area. Get used to that—this level is full of them. They can be a bit tricky to defeat. Their swords will pretty much deflect a sword attack every time you swing, but it will also launch their arm back, leaving them open for an attack. If you're playing multiplayer, have one player attack from behind while you keep the Soldier busy. If you're playing single-player, you can position a Doppel behind it, switch to your Doppel, and use the Doppel to slash the Soldier. When the Soldier turns its attention toward the Doppel, switch back to your other Link, slash the Soldier in the back, and repeat. It's a slow process, but it's the easiest way to defeat these aggravating enemies.

Once you've defeated the Soldier, head to the right and grab the Sub-Weapons off of their pedestals. (Anyone wearing a Boomeranger outfit should grab the Boomerang, of course.) After grabbing all three Sub-Weapons, the gate to your right will lower.

You'll face off with two red Spear Throwing Soldiers in this next area. They won't give you as much trouble as the green Soldiers, but they can be a pain in their own right. They'll constantly run away from you as you approach them, making them hard to hit. This is where your Gust Jar and Boomerangs will come in handy. Stun the Soldiers to get in close, then swing away.

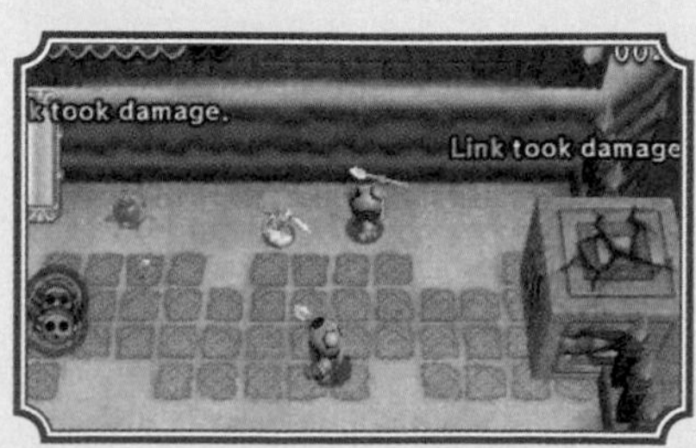

Use the Bomb Flowers to break the cracked block on the right side of the area to progress.

You'll run into three more Soldiers here: two green and one red Spear Throwing Soldier. Use your Sub-Weapons and sword to stun them and press them back against the gate; the Gust Jar is particularly effective against them. Keep the pressure up and all three enemies will eventually fall.

Now, make a two-Link Totem and hit the orb switch on the right side of the bridge to lower the gate. You'll find the Triforce gateway on the other side of the gate.

ROOM 2

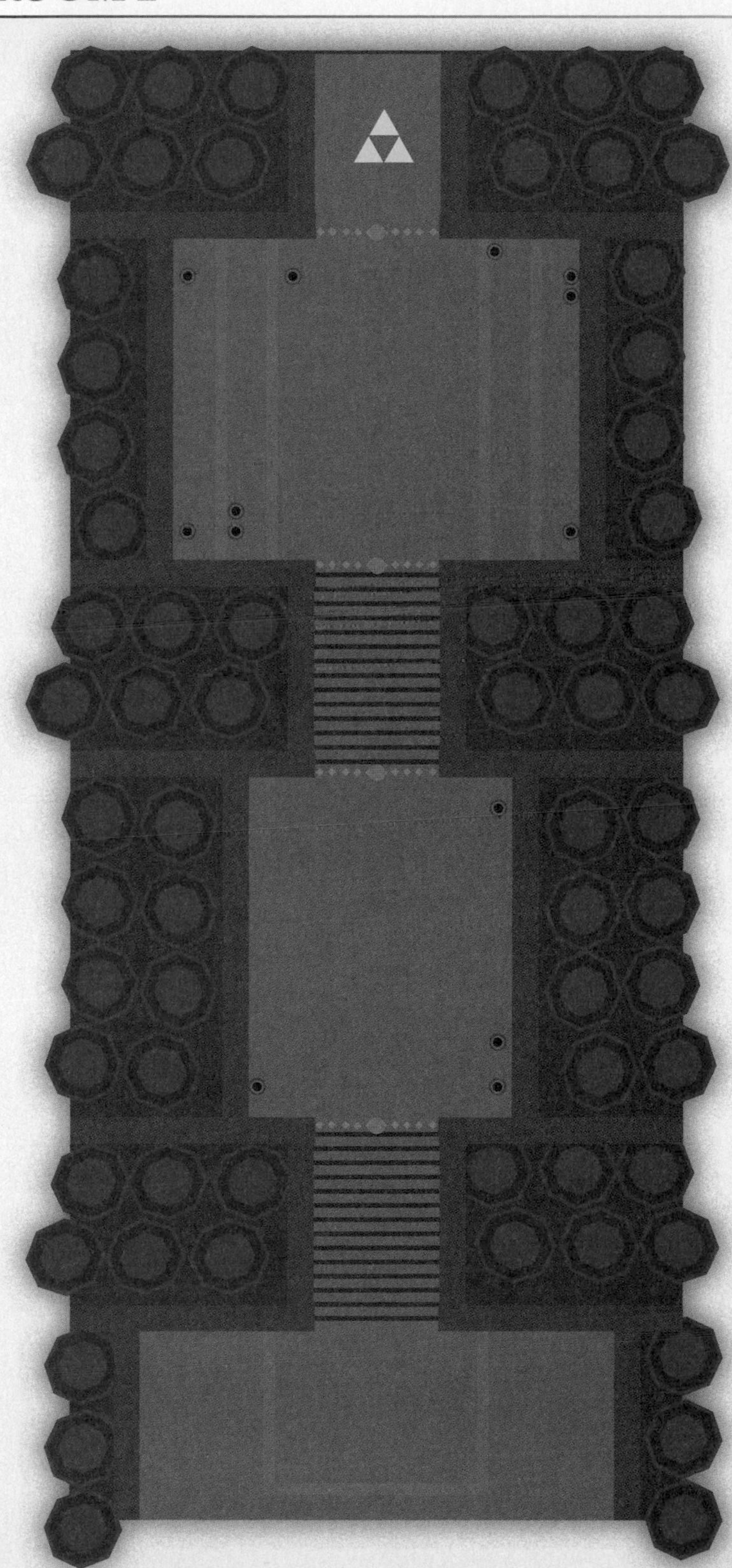

You'll have to face off with a Silver Ball & Chain Soldier in the area at the top of the stairs. You can use your Gust Jar or Boomerangs to stun it, then move in close to get a few hits in. If it starts to shake, get back. It means it's about shake out of its stun, and these guys tend to come out swinging. Literally!

Once it's been defeated, head farther north. You'll have to defeat a variety of Soldiers in this room to move on. Specifically, you'll have to defeat two green Soldiers, two red Spear Throwing Soldiers, and two Bomb Soldiers. You can utilize the Bombs being thrown at you to help you defeat this onslaught of enemies. You can also throw your Links onto the tiered platforms on either side of the room and take out the Bomb and Spear Throwing Soldiers. Whatever method you choose, as soon as you defeat all six Soldiers, the northern gate will lower and you'll be able to reach the Triforce gateway.

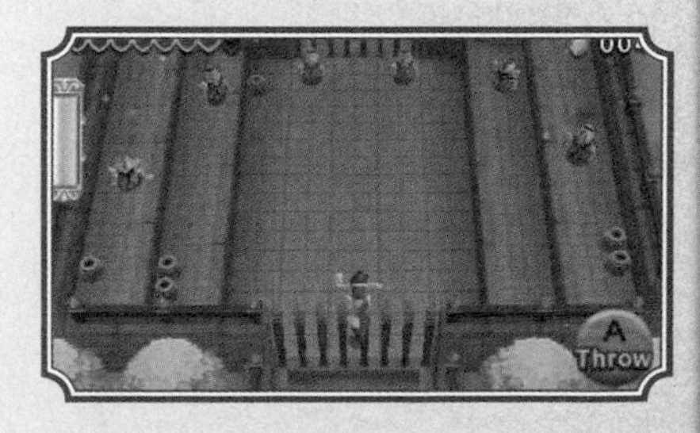

ROOM 3

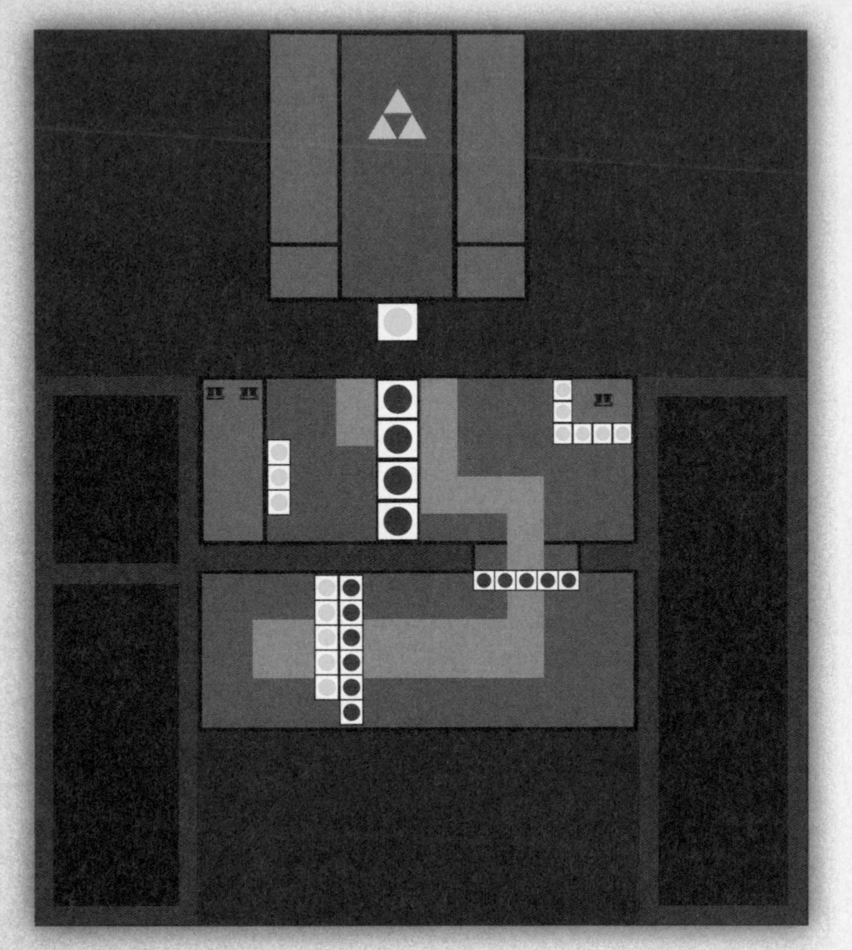

You'll encounter color-changing orb switches at the start of this room. These switches change color when you hit them and the color corresponds to platforms of the same colors. If the orb is purple, the purple platforms will move up; if the orb is yellow, the yellow platforms will be up. Simple enough, right? But these things can make some pretty devious puzzles.

Hit the orb switch to turn it purple, then have all three Links stand on the submerged yellow platforms. Now hit the orb again and the yellow platforms will jet out of the ground, raising all three Links up with them. Now simply drop into the area to your right with the Soldier, red Spear Throwing Soldier and the Squiddy.

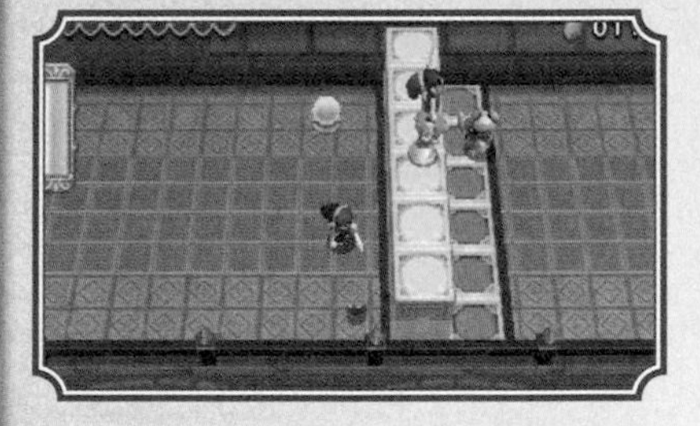

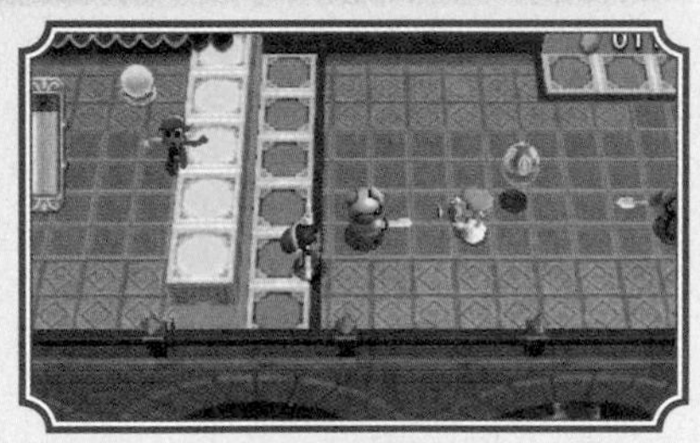

As much as we want to encourage you to take out a withdrawal from the First Hytopian Bank of Squiddy, wait until you take out the two Soldiers in this area first.

Once you've made your Rupee withdrawal from Squiddy, make a three-Link Totem, stand on the purple platform on the north side of the room, and then throw the top two Links over to the other side. Have those two Links clear out the Soldiers, and then have one hit the color orb switch on the right side of the room to allow the lone Link to rejoin his comrades.

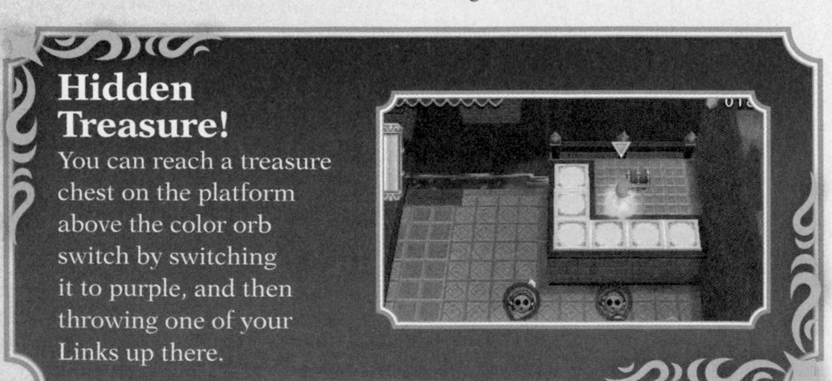

Hidden Treasure!

You can reach a treasure chest on the platform above the color orb switch by switching it to purple, and then throwing one of your Links up there.

Change the color orb switch to yellow, then have all your Links stand on the purple platforms in the center of the room. A Bomb Soldier will be doing its only job by throwing Bombs at you from the north end of the room. Pick a Bomb up and throw it onto the color orb to your left, then wait for it to explode. The orb will change to purple and all of your Links will be elevated.

Hidden Treasure!

You can reach the treasure chests on the left side of the room by setting the color orb to purple and standing on the yellow platforms along with one other Link. Have the remaining Link hit the color orb to raise the yellow platforms, then have one of the Links on top throw the other up. Voila!

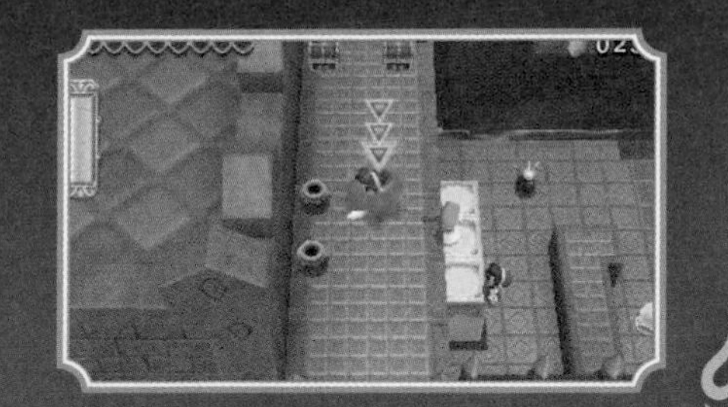

Make a three-Link Totem and throw the top two Links over the gap to the north side of the room. Have them quickly stand on the two pressure switches just below the Triforce gateway. Two sets of stairs will rise out of the water in the gap, giving the lone Link the ability to rejoin his friends.

Ignore all of the Soldiers as best as possible, and have all three Links stand on the Triforce gateway at the north end of the room.

ROOM 4

You'll have to ride an elevator on the north side of the room while dodging two silver Bomb Soldiers' Bombs. If their Bombs land on the elevator, quickly pick them up and throw them off.

Defeat the silver Bomb Soldier at the top of the elevator once you get off of it, then line up the two Boomerang Links at the end of the northern platform. Use your Gust Jar Link to blast them across the gap, then have the Boomerang Links step on the two pressure switches to create a bridge across the gap.

Two giant, hanging weights will be blocking your path ahead. To get past them, have your Gust Jar Link head to the platform to the right, then air blast each weight to cause them to swing. They'll keep swinging back and forth, giving you a chance to slide in between them into the next area.

When all three Links enter the northern area of the room, two Silver Ball & Chain Soldiers will appear. Keep your distance and try to stun both of them before attacking either of them. If you leave one un-stunned, it will bash you while you're trying to hit the other one.

Once you defeat both silver Soldiers, the northern wall will shift away and the Triforce gateway will be at your fingertips. Stand on it to finish the level.

Level 2: Bomb Storage

Challenges

Win without using a sword

Transport the orb quickly

Don't fall at all

Sub-Weapons

 Bombs

 Gust Jar

 Gust Jar

Materials

 Stiff Puff

 Stiff Puff

 Royal Ring

Recommended Outfits

 Big Bomb Outfit

 Legendary Dress

This stage is full of puzzles and platforming that will drain your Heart Containers pretty quickly. The Legendary Dress will help to keep your health up during the more challenging areas. The Big Bomb Outfit has limited use in this level, but enough to warrant wearing it if you have it.

ROOM 1

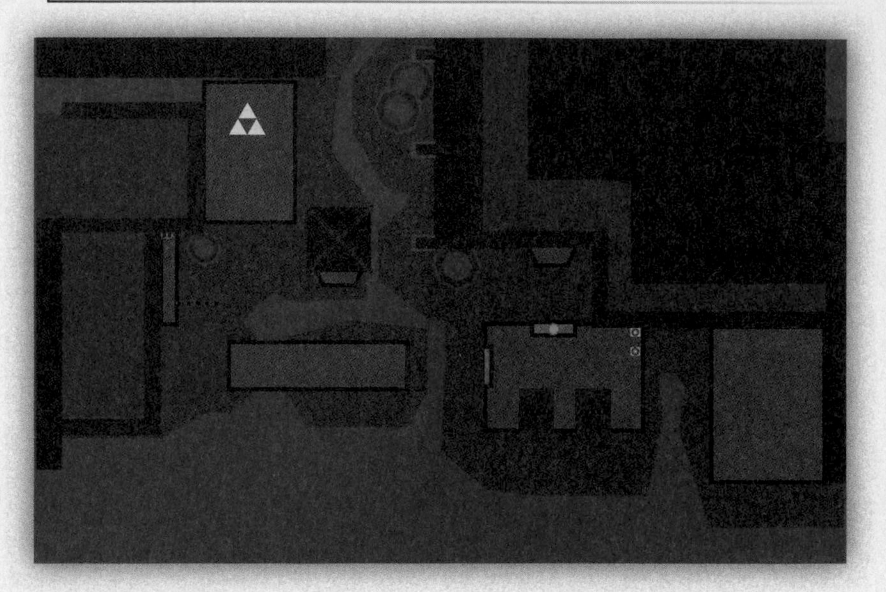

Grab the Sub-Weapons ahead of you, then line up the Bomb Link and a Gust Jar Link on the northwest side of the landing. Use the remaining Gust Jar Link to blast the other two Links over the gap. Have those two Links stand on the two pressure switches on the other side of the gap to extend a bridge to the remaining Link.

You'll find an elevated bridge on the left side of the room and a cracked window slightly northeast of that. You'll need to break the northern window and hit the orb switch behind it to lower the bridge. To accomplish this, have a Gust Jar Link blast the Bomb from the Bomb Flower across the gap and onto the balcony below the window. The window will break and reveal the orb switch. Shoot another Bomb over to the balcony and it will activate the orb switch, which lowers the bridge.

Clear out the two Hardhat Beetles on the other side of the bridge, then stand just below the cracked window. This can get a little tricky: Have your Bomb Link stand to either the left or the right and then have him throw a Bomb onto the steel slab just below the cracked window.

Now have a Gust Jar Link blast the Bomb across the gap and onto the balcony in front of the window. (The Bomb Link will have to be pressing up against the railing to make this work properly.) The window will break and reveal another orb switch. Repeat the process to activate the orb switch and create a bridge on the left side of the platform.

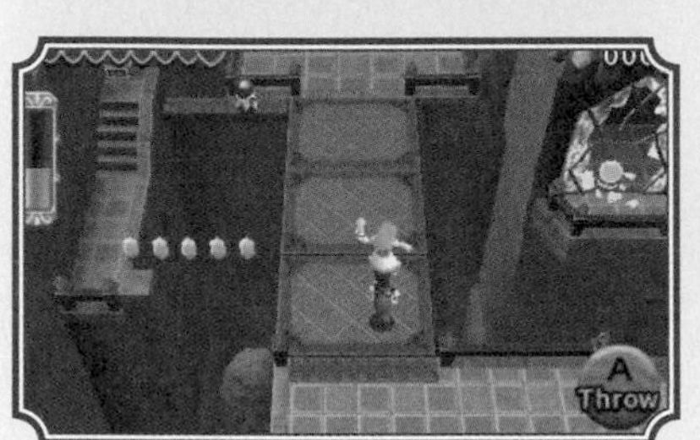

Continue north to find the Triforce gateway.

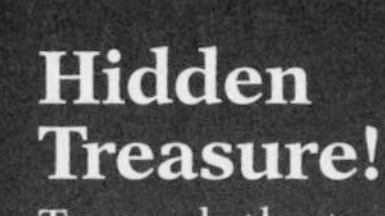

Hidden Treasure!

To reach the treasure chest on the left side of the bridge, make a two-Link Totem, then cross the narrow girder at the north end of the bridge. Throw the top Link up to the treasure chest and it'll be as good as yours!

ROOM 2

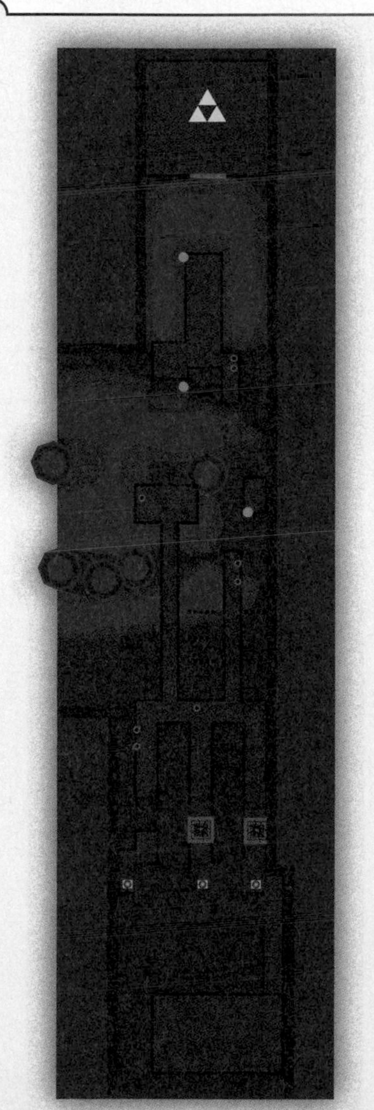

Head north until you reach a set of platforms with pressure switches and steel slabs. Use one of the Gust Jar Links to blast the other Gust Jar and the Bomb Links across the gap on the left.

Now have the Gust Jar Link you just blasted over blast the Bomb Link across the gap on the left side of the center platform. Next, have all three Links stand on their respective pressure switches. The northern wall will retract and each Link will have to traverse their own path.

The Links on the center and right paths both have cracked blocks. Have the Bomb Link throw a Bomb to the center path to destroy the center block, then have him throw another, but this time have the center Gust Jar Link throw the Bomb to the right path to destroy the cracked block there.

Have the center Link use his Gust Jar to put out the flames on the left Link's path. Now all three Links can move forward. Carefully defeat the Hardhat Beetles on each path, then move on.

Eventually the two Gust Jar Links' paths will merge, then come to an abrupt end. The Bomb Link will have to give them a hand by throwing a Bomb next to the orb switch ahead of the Gust Jar Links' path.

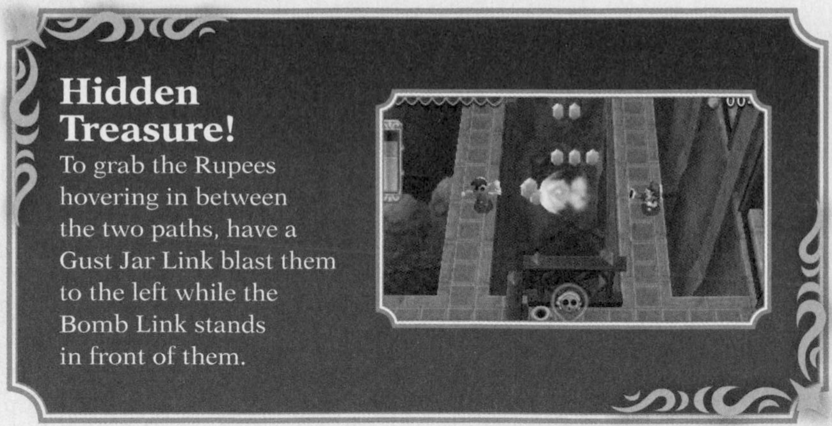

Hidden Treasure!

To grab the Rupees hovering in between the two paths, have a Gust Jar Link blast them to the left while the Bomb Link stands in front of them.

A moving platform will allow the Gust Jar Links to head north across the gap, while the Bomb Link has to stay behind and wait patiently.

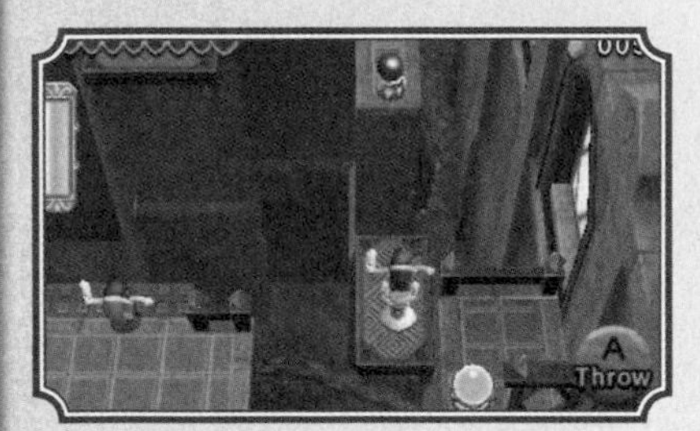

You'll find a couple of Hardhat Beetles and orb switches on the other side of the gap. Defeat the Hardhat Beetles carefully, then make a two-Link Totem and throw the top Link onto the platform with the orb switch on it. Hitting that orb switch will activate another moving platform, which will allow the Bomb Link to rejoin his pals.

With all three Links together again, make a three-Link Totem and hit the orb switch at the end of the path. A bridge will lower, giving you access to the Triforce gateway.

ROOM 3

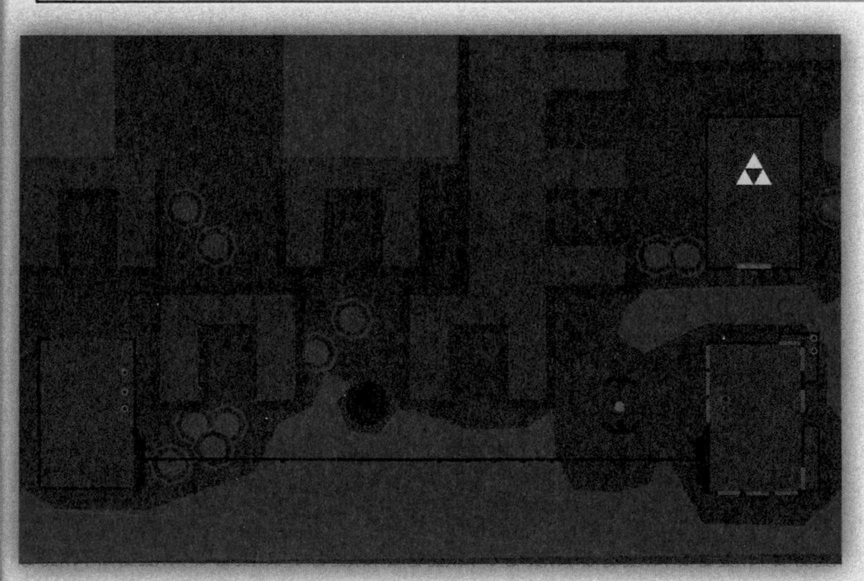

When you appear in this room you'll see a tram car hanging from its track. To move the car you need to have one of the Gust Jar Links point at the tram car's left end, and then fire an air blast. You'll have to continue using the Gust Jar to keep the car moving.

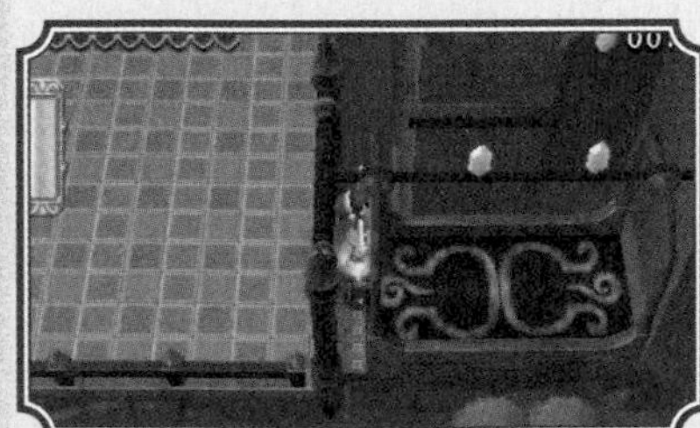

Hidden Treasure!

You've probably seen all those wonderful Rupees sitting on the tram's track and wondered, "How the heck do I get all of that sweet, sweet cash?" Well wonder no more! Make a three-Link Totem with a Gust Jar Link on top, then stand directly under the track and throw your top Link up! Easy as that! Have that Link walk carefully, because it's actually pretty easy to fall off.

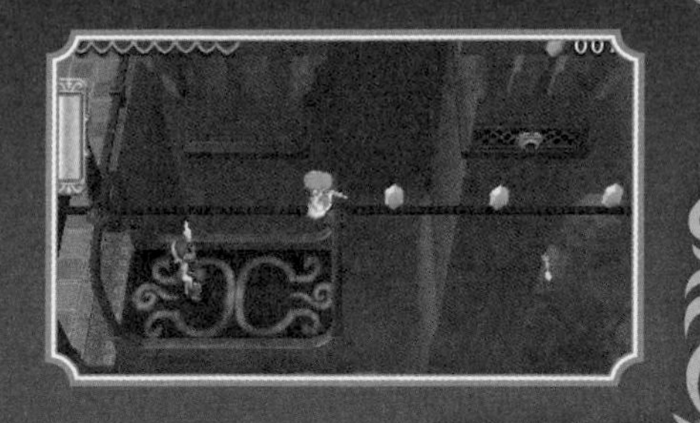

Around the center of the track, you'll find a shy orb switch. Have your Bomb Link lob a Bomb next to the switch, then stand to the south end of the car to activate it. A tower will shift and reveal another orb switch a bit farther down the track.

You'll need to have the Bomb Link throw a Bomb into this tower. The problem is the tower's exterior is rotating. You'll need to time your Bomb tosses carefully in order to land a Bomb inside the tower. Make a three-Link Totem with the Bomb Link on top and throw a Bomb into the tower when you get a clear shot. Once you've activated the switch, a bridge will lower on the northeast corner of the room, giving you access to the Triforce gateway.

Make sure to give a Squiddy a quick shakedown on your way out of the room.

ROOM 4

BOSS FIGHT: THE HINOX BROTHERS

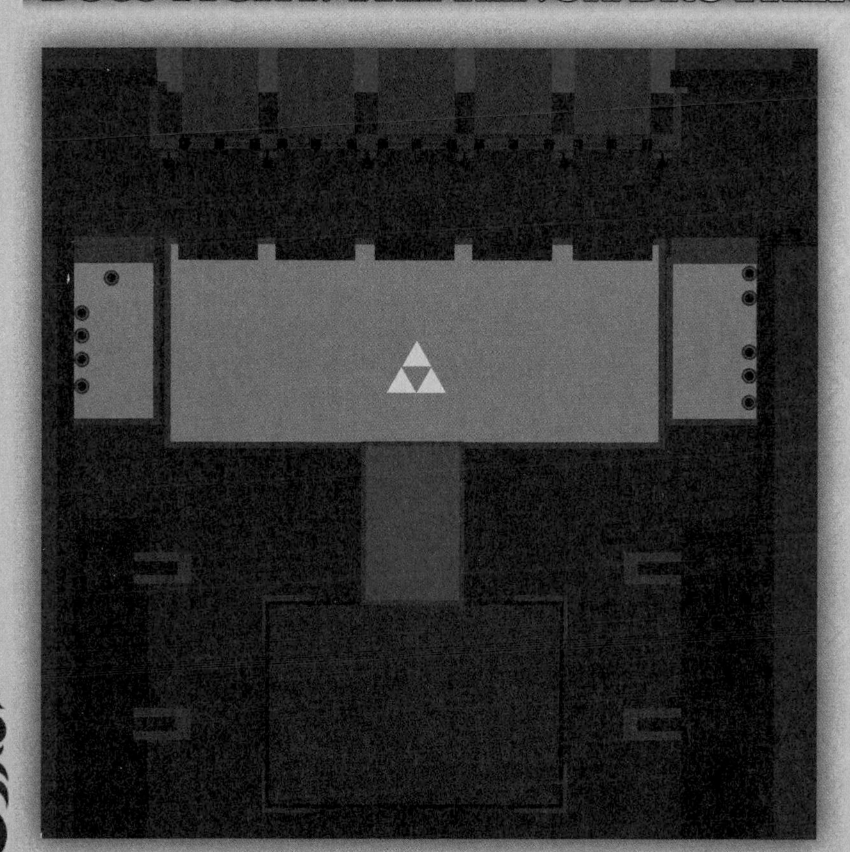

Everybody's favorite Bomb-throwing crew is back! It's the Hinox Brothers, ready and willing to pelt you with Bombs. Luckily they aren't on a minecart this time, so it's significantly easier to dodge their Bombs.

Hinox the Eldest and Hinox the Elder will pop out of the second and fourth windows of the northern building and begin tossing Bombs your way. Simply picking the Bombs up and throwing them back won't work this time—you'll have to get crafty. To stamp a big ol' "Return to Sender" on the Hinox Brothers' Bombs, use the Gust Jar to blast the Bombs back at them.

To speed this fight up, you can have the Bomb Link stand on the steel slabs to the left or right of each Hinox Brother and then throw a Bomb onto the slab in front of them. Have a Gust Jar Link blast the Bomb Link's Bombs back at the Hinox Brothers to make short work of them.

If you're struggling to hit Li'l Hinox with his own Bombs, you can switch back the method you used on the elder two Hinox Brothers. You'll need to be a bit more observant to figure out where Li'l Hinox is going to appear, but the strategy works just as well as before.

Once the Elder and Eldest Hinox brothers have been defeated, Li'l Hinox steps in to get some very explosive revenge. Li'l Hinox is a bit of an overachiever. He throws Bombs at you, just like his brothers, but they are mondo, massive, behemoth Bombs that put even your Big Bomb Outfit Bombs to shame. You'll need to air blast these Bombs several times to get them to move toward Li'l Hinox. Right as they are about to detonate, air blast them off the edge toward Li'l Hinox to damage him.

Multiplayer Method

You can still air blast Bomb Link's Bombs over to the remaining Hinox Brother, but you'll need to have the remaining Link move Li'l Hinox's Bomb away from the other Links. Just make sure not to knock it off the edge outright, or Li'l Hinox will disappear and reappear at another window with another giant Bomb.

You'll have to watch out for Hardhat Beetles during this phase of the fight. They'll start appearing on the far left and right sides of the platform, making it difficult to blow Li'l Hinox's Bombs back at it.

In Case of Emergency

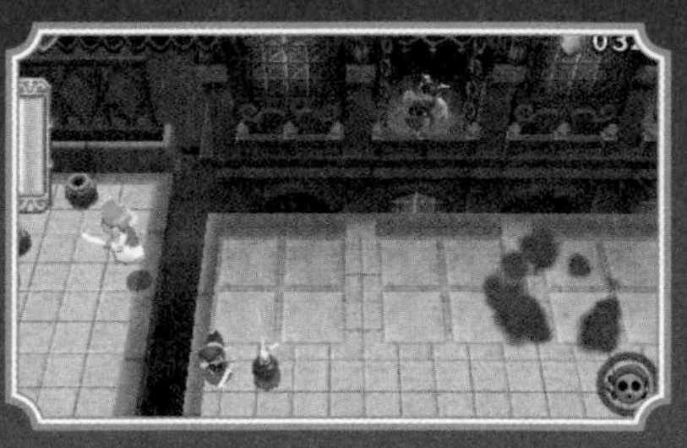

If you're getting low on health, make a three-Link Totem and throw the top Link on one of the platforms to the left and right sides of the room. You'll find jars on each of the platforms that potentially hold Hearts, especially if opened by a Link wearing the Legendary Dress.

After hitting Li'l Hinox with Bombs a handful of times, he'll be defeated and the Triforce gateway letting you out of this room will appear.

Questing for Outfits

You should take the time to grab a Royal Ring from this level if you didn't get one, then grab a Stiff Puff from this level or the Sealed Gateway, and then grab a Silver Thread from the Sealed Gateway to create the Sword Suit at Madame Couture's. This Outfit will let you do double damage with your sword and allows you to fire energy beams from it when you're at full health. It's a very helpful Outfit that you should wear pretty much every chance you get, unless a level would benefit from another Outfit more.

Level 3: Training Ground

Challenges

Clear within the time limit

Halved attack and defense

Don't drop the pot

Sub-Weapons

 Bow

 Gripshot

 Gust Jar

Materials

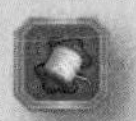 Silver Thread

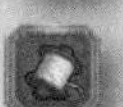 Silver Thread

 Antique Coin

Recommended Outfits

 Kokiri Clothes

 Goron Garb

This is undoubtedly one of the toughest levels in the game. Some of the puzzles here are outright devious! Bringing the Goron Garb will be a huge help for some of the puzzles, but if you can only pick one Outfit, go for the Kokiri Clothes. The Goron Garb helps, but you can still get past the puzzles without it; the Kokiri Clothes will make a lot of the fights and a puzzle or two significantly easier.

ROOM 1

Head north and stand on the three-man pressure switch in the center of the platform. This will raise a Totem Armos up to the platform. Stand on the upper level behind the Totem Armos, then drop down on top of it. The Totem Armos can be pretty tough to control, but once you get the hang of it, it's your own stompy, baddie-busting, all-terrain vehicle.

Steer the Totem Armos across the bridge to the right side of the room, then steer it up to the glowing eye symbol on the ground. You can speed the Totem Armos up by holding the R-Button while riding it.

When the Totem Armos reaches the symbol, it will park and Link will leap off. This is the only way to get off of the Totem Armos once you're on it (aside from being hit off of it by an enemy). You'll find the Bow at the top of the stairs. Grab it with the Link wearing the Kokiri Clothes. Have all three Links walk up to the upper level above the Totem Armos, make a three-Link Totem, and then hop back on it.

Steer the Totem Armos into the lava and drive it to the north side of the room. Head up the stairs, then follow the wall to the west side of the room. You'll find another eye symbol for you to park the Armos.

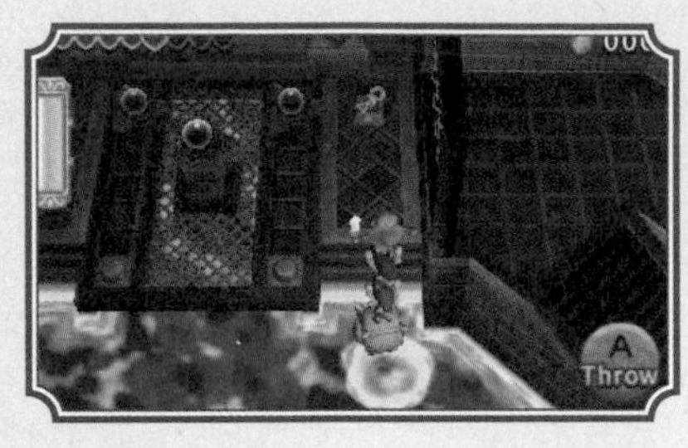

You'll find the Gust Jar and Gripshot, along with three shy orb switches, on the north end of the room. You can hit the two pressure switches to bridge the gap to where you originally got on the Totem Armos.

To reach the Triforce gateway, you'll need to hit all three orb switches in roughly three seconds. Have the Bow Link (with the Kokiri Clothes) stand in the center of the south end of the bridge you just extended, then have the other two Links make a Totem. Have the Totem stand off to the left or right of the elevated orb switch, far enough away to keep the orbs from hiding.

Now have the Totem fire the Gust Jar or Gripshot at the orb switch, then immediately have the Bow Link fire his arrows. The arrows will split and hit the back two orb switches, while the Totem Links take care of the elevated switch. If your timing was tight enough, the wall on the north end of the room will recede and reveal four more pressure switches.

You'll need to drive the Totem Armos onto the eye symbol in the north point of the room to activate that pressure switch. Once that's done, have each Link stand on a pressure switch to make the wall recede and reveal this room's Triforce gateway.

ROOM 2

Ride the elevator on the north end of the room to the room's upper level. Before you walk off the elevator, there are things you should know. Six red Hardhat Beetles will appear along with two blue Sword Soldiers. You can't hit the Hardhat Beetles without stunning them first or you'll get burned, and the blue Soldiers have shields that will deflect any frontal assault. What can you do about all of this? Immediately rush to the Totem Armos in the center of the room and throw one or two Links on top of it. The Armos will do damage to any enemies it bumps into and, best of all, you won't take damage from the fiery, red Hardhat Beetles.

Have the remaining Link use his Sub-Weapon to defeat the Hardhat Beetles and stun the blue Sword Soldiers while the Totem Armos mows enemies down. (Remember to hold the R-Button to speed up while on the Armos.)

Once the enemies have been defeated, the giant doors on the north side of the room will open, revealing the Triforce gateway.

ROOM 3

If one or more of your Links is wearing Goron Garb, this room will be a whole lot easier. You'll see a Beamos on top of a Totem Armos ahead of you. Beamos are another Zelda staple enemy. They'll look around a room in a circle and shoot lasers from their eye whenever they spot a Link. If you wait for their eye to pass, you can sneak past them or even destroy them.

Make a two-Link Totem and wait for the Beamos's eye to pass your area, then move in and slash it or shoot it with arrows until it falls off of the Totem Armos. The Beamos will begin to flash and roll toward you. Get as far away from it as you safely can—the Beamos will explode after flashing for a few seconds.

Now throw two of your Links on top of the Totem Armos and have them steer up the narrow path on your right and have it bounce in front of the tunnel that the giant steel balls are coming out of. If you're in multiplayer, you'll want to have whatever Links aren't on the Totem Armos follow behind it to keep from getting knocked off the path and into the lava by the steel balls. If you're in single-player, switch to the other Links while the Totem Armos Link bounces in front of the tunnel. Move the other Links to the other side of the path, then switch back to the Totem Armos and steer it onto the eye symbol on the right side of the of the area.

This next part can be brutal in multiplayer without the Goron Garb, so we hope at least one of your Links is wearing it. Single-player is a good bit easier than multiplayer and is made even easier with the Goron Garb, but it's not absolutely needed.

Hidden Treasure!

To get the treasure on the south side of the room, drop down to the platform below, then hit the orb switch to ride that platform up to the treasure chest. Easy!

Multiplayer Method

The following strategy works in multiplayer for the most part, but the Totem Armos won't stop moving once a Link is on it. That means you'll need to do everything in one go without time to think about your next step. Take the time to read ahead before trying to take on this challenging puzzle.

Throw one of your Links on top of the Totem Armos and don't steer it at all! It will automatically move to the right, which is exactly what you want. The Totem Armos will move past the flame rods and block them momentarily. You'll need to walk along with the Link riding the Totem Armos as it passes over the flame rods. If you switch from the Link controlling the Armos to either of the other two Links, the Totem Armos will stop in its tracks. To get it moving again, switch back to the Totem Armos's pilot and it will continue hopping forward.

Try, Try Again

If the Totem Armos gets ahead of you and you can't get past a flame rod, you'll have to drop down onto the platforms south of you and use the elevator platform to go back to the start. Then you'll need to steer the Totem Armos back to the eye symbol at the start and try again from the start. If your pilot Link is burned while on the Totem Armos, he'll fly off of it and the Totem Armos will disappear from its location and reappear on the eye symbol on the left side of this area.

As soon as you pass the first flame, rush over and hit the color orb and switch it to yellow. This will raise a bridge to keep the Totem rider from being burned by the second flame rod and will also block the second flame rod, so you can keep walking along with the Totem Armos.

Move the Totem Armos past the second flame rod, then hit the color orb ahead to lower the bridge again. This will keep the pilot from being burned by the third flame rod. The two Links on solid ground can walk under the third rod safely, so don't worry about trying to block it.

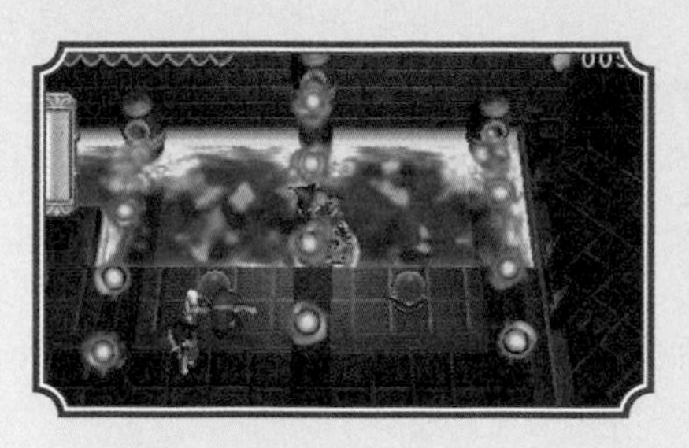

As soon as the Totem Armos passes under the third flame rod, use one of the other Links to hit a color orb to raise the bridge again. Now move the Totem Armos in front of the fourth and final flame rod to block it and get the other two Links to the east side of the room.

Have the Totem Armos come to a stop in front of the elevator platform in the center of the landing, then have your other two Links make a two-Link Totem, hop onto the elevator, and then drop down onto the Totem Armos. Steer the Totem Armos into the eye symbol on the north side of the area and all three Links will hop off onto the upper landing. This is where you will find the Triforce gateway.

ROOM 4

Each Link will start on a platform above a Totem Armos. Move a Link onto an Armos, and then get ready for some Armos jousting! Several Soldiers will appear, each on a Totem Armos of its own. Using your Bow Link to fight the Soldiers from a distance is a particularly good strategy, but sword slashes work too.

After defeating the first wave of Soldiers, a second wave will appear on the north side of the room. Once you've defeated all of the Soldiers, park each Totem Armos on an eye symbol on the north end of the room, then use the Triforce gateway to exit the room.

Level 4: The Lady's Lair

Challenges

Evade the Wallmaster

Fewer Heart Containers

Only Bombs—no swords

Sub-Weapons

 Gripshot

 Boomerang

 Gust Jar

Materials

 Royal Ring

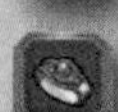 Royal Ring

 Fancy Fabric

Recommended Outfits

 Sword Suit

 Big Bomb Outfit

 Boomeranger

None of the Outfits recommended for this level are going to help tremendously, but if you have to pick one, you should pick the Sword Suit. There are plenty of enemies in the level and the Sword Suit will make them easier to deal with.

You can also bring the Big Bomb Outfit to make the boss easier, or you can grab the Boomeranger Outfit for the Link that uses the Boomerang. The Sword Suit would be the best of these choices, but these two Outfits are here if you don't have access to it yet.

ROOM 1

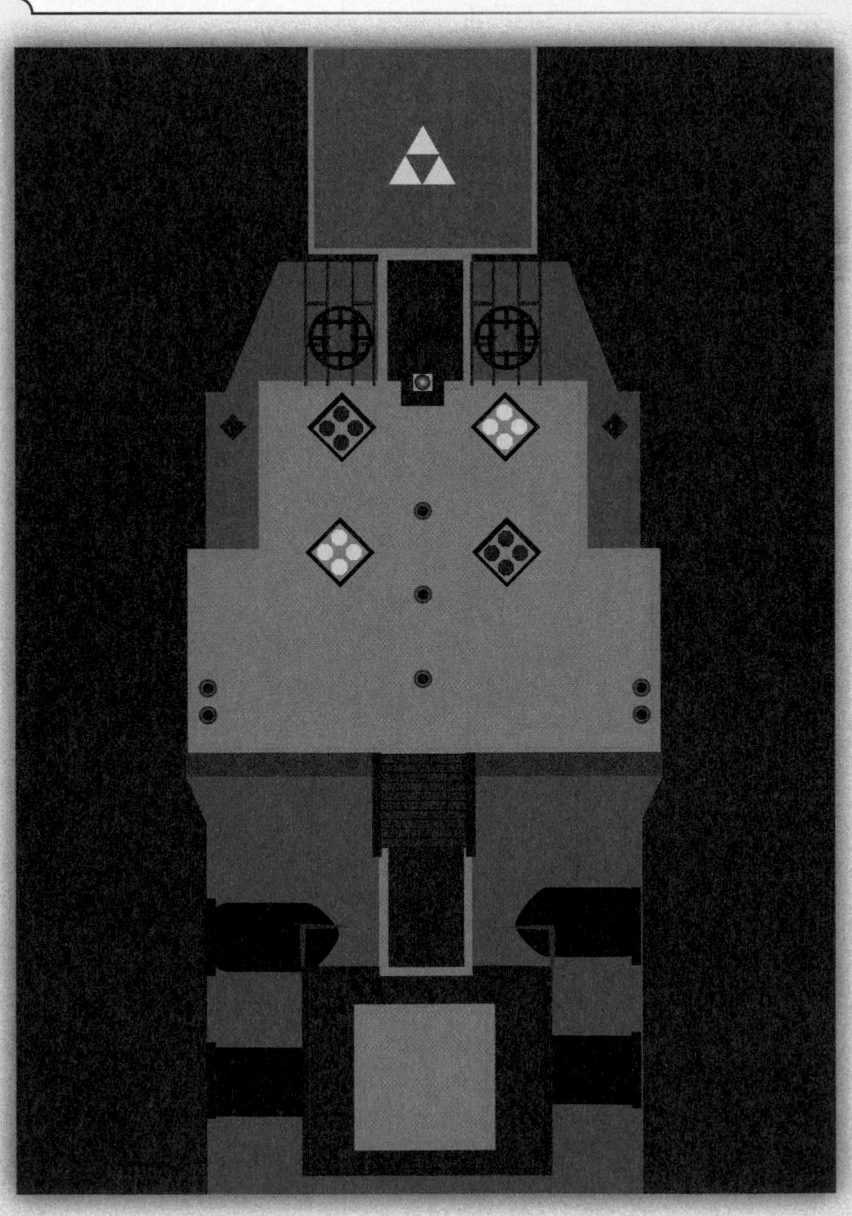

Head up the stairs to the north, then continue on to the north end of the area while avoiding the giant steel balls that are rolling south from tunnels on the north side of the room. Have a Link stand in front of the color orb across the northern gap, then make a Totem with the other two Links.

A bridge will lower in front of the lone Link, allowing you to cross to the other side.

Now have the Totem Links stand on one of the lowered colored platforms, and then let your lone Link hit the color orb. The colored platform will lift the Totem Links up within range of an orb switch. Hit the switch, then immediately head over to the colored platform on the opposite side of the room. Have your lone Link hit the color orb again to raise the other platform the Totem Links are on, then have the Totem Links hit the second switch. The time limit is pretty generous here, so you should plenty of time to hit both switches.

ROOM 2

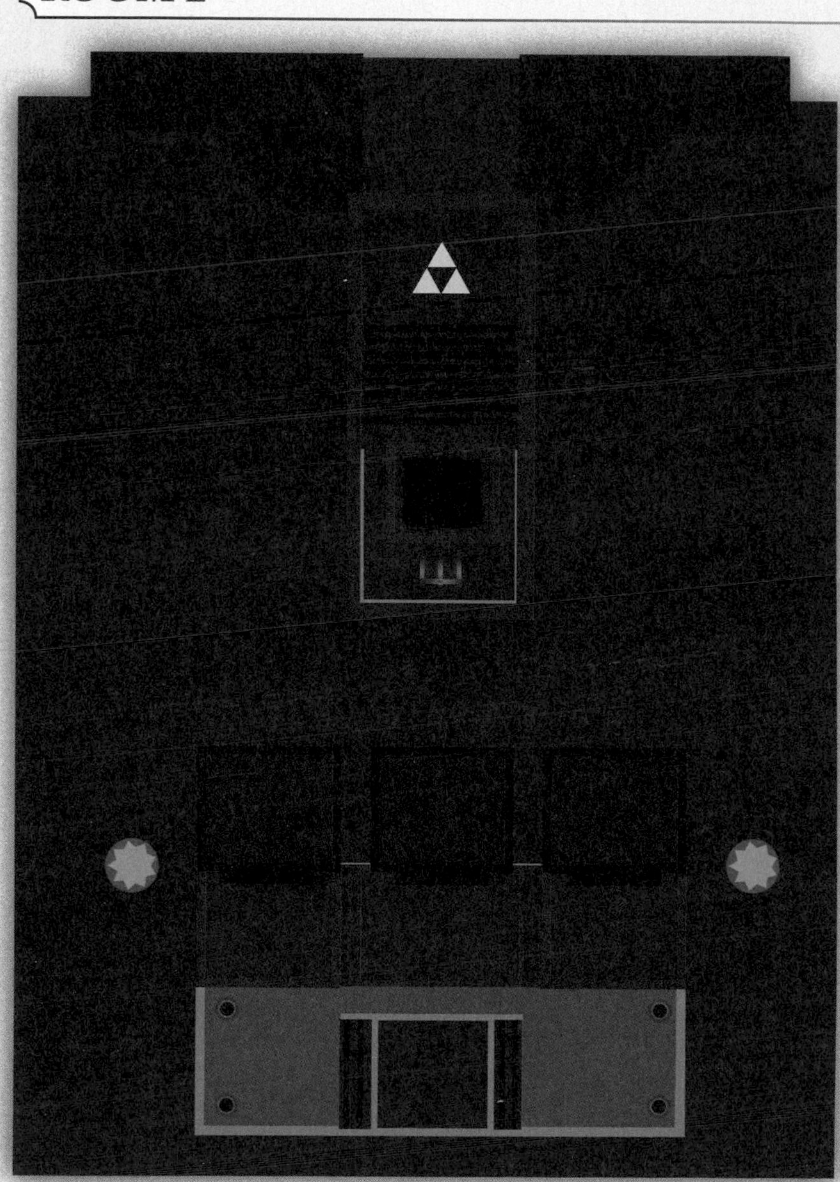

You'll have to fight Soldiers in a sort of Ferris wheel on the north end of the room. They'll throw spears and Bombs at you and you should return the favor by throwing Bombs of your own inside their compartments. To make this easier, make sure to throw the Bombs at the bottom of the steel slabs (the ones that line the north side of the landing you're currently on), instead of directly on top of them. The closer you are to the edge of the landing, the harder it is to land the Bombs inside the Soldiers' compartments.

If you defeat the Bomb thrower before the other Soldiers, you can grab Bombs from the Bomb Flowers on the left and right sides of the room.

After you defeat all of the enemies, a three-man pressure switch will appear. Have all three Links stand on the pressure switch to activate it. The platform the pressure switch is on will lift you to the upper levels of the room where the Triforce gateway is.

ROOM 3

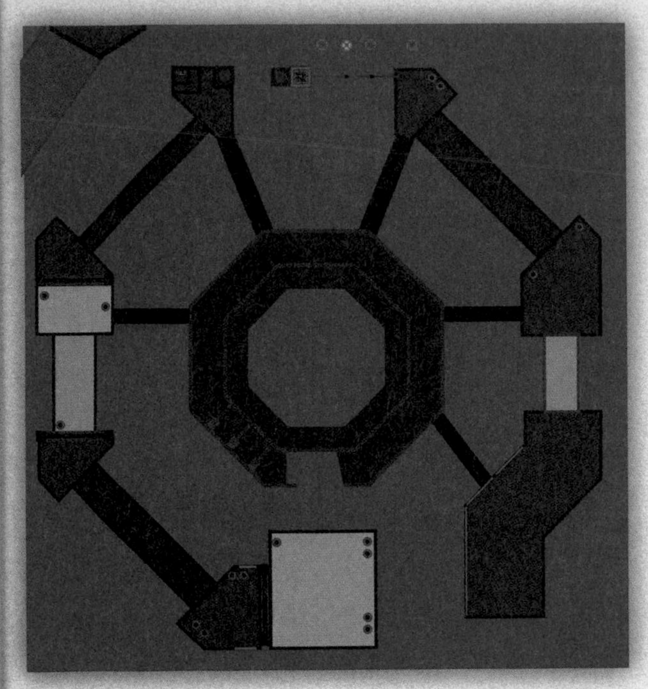

This room is very big, but it is also quite simple. You'll have plenty of enemies to fight, but nothing you haven't had to deal with before.

Head up the path until you reach a tightrope. Walk onto the tightrope with a single Link to goad the Crows into swooping at you so you can take them out. If you were in a Totem, the Crows would swoop too low for you to hit and your Links would plummet into the darkness below. Now make a three-Link Totem with the Gripshot or Boomerang Link on top and begin to slowly walk along the tightrope.

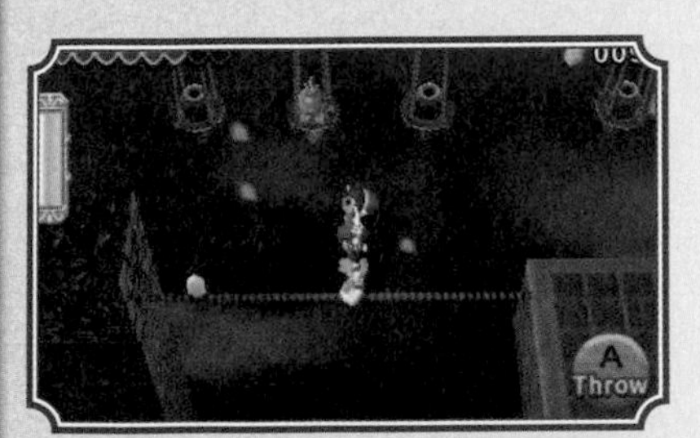

When you are parallel with the Bomb Flower in the hanging sconce, turn and use the Boomerang or Gripshot to pull it out of the sconce, then throw it on the cracked block ahead.

Slowly walk across the tightrope to the pressure switch that was under the block and press it. The pressure switch will activate a moving platform that you can use to get to the left side of the room. Once you're over there, you can throw your Links onto the tiered tower to grab the treasure chest.

Head up the stairs and onto the bridge. When all three Links are standing on the bridge, the gates on both ends will close and three blue Hardhat Beetles and a blue Sword Soldier will appear. Defeat them to lower the gates, then continue south.

Head up the next flight of stairs and enter the checkered room. As soon as all three Links are in this room, the gate behind you will close and two Hinox and a Gold Ball & Chain Soldier will appear. The Hinox you know, but the Gold Ball & Chain Soldier comes with a twist: its ball and chain are engulfed in flames, making it a particularly dangerous foe.

Use your Boomerang Link to continuously stun the Soldier while you slowly make your way toward it. When you are near it, hit it toward a wall and keep up the pressure. Every time you hit the Soldier, it will restart its swinging attack. If you keep hitting it rapidly, it'll continuously restart its attack, keeping you from getting hit by it.

Once all the enemies in the room have been defeated, the Triforce gateway will appear in the center of the area.

ROOM 4

BOSS FIGHT: THE LADY'S PETS

You'll meet the wicked witch herself as soon as you enter this room: The Lady! She's the one who cursed poor Styla with that awful set of black tights! If you defeat The Lady, you'll save Styla and Hytopia!

The Lady isn't about to let you defeat her easily! She's keen to your three-player game and she's eager to play one of her one. Enter, The Lady's Pets!

The Lady's Pets aren't anything you haven't seen before. Literally! You'll be fighting fancier, faster versions of Margoma, Moldorm, and Arrghus. The strategies for those bosses still apply here, but if you need a refresher, we've got you covered.

The first of The Lady's Pets is a Margoma wearing a tablecloth. It looks fancier, sure, but that doesn't mean it's got any real new tricks. It can now spin around in place and create wind that blows your Links back instead of charging toward you, and it will also be a lot more mobile, but everything else is pretty much the fight you remember.

Use the Bomb Flowers on the left and right sides of the room and drop Bombs in the hatch at the center of Margoma's head. To do this, grab a Bomb with the Gripshot or Boomerang, then toss it in. Margoma will retract the spikes on its head, a red orb will pop out of its head, and it will be temporarily stunned. Throw a Link on top of the glorified table and smack its eyeball.

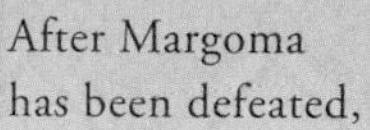

Get on Margoma's head two or three times and beat the ever-loving fashion out of it to defeat it.

After Margoma has been defeated, Moldorm tries its hand at the Links. There are some key differences. There is fire in front of Moldorm's face. Its tail starts higher up than your first fight. But it's easier to get behind it, even while it's chasing you.

Make a two-Link Totem and chase after the orb at the end of its tail. After a few hits, Moldorm will go completely nuts and start bouncing around the room at a rapid pace. Its tail will also rise, so you'll have to turn your two-Link Totem into a three-Link Totem to hit it. A few more hits and Moldorm will be squashed.

You'll now have one last boss to fight: Arrghus. The nine-eyed octopode has gone under the most significant changes of all three bosses—namely, it no longer has nine eyes (or any eyes at all for that matter). Not real ones anyway!

Arrghus's "eyes" come in two flavors: Fire and Ice. You can use the Gripshot on Arrghus's main red-jeweled eye at any point, but you run the risk of grabbing the fire and ice eyes. Your best bet is to try and take out the eyes before going for its main eye. You can use the Bombs on the left or right sides of the room, wait until they're about to blow, and then throw them up at Arrghus to destroy its eyes. You can also blow the ice eyes off of the platform if you the opportunity presents itself.

The fire eyes can be destroyed after you put them out with the Gust Jar. Arrghus is pretty keen on throwing its eyes at you, so sooner or later the fire eyes will be in front of you, which is the perfect time to put them out and start slashing them.

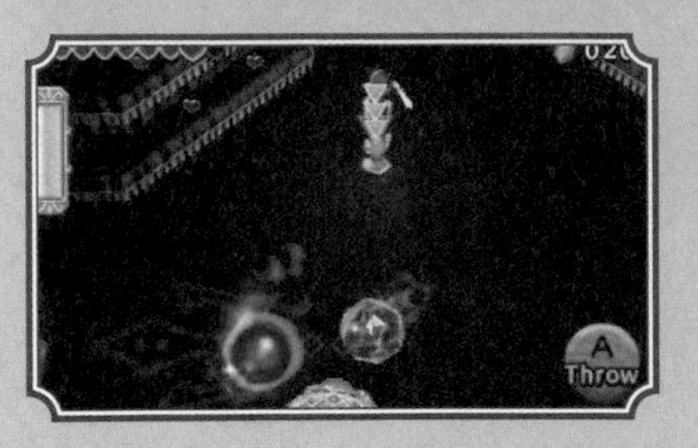

Once all of Arrghus's eyes have been cleared out, make a three-Link Totem and hit Arrghus's red-jeweled eye with a Bomb or a Sub-Weapon to stun it, then throw your top Link down and have him slash away at the squirrely squid. If you get too close to Arrghus, it'll close its eye, so try and maintain your distance while still being in reach of his eye. You'll have to watch out for its dark beam attack, but from this point on the worst is over. You can also use Bombs to stun Arrghus in place for a few seconds. It will keep its eye open during this time, so it's the perfect time to hit it.

After knocking it down two or three times and giving it a fantastic sword slapping, Arrghus will perish once more and the fight will be over.

Naturally, The Lady escaped, but you'll find The Lady's Collar in the treasure chest in room 5. You're only one Material away from creating The Lady's Ensemble!

You'll unlock worlds 6 and 7 and a slew of new Outfits after completing this world. Make sure to head to Madame Couture's to check them out!

Questing for Outfits

If you're willing to commit the time, you can make the Rupee Regalia with a Royal Ring from levels 2 and 4, an Antique Coin from level 3, and Fancy Fabric from level 4. The Rupee Regalia increases the likelihood of enemies and destructible objects dropping Rupees. Not only that, it will double the amount of Rupees every time a Rupee would normally drop. Top that off with an increased likelihood of finding purple Rupees and you pretty much become a walking bank. This outfit is perfect to use whenever you're running low on cash, but you really want to get a new Outfit or Material from the Street Merchant.

WORLD 6: THE DUNES

Level 1: Infinity Dunes

Challenges

Adventure in the dark

Guard the orb

Fewer Heart Containers

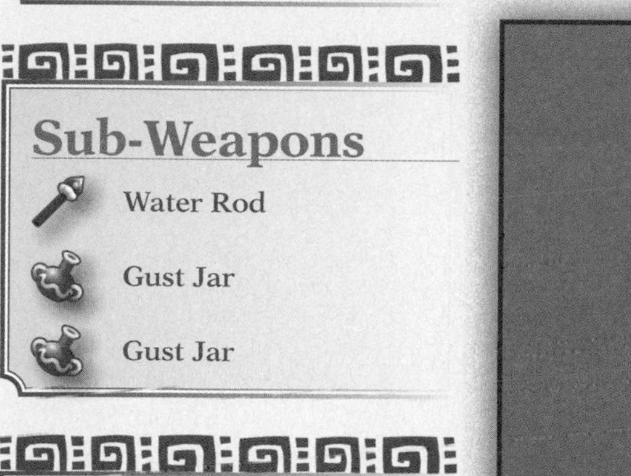

Sub-Weapons

Water Rod

Gust Jar

Gust Jar

Materials

Palm Cone

Palm Cone

Ancient Fin

Recommended Outfits

Torrent Robe

Legendary Dress

Sword Suit

Having one Link wear the Torrent Robe will be pretty helpful in this level. There's a good bit of puzzle solving and platforming that require the use of the Water Rod, and having the Water Rod Link wear the Torrent Robe will make it that much easier. It's not required by any means, so if you want to wear a general Outfit like the Sword Suit, Legendary Dress, or the Rupee Regalia, you can feel safe knowing it's not going to come back to bite you in the hindquarters.

ROOM 1

Drop into the pit to the north and grab the Sub-Weapons. Use the Water Rod to get your Links back up to the surface, then start heading north. It's worth exploring the area for breakables and Rupees, but whatever you do, don't stop moving! The sand is actually quicksand, and standing still in it for more than a couple of seconds will see your Link swallowed whole by the sand. It is safe to stand on any stone platforms you see around the area, but the sand is always bad news.

Buried Treasure

The mounds of sand you'll find all over this level can be destroyed to uncover Rupees and Hearts. Just use the Water Rod or Gust Jar on a mound to remove it.

Once you reach the sand river in the center of the room, have your Water Rod Link create a water bridge across to reach the other side of it. To get across faster, you can make a two-Link Totem with your Gust Jar Links, create the bridge, and then pick up the Totem and run across.

Continue north and avoid the skeletal Sandfish, which are just Skullfish except they swim in sand instead of water. After walking north for a while, you'll reach a gap that you can't cross. There is a pressure switch on the leftmost brick platform, but it doesn't do anything when you press it. Use your Gust Jar or Water Rod to destroy the sand mound on the brick platform to your right, then use the Water Rod or throw your Link onto the elevated platform on the far right. Destroy the sand mound up there as well and you'll now have three pressure switches around you. Step on all three to create a bridge across the northern gap, then continue north.

ROOM 2

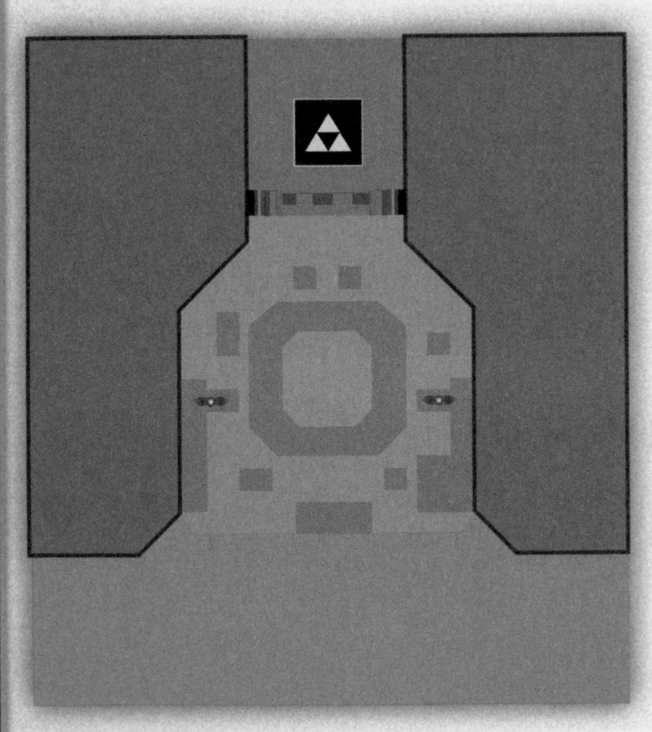

You'll have to defeat all the enemies in this room to be able to leave it. You'll face off with two Life Likes, two Leevers (plant-like creatures that dig under the ground, then rise to the surface somewhere else in the room), and a Vulture, which is not at all unlike the Crows you've encountered in past levels.

The Leevers only need a couple of sword slashes to be defeated, so they aren't much of a threat. If a Life Like grabs you, immediately switch to one of your Doppels, or have one of your teammates hit it to get it off of you. You can use the Water Rod to grow the saplings on the east and west sides of the room. They'll turn into Bomb Flowers, which you can use to throw into the mouths of the Life Likes. You can also use the Water Rod under the Vulture to stun it and bring it to a place you can reach it reliably.

Once all of the enemies have been defeated, a gate on the north end of the room will open and reveal the Triforce gateway.

ROOM 3

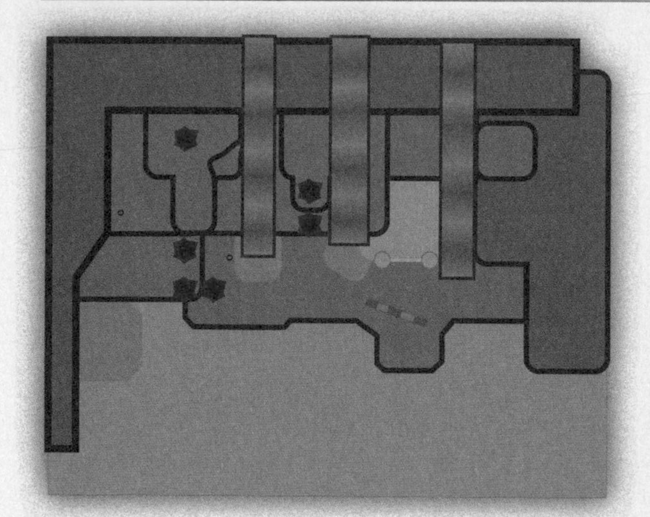

This room is very big and can seem pretty daunting, but if you know what you're doing, it's actually a breeze. Head west until you see a sapling. As you make your way west, a giant door will slide shut, blocking the Triforce gateway. Your goal is to reopen that door.

Use your Water Rod on the sapling to make it grow into a moving platform. Hop on the platform and ride it up the Cliffside. You'll find another sapling, some Rupees, and our good friend Squiddy at the top of the platform's path. Remind Squiddy of the good ol' days, grab the Rupees, and then use your Water Rod on the sapling to create another moving platform.

This is where things get a little tricky. There are a handful of sand waterfalls along this wall, and falling into any of them will take you back to the bottom of the room almost every time. Be very careful if you don't want to have to climb the cliffs over and over.

Stand a Gust Jar Link and the Water Rod Link right by the waterfall without touching it, then use the remaining Gust Jar Link to blast both Links across to the platform on the other side.

You might have noticed the shy orb switch below your lone Link. Well, we're about to take care of that. Have the Water Rod Link water the saplings to create Bomb Flowers. Next, have the Gust Jar Link on the other side of the waterfall air blast the Bomb over to your lone Link, then use the lone Link to pick up the Bomb and throw it onto the orb switch's platform. The switch will activate and open one layer of the locked door at the southeast side of the room.

Now have the Water Rod Link drop south off the platform and use the Water Rod on the sapling below. This will allow the lone Link to rejoin his friends.

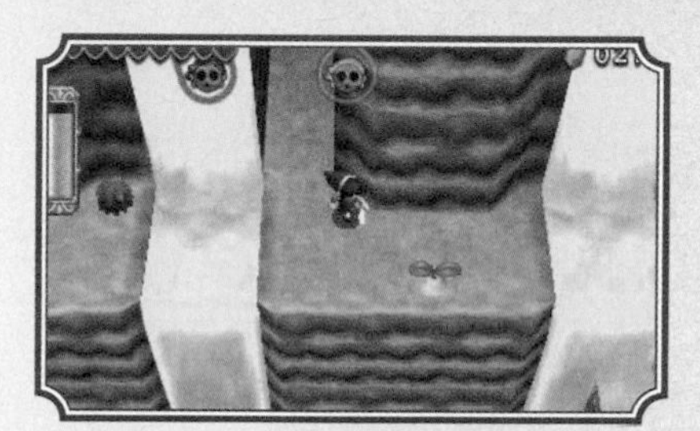

Have the lone Link walk off the right side of the landing onto the landing slightly below it, then walk to the landing's south end and fall off of its right side. This will put you on the same level as the sapling your Water Rod Link just watered.

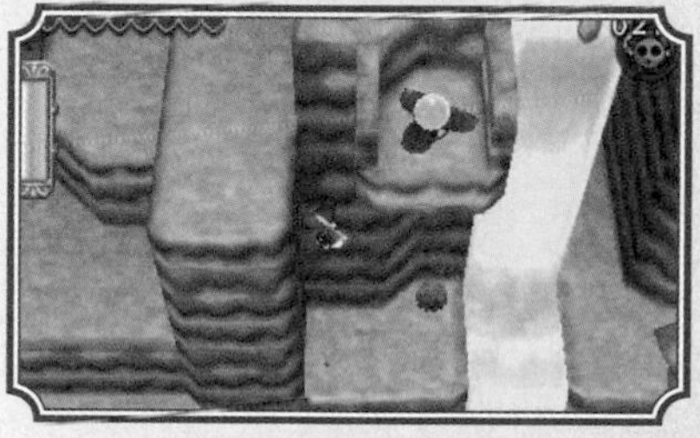

Now have the Water Rod Link create a bridge over the sand waterfall to allow the lone Link to cross. Have both Links ride the leaf platform back up to where the other Gust Jar Link is.

Once all three Links are back together, line up a Gust Jar Link and the Water Rod Link in front of the sand waterfall on the right, then use the remaining Gust Jar Link to blast them over.

You're supposed to blast a Bomb over to the two Links, have them create a water pillar, hop on it, and then throw a Bomb onto the second orb switch, but there's an easier way to deal with this switch. Have your Water Rod Link create a platform in front of the orb switch, just before the sand waterfall. Pick up the Gust Jar Link, aim him towards the orb switch, and then have him fire an air blast to hit the switch. This will keep you from having to deal with the tight timing of blasting a Bomb over, creating a platform, picking up the Bomb before it blows, and then throwing it near the switch.

With the second switch hit, the southeast door will open, revealing the Triforce gateway. Drop off the cliff and head to the next room.

Hidden Treasure!

You can ride the far right sand waterfall down to reach a platform with a treasure chest on it. Bonus: It is right next to the door you're heading to! Not too shabby!

ROOM 4

You'll face a new type of enemy in this room: a Hokkubokku. To defeat it, you need to hit each part of its body until its head is on the ground. The catch is that every time you hit one of its body parts, it'll go soaring around the room, damaging you if it hits you. The Hokkubokku will also dig into the ground and try to resurface under you to deal damage.

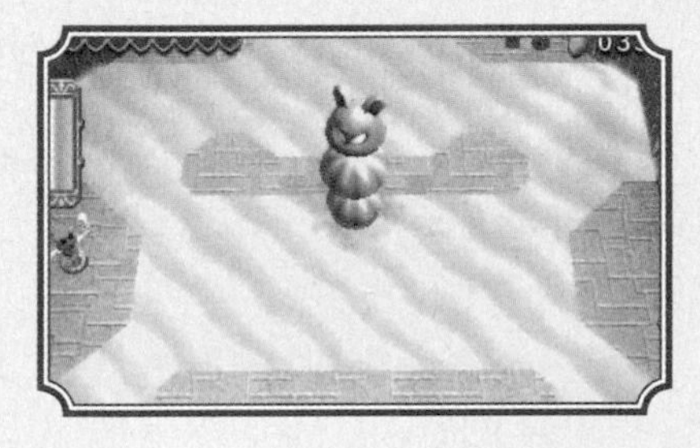

The easiest way to beat this enemy is to use your Water Rod to create a platform underneath it. It will stun the Hokkubokku in place for a moment, giving you plenty of time to smack its body parts out from underneath it. But sword slashes work just as well.

Once you defeat the first one, three more Hokkubokkus will enter the room. Try to take one down at a time to avoid having Hokkubokku body parts bouncing all over the room.

Once you've defeated these three, the northern gate will open to reveal the Triforce gateway.

Level 2: Stone Corridors

Challenges

Clear within the time limit

Evade the Wallmaster

Don't fall at all

Sub-Weapons

 Gripshot

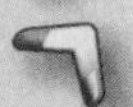 Boomerang

 Gust Jar

Materials

 Palm Cone

 Palm Conc

 Vintage Linen

Recommended Outfits

 Boomeranger

 Sword Suit

This is one of the most challenging levels in the game. There are several rocking platforms that you'll need to try and balance in order to progress. If you can't keep them balanced, they'll drop you in the abyss below the clouds.

You can bring the Boomeranger Outfit, since the Boomerang gets a lot of play in this level. It's more of a convenience item during this level, but if you're not an excellent shot with the Boomerang, this will more than make up for it.

ROOM 1

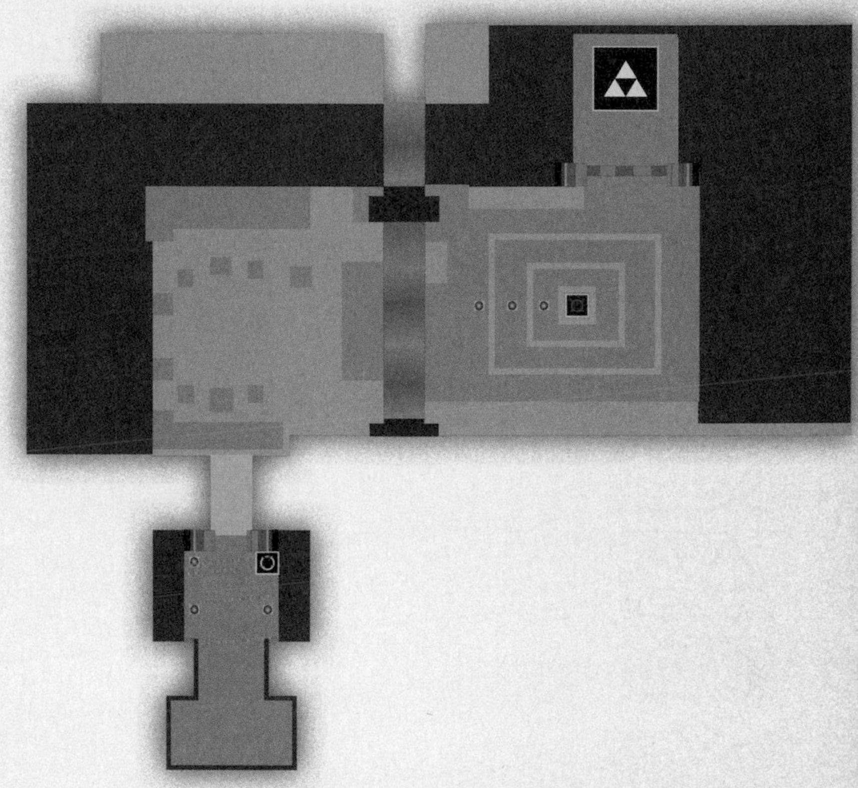

Grab the Sub-Weapons in front of you, then head north. You'll find three switches, a very tall mound of sand, and a strange pedestal in the top-right corner of the room. Use the Gust Jar to blow the sand mound away and reveal a cat-like statue. You'll need to pick up the statue, place it on the pedestal, and then stand on all three switches.

Once you've done all of that, a bridge will rise and fill the gap between the area you're in and area to the north. Cross the bridge and head directly to the north end of the room, taking care not to stand still in the quicksand or get attacked by the Sandfish. In the northwestern corner of the room, you'll find another giant sand mound. Use the Gust Jar to blow the sand away and reveal another statue.

Grab the statue and have all of your Links head right along the northern wall until you reach a river of sand. You'll need to have all three Links cross and also get the statue to the other side with you.

Use the Gust Jar Link to blow the statue and the other two Links across the sand river, then use the Boomerang Link to grab the Gust Jar Link. Make a three-Link Totem, and then head slightly south to the pyramid-like structure near you.

Step on the switch on the left side of the pyramid, turn to the right, and throw each of your Links up, one by one, until all three are standing on the switches. Now throw the statue into the pedestal at the tip of the pyramid.

With the switches pressed and the statue in its pedestal, a door north of you will open, revealing the Triforce gateway for this room.

ROOM 2

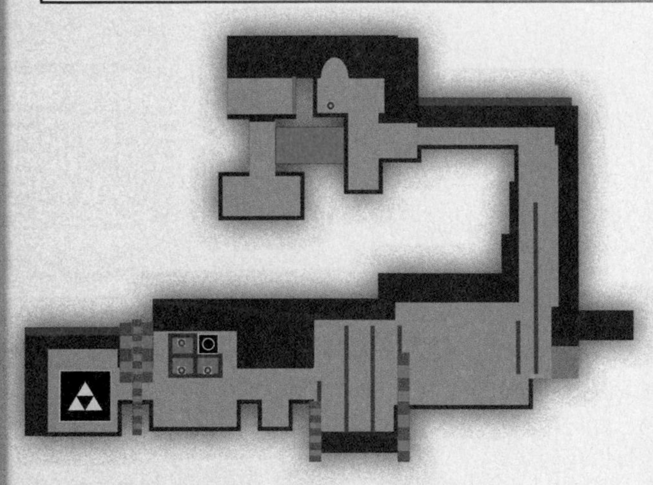

Head north, then make a three-Link Totem with the Gripshot Link on top. Use the Gripshot on the revolving frame of the fence to pull the Gripshot Link through to the other side.

Use the Gripshot to grab the cat-like statue on the other side of the gap to your right, then step on the pressure switch. The switch will raise a set of stairs below you, allowing your other Links to rejoin your Gripshot Link.

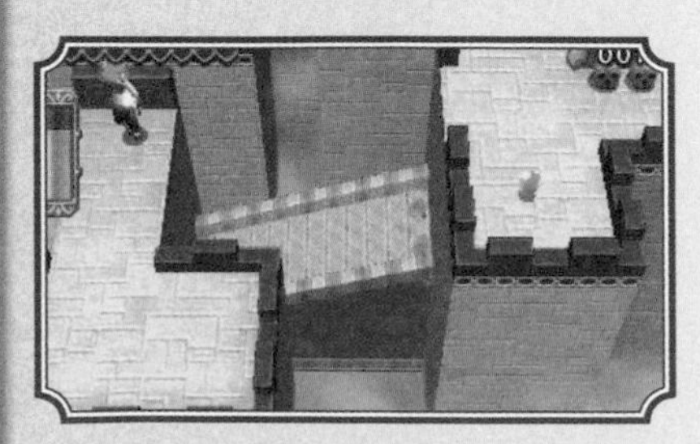

Unfortunately, this will also activate a nearby arrow trap. Pick up the cat statue and throw it against the wall in front of the arrows.

Now use the Gust Jar Link to blast the statue forward until you reach the source of the arrows. Get all of your Links together below the arrow trap, then grab the statue and head south.

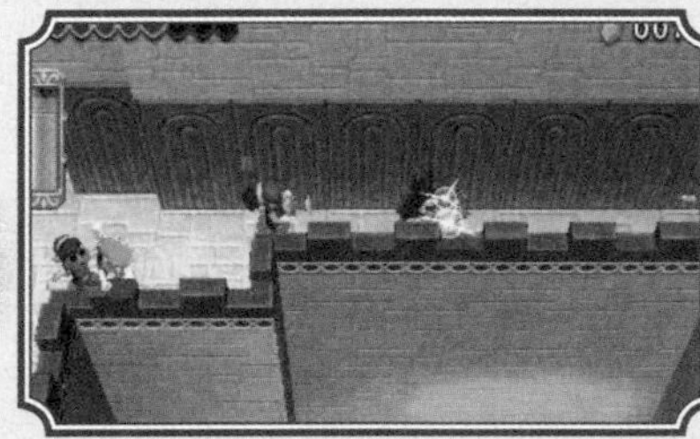

You'll need to be careful here. A spiked log is rolling back and forth in this corridor and the only way to pass it is to wait until it reaches the south end of its track, then you can slide into the room on your left.

You can use the Gust Jar on the giant sand mounds to uncover some Rupees. Once you're ready, stand in the doorway in front of the next spiked log and wait. This thing is moving way too fast for you to pass safely, so you'll have to be clever. Wait for the log to roll south, then throw the cat statue south in front of it. The log will bounce off of the statue, allowing you to pass safely.

You'll want to try and position the statue in line with the southwest exit of the room. After you make your way out of the room through that exit, you can use the Boomerang to grab the statue and continue on.

Make a three-Link Totem with the Link carrying the cat statue on top, then throw each Link up to the tiered platforms and put the cat statue on the pedestal at the top of the platforms. A gate will open on the west side of the room, giving you access to the Triforce gateway.

ROOM 3

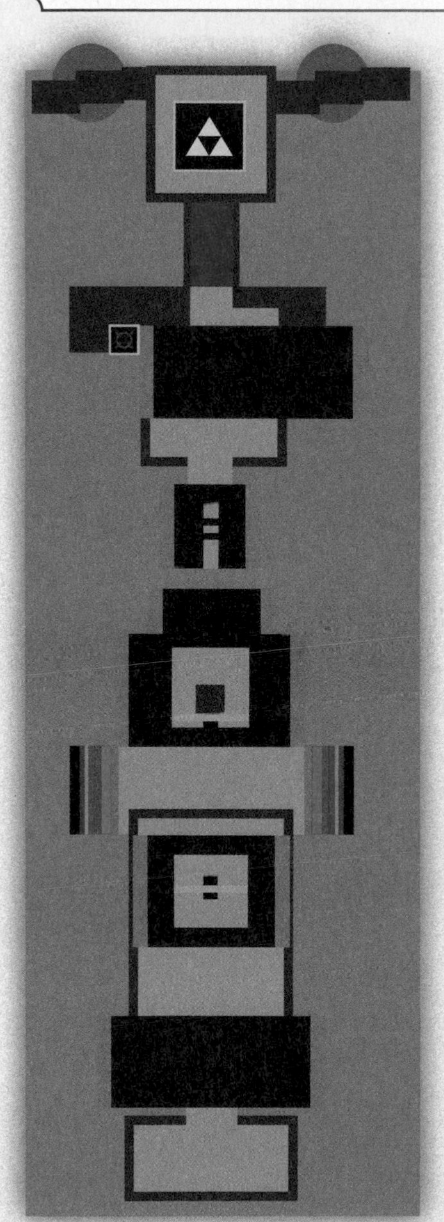

You'll have to be very careful in this part of the level. Most of the platforms will rock back and forth depending on how weight is distributed on them. Have too many Links on one side and the platform will turn in that direction, dumping everyone off the edge.

Balancing Act

There are some general rules for dealing with balancing platforms that you're going to want to keep in mind whenever you're faced with one of these terrible obstacles.

1. If you have a Link on the left side of the platform and you move a Link onto the right side, so long as those two Links are on their sides of the platform it will stay balanced, no matter where they are on their sides of the platform.

2. Never add Links or objects to the platform without being prepared to counter-balance it. For every Link on one side of the platform, there needs to be a Link on the opposite side. The cat statues also count as a Link-worth of weight, meaning having one on a platform is like having an extra Link. You'll need to counter-balance immediately or risk being dropped into the sandy abyss below.

3. The middle section of every balancing platform is a safe zone, meaning the platform won't need to be counter-balanced if a Link or a statue is in the center of the platform. Keep this in mind while solving these puzzles—it'll definitely make things a lot easier for you from here on.

You can safely run up the center of this platform if you're just looking to get across to the other side. But if you're looking to grab Rupees, you can rock the platforms back and forth by going back and forth on both sides of the platform. Use your Boomerang Link to nab up the Rupees when the platform is on the same level as it.

After you pass the first rocking platform, you'll find another cat statue. You can use the cat statue as a counterweight on the platforms. Pick up the statue with a Link, then make a two-Link Totem with the remaining Links. Now have one pair walk onto one side of the platform and immediately have the other pair step on the opposite side. You should be perfectly balanced at this point. Just move each pair up to the end of their side of the platform, very quickly walk one pair onto the landing ahead, and then switch to the other pair and move them onto the landing as well. If you are quick enough, everyone should come out unscathed.

Your best bet for most of these platforms is to try and stay in the middle section of the platform as much as possible. Staying in the middle will keep the platform from tipping. You can even have a three-Link Totem with the cat statue on top and the platform won't drop you.

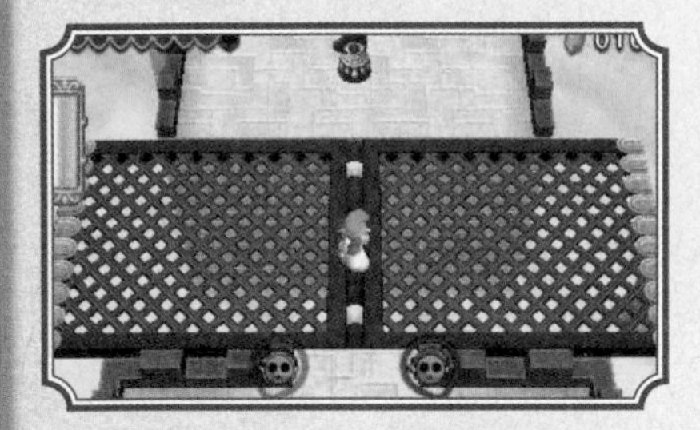

For this next platform, grab the cat statue with the Gust Jar Link, then have another Link pick up the Gust Jar Link. Throw the statue-holding Gust Jar Link onto the red landing in the opening at the center of the balancing platform.

Now place one of the two remaining Links on one side of the platform while you rush the last Link to the opposite side of the platform. You should be completely balanced. Have both Links make their way up to the north side of the platform. Move both Links onto the balancing platform's center line. The platform should have no trouble balancing if both Links are standing in the center. Have the Link on the red landing throw the cat statue up to the other two Links.

Have the Boomerang Link grab the Link on the red landing. You should have two Totems now: One with a Link holding a cat statue and one with a Link holding another Link. Move both Totems away from the center line so that they are lined up with the left and right sides of the platform ahead. Now quickly throw the cat statue on one side and the top Link of the other Totem on the other side of the platform ahead. Both platforms should be balanced if you were quick enough.

Move the Links on the lower platform back to its center line and make a two-Link Totem with the Boomerang Link on top. Now move the Link on the upper platform to that platform's north end, but don't step off of it yet! Face the two-Link Totem to the side of the platform the other Link just moved up, then, very quickly, throw the Boomerang Link onto the upper platform and immediately have the northern Link step onto the landing ahead.

Now move the Boomerang Link to the north end of the platform, turn diagonally toward the cat statue, Boomerang it, and then quickly walk to the landing ahead. Safely place the cat statue down on the landing, then have the Boomerang Link head back to the platform's center line.

Make sure the Link on the lower platform is as close to the edge as possible. Now have the Boomerang Link grab the lower Link and bring him to the northern landing.

Take a deep breath: This is your last platform for this room. You'll need to deposit the cat statue into its pedestal on the top-left corner of the platform. Make two Totems again, one holding the cat statue and one holding another Link. Walk both Links up the center line of the platform, then, very quickly, have the Totem with the cat statue move to the left side of the platform while the Link-holding Totem moves to the right side. You should be balanced right now.

Now quickly run the cat statue toward its pedestal and throw it in. A door will open, allowing you access to the Triforce gateway, but you're not done yet! Race that lone Link to the northern landing, then have the Totem Links join him. If you were fast enough, everyone should be on the north landing, safe and sound. If not, well, you'll take a Heart or two of damage, but the worst is over.

Head to the Triforce gateway to move on to the next room.

ROOM 4

BOSS FIGHT: VULTURE VIZIER

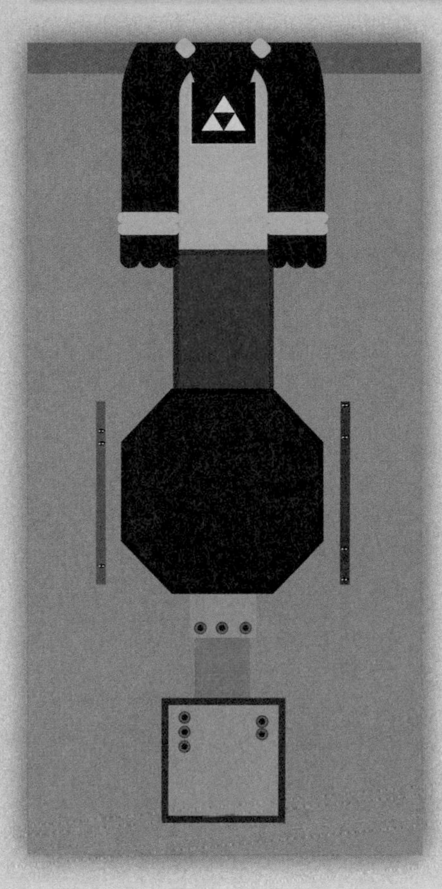

Unfortunately, your platforming antics aren't over yet. In fact, you'll have to take everything you've learned and apply it to this room, because you're about to fight a boss on one of these platforms.

There isn't a lot to this fight, but that's probably because the agonizing act of balancing on this platform is more than enough to make the fight a challenge.

Vulture Vizier will perch on one of the perches on the left or right side of the room. The left side is lower and the right side is higher, so you'll need to rock the platform lower or higher based on where the boss currently is.

Vulture Vizier will sometimes take a massive breath and then begin spitting bursts of air out onto the platform. Needless to say, if you get hit by one you'll be blasted backwards, potentially unbalancing the platform. Vulture Vizier will also, on occasion, smack the edge of the platform with its beak, which will rock the platform violently back and forth.

This fight is best done with only two Links; the third Link unbalances the platform, making it so everyone can fall pretty easily. If you're playing multiplayer, just have the second Link do everything we're about to describe by himself.

The Boomerang Link should be in charge for pretty much the entire fight. Pick up one of the other Links, then walk up the center of the platform. Now throw the Link to the side opposite of where Vulture Vizier is. So if Vulture Vizier is left, throw the Link right and vice versa.

Have the Boomerang Link walk back and forth on his side of the platform to get it to rock and then, when the platform is low or high enough, throw the Boomerang at Vulture Vizier. If you land the hit, Vulture Vizier will lower its head, leaving it open for you to hit. Keep rocking the platform back and forth to be able to reach it.

When Vulture Vizier leaves its perch and starts flying over the platform, immediately race over, Boomerang the Doppel Link, and then wait on the solid platform on the south side of the room. Sometimes Vulture Vizier will drop cat statues, which will unbalance the platform and drop one or both Links into the clouds below.

Repeat this process several times until Vulture Vizier starts violently flashing red. Vulture Vizier will fly over the platform and fall directly onto its center. Hit it with your sword about five times and the fight will be over.

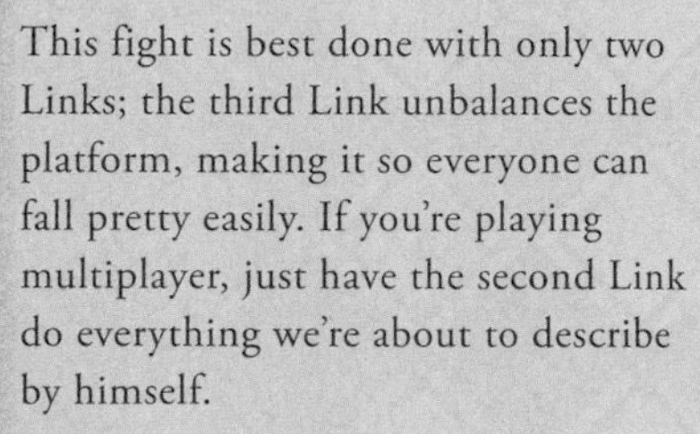

Level 3: Gibdo Mausoleum

Challenges

Clear within the time limit

Avoid falling and quicksand

Only Bombs—no swords

Sub-Weapons

 Gripshot

 Gust Jar

 Fire Gloves

Materials

 Ancient Fin

 Ancient Fin

 Gibdo Bandage

Recommended Outfits

 Sword Suit

To make up for how rough the last level was, *Tri Force Heroes* gave you a much easier level as a way of apologizing. Awww, isn't that nice? This stage will pose little difficulty to you, but if you want to wear an Outfit that will truly help, wear the Sword Suit. There are plenty of enemies to fight in this stage, so wearing the Sword Suit will make those fights significantly easier.

ROOM 1

As soon as you grab all three Sub-Weapons, a key will drop from the ceiling. Karat Crabs covered in Sand Dunes will quickly snatch up the key. Use the Gust Jar and the Bomb Flowers to remove the Sand Dunes from on top of the Karat Crabs, then defeat them. One of the Karat Crabs will have the key on top of its head. Defeat that one, grab the key, and head to the lock on the north end of the room to move on to the next one. Just make sure to watch out for the spikey balls called Morths. They'll slow any Link that they cling to. You'll need to have a friend hit them off, or switch to another Doppel.

ROOM 2

You only need to defeat all the enemies in this room to move on to the next one. You'll have to fight a Fire Keeleon, more Morths, Skullropes (snakes with skulls on their heads), and Stalfos (skeleton monsters).

Stalfos can be a particular pain, because they jump backwards every time you swing at them. Sometimes they'll add insult to injury and throw a bone at you after they jump. Using your Sub-Weapons to stun them is the best way to take them out.

After you've cleared the room of enemies, the northern doors will open up and you'll have access to the Triforce gateway.

ROOM 3

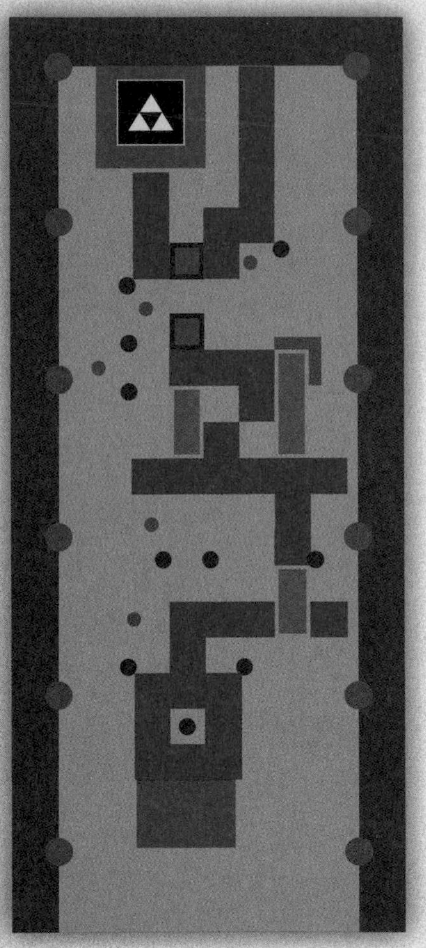

This room looks trickier than it actually is. As you start the room, you'll notice a severe lack of flooring. The floors are actually there—they're just invisible. The trick to figuring out where it's safe to walk is to use your Fire Gloves. Throw a fireball ahead of you and if there's a platform to walk on, it will light up and become visible temporarily.

From there, all you need to do is make your way to the northern part of the room, where you'll find a moving platform that will take you to the Triforce gateway. Truly, the hardest part of this room is the Fire Keeleons that litter the area. Use your Gust Jar to put their fire out, then slash away. Just don't let them start you on fire or you'll fall for sure.

There's a Squiddy off to the right of the Triforce gateway, but (and we can't believe we're saying this) it's not worth it to try and hit it. The Squiddy is almost guaranteed to fall into the pit below, and even if you defeat it, half of the Rupees would fall. Sigh... Just let this one go, friends. There will always be another...

ROOM 4

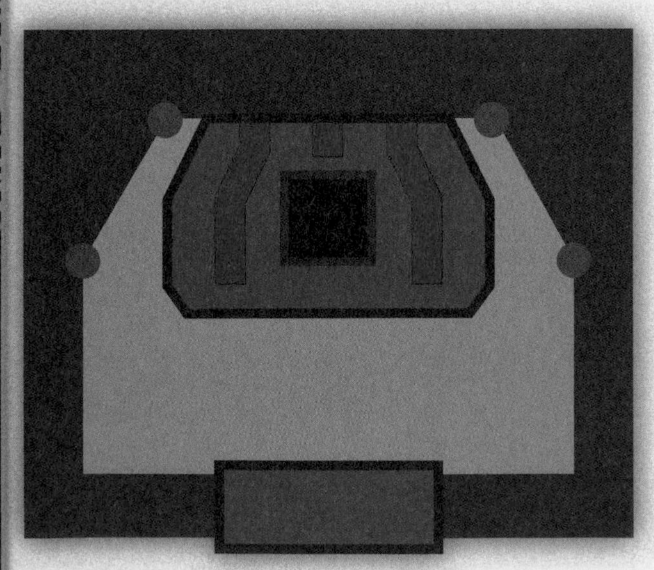

Defeat the enemies in this room to complete it and the level. You'll face off with a new enemy here called a Gibdo. These bumbling mummies have been around the Zelda series since the first game and their erratic movements have not changed much since.

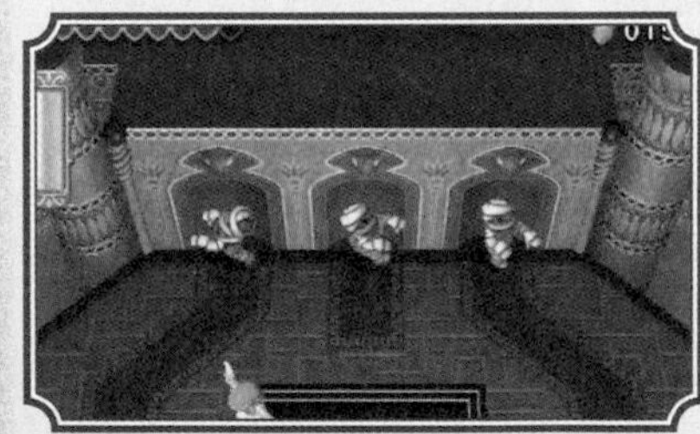

Keep your distance from them and use either your Fire Gloves or Gripshot to remove their bandages and reveal the much weaker Stalfos hiding in each of them.

Once you defeat two of the three Gibdos, two more will join in on the fun. Defeat the remaining Gibdos and a Triforce gateway will appear, meaning you've pretty much completed the level.

Level 4: Desert Temple

Challenges

Fewer Heart Containers

Don't pop any balloons

Clear within the time limit

Sub-Weapons

 Boomerang

 Magic Hammer

 Magic Hammer

Materials

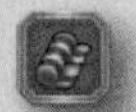 Vintage Linen

 Vintage Linen

 Stal Skull

Recommended Outfits

 Hammerwear

There's a good deal of hammering to be done in this stage and the Hammerwear will make all of it a lot faster. This level has puzzle solving with the Magic Hammer, defeating enemies with the Magic Hammer, smashing obstacles and platforms with the Magic Hammer—almost everything uses it to some capacity in this stage! Bring the Hammerwear if you want it all to go much smoother.

ROOM 1

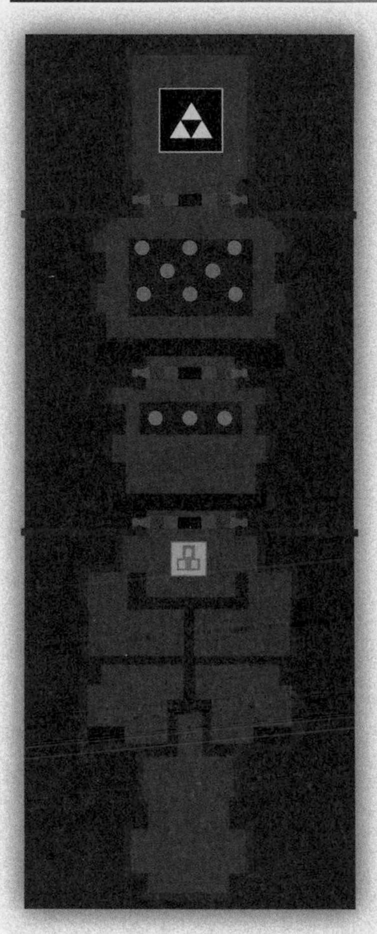

All three Sub-Weapons are in this room, but two of them are locked behind peg fences. Have a Link pick up the Magic Hammer ahead and smash down the pegs so that the other Links can retrieve the remaining Sub-Weapons.

Once you've collected all three, stand on the three-man pressure switch on the north side of the area. It's now time to play a rousing game of Whack-a-Mole! A little creature will pop out of one of the three hatches randomly. Your job is to bop it on the head with your Magic Hammer.

You can use your Boomerang to stun the creature when it pops up, then switch to your Magic Hammer Link and smash it while it's still stunned. Once you've smashed the creature, the northern gate will open and you'll have to smack multiple creatures with your Hammer. Plus, they're faster now. Good luck!

Electrified creatures will pop out of the hatches at times, so take care to watch what you're swinging at. Use the Boomerang to stun one of the creatures, then switch to your Hammer and bop it, just like you did in the last area. You'll need to smash three of the creatures to complete this mini-game and open the gate on the north side of the room.

ROOM 2

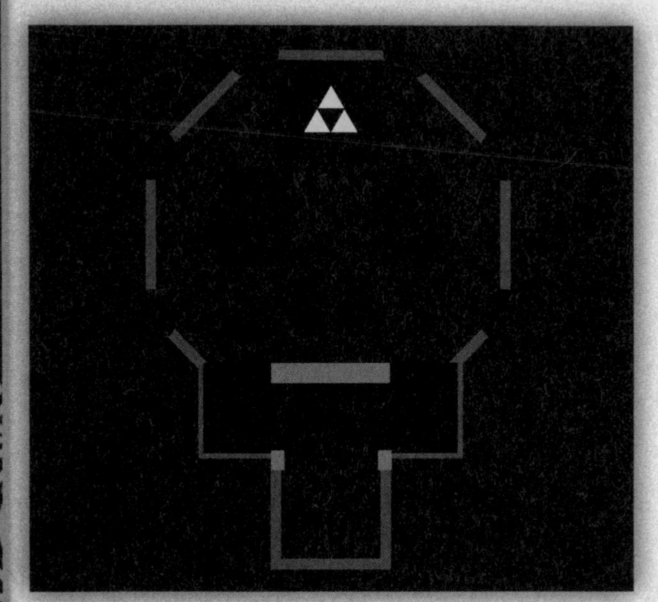

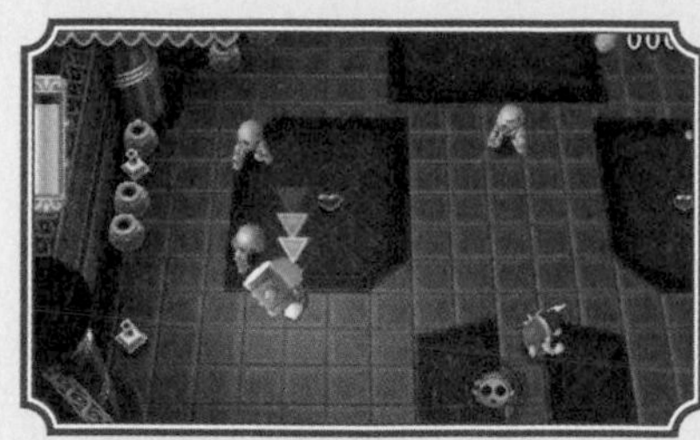

To complete this room you'll have to defeat a large group of Stalfos. Lucky for you, you have just the Sub-Weapons to do it with ease. Stalfos don't jump away from Hammers, meaning you can get in nice and close, then pound the Stalfos into the ground like tent stakes. The Boomerang also works well in stunning the bone bags. However you tackle this room, once you've cleared out the Stalfos, the Triforce gateway will appear on the room's north end.

ROOM 3

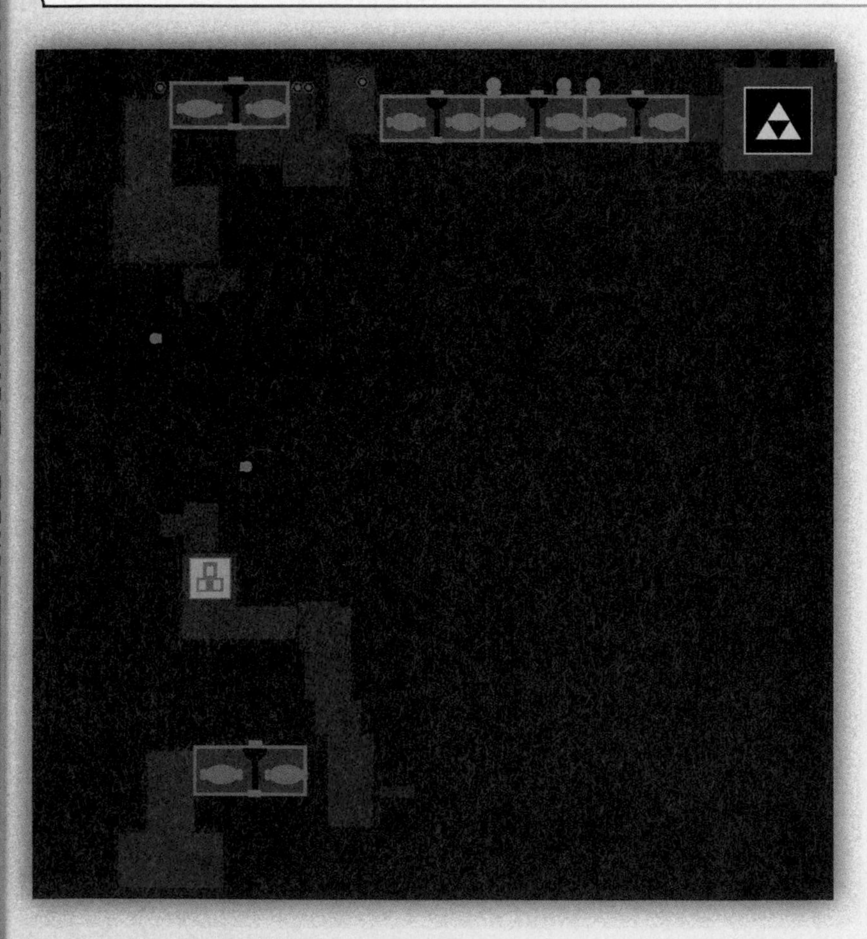

Head north until you reach the platform with eye symbols on it. These work similarly to the rocking platforms from the first level of this world. Don't panic! That doesn't mean you have to do any balancing! It's all about positioning. Use your Magic Hammer on the left side and the right side will rise. Do the same on the right side and, well, you get the idea.

Use the Hammer on the right side of the platform to lower it, then use the Boomerang Link to hit the switch. The switch will cause platforms to fall down and create a bridge north. Hit the left side of the platform and raise the right side up, then throw your Boomerang Link over. Have the Boomerang Link grab the other two Links, then head north.

Have all three Links stand on the three-man pressure switch to cause moving platforms to make their way to you. Now, hop on the first platform and immediately stand on its left point to avoid getting burned by the flame rod ahead.

Once you pass the first flame rod, move to the north end of the platform, hop onto the platform ahead, and then stand on that platform's right side. This will keep you from being burned by the second flame rod.

Once back on solid land, you'll run into everyone's favorite Squiddy: The Squiddy! Ask it politely to lend you some Rupees, then continue north until you reach another eye platform.

There are three orb switches surrounding the eye platform and you'll need to hit all three before time runs out. Start by hitting the right side of the platform with your Hammer. Create a two-Link Totem with the Boomerang Link on top.

Now, with your remaining Link, hit the lower-right orb, switch to the Totem, and head to the left side.

Use the Boomerang to hit the upper-left orb, switch back to your lone Link, and smash the left side of the platform with your Hammer twice. Now switch back to the Totem and hit the orb switch on the upper right. Once all three switches are hit, platforms will form just below you. Follow them to get around the right wall.

You can use your Boomerang Link to grab the purple Rupee south of you. Now head up to the orb switch above you and hit it to level out all of the eye platforms to your right.

Smash the left side of the first eye platform to raise the right side up to the platform above it. Make a three-Link Totem and throw one of the Magic Hammer Links to the platform above as soon as the flame rod retracts.

Now have the Hammer Link on the upper platform smash down the platform's left side. This will bridge the gap between the upper and lower platforms, allowing the lone Link to rejoin his Link-y brethren.

Repeat this process until you reach the top of the room and you'll find the Triforce gateway.

ROOM 4

BOSS FIGHT: STALCHAMPION

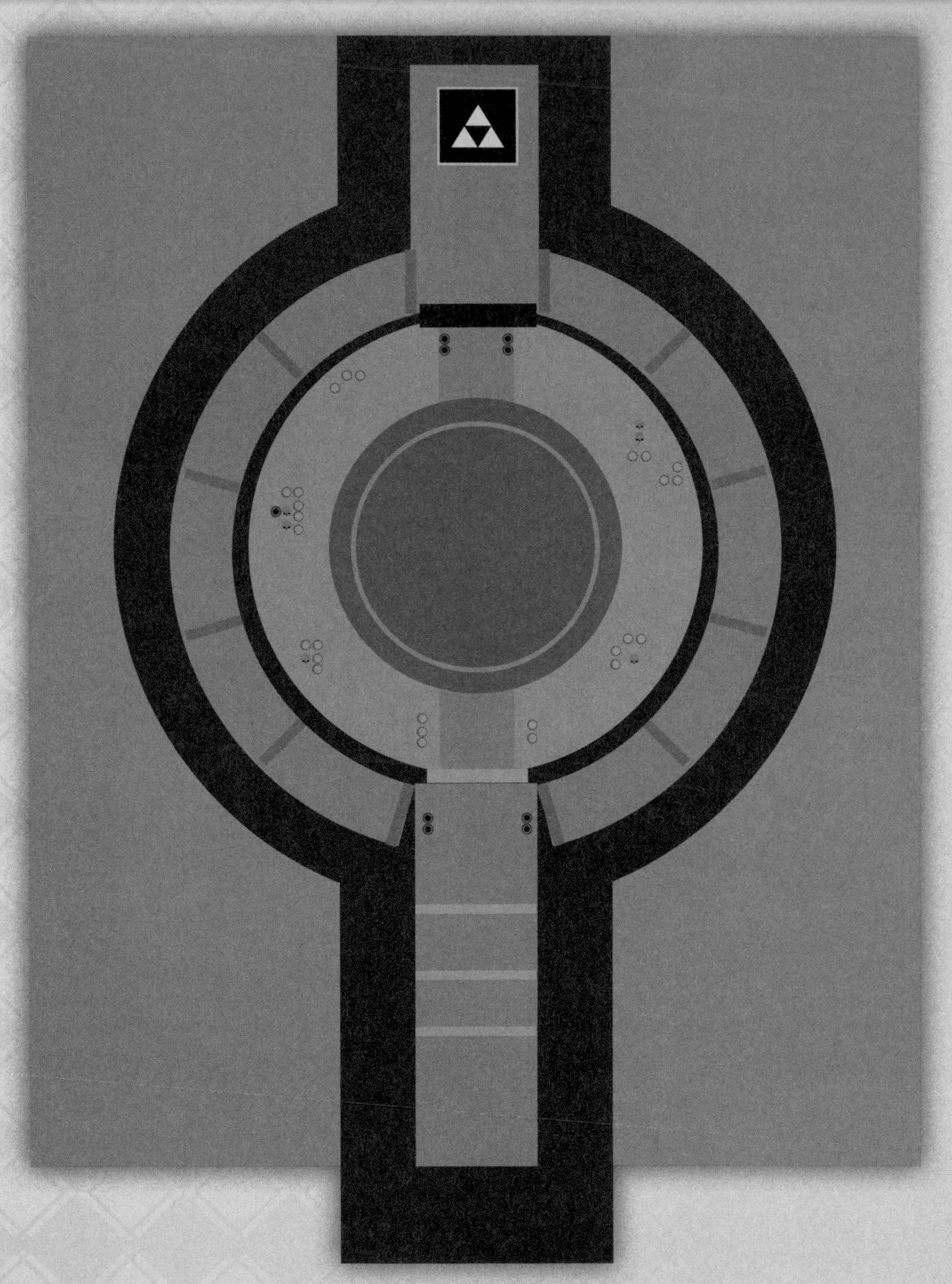

Head down the steps and crack open the pots if you're in need of health. As soon as you enter the circular portion of this room, you'll have to face the massive Stalchampion.

Stalchampion likes to create shockwaves and throw its bones like Boomerangs. The Boomeranging bones are easy enough to dodge, but the shockwaves can be a bit trickier. It'll often do a one-two combo by throwing a bone at you and then slamming the mace that is connected to its right hand to the ground to create a small shockwave. Its shockwaves deal damage and knock you backwards.

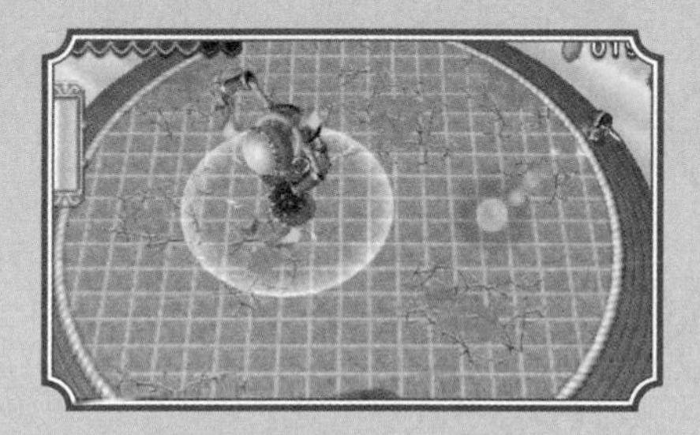

If you attack Stalchampion while it's in the middle of this attack, it'll either deflect it outright or bounce high into the air and create a shockwave as it lands.

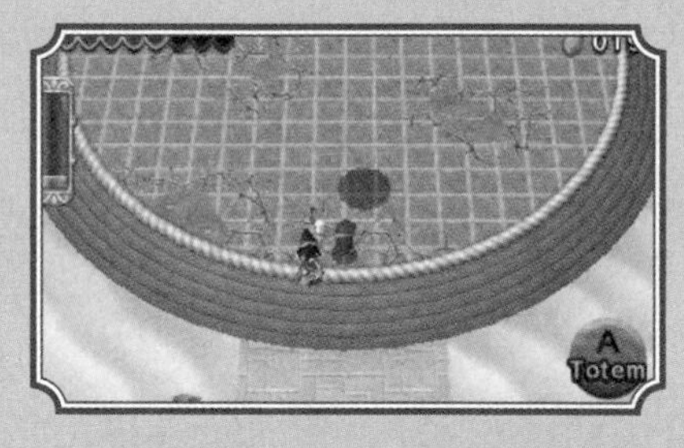

The way to defeat the Stalchampion is to hit it in the back. The best time to do this is when it's in the middle of its one-two combo. When you hit it, it'll begin to bounce around on one foot. Hit it again and it'll fall to pieces. (The Boomerang is particularly excellent for hitting it this second time.)

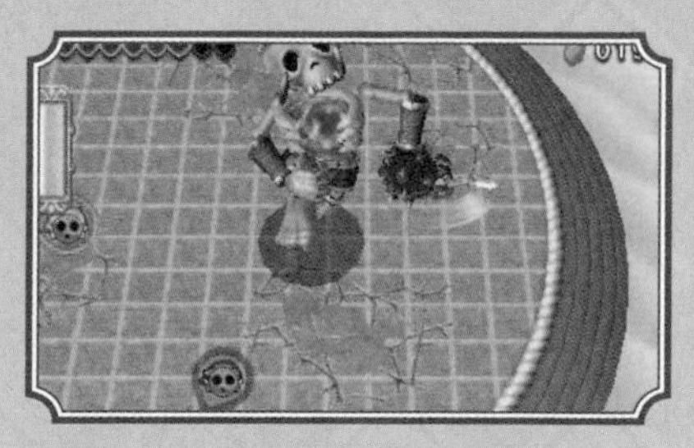

When the Stalchampion comes undone, have your Hammer Links smash its chest piece to do damage to it. Just watch out for the spiked mace, as it will slowly roll after you while the Stalchampion is in pieces. When Stalchampion comes back together, it'll immediately jump into the air and create a small shockwave upon landing.

After beating up the Stalchampion for a bit, it'll get angry and jump into the air. Get every active Link off of the center platform swiftly! When Stalchampion lands, it'll create a massive shockwave that will hit anyone standing on the center platform.

The Stalchampion now will become a bit quicker and more difficult to hit in the back. If you're playing single-player, you'll want to spread your Links out along the edges of the center platform. While Stalchampion is looking at one of your Links, switch to another and quickly strike its back.

Every time Stalchampion rebuilds itself in this phase, it'll jump into the air and create a shockwave that encompasses the whole center platform, so make sure to get off of it while it's in the air.

After breaking Stalchampion down a few more times, its body will fall apart and it'll chase you down with its floating head. Oh, did we mention its head is now on fire? Make a three-Link Totem with the Boomerang Link on top, then throw the Boomerang at Stalchampion's head. The flames will recede while it's stunned, which will give you a chance to slash it as it hovers in the air.

Keep stunning and attacking Stalchampion's head and it'll at last be defeated.

WORLD 7: THE RUINS

Level 1: Illusory Mansion

Challenges

Fewer Heart Containers

Don't fall at all

Clear within the time limit

Sub-Weapons

 Boomerang

 Boomerang

 Boomerang

Materials

 Carrumpkin

 Carrumpkin

 Mystery Extract

Recommended Outfits

 Tingle Tights

This place is tricky and there are an awful lot of pits to fall into. In fact, there is an enemy at the end of the level that specifically uses pits to damage you and your Links. That's why we can't emphasize enough that you use Tingle Tights for this stage above all other Outfits. They're listed three times in the "Recommended Outfits" box, so you know we mean business.

ROOM 1

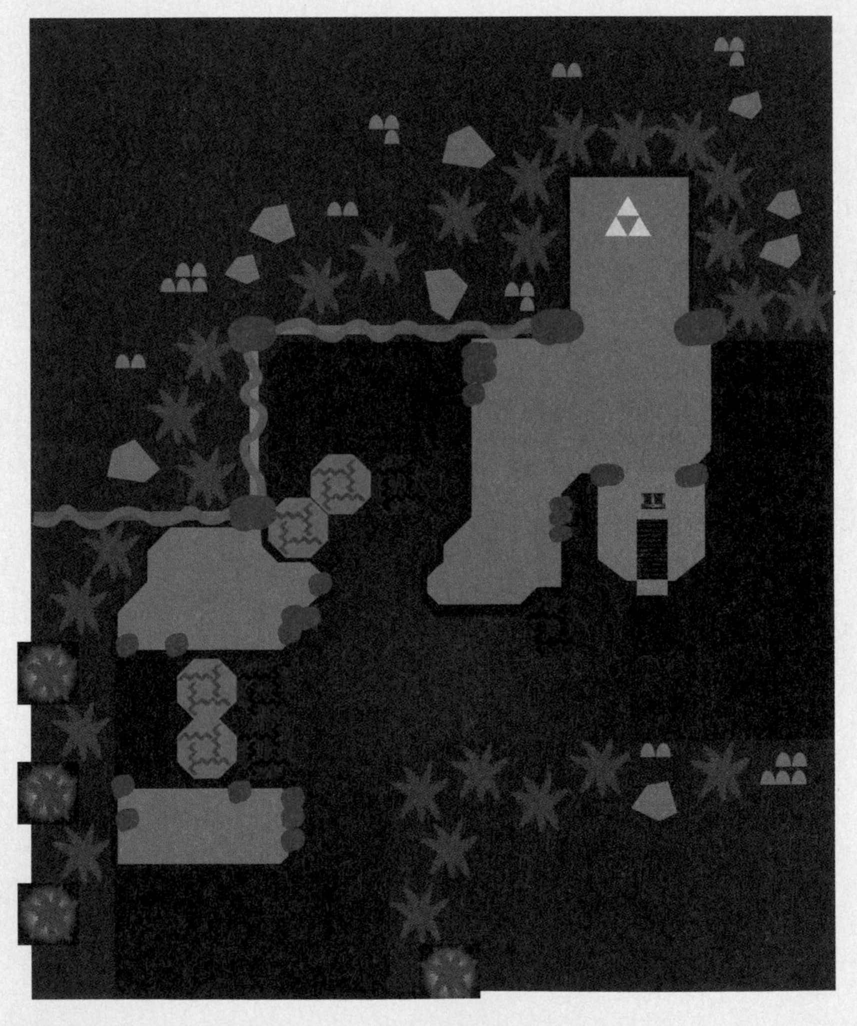

The colored platforms ahead correspond to each color of Link. Only a Link of the same color as the platform can cross each type of platform. For example, the green Link can walk on the green platforms, but not the red or blue ones. This makes for some tricky puzzle solving later in the level. For now, make a three-Link Totem and walk all three Links across the platforms that are the same color as the Link on the bottom of the Totem.

Grab the Boomerangs off their pedestals before moving on. Now you'll need to make a Totem to match the order of the colored platforms ahead (green on bottom, blue in the middle, and red on top). Walk across the green platforms and throw the top two Links onto the blue platform ahead. Now throw the red Link over the gap to the right.

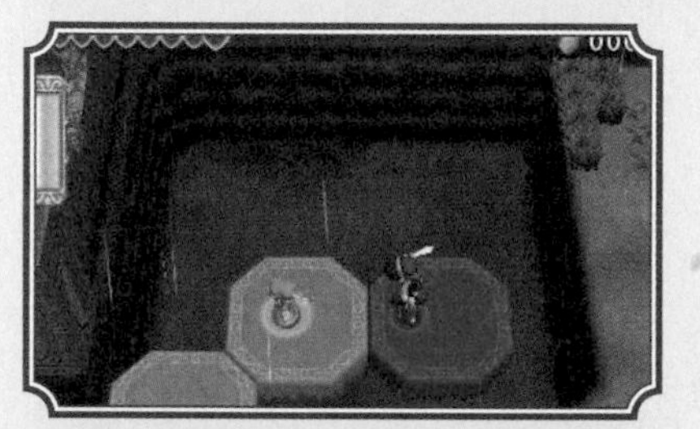

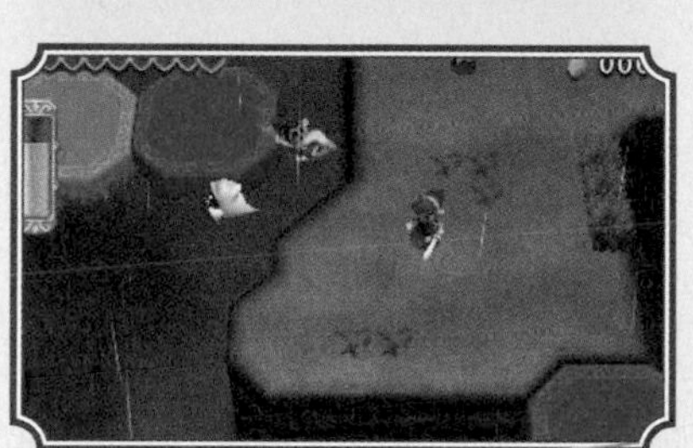

Now, as the blue Link, turn around, Boomerang the green Link, and throw him over to where the red Link is standing. Now use the red or green Link to clear out the ghostly Poes floating around the area, then Boomerang the blue Link over the gap.

Normal Poes don't pose much of a threat. (Pun intended? We like to think so.) A couple of hits and they'll walk into the light, so to speak.

You'll need to open the treasure chest on top of the tower on the east side of the room. The northern gate is locked and the key is inside the chest on top of that tower.

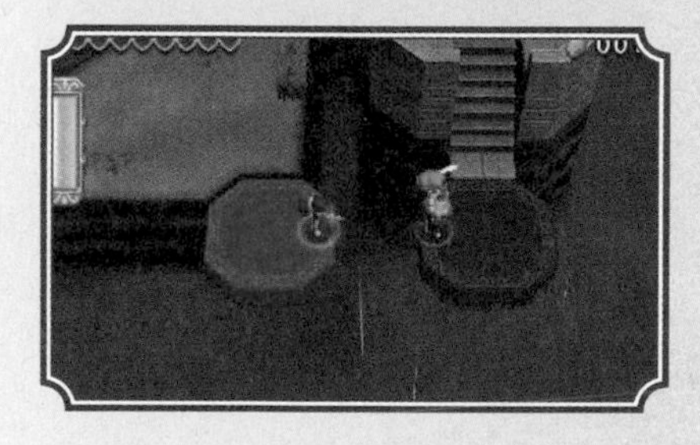

To reach the treasure chest on top of the platform on the right side of this area, make a Totem with the blue Link on the bottom and the red Link on top. Walk onto the blue platform to the south, then throw the red Link onto the red platform. Have the red Link head up the stairs and grab the treasure, throw it north onto the landing below, and then move back onto the red platform. Now have the blue Link Boomerang the red Link back to the blue platform and you're good to go.

Use the key to open the gate, then move on to the next room.

ROOM 2

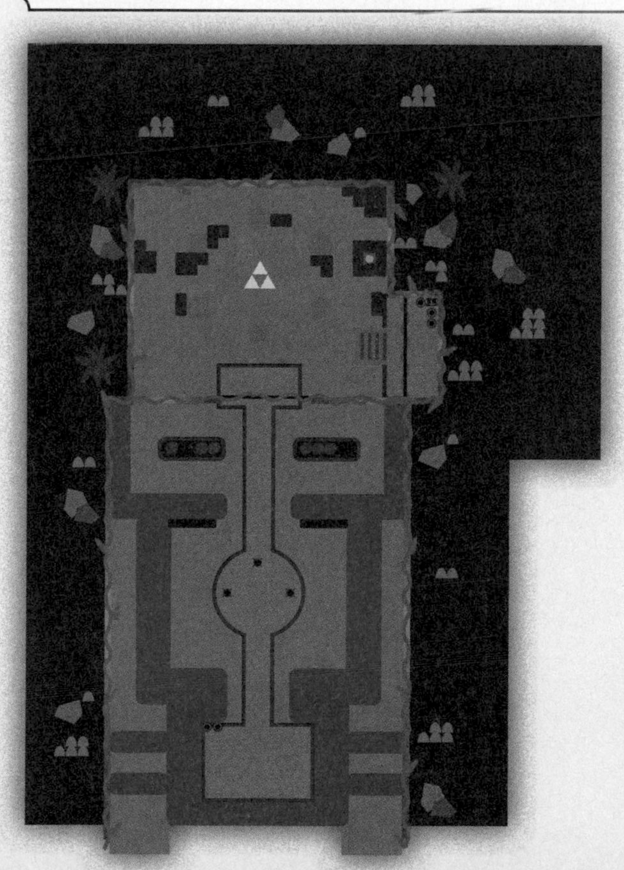

As you head north, three colored Poes will appear near three unlit torches. To defeat these colored Poes, you'll need to attack them using the Link that matches the color of each of the Poes (the green Link attacks the green Poe and so on). The colored Poes are not different from the normal white Poes in behavior, so a couple of slashes from your sword will take them out.

As you defeat each Poe, a torch will light. Once you defeat all three Poes, a key will fall between the torches. Pick up the key and head north.

As you approach the northern gate, two white Poes will appear and try to attack you. Defeat them, "have a word" with Squiddy, and then unlock the north gate.

Hidden Treasure!

To reach the treasure chest behind the gate, you need to hit the pressure switch in the patch of grass just north of the gate. Once you hit the switch, the gate will open and the treasure will be yours.

When you enter the next area, six colored Poes will appear at varying heights. You'll need to make a Totem with the Link that matches the Poe you're trying to attack on top. This is not a particularly difficult fight, so you should be able to mop the Poes up quickly. Once you do, a Triforce gateway will appear in the middle of the area.

ROOM 3

Have the blue Link walk on the blue platform ahead of your starting point. Now grab the Bomb ahead of you and run it back to the cracked block on the left side of your starting point to blow it up.

You'll find a three-man pressure switch behind the block. Have all three Links stand on it and several more colored platforms will appear in the area north of you.

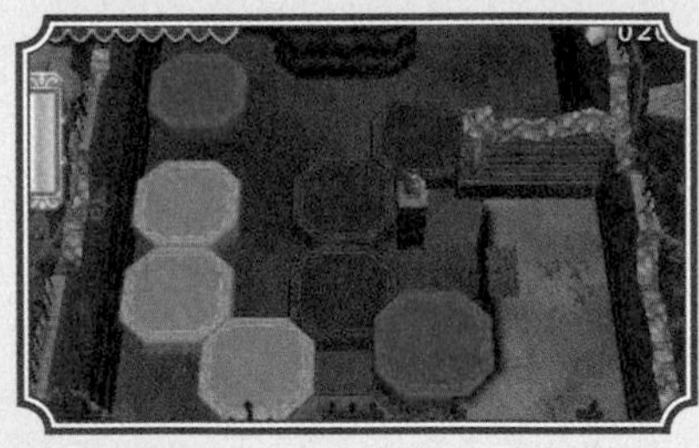

Make a Totem with the blue Link on the bottom, the green Link in the middle, and the red Link on top, then walk onto the blue platform. You'll want to defeat the one-eyed, Keese-like Chasupas flying around the platforms; they'll cause you plenty of grief if you don't. Once the coast is clear, throw the top two Links onto the green platform, then have the green Link turn and throw the red Link onto the red platform.

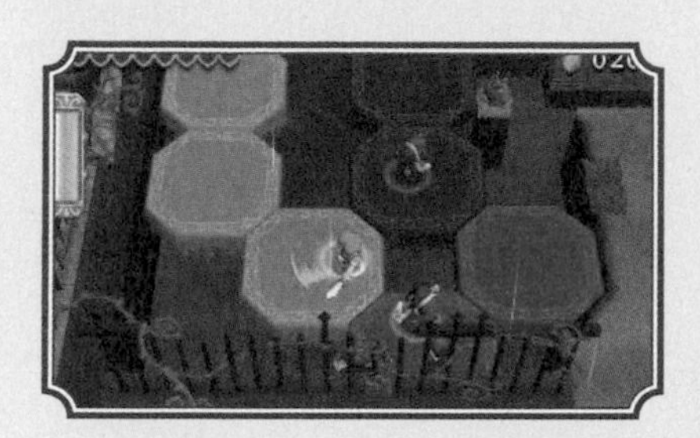

Now have the green Link Boomerang the blue Link and carry him north up the green platforms. At the end of the platforms, throw the blue Link onto the blue platform ahead, then have the blue Link Boomerang the green Link over to him.

Throw the green Link onto the landing ahead, then have the green Link Boomerang the blue Link over. Now wait near the cracked block. Have the red Link Boomerang the Bomb in the center of his row of platforms, then throw it over to the other two Links. Next, get the green or blue Link to throw the Bomb in front of the cracked blocks to destroy them. Now have the green or blue Link Boomerang the red Link off of his platforms, then head north.

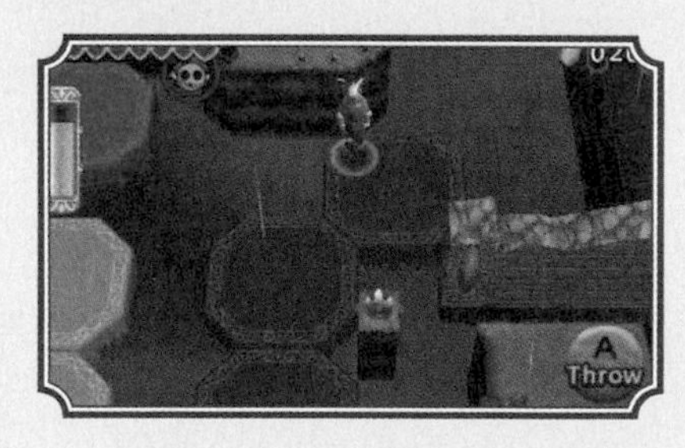

Take care not to get ambushed by the Life Like on the north end of this area. You'll know where it is when you see the fake Heart wobbling on the ground in the middle of the grass ahead.

Make a Totem with the green Link on the bottom, the blue Link in the middle, and the red Link on the top, then walk onto the green platform on your right.

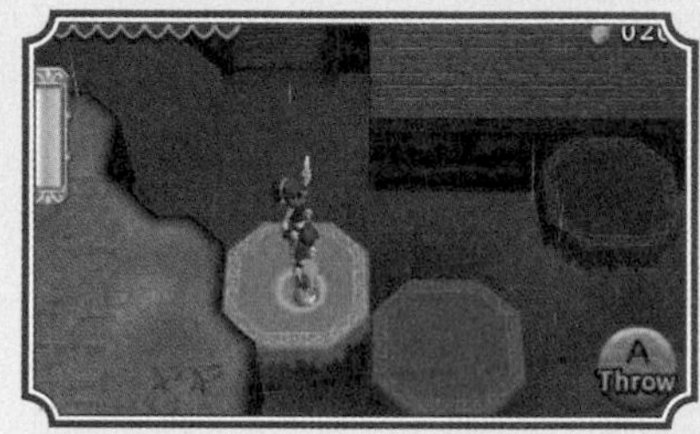

Throw the top two Links onto the blue platform, then have the blue Link throw the red Link onto the red platform.

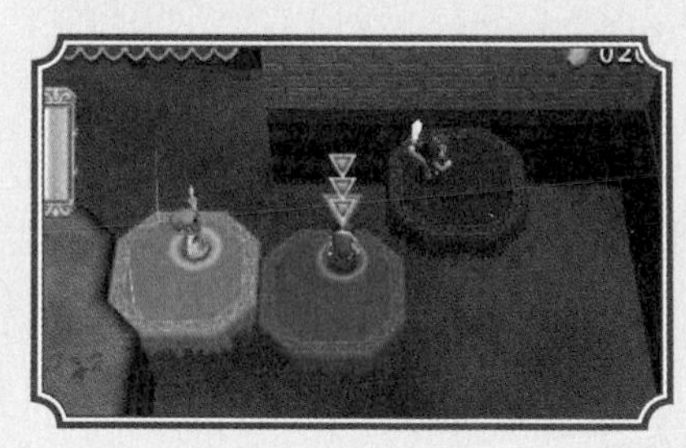

Now have the blue Link Boomerang the green Link, then walk to the northeast corner of the blue platform and have the red Link pick up the blue Link's Totem.

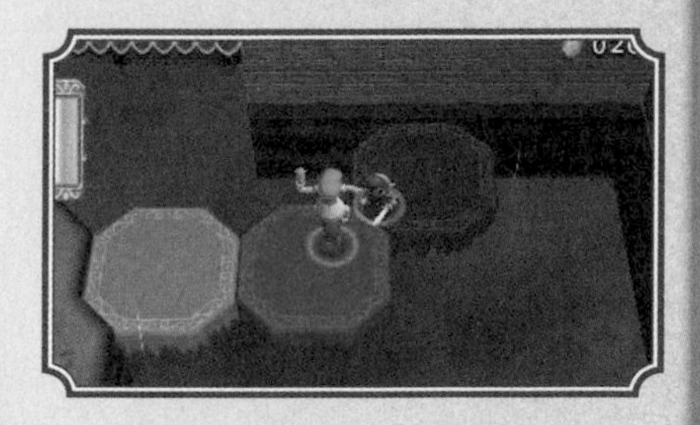

Face north, then have the blue Link throw the green Link onto the platform above.

Have the green Link step on the pressure switch to create a bridge for the other two Links to use to reach the Triforce gateway above.

ROOM 4

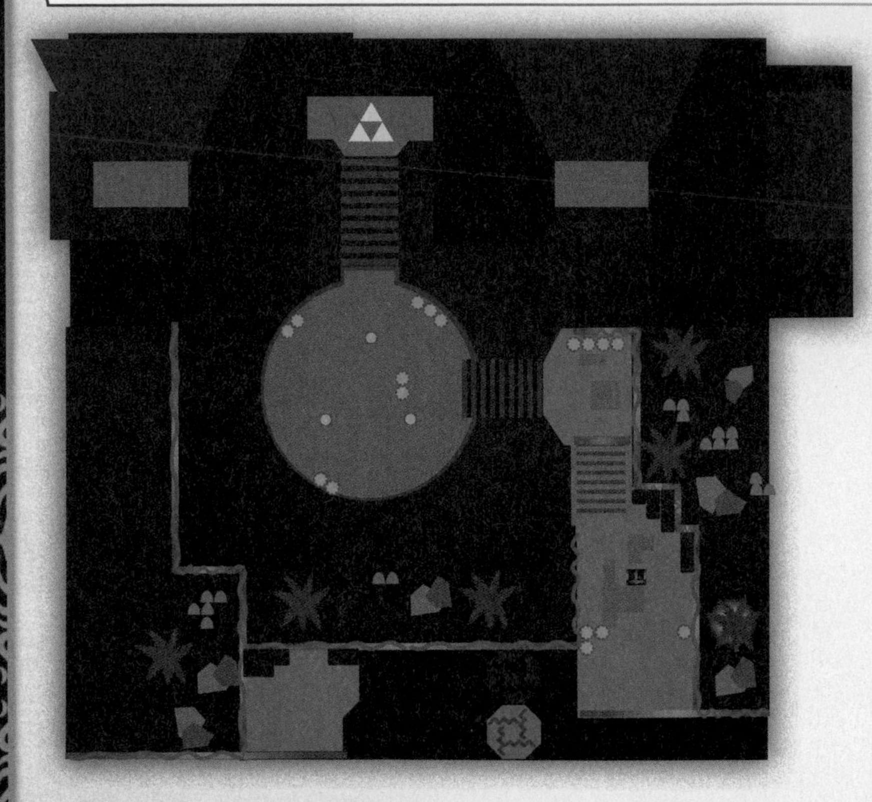

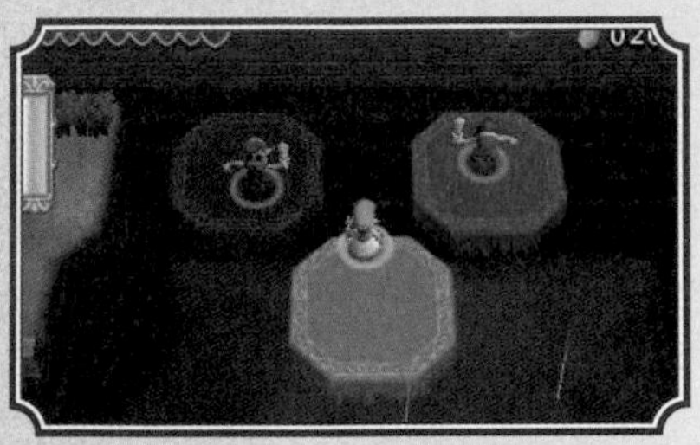

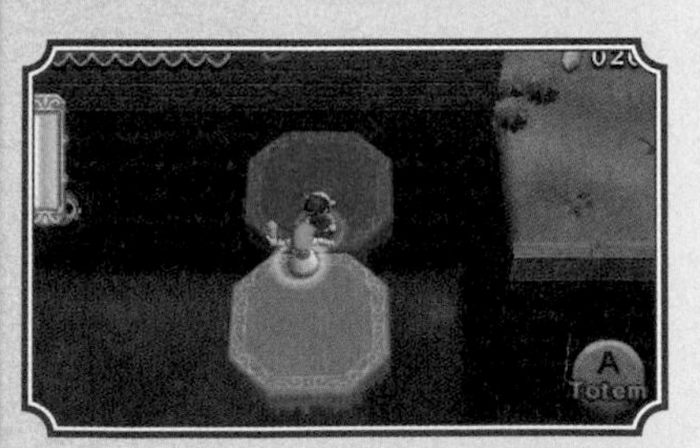

Make a three-Link Totem with the red Link on the bottom, the green Link in the middle, and the blue Link on top, then step onto the red platform. Have the red Link throw the green and blue Links onto the green platform below you, then have the green Link throw the blue Link onto the blue platform.

Boomerang the red Link with the green Link to create a Totem. Walk to the northeast edge of the green platform, then have the blue Link pick up the Totem and walk onto solid ground on the right side of the room.

An ambush of Poes will appear in the center of the area. Defeat them and a treasure chest appears. Head up the stairs and drop down onto the circular platform on the left.

Have each Link stand on one of the pressure switches to activate them. When the switches are activated, the bridge you dropped from will retract and three new enemies, Prankster Poes, will appear.

There's no other way to describe these enemies except to call them massive jerks. They will chase after a Link like Ganon chases after the complete Triforce, and they won't stop until they reach him. But the fun doesn't stop there! Once they have their horrible little hands on your Link, they'll pick him up, usher him to the nearest pit, and toss him right in. Out of all the enemies that have ever graced a Zelda game, none have been nearly as rude as the Prankster Poes.

If you slash them, they'll disappear momentarily, then reappear behind whichever Link slashed them. You'll need to be quick to catch them before they catch you. When a Link gets picked up, if you're playing single-player, you can switch to another Link and quickly slash the Poe to get it to drop the Link. In multiplayer, you'll need a friend to slash the Poe for you.

Once you've defeated all of the Prankster Poes (good riddance!), a bridge will extend from the north, giving you access to the Triforce gateway for this room.

Level 2: Palace Noir

Challenges

Pop all balloons

Halved attack and defense

Transport the orb quickly

Sub-Weapons

 Bow

 Gust Jar

 Fire Gloves

Materials

 Carrumpkin

 Carrumpkin

 Spider Silk Lace

Recommended Outfits

 Kokiri Clothes

 Tingle Tights

 Gust Garb

This level is dark. Really dark. It also has a good deal of tricky puzzles, made trickier by the lack of light. The Outfits you wear in the stage aren't going to have a major impact, but we went ahead and listed a few that offer a bit of help. You can feel free to wear any Outfit with a general benefit (Sword Suit, Legendary Dress, etc.) if you'd prefer. Most of this level is about being patient and not walking off of the edge of a platform.

ROOM 1

The white Poe holding the lantern is harmless. In fact, it's actually pretty helpful in this dark room. You can use the Poe's light to see around whatever area the Poe is in, but we won't need it.

You'll find the first Sub-Weapon for this level, the Bow, directly ahead of you. The Gust Jar is in the top-left corner of the room, and the Fire Gloves are on the top-right corner of this downstairs area.

Have the Fire Gloves Link light the two torches in the north side of the room to help dispel this darkness.

Now head up the stairs on the right side of the room and a small cutscene highlighting another unlit torch will play. Have the Bow and Fire Gloves Links line up at the left edge of the floor, then have the Gust Jar Link blow them over.

Once on the other side, have the Bow Link throw the Fire Gloves Link across the gap on your left. Now have the Fire Gloves Link light the torches on his platform.

Have the Fire Gloves Link drop down to the bottom floor, head up the stairs on the right side of the room, and then let the Gust Jar Link air blast the Fire Gloves Link back to where the Bow Link is. Have the Fire Gloves Link throw the Bow Link across the gap this time. Now have the Bow Link stand in front of the bottom torch of the platform, face to the right, and fire an arrow through the torch. The arrow will light one of the two remaining torches.

Have both the Fire Gloves Link and the Bow Link head back up the stairs to where the Gust Jar Link is standing. The last torch that needs to be lit is directly south of your position, sitting on top of one of the white pillars in the center of the room.

In single-player, this part is quite tricky. You'll need to position your Fire Gloves Link on the very edge of the opening in the balcony while facing north. Your Bow Link will need to stand against the north wall directly in front of the Fire Gloves Link, but have your Bow Link face south.

Now have the Fire Gloves Link throw a fireball toward the Bow Link, then quickly switch to the Bow Link and fire your arrows. If your timing was right, your Bow Link's arrows will shoot through the fireball, catch fire, and then hit the torch on top of the column. It might take a few tries, but you'll get it eventually.

Multiplayer Method

While playing multiplayer, you only need to have the Fire Gloves Link stand to the left or right side of the balcony's opening while holding out a fireball to solve this puzzle. Definitely a simpler task than bouncing fireballs off of walls for some sort of Bow trickshot.

Once all of the torches in the room are lit, the Lantern Poe will pop and the gate on the north side of the room will open. You'll be able to reach the Triforce gateway just behind the gate.

ROOM 2

This room is also dark, and to make matters worse, the pathways here are very narrow. There is a three-man pressure switch directly ahead of you. Have all three Links stand on it to activate it. Activating this switch will cause a key to fall onto a column in the center of this area. You'll need to grab that key to unlock the door blocking the Triforce gateway on the north end of the room.

The key will shortly thereafter be engulfed in fire. In order to reach it you'll need the Gust Jar Link to put the fire out. Have one Link (but not the Gust Jar Link) head left along the pathway until you encounter a moving platform. Have that Link stand on the middle of the platform while the other two Links head to the right.

Make a Totem with the Gust Jar Link on top. Now walk the Totem onto the moving platform on the right side of the room and face the key. When the left platform is just about parallel with the platform the Totem is on, fire the Gust Jar at the key. If you're close enough, the key will launch off of its column and land on the moving platform on the left side of the room. Having the Link over there will help you catch it.

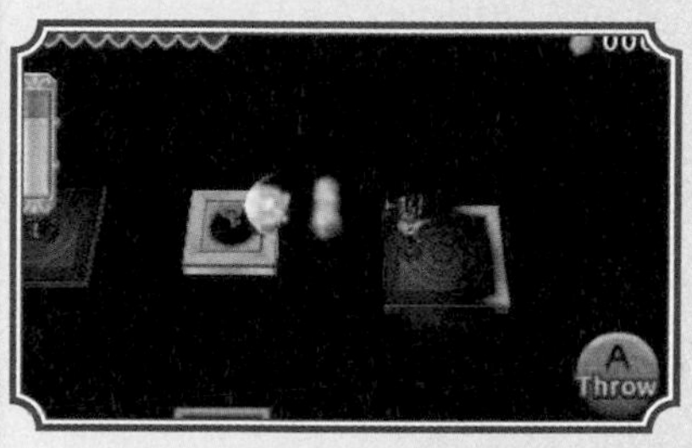

With key in hand, have all three Links use the left platform to reach the northwest corner of the area, then follow the path east. You can find another unlit torch at the end of this path. Lighting it will make things a bit easier.

To get across the gap on the far right side of the room, put the key safely on the ground, make a two-Link Totem (but don't add the Gust Jar Link to it), and have the Totem stand at the edge of the red platform. Now move your Gust Jar Link onto the landing above the red platform and air blast the top Link of the Totem across the gap.

Have the Link that crossed the gap hit the pressure switch to make the red platform move. Now grab the key, hop on the red platform, and cross to the other side of the room. Put the key in the lock on the northern gate to open it and gain access to the Triforce gateway.

ROOM 3

This room is large, but simple. Three Key Bandit Poes are holding three keys, all of which you need to unlock the gates on the north side of the room. This room is a bit of a maze, complete with pitfalls and enemies, but none of it is too challenging if you mind your step.

The Key Bandit Poes are similar to the Prankster Poes, except they've only got eyes for keys. The second you pick one up, a horde of Key Bandit Poes will try to attack you to take the key back.

Once you have a key, immediately take it to one of the locks on the northern gates. Grab all three keys and escort them to the gates to exit the room. The last lock requires a two-Link Totem be made in order to reach it, so quickly race to one of your other Links, have one of them pick up your key-holding Link, then race back to the lock.

Once all three gates are open, a Squiddy will appear directly below the gates. Speak with the Squiddy in a language it understands, then exit the room.

In Case of Emergency!

If you're low on health, you can throw a Link onto the bookshelves littering the room to break pots that likely contain Hearts.

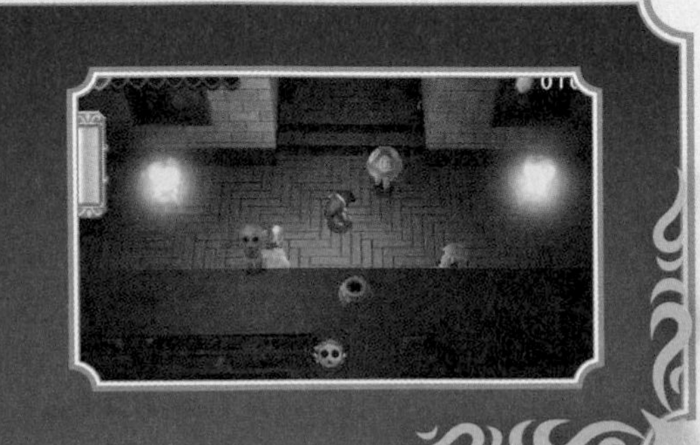

ROOM 4

BOSS FIGHT: GRIM REPOE

Each Link starts in a different area of this room. When all three Links enter the center of the room, three colored Poes appear, but these ones are a little different than the ones you've faced up to this point. These Poes will run away from you as you approach, so you'll have to herd them into one of the alcoves surrounding the room to hit them.

In single-player, you can force them toward an alcove with one Link, then leave that Link in between the wall and the bookshelf to basically create a barricade that the Poes won't cross. Control a different Link and move him to the opposite side of the bookshelf to keep the Poes from moving through that side as well. Now take your third Link and attack. Keep pressuring the Poes back, then block them in until all three are defeated.

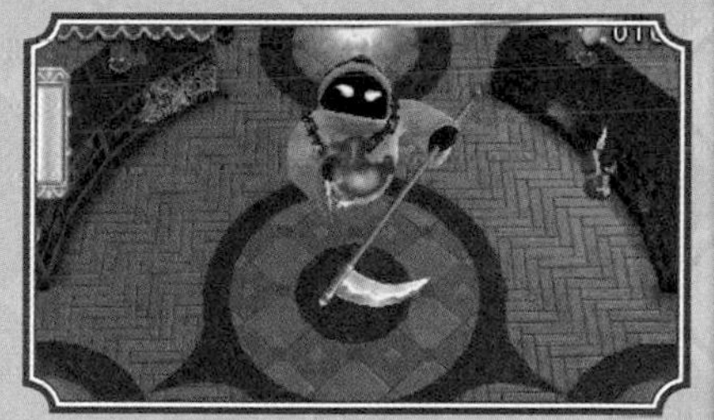

After each of the three Poes have been defeated, Grim Repoe will appear to avenge its fallen brethren.

The Grim Repoe will promptly disappear after the fight begins, leaving only its scythe visible. To make Grim Repoe visible again, you'll need to have the Fire Gloves Link relight all three torches surrounding the center of the room.

When all three torches are lit, Grim Repoe will reappear, but it'll still be untouchable. Have the Gust Jar Link hit it with an air blast and it'll be completely visible, meaning you can hit it with your sword. After a handful of hits, Grim Repoe will blow the lights out and become invisible once again.

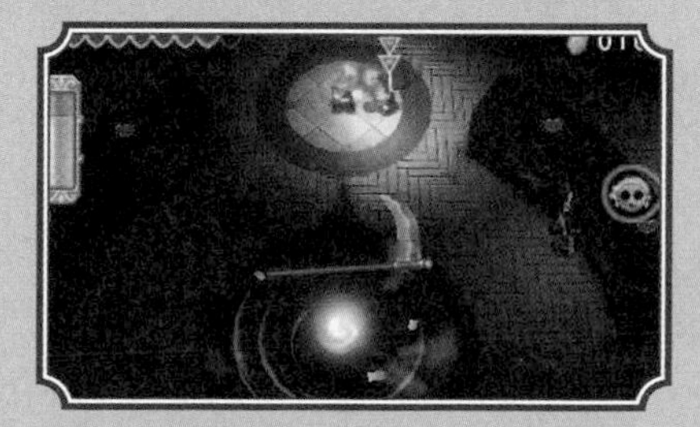

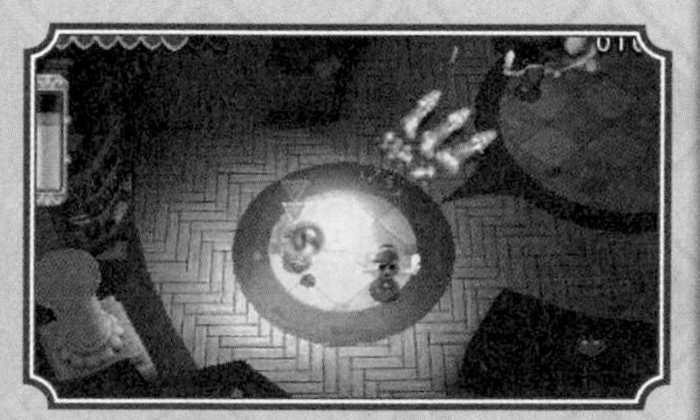

You'll need to relight the torches, but Grim Repoe will try to put them out with its spin attack. You'll need to be quick if you want to relight all three before Grim Repoe can put one out again. If you equipped the Kokiri Clothes, you can light one of the torches, then shoot through the torch toward the other two to quickly light them. It takes some good aim, but it's the fastest way to get the torches up and running again. You can also do it without the Kokiri Clothes, but the Outfit makes it easier.

You only need to make Grim Repoe visible and attack it with your sword one or two more times to defeat it.

Level 3: Lone Labyrinth

Challenges

Don't drop the pot

Guard the orb

Adventure in the dark

Sub-Weapons

 Gripshot

 Gust Jar

 Fire Gloves

Materials

 Mystery Extract

 Mystery Extract

 Poe Soul

Recommended Outfits

 Tingle Tights

 Legendary Dress

 Sword Suit

There are a lot of narrow pathways in this level and a lot of tricky combat situations. Really, any of these Outfits will do to help you complete this level, but if you want some guidance, the Tingle Tights or the Legendary Dress will help you keep your Heart Containers full.

ROOM 1

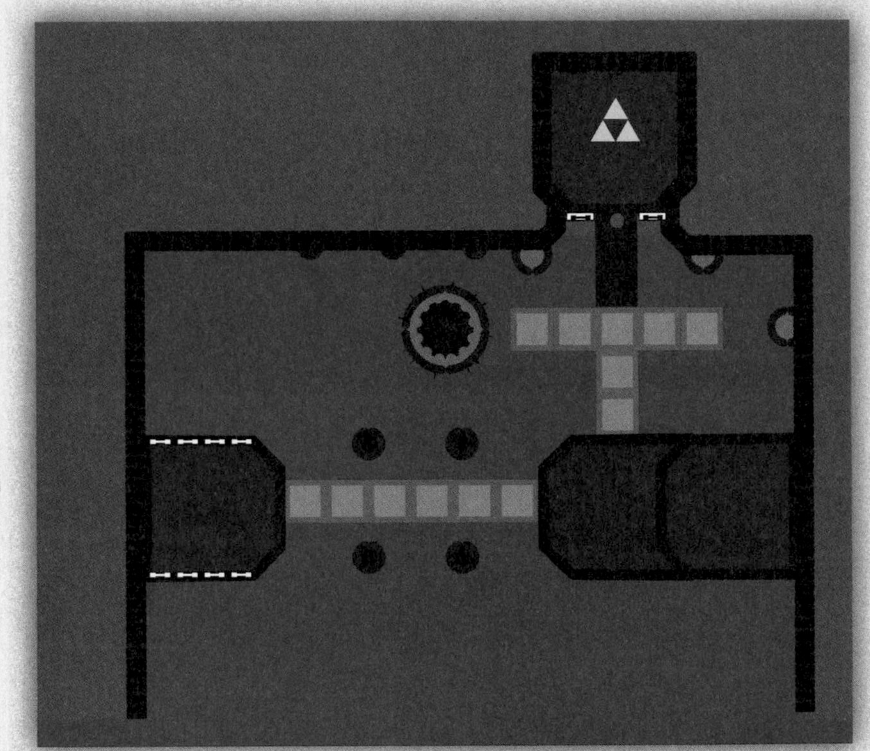

At the start of this level, hit the orb switch next to you to create a bridge to the east side of the room. You'll find all three Sub-Weapons on the other side of the bridge. Grab them, but hold off on hitting the orb switch.

The orb switch will make a bridge to the north, but the bridge will disappear after a short time. You can make the bridge reappear by hitting the orb switch again.

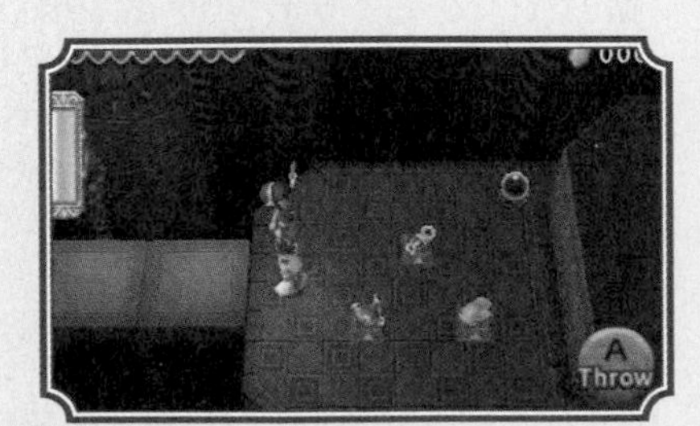

You can throw a Link onto the ledge to your right to reach a Squiddy. Have a heart-to-heart with the jewel-filled jelly, then hop back down and wait in front of the northern bridge.

There are two switches you'll need to hit to advance. One is in a structure on the left side of the bridge and one is on the right. You'll also need to light a torch on the right side of the platform. Make a three-Link Totem with the Gripshot Link on the bottom and the Fire Gloves and Gust Jar Links on top. Head to the north end of the bridge and throw the top two Links to the right, while heading to the left with your Gripshot Link.

Use the Gripshot to grab the Bomb from the Bomb Flower on the left side of the platform. Now throw the Bomb into the pillar housing the orb switch.

Now switch to your Gust Jar Link and hit the right switch with the Gust Jar. Switch to your Fire Gloves Link and have him light the torch on the northern wall. If you were fast enough, a bridge will extend from the north side of the room to give you access to the Triforce gateway.

ROOM 2

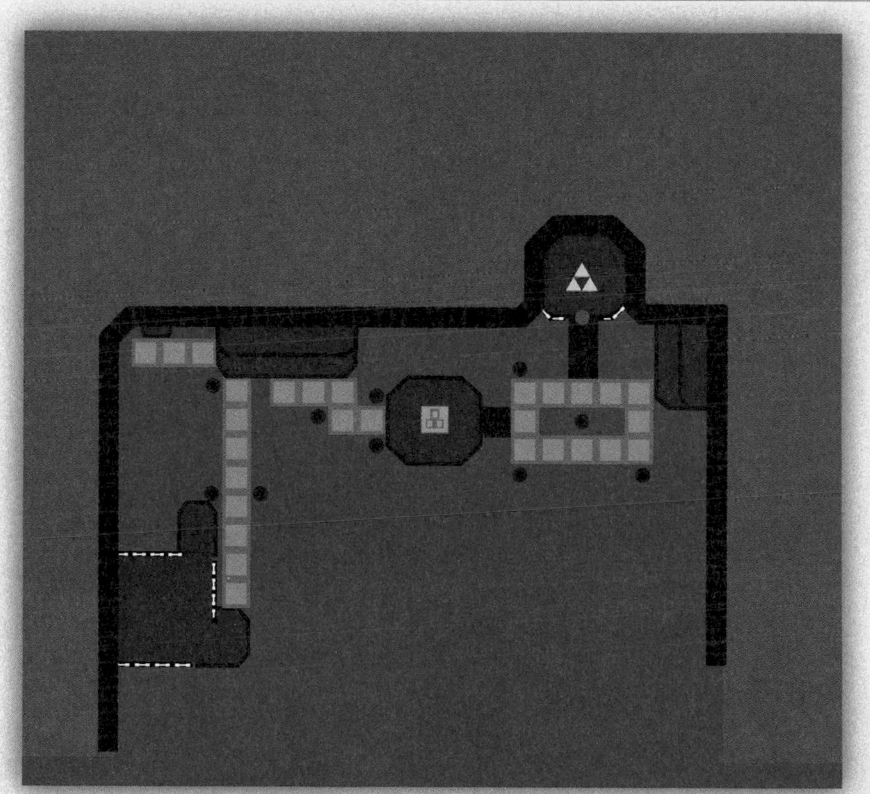

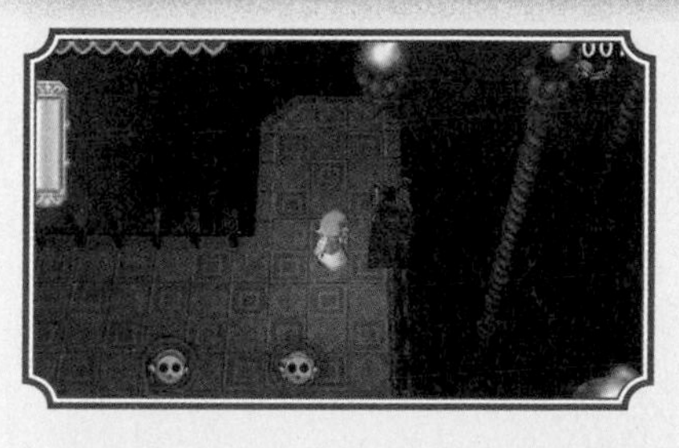

Head to the upper-right corner of the landing you start this room on, make a two-Link Totem with the Fire Gloves Link on top, and then light the torch.

Another bridge will form to your right, but this one's platforms will disappear and reappear one at a time in succession. Watch the platforms to get an idea of when they're going to disappear, then head across the bridge to reach the north side of the room. As a general tip, when you see the white border appear on one of the platforms, that means it's about to disappear.

You can grab the treasure chest and light the torch on the ledge ahead, but lighting the torch is unnecessary for completing this room. It will, however, cause a treasure chest to appear on a column to your left. You can use the Gust Jar Link to send a Link over to the column to reach it. Once you open the chest, disappearing platforms will appear, making a path back to your other Links.

Drop onto the second set of disappearing platforms south of you and follow them to the right. You'll come across a three-man pressure switch. Have all three Links stand on it to activate it. Three white Poes will appear around you and the pressure switch. Defeat them and another bridge of disappearing platforms will appear to your right.

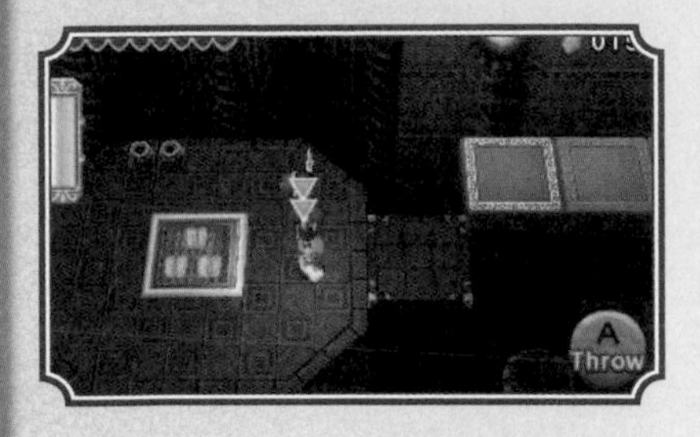

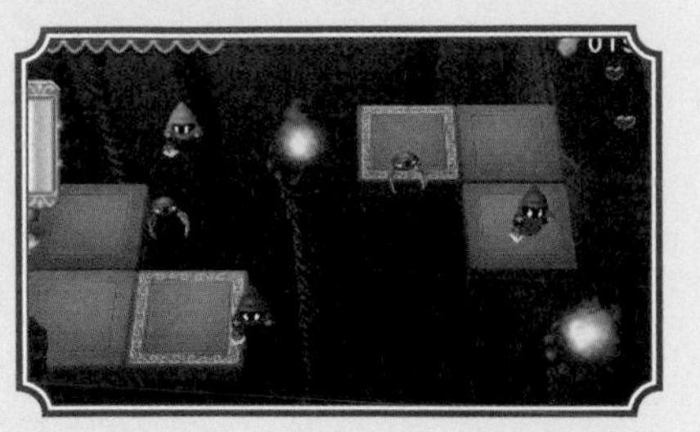

As soon as you approach the bridge, two Chasupas and three colored Poes will appear. This fight can be very tricky, since you can't damage a colored Poe that doesn't match the color of your current Link. Try and take out the closest Poes first, then head for the one on the far side of the platforms.

Once you've defeated all three Poes, a bridge will extend from the north, giving you access to the Triforce gateway.

ROOM 3

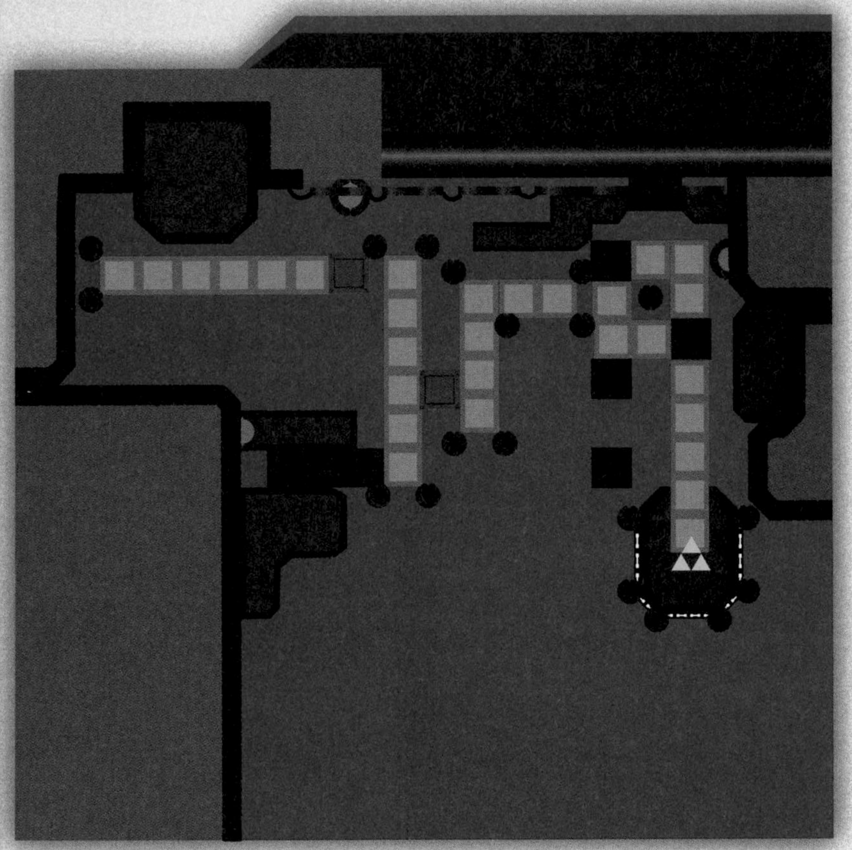

Drop down onto the disappearing platforms below your starting location, then immediately head to the right until you reach a solid platform. Use the Fire Gloves Link to light the torch above you, which will cause more disappearing platforms to appear on the right.

The platforms will disappear in succession downward, stop, start disappearing one at a time upward, and then repeat. Drop down onto the platforms when the coast is clear, then stand on the solid platform at the center of the disappearing-platform bridge.

Wait for the disappearing platforms to reappear south of you, make a three-Link Totem with the Gripshot Link on the bottom, and head south on top of the platforms. Throw your top two Links onto the landing to the left, then use the Gripshot to pull the remaining Link over.

This will cause another set of disappearing platforms to appear to the right of the platforms you used to get to this landing. It will also create a bridge back to the disappearing platforms, so you don't need to throw any Links over any gaps to get back onto the platforms.

When you're ready, and when you're sure it's safe to go, walk onto the disappearing platforms, then head back to the solid platform.

Make a three-Link Totem with the Gripshot Link on the bottom, then head north up the disappearing platforms on your right. Throw your top two Links onto the landing on the north side of the room, then Gripshot onto either the Links or the fence surrounding the back of the landing.

Proceed to the right end of the landing, then line up the Gripshot and Fire Gloves Links on the right ledge. Use the Gust Jar Link to blow the other two Links across the gap.

Make a Totem with the Fire Gloves Link on top, then light the torch just south of your location. A platform will bridge the gap you just crossed. Head back over to your lone Link.

You'll have to defeat three more colored Poes to progress. The catch is that the three-piece sections of disappearing platforms the Poes are floating around disappear at the same time.

The safest way to deal with this section is to have two Links stay on the solid platforms on the upper-left and bottom-right corners of this area, while the third Link goes after the Poe of his color. (If you're playing single-player, this is the way you have to solve it anyway, of course.)

Once you've defeated all three Poes, another bridge of disappearing platforms will appear below you and the sections of platforms that the Poes were floating over will stay visible permanently. From here you can throw the Gripshot Link onto the ledge to your right to grab the treasure chest, then have him Gripshot back to the other Links.

Now walk to the south end of the bridge and wait for the platform to disappear underneath you. You'll fall onto a row of Rupees and land on the Triforce gateway below. You can hit the orb switch to take a platform back up to the upper levels of the room, if you desire.

Once you're ready, head to the next room.

ROOM 4

This room is monstrous in multiplayer and requires a lot of cooperation; in single-player it's pretty simple. As soon as all three Links drop into the room, a ReDead will appear. These undead creeps may be rotting, but they're not to be taken lightly.

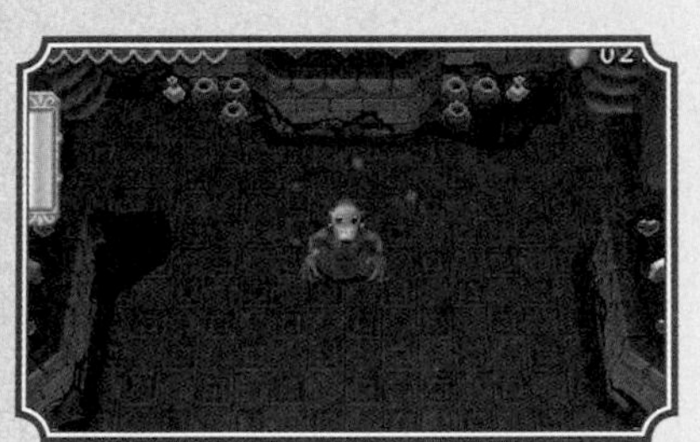

They move incredibly slow—that is until they let out a terrifying, blood-curdling screech, which will stop any Links within its range in their tracks for a limited time.

The ReDead will pick up its pace when it freezes a Link. When the ReDead reaches a Link, it will wrap itself around the Link and begin to drain his health. If you're in single-player, you can just switch to a different Link to get the ReDead to stop coming after your frozen Link, or to let him go. If you're in multiplayer, however, you'll need a friend to hit the ReDead with a Sub-Weapon to get it off of the Link. (Sword slashes take too long, so stunning the ReDead is the best way to stop them from draining your Heart Containers.)

In the same fashion as a Life Like, the ReDead won't stop draining your health until it is knocked off of a Link by another player, so if a Link gets grabbed, immediately race to his aid.

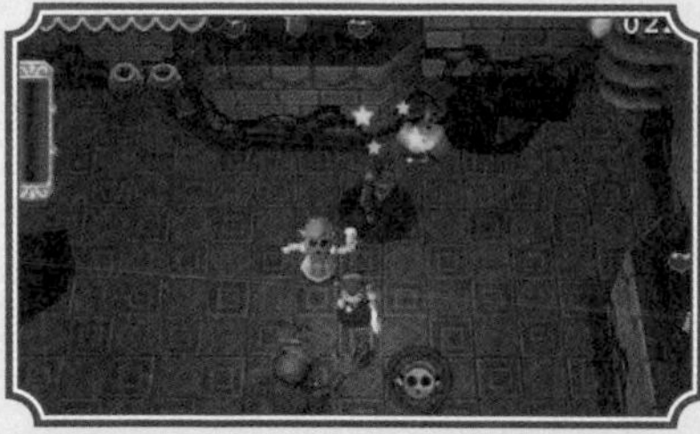

Every time you hit a ReDead, it will dig into the ground and move to another location in the room. When it pops up, if any Links are near, that's when it's most likely to scream, so try and keep your distance from a digging ReDead.

Once you defeat the ReDead, four more will appear and take its place. Focus on one ReDead at a time. The more you lower the number of ReDeads in the room, the easier this fight will get.

Once all the ReDeads have been defeated, a Triforce gateway will appear in the room.

Questing for Outfits

If you have a Carrumpkin from levels 1 or 2, a Spider Silk Lace from level 3, and a Poe Soul from level 3, you can head to Madame Couture's to create the Light Armor. This Outfit creates an aura of light around whatever Link is using it, perfect for lighting dark places. You won't get a lot of use out of it for the remainder of this world, but if you're hoping to complete this world's challenges (and many other challenges), this will help light your path.

Level 4: Grim Temple

Challenges

Fewer Heart Containers

Don't fall at all

Clear within the time limit

Sub-Weapons

 Gripshot

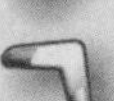 Boomerang

 Fire Gloves

Materials

 Spider Silk Lace

 Spider Silk Lace

 Twisted Twig

Recommended Outfits

 Tingle Tights

 Sword Suit

 Light Armor

The platforming can get a little hairy in this level, which is why we've suggested the Tingle Tights. There are also some pretty challenging fights throughout this stage, so the Sword Suit will help end those sooner rather than later. You can also wear the Light Armor to help see in the dark in the earlier portions of this level. Any choice will do, so pick your poison!

ROOM 1

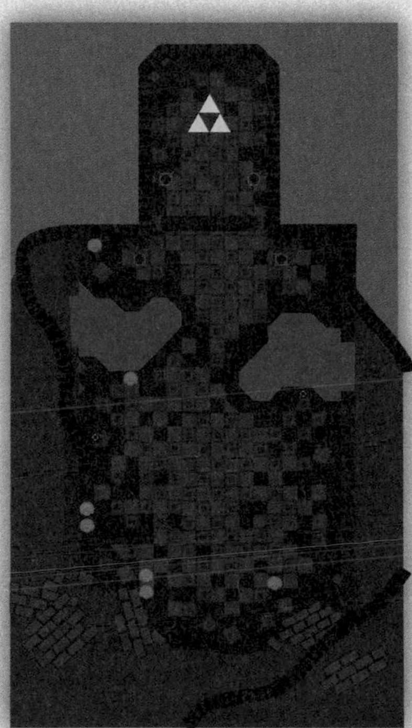

All three Sub-Weapons are directly above your starting location. Grab them, switch to your Fire Gloves Link, and light the torch slightly north of the Sub-Weapons.

To exit the room, you'll need to defeat all of the Stalfos roaming around it. Don't bother swinging at them with your sword, throwing a Boomerang at them, or using your Fire Gloves on them; they'll just jump away, dodge, and avoid most of your attacks. Instead, hit them with the Gripshot to stun them, then hit them once with your sword. Hit them with the Gripshot again, then the sword again. Repeat this process until they have been defeated.

Once you've defeated all the Stalfos, a gate will open on the north side of the room, revealing the Triforce gateway behind it.

ROOM 2

Each Link will start on a different area of the room, but a bridge of disappearing platforms connects all three landings the Links are on. Three colored Poes float around the platforms, and you'll need to defeat each one with the appropriate Link. After you defeat all three, a couple of white Poes will appear. Defeat them to proceed.

Once you've defeated all five Poes, a bridge of disappearing platforms will form north of you. Cross the bridge and hit the orb switch at the end of it.

Another disappearing-platform bridge will appear. You'll need to quickly cross this one before it disappears. Once it does, it won't reappear until you hit the orb switch again.

There's a handful of Gibdos on the other side of the bridge. You'll need to be careful, because the disappearing platforms in the center of this area, well, disappear!

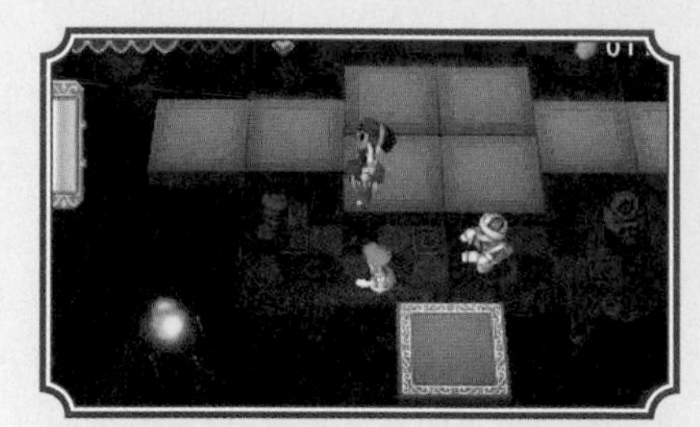

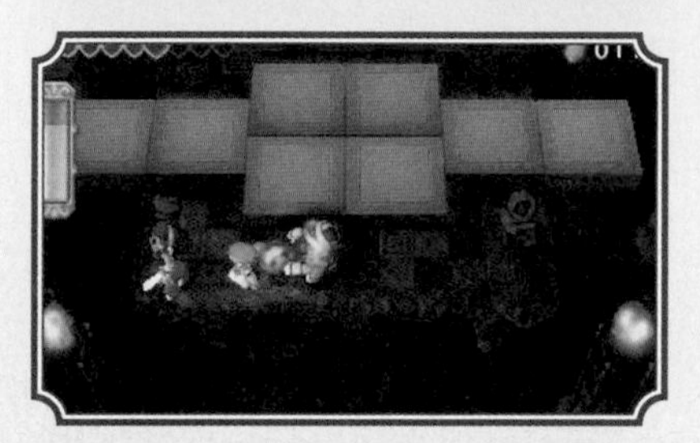

Remember: You can use your Fire Gloves or Gripshot to remove a Gibdo's bandages, making it just a plain ol' Stalfos. Use your Gripshot to stun the Stalfos, hit it with your sword, and repeat to defeat it. You can also use the Gripshot to push the Stalfos off the ledge, provided that you keep hitting it until it finally takes the plunge.

Once all the Gibdos have been defeated, a bridge to the Triforce gateway will form ahead of you.

ROOM 3

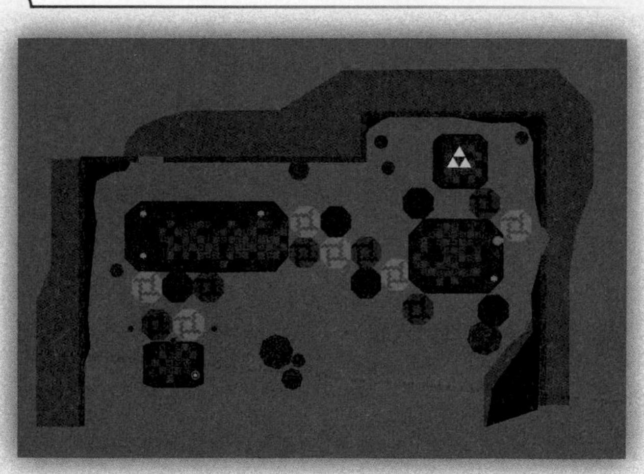

You'll have to deal with more of those colored platforms you tangled with in the first level of this world. These are bit tricky. You'll need to form a Totem with the Boomerang Link on the middle or top, then throw him to the platform that matches his color. Use the Boomerang Link to grab any remaining Links and pull them over to the Boomerang Link's side.

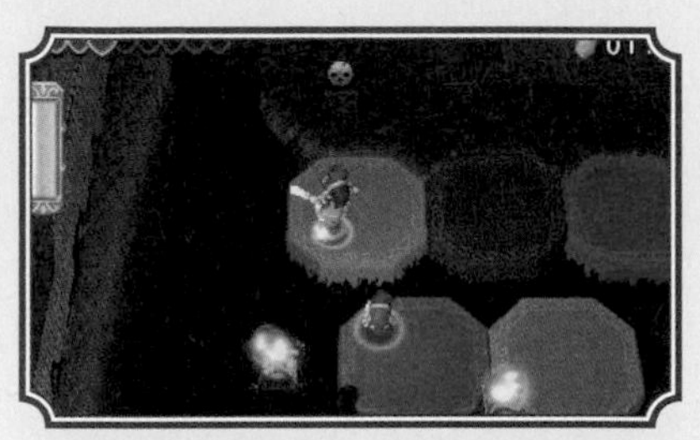

Once all three Links are across the gap, three of those terrible, troublesome Prankster Poes will appear. As a refresher, Prankster Poes will race toward Link and try to throw him off of a ledge. If you slash them, they'll disappear and reappear behind whatever Link did the slashing. You can save a Link that has been grabbed from being tossed into a pit by quickly switching to another Link and slashing the Prankster Poe, or by having a teammate slash it.

Once the Poes have been defeated, more colored platforms will appear on your right and a Squiddy will appear on your left. Show Squiddy how sharp your sword is, then head to the right.

Make a Totem with a green Link on the bottom, red Link in the middle, and blue Link on top. Approach the higher of the two sets of colored platforms, then, one at a time, throw each Link onto their respective platforms ahead.

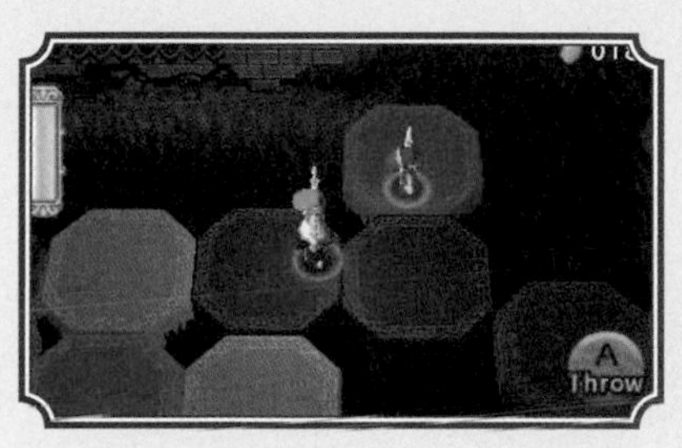

Now have the green Link get to the right edge of his platform and have the red Link come pick him up. Have the red Link approach the right side of his platform, then have the blue Link pick their Totem up.

Wait until a red platform approaches the right side of the platform your Totem is currently on, then throw the red Link and green Link onto it, or throw them onto their own individual platforms. If you're playing single-player, only have one Link do all the fighting; leave the other two Links on their platforms and out of the way for now.

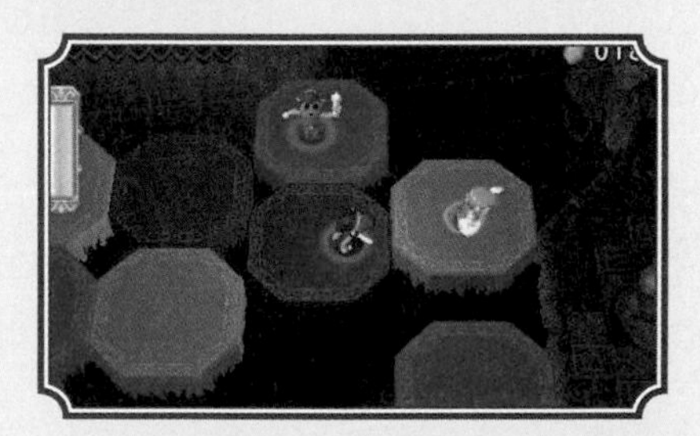

When a blue platform approaches your right, hop on it with the blue Link and get ready for another ReDead fight—this time on a very small landing.

The easiest way to deal with the ReDeads is to use your Sub-Weapon to slowly push them off of the edge of the landing. Don't bother using your sword at all, because a single slash will break a ReDead's daze, allowing it to immediately counter-attack with one of its paralyzing screams.

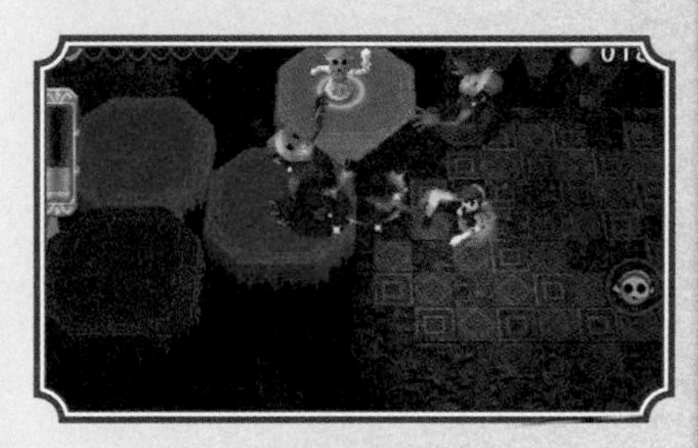

As a reminder, if a ReDead stuns you in single-player, immediately switch to a different Link to get it off of you. If one of your teammates in multiplayer is being eaten, you'll need to quickly hit the ReDead doing the eating with a Sub-Weapon.

Once the ReDeads have been defeated, the Triforce gateway will appear on the north side of the room. Make a Totem, wait for the appropriate colored platform to come your way, and then cross to the north side of the room.

ROOM 4

BOSS FIGHT: PRISMANTUS

Cut the bushes and break the skulls ahead of you to try to refill your health. You're going to need it, because you're about to face the Grim Temple's boss.

This boss isn't terribly complicated, but it can run your Heart Containers down pretty easily if you're not careful. Each of its three limbs have a colored orb at the end of it. You'll need to use the Link with the matching color to hit each orb twice.

Prismantus has two speeds during this phase: Spin fast and spin faster. If you see Prismantus start spinning faster, that means it's about to spin your way. Hitting its orb while it's spinning at this speed is not wise. Instead, wait for it to slow its speed a bit before trying to attack its orbs.

Every time you hit an orb twice, that orb will darken. Once you've darkened all three orbs, Prismantus will be momentarily stunned. Grab a Link and throw him on top of one of Prismantus's limbs. Now have the Link slash away at its eyeball to damage it.

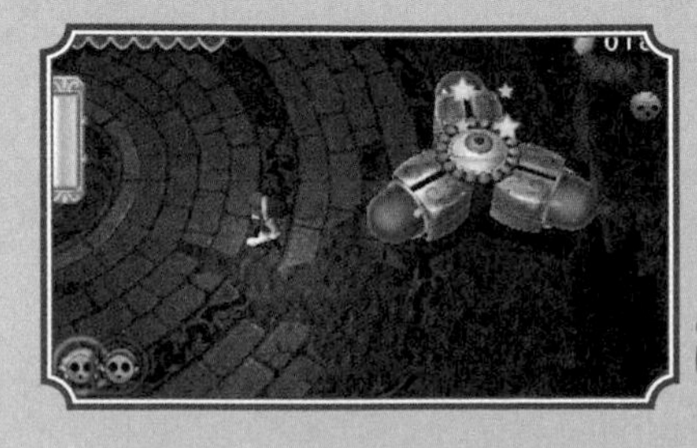

After hitting Prismantus's eye a handful of times, it will knock Link off of it and turn upright. Now hitting the orbs at the ends of its limbs is tougher. You can slash the orbs as it rolls around the room, but you'll have to be careful not to get crushed by them.

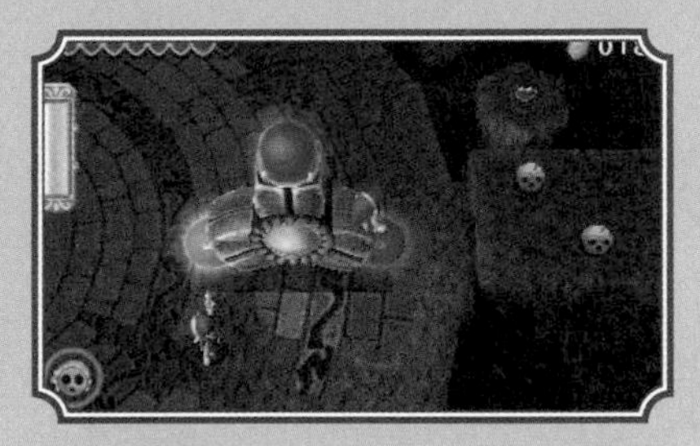

Prismantus will eventually come to a stop momentarily. This will give you a chance to slash its orbs. To reach the top one, you'll need to make a three-Link Totem with the Link of the right color on top.

Once you've deactivated all three orbs, Prismantus will fall over stunned once again. Throw a Link on top of it and go to town on its eyeball.

After a few more hits, Prismantus will stand upright once again, but this time it will only be on one of its limbs. You'll want to stay as close to Prismantus's back as possible at all times during this phase. It will move much faster when it marches around the room. When it comes to a stop, it will shoot out a giant laser beam from its eye and will spin around the room slowly while doing it.

It's incredibly difficult to hit Prismantus's orbs while it's marching during this phase of the fight. Your best bet is to wait until it holds still, make a three-Link Totem, and then attack the orbs one by one.

Once all three orbs have been put out again, Prismantus will fall to the ground, stunned once more. Throw a Link onto it and have him slash away at its eyeball. A few more hits and Prismantus will be finished!

Questing for Outfits

If you're willing to wrangle an Ice Rose from world 4's challenge levels and, from this world, a Carrumpkin from levels 1 or 2, a Mystery Extract from levels 1 or 3, a Poe Soul from level 3, and a Twisted Twig from level 4, you can take them to Madame Couture to have her make the Serpent's Toga.

The Serpent's Toga turns you into a statue while you are motionless, meaning you can't take damage. This is an excellent Outfit for just about any level.

WORLD 8: SKY REALM

Level 1: Floating Garden

Challenges

Win without using a sword

Evade the Wallmaster

Don't fall at all

Sub-Weapons

Bow

Bombs

Gripshot

Materials

Cucco Feathers

Cucco Feathers

Carmine Pearl

Recommended Outfits

Tingle Tights

Sword Suit

Legendary Dress

This level, and every other level in this world, is very challenging. Everything you've learned up to this point will be put to the test and you'll even have plenty of new challenges thrown your way.

The Tingle Tights will help a lot in this level, because there are plenty of places to fall from and plenty of puzzles that have you dangling over pits and endless drops. There are also plenty of really challenging enemies to face in this level, so the Sword Suit is quite handy. To round it off, the Legendary Dress will keep your health as full as possible when everything else is trying to deplete it.

ROOM 1

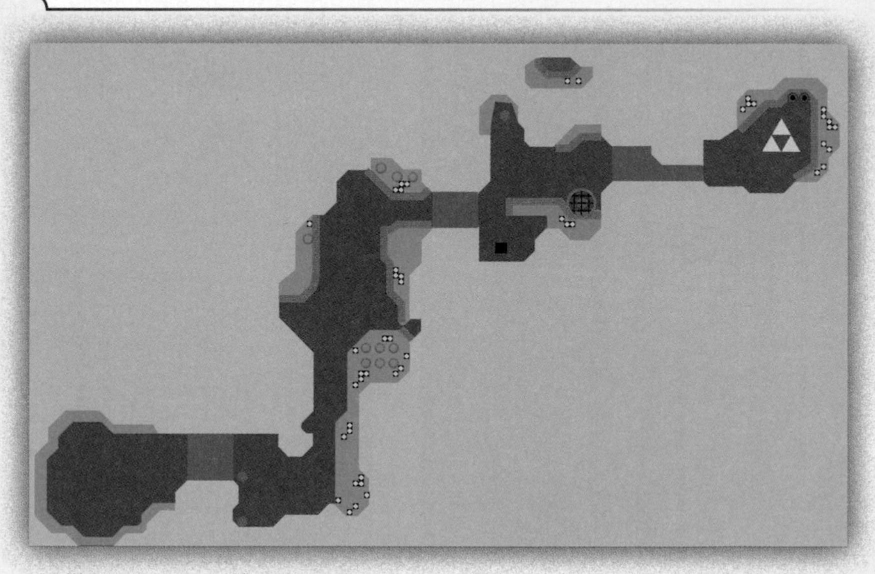

You'll have to contend with strong winds in this level. The winds will gladly try to blow you off of any surface you're standing on if you get in their path.

You'll need to hit the two orb switches across the gap ahead in order to reach the landing on the other side. You need to shoot both switches with the Bow, but the wind will make your arrows fly at a curve. To hit both switches, stand in the positions illustrated in the following screenshots, then fire.

When both switches have been hit, a bridge will extend from the right landing and you'll be able to cross. Just be careful while you do. The wind will knock you off that bridge faster than you can say, "I should've worn Tingle Tights!"

Head up the path and defeat the two Soldiers ahead. Throwing the Bomb Link on the elevated landing to your right and having him throw Bombs at the Soldiers is a slow, but easy way of taking them out without any real hassle. You can also use the Gripshot to rip the Soldiers' shields away, making it harder for them to deflect your attacks.

Life Like Ahead!

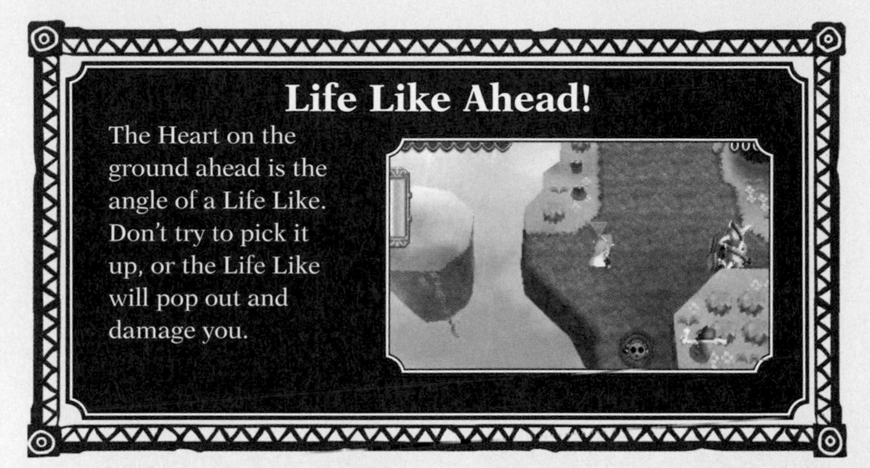

The Heart on the ground ahead is the angle of a Life Like. Don't try to pick it up, or the Life Like will pop out and damage you.

Once the Soldiers have been defeated, make a three-Link Totem with the Gripshot Link on top. Throw the top two Links onto the elevated platform to the right.

Now have the Gripshot Link hook onto the peg to your right to pull himself to the island on your right.

You'll need to position your Gripshot Link near the orb switch on the top-left corner of the island. Now switch to your Bomb Link and have him throw a Bomb near the edge of his island. Quickly switch back to the Gripshot Link, grab the Bomb, and throw it near the orb switch on the top-left corner of the island to extend a bridge for the other Links to cross.

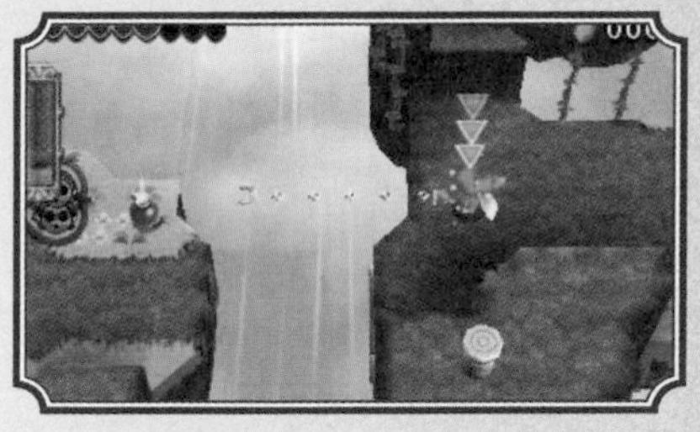

Move the other Links across the bridge onto the island on the right. You'll need to activate the orb switch under the grate on the lower-right side of the island, but strong winds blowing over the grate will push your Bombs off the island. You'll have to throw your Bomb above the grate and let the wind slide it over the grate. You can also wait for the Bomb to nearly explode, then throw the Bomb toward the grate and activate it that way, but you're more likely to blow yourself up in the process. Regardless, the choice on how to handle the switch is yours.

Once you activate the orb switch, a bridge will extend from the island on the right to your island. You now can reach the Triforce gateway on the other island.

ROOM 2

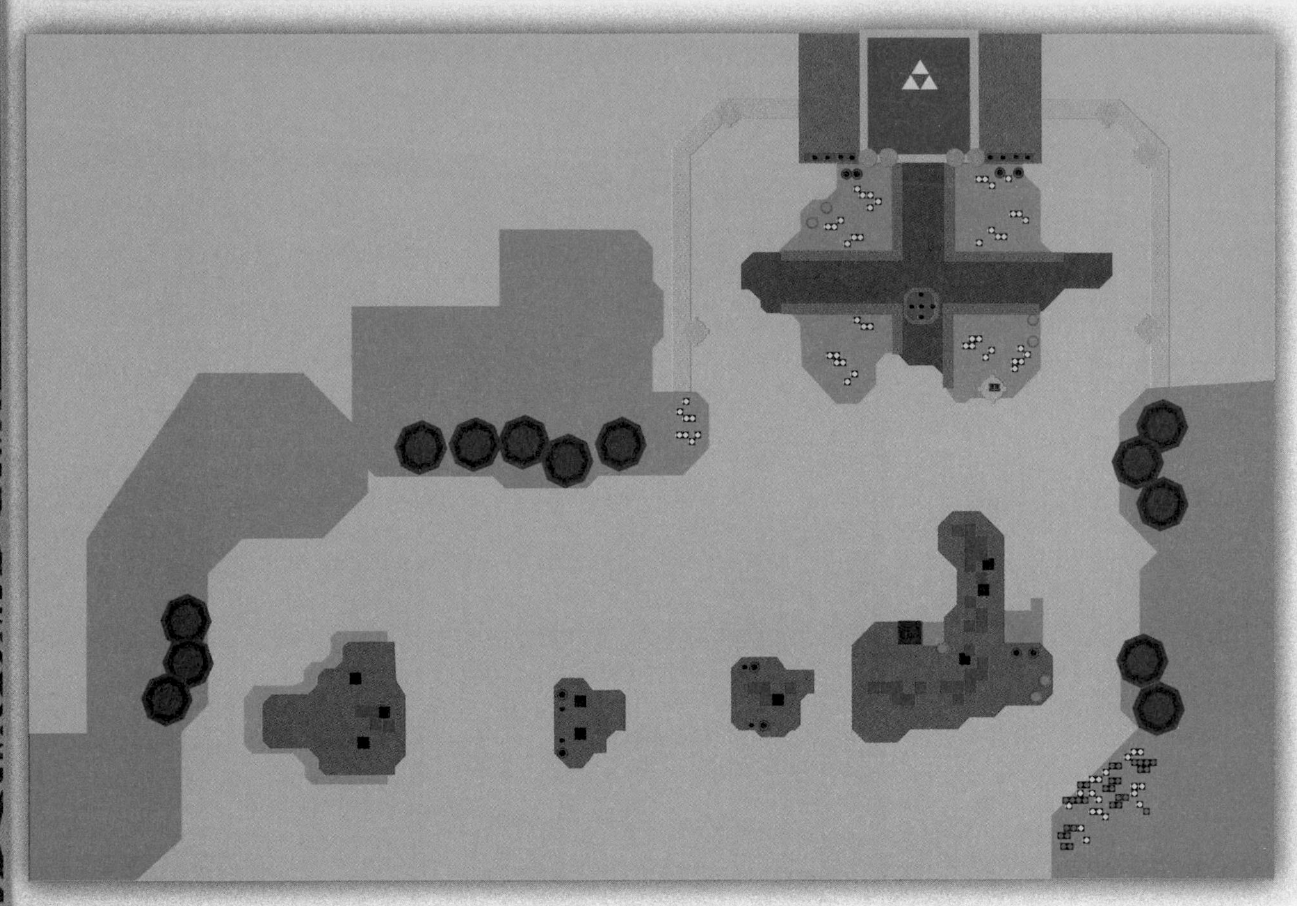

This room is a blast. You'll need to pick up one of the chicken-like Cuccos, make a three-Link Totem with the Cucco-holding Link on top, and then jump off the right side of the island.

Jump from island to island until you land on the large island with the stone structures.

Ride up the gold platform to reach the top-left structure, then jump to the right to reach the other structure. Head to the northern tip of the structure, then jump north.

If you angle your flight path slightly to the left, you can land on a pillar on the northern island that has a treasure chest on top of it.

When all three Links land on the northern island, new enemies called Helmasaurs will appear. These enemies are rough. The helmets on their heads will defeat any slash with your sword and they'll chase you for a good long while. You'll need to slash them from behind, throw Bombs at them from a distance, or, the easiest method, Gripshot their helmets off. Once the helmet has been removed, you can attack any part of their body without bouncing off.

Once you defeat all of the Helmasaurs, the doors on the north side of the room will open and you'll be able to reach the Triforce gateway.

ROOM 3

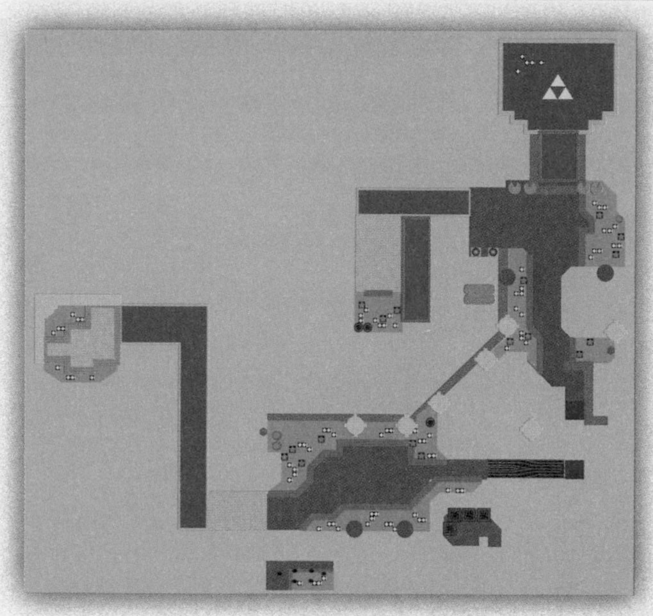

You'll have to shoot another arrow through a wind tunnel and hit an orb switch here. This one is far trickier than the first two. Make a two-Link Totem with the Bow Link on top. Walk out onto the pathway the wind is blowing on and fire your Bow to the right, just as you reach the line between the third and fourth gold tiles on the pathway. (Use the following screenshot to see where to position yourself.)

After you hit the switch, a stairway appears on the southern side of the pathway. Cross it to reach the island on your right and Squiddy: The magical, floating piggy bank!

Head to the right side of the island and you'll see a group of cracked blocks and a couple of Cuccos south of you. Use the Bomb Link to blow up the cracked blocks, then throw a Link up to the Cuccos. Have that Link grab one of them, then approach the right edge of the landing he's standing on.

You need to time your jump so that you can land on the gold platform to the northeast while it's at the south end of its path. If you try to fly to the northern island outright, you'll fall for sure.

Once you land on the gold platform, let it take you to the northern island. When you reach the northern island, hit the orb switch ahead to create a bridge that will allow your other Links to reach the gold platform.

You'll have to take out two more Sky Shield Soldiers up ahead. Use Bombs or pull away their shields with the Gripshot to make this fight as painless as possible.

This next part is tough. Really tough! You'll need to have the Bow and Bomb Links stand on the pressure switches on the left. This will extend out a bridge and retract the housing surrounding the key you need to open the northern gate.

Now have the Gripshot Link stand in the wind tunnel and face right. As soon as you reach the second-to-last gold tile on the platform, fire your Gripshot to the right, then immediately hold Up on the Analog Stick. If your timing was right, you'll have the key in hand. If not, try and try again. This is a very challenging room, so don't lose heart if you struggle to get the key.

Once you have the key, walk it back to the northern gate to open it and reach the Triforce gateway.

ROOM 4

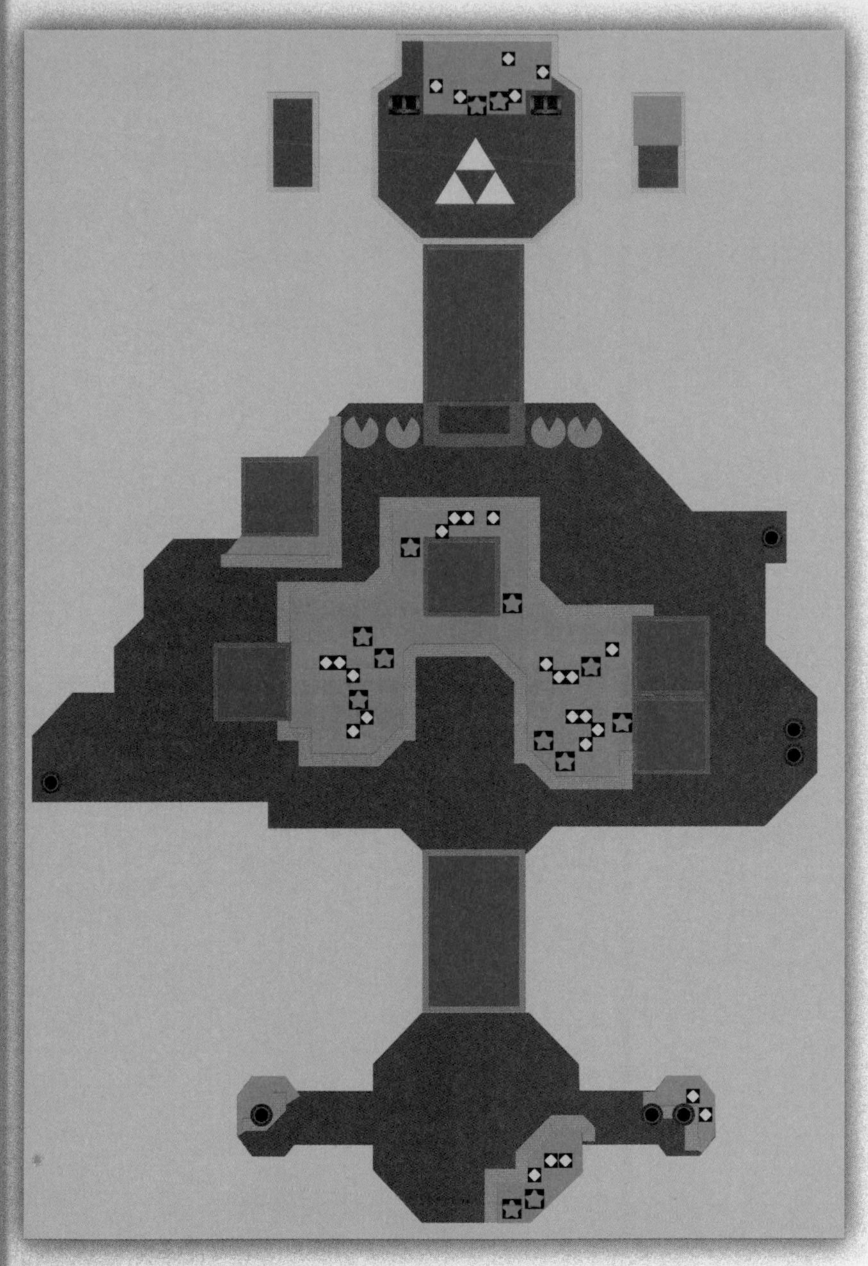

You'll need to use your Bow to take out the Fire Keeleons since you don't have a Gust Jar to put their flames out. Just keep your distance, make a Totem, and shoot them with your Bow to take them out.

Unfortunately, once you take out the first wave of Helmasaurs and Keeleons, another wave will appear and, to make matters worse, all of the elevated platforms will lower until they fall off the island entirely.

Use the same strategies you just used to defeat this wave of enemies. Once you defeat them, the northern doors will open and you'll be able to reach some treasure and the Triforce gateway.

This is another combat room—a particularly challenging one, if we do say so ourselves. You'll have to defeat Helmasaurs and Fire Keeleons, which is no small task. Your best bet is to lure the Helmasaurs away from the Fire Keeleons, then pull their helmets off and defeat them one at a time. Things can get pretty hectic with the Helmasaurs charging at you and the Fire Keeleon spitting fireballs in your direction.

Level 2: Deception Castle

Challenges

Clear within the time limit

Don't fall at all

Don't pop any balloons

Sub-Weapons

 Gripshot

 Gripshot

 Gust Jar

Materials

 Cucco Feathers

 Cucco Feathers

 Sky Dragon Tail

Recommended Outfits

 Tingle Tights

 Legendary Dress

This level is grueling. You'll have to contend with more balancing platforms, but these are significantly tougher. That's why we suggest you wear the Tingle Tights or the Legendary Dress. You'll need all the Hearts you can get!

ROOM 1

You'll have to do some fighting with a couple of Totem Armos-riding Soldiers while standing in a giant wind tunnel. Yup, you read that correctly. Before you drop down, make a two-Link Totem—it'll save you the hassle of trying to create one while in the wind tunnel. Now drop into the room on your left with your Totem and leave the other Link behind.

Immediately go for the shorter of the two Armos riders and defeat it swiftly. Now head to the top of the room, switch to your lone Link and have him race to the Totem Links and pick them up. Now attack the other Soldier to get the wind to stop blowing and to open a door on the upper-right corner of the room.

There are three pressure switches in this area, and all of them need a Link firmly planted on them. Have one of the two Gripshot Links shoot the fence ahead, then have the Gust Jar Link blast him to the pathway on the north side of the area.

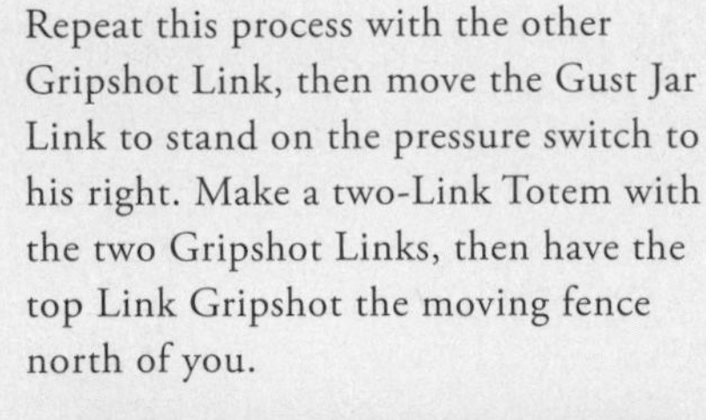

Repeat this process with the other Gripshot Link, then move the Gust Jar Link to stand on the pressure switch to his right. Make a two-Link Totem with the two Gripshot Links, then have the top Link Gripshot the moving fence north of you.

Next, drop that Gripshot Link off of the fence onto the landing to the right and move all three Links to stand on their respective pressure switches. Platforms will bridge the gaps between all three Links and give you access to the Triforce gateway.

ROOM 2

You can easily use the Gust Jar to blast the Bombs off of the Bomb Flower and into the Ball & Chain Soldier's balcony. It'll keep you much safer than trying to throw Bombs onto its balcony.

To take out the west Soldier, pick up the Bombs the north Soldier throws at you and then throw them at the west Soldier.

Once you've defeated the east and west Soldiers, make a three-Link Totem and either Gust Jar the Bomb Flower in front of the north Soldier into its balcony, or Gripshot the Bomb Flower and throw the Bomb next to it.

After defeating all three Soldiers, a Triforce gateway will appear in the center of the spinning platform.

Head to the right, jump on the wind turbine, and float your way to the spinning platform ahead. Once all three Links are on the platform, three Soldiers will appear in the balconies on the north, east, and west sides of the room, while a Vulture flies around in the spinning platform in the center of the room.

You'll need to use the Bomb Flowers lining the room and get their Bombs onto each Soldier's balcony. Your best bet is to focus on one Soldier at a time. Save the Soldier on the north side of the room for last and focus on the east and west Soldiers first.

If you decide to tackle the east Soldier first, only ever get close enough to it to throw a Bomb onto its balcony. It's a Sky Ball & Chain Soldier, and it will gladly hit you with its weapon if you get too close. After it spins the ball and chain over its head a few times, it'll try to throw it at you and pull it away twice. If you stand behind the dark outer ring of the spinning platform, the Soldier's ball and chain won't be able to reach you.

ROOM 3

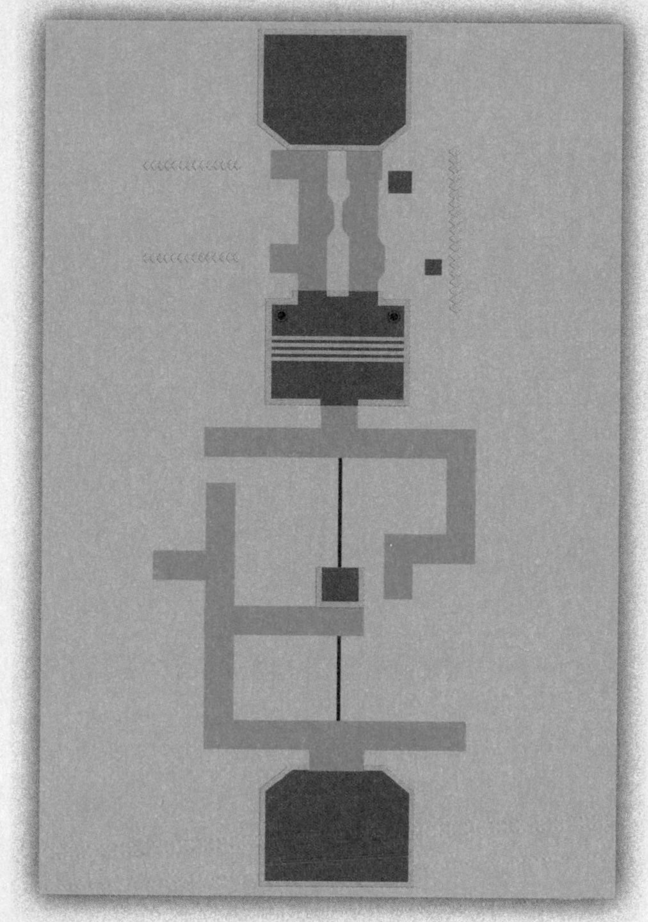

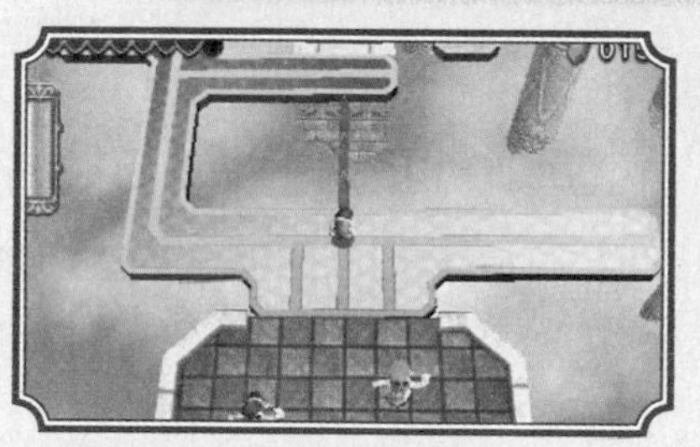

We've got bad news: This room has balancing platforms for you to walk across and they're tougher than the ones you did in world 6. We weren't joking when we said this world puts everything you've learned to practice. Don't worry. We're going to try and make this as painless as possible!

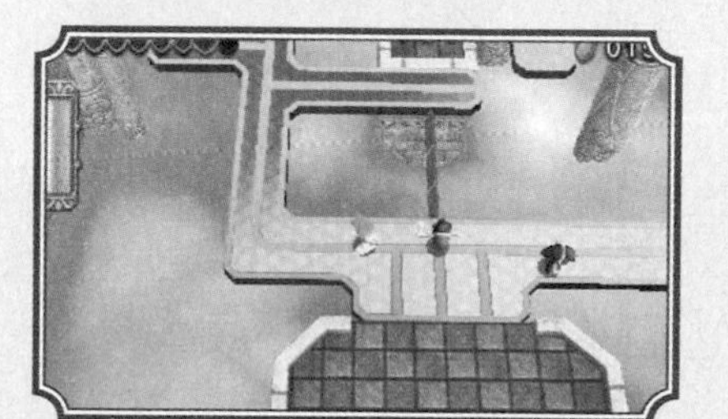

Have a Gripshot Link stand just below the balancing rod that is visible between the north and south sides of the platform.

Now have the other two Links make a Totem, and be sure to have the remaining Gripshot Link on top. Quickly throw the top Link onto the right side of the platform while you move the bottom Link to the left.

That platform should remain balanced while the left Link makes his way north to the center landing.

Quickly have the Gripshot Link on the right side of the platform approach the center of the platform (where the other Gripshot Link is) and Gripshot the northern Link.

Now have the Gripshot Link that is standing below the balancing rod Gripshot north to rejoin his cohorts. This is where things get extra hairy.

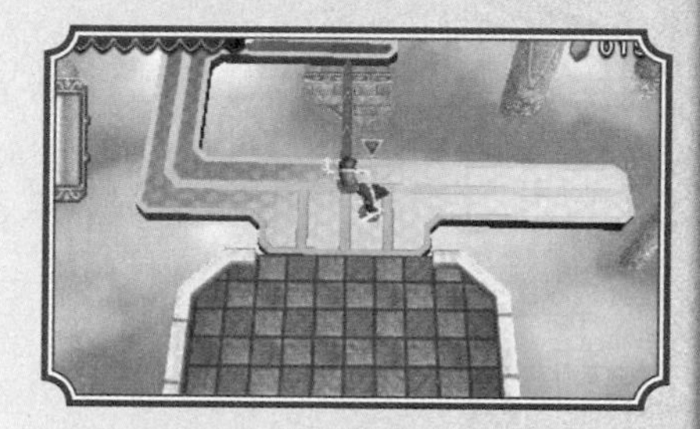

Have a Gripshot Link wait on the landing while you make a Totem with the Gust Jar Link on top. You'll need to be very quick with this next part. Throw the Gust Jar Link onto the segmented part of the platform to your right, then immediately race to counterbalance the platform by setting the other Link on the lower left side of the platform.

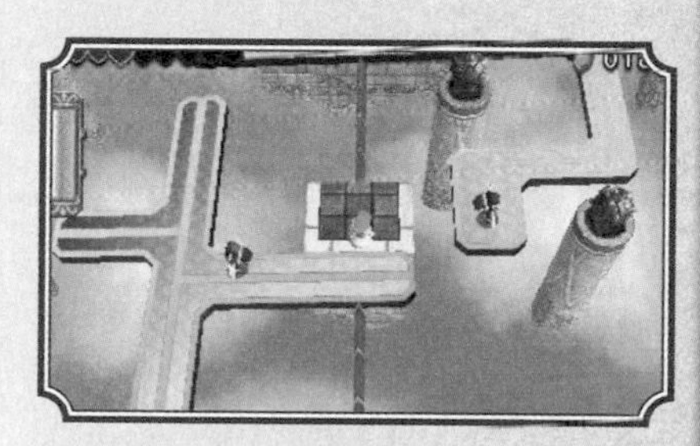

Quickly run the Gust Jar Link up to the north-center end of the platform, then switch to the Link on the left and have him make his way back to the center landing.

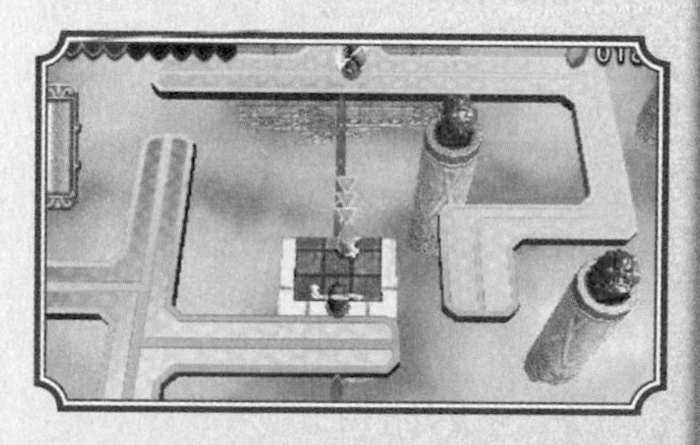

Have the two Gripshot Links hook onto the Gust Jar Link to get across to the other side. The worst is mostly over. You have one more balancing platform to contend with in this area, but it's not as bad as the one you just crossed.

You'll have to destroy four Mini-Margos scattered on the left and right sides of the room and you'll have to do it without falling off of the balancing platform. Have the Gripshot Link grab the other Gripshot Link to make a Totem, then step on the right side of the platform and throw the top Link to the left side.

You'll be able to make minor adjustments while on this platform by adjusting the Links on either side. For now, face the left Link to the left, then have the right Link Gripshot the Bomb Flower on the right.

Now throw the Bomb over to the left Link and have the left Link throw the Bomb into the center of the Mini-Margo ahead. The Mini-Margo should be destroyed now, but there are still three left! Move your left Link north up the platform and have him face left toward the next Mini-Margo. Make sure to leave the right Link where he is.

Have the right Link Gripshot a Bomb and throw it diagonally to the left Link. You can also have the right Link run up the platform and throw the Bomb to the Link that way, but you'll reduce the amount of time you have before the Bomb explodes.

Have the left Link throw the Bomb into the Mini-Margo's center, then have the left and right Links move back to the south.

Now have the Gust Jar Link pick up another Link, walk onto the right side of the platform, and immediately throw the top Link to the left.

Move the Gust Jar Link north and line him up with the northern Bomb Flower. Have him blast the Bomb Flower with his Gust Jar into each Mini-Margo as it lines up with the Bomb Flower.

It might take a few tries, but keep at it! Both Mini-Margos can be destroyed with this Bomb Flower. When the last two Mini-Margos are destroyed, a key will fall onto the scale near the center of the balancing platform. Leave the key where it is! It's important that you don't Gripshot the key, or you'll make this next part more challenging for yourself.

You'll need to be quick with this next part. Have the Gripshot Link that is on the south landing Gripshot to the Gust Jar Link, then have the Gripshot Link throw the Gust Jar Link to the northern landing. Leave the Gust Jar Link where he is—you'll need him in a moment.

Have the left Gripshot Link hook onto the right Gripshot Link, pick him up, and throw him up with the Gust Jar Link. Immediately have the lone Link Gripshot hook onto either Link on the northern landing to get him to safety. All three Links should now safely be on the landing.

Gripshot the key to pull it up to you, then open the locked gate with it. The Triforce gateway is behind the gate.

ROOM 4

BOSS FIGHT: GIGALEON

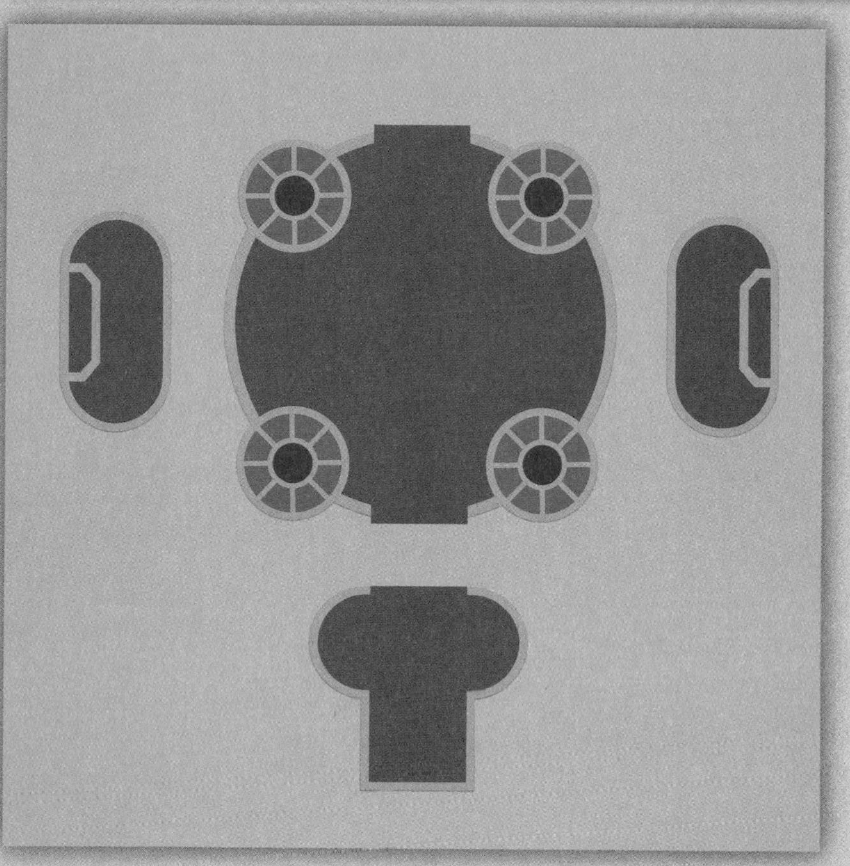

Break any pots you see to refill your health. As soon as all three Links enter the center of the room, the massive Keeleon, Gigaleon, will enter the room.

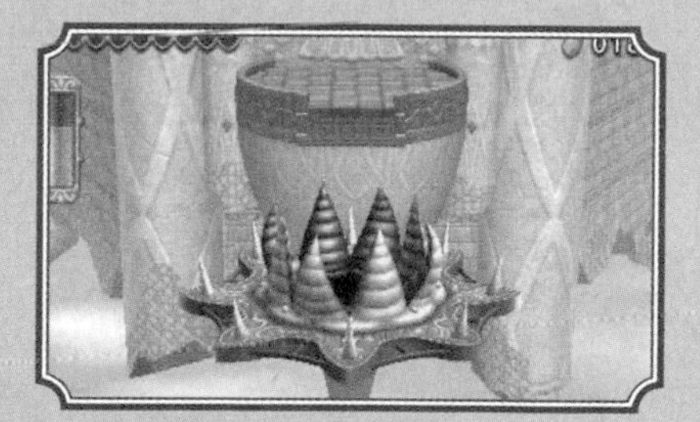

Gigaleon seems tough, but it's actually pretty easy to beat. It'll spit fire at you while it's in the air, but the fire isn't too hard to dodge.

Use the Gust Jar Link on the turbines in the four corners of the room as Gigaleon passes them. If you activate one while Gigaleon is above it, it'll stun the gigantic Keeleon.

Now quickly switch to a Gripshot Link, Gripshot a Bomb from the Bomb Flowers nearest you, and then throw it onto the turbine. Repeat this process to move Gigaleon into its next phase.

After throwing a few Bombs at Gigaleon, it'll destroy the two platforms that the Bomb Flowers are on. You'll have to do this the old-fashioned way: With your sword. Gigaleon will flip, exposing its eye. It'll move faster now and shoot out a lot more fire, so be on your guard.

Switch back to your Gust Jar Link and activate the turbines as Gigaleon passes over them to stun it again. Now throw a Link onto the turbine and it will lift that Link on top of Gigaleon. Now slash away on Gigaleon's eyeball to damage it.

After repeating this process a few times, Gigaleon will fall to the ground. Hit it with your sword like you're talking with Squiddy and you'll ground Gigaleon for good.

A bridge of wind turbines will appear in the north side of the room. Cross it to reach the Triforce gateway.

Level 3: Dragon Citadel

Challenges

Avoid the volcanic rocks

Halved attack and defense

Don't fall at all

Sub-Weapons

Water Rod

Boomerang

Magic Hammer

Materials

Carmine Pearl

Carmine Pearl

Pretty Plume

Recommended Outfits

Hammerwear

Sword Suit

Tingle Tights

Legendary Dress

This is likely the longest level in the game, and it's quite a challenge. There are plenty of tough enemies in it, which is why we suggest Hammerwear, at least for whichever Link grabs the Hammer. The Magic Hammer in the hands of a Hammerwear-wearing Link is a force of nature. Very few enemies can survive a direct hit from a Hammerwear Link's giant Hammer.

The other Links can either wear the Sword Suit for added damage or Tingle Tights if you struggle with narrow platforms and wind tunnels. It also wouldn't be a bad idea to bring the Legendary Dress along to keep your Heart Containers full. Whatever you choose, be ready for one of the toughest levels in the game.

ROOM 1

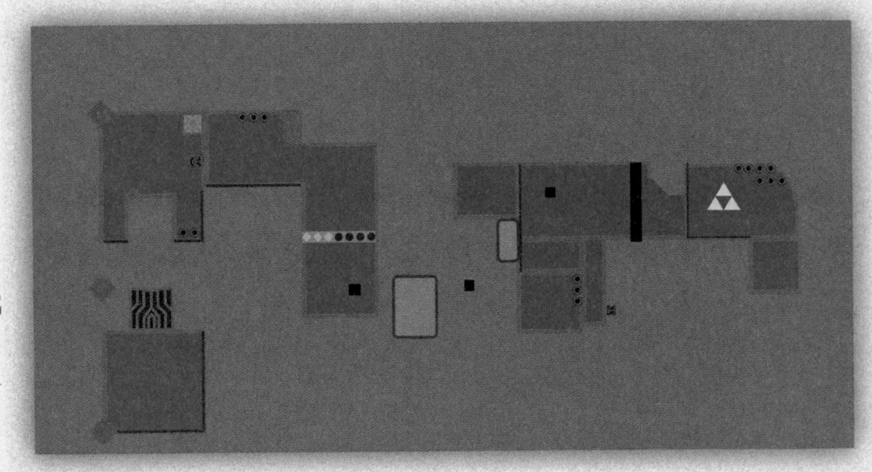

Have all three Links stand on the blue platform ahead, then slash the orb switch to activate the platform. The platform will take you up to the Sub-Weapons for this level.

Grab the Sub-Weapons, make a three-Link Totem with the Hammer Link on top, and then smash the spring platform to your right. Have the Totem walk onto the spring platform and wait for it to launch you up to the upper landing. Now hit the switch in the upper-right corner of the landing to open the gold gate on your right.

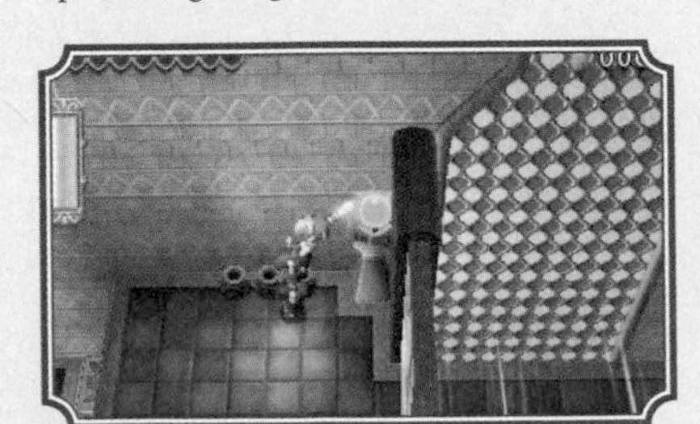

This will also activate a moving platform to your left, which will allow you to reach the blue Rupees on the ledge above.

Step into the wind tunnel to your right and let it push you against the yellow wall. Throw the top two Links north so that the wind pushes them back against the yellow wall.

Have the lone Link hit the color orb below you to raise the purple wall, then grab your Totem as it slides south.

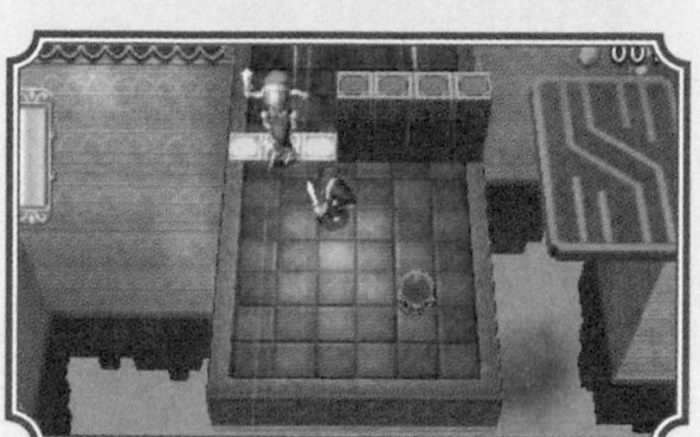

Throw the top two Links onto the golden moving platform to your right (making sure that your Boomerang is one of the top two Links), then use the Boomerang Link to pull the lone Link onto the golden platform as well.

Use the Boomerang Link to hit one of the color orbs on your left or right to raise the yellow wall again. This will block a wind tunnel to your right, which will allow you safely throw Links onto the landing on your right.

Make a three-Link Totem with the Boomerang Link in either the middle or the top position, then throw the top two Links onto the upper-right landing. Boomerang the lone Link off of the golden platform.

Make another three-Link Totem, this time with the Hammer Link on top, walk onto the small golden platform south of you, and ride the platform to the south landing.

Have your Boomerang Link hit the color orb on your left again. This will raise another colored wall at the top of the north set of landings, which will make it easier to climb.

Make another three-Link Totem, but this time have the Water Rod Link on top. Have the Water Rod Link create water pillars up the landings until you reach the top.

You can reach a treasure chest near the south end of this landing. Just have a Link slide down via wind power to the south tip of the landing and grab the treasure chest.

Take the Hammer Link to the right and smash down the pegs. Have all three Links cross the broken pathway on your right to reach a three-man pressure switch. Activate the switch to reach the Triforce gateway.

ROOM 2

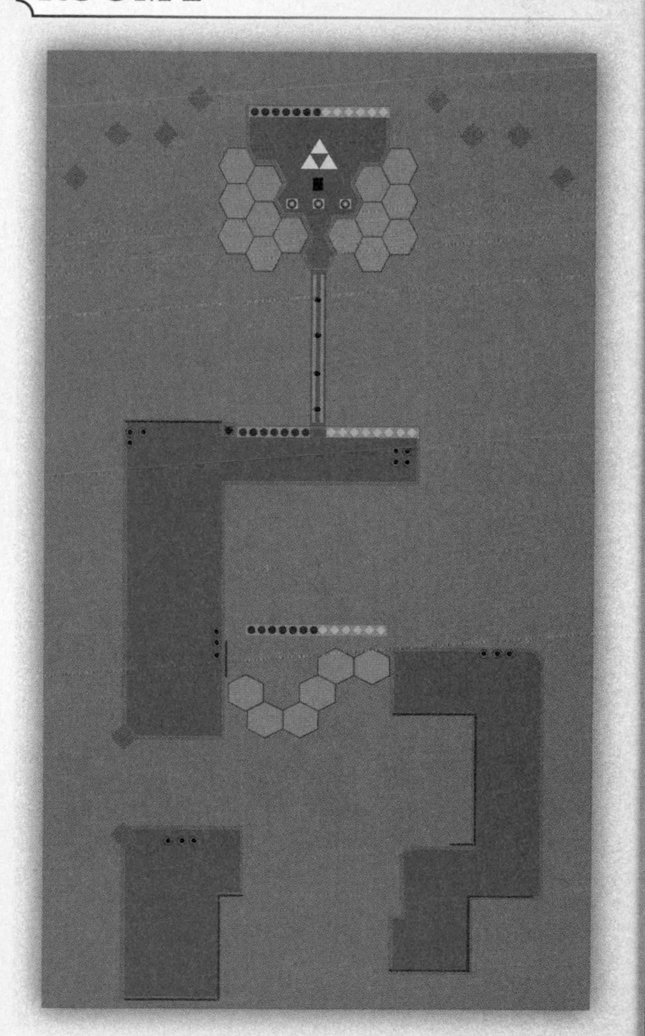

Unfortunately, this next area has disappearing platforms AND a wind tunnel blowing over it. It's not as difficult as it sounds though. It's like every wind tunnel you've done up to this point—you just need to wait until the platforms are reappearing on your side of the area before trying to cross them.

If you're feeling confident, you can make a three-Link Totem and cross with all three Links at the same time. If you're nervous about falling, however, you can just take it one Link at a time.

A Smashing Good Time!

The Hammer is a particularly effective tool against Soldiers. If you're having a hard time fighting any of the Soldiers in this level, have your Hammer Link deal out some swift justice. It'll save you Hearts and time in the long run.

Once you're on solid ground again, head north and defeat the Soldier ahead. This next part can get a bit tricky. You have to walk along platforms that look an awful lot like ice sheets while a wind tunnel tries to push you off of them. If you stand on these sheets for too long, they'll break beneath your feet.

This is about as difficult as crossing the invisible platforms a moment ago. There's a color orb switch that you can use to change where the wind is blowing, but don't hit it! It'll make things a lot harder if the wind is blowing on the first half of the platforms rather than the second half.

Either make a three-Link Totem and cross the platforms like you did with the invisible platforms, or take it one Link at a time. Once you reach the other side, you'll find our good friend Squiddy. Extort Squiddy for all it's worth, then head north.

You'll find two more Soldiers on the north end of the corridor. Defeat them, then hit the color orb to switch it to purple. Make a three-Link Totem and head up the narrow pathway to your right.

There are three pressure switches and another wind tunnel here. This may seem tricky at first glance, but it's pretty simple. Just have two Links stand on the two pressure switches that are not in the wind tunnel, then have the third Link step on the final switch.

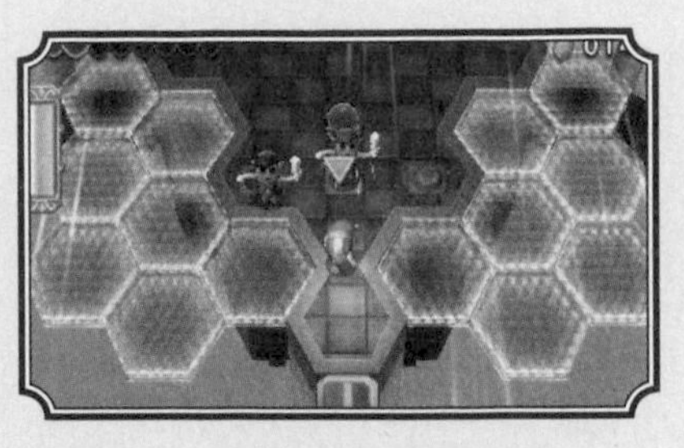

As soon as you hit all three switches, four Ice Wizzrobes will appear. This fight can get pretty mean if you're not extremely careful. You'll need to use the color orb to switch where the wind is blowing, but you'll also need to keep track of where your other Links are. If you hit the color orb while your other Links are behind the wall that lowers, they'll get blown off the edge and you'll take damage. You'll also have to be extremely careful not to get frozen by the ice waves from the Wizzrobes. Depending on where you are on the platform, you'll likely be pushed off a ledge by the wind while frozen, meaning you take two Hearts of damage for every one ice wave that hits you.

You can make this a lot easier on yourself by positioning the two Links you're not controlling directly in front of the color orb. They'll be safe from the wind's effects here, meaning you won't have to worry about them getting blown off the edge.

Once you defeat the four Wizzrobes, a Triforce gateway will appear on the north side of the platform.

ROOM 3

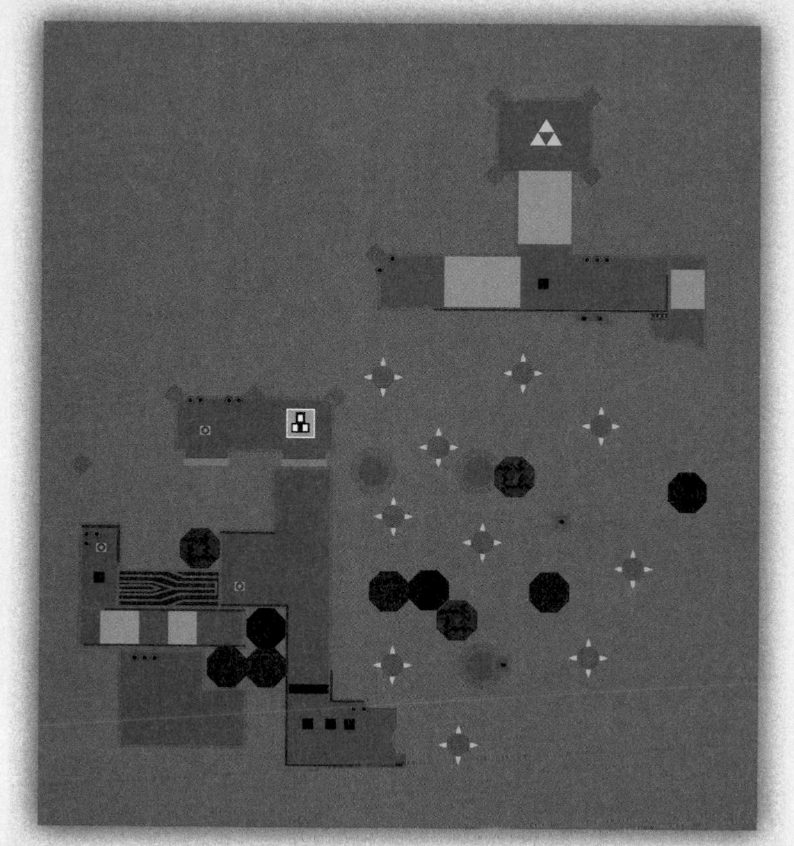

Defeat the Soldiers in the area, then switch to the Boomerang Link and target the orb switch on the north wall ahead.

Switch to the Hammer Link, head south, smash the pegs, grab a Cucco, and go back to your other Links. Jump off the ledge to your left and fly through the passage on the north wall. Stand on the pressure switch to open the door on the right. Now have all three Links stand on the three-man pressure switch to activate the wind turbines on the east side of the room.

Head south back to the Cuccos. This next part is a bit tricky. You'll need to grab a Cucco, then jump off the ledge and use the wind turbines to propel yourself higher into the air. That part is actually pretty straightforward. If you take your time to look ahead and figure out where the next wind turbines and platforms are, you shouldn't have too much trouble with it. The challenge comes from the platforms you need to land on. They are colored, meaning only specific Links can land on each one.

The platforms ahead are colored platforms, so don't accidentally walk onto them with the wrong Link if you want to avoid taking damage. Make a three-Link Totem with the red Link on the bottom and the green Link in the middle. As soon as the red platform meets the green platform, throw the green Link onto the green platform. Now have the green Link pick up the Totem and carry all three Links onto the landing to the left of the green platform.

Head up the stairs and hit the pressure switch at the end of the path. A blue-colored platform will appear. You'll need to get the Hammer Link to the other side of the gap. To do that, if your Hammer Link doesn't match the color of the platform, you'll need to have the Hammer Link grab the nearby Cucco, then have the blue Link pick up the Hammer Link and jump off the ledge toward the blue platform.

Throw the Hammer Link over the short pegs on your right, or if the Hammer Link is blue, have him smash the pegs right then and there. Now hit the pressure switch just below you to create a bridge across the gap. Make a two-Link Totem with the Hammer Link on top and smash down the tall pegs to let all three Links pass unimpeded.

Your goal is to head to the north side of the area. There are Rupees scattered around the area, but you'd be better off ignoring them. Trying to go for the Rupees is what will do the most damage to you. Take it one Link at a time and just go straight for the north side of the room.

Hop off the landing toward the first wind turbine.

Now float over to one of the platforms ahead, taking care to only land on one that matches your current Link's color. Now float to the wind turbine directly north of you.

Float to the turbine slightly northeast of you, then float to the turbine slightly northwest.

Now float to the landing north of you. You can head to the east side of the landing to find a couple of treasure chests. Once you're ready, head through the north passage to reach the Triforce gateway.

ROOM 4

You'll have to battle a new enemy here called an Aeralfos and they're incredibly tough. They will flap their wings to create two mini-tornadoes that will zigzag across the room. They will also dive at you, then immediately fly back into the air. The attack you want them to do is a dive, followed by a three-swing sword combo. This is when you'll have your opportunity to strike. You can either hit the Aeralfos with your Boomerang Link to stun it and then hit it once with your sword or, if you're wearing the Hammerwear, you can Hammer the Aeralfos while it's in the middle of its combo. Just watch out for its third swing in the combo—it's a spin attack not unlike Link's and it will definitely hit you if you're near the Aeralfos when it performs this attack.

Once you defeat all of the Aeralfos in the room, the Triforce gateway will appear and you will have finished one of the toughest stages in the game. Congratulations!

Level 4: Sky Temple

Challenges

Clear within the time limit

Clear without any items

Fewer Heart Containers

Sub-Weapons

All

Materials

 Sky Dragon Tail

 Sky Dragon Tail

Mock Fairy

Recommended Outfits

 Hammerwear

My goodness is this level challenging! Or rather, it would be if you didn't bring the Hammerwear. So bring the Hammerwear, because you want to knock this level out with ease. (Don't you?) Only one Link should wear the Hammerwear, while the others should wear the Sword Suit, the Legendary Dress, or some combination of the two.

This level is made up entirely of battles against a variety of enemies. You'll be able to choose from every Sub-Weapon in the game a handful of times throughout the level. We'll make sure to let you know what the best Sub-Weapons to choose for each area are.

ROOM 1

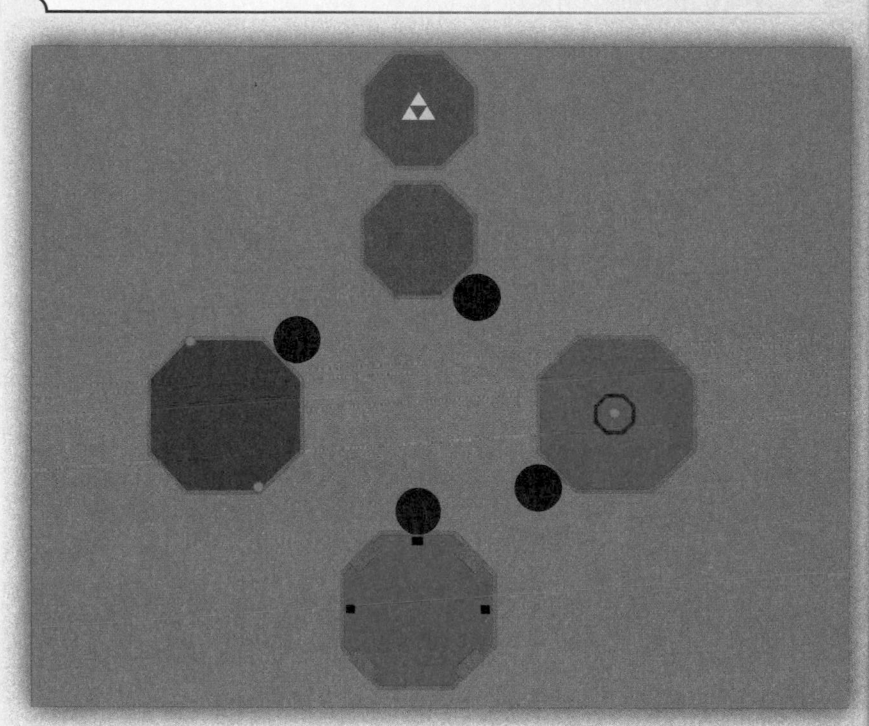

Platform One: You'll find all of the Sub-Weapons in the game on this platform. You'll want to pick the Bow, Magic Hammer, and Water Rod. As soon as you pick up three Sub-Weapons, a translucent platform will appear. Make a three-Link Totem with your Bow Link in the center, then step onto the platform.

Platform Two: You'll land on a small elevated platform in the center of a larger platform. Two Mini-Margos will appear and two Totem Dekus can be found on the left and right sides of the larger platform. You'll want to take out the Totem Dekus first and foremost; they'll make defeating the Mini-Margos far more challenging that it needs to be. Throw your top Link off of the Totem. Your Bow Link should now be on top. Aim at the taller Totem Deku on the right and shoot it with your Bow.

WALKTHROUGH

Now drop off the middle platform and take out the Totem Deku on your left. With both Totem Dekus out of the way, you'll have a much easier time defeating the Mini-Margos. Throw a Link onto the middle platform again, then have that Link grab a Bomb and toss it toward one of the Margos as it stops.

Once you've defeated the Mini-Margos, another translucent platform will appear. Make a three-Link Totem, then walk onto the platform.

Platform Three: You'll have to face three Water Tektites, two Water Octoroks, and a Keeleon on this watery platform. This fight is actually quite simple if you switch to your Water Rod Link. Just create water pillars under each enemy, then slash the enemy with your sword until it is no more.

Once you've defeated all six enemies, another translucent platform will appear. Make a three-Link Totem and hop onto the platform.

Platform Four: You'll face two Freezards, two Ice Wizzrobes, and three Terrorpins on this iced platform. Use the Hammer to flip the Terrorpins, then slash them with your sword. The Ice Wizzrobes just need a good ol' fashioned slashing to be defeated.

You can use your Hammer to smash the Freezards, but you run the risk of getting too close and taking damage by way of touching the Freezards. If you want to play it extra safe, you can always use Bombs. There is a Bomb Flower on both the north and south sides of the platform. You'll need to pick one of the Bombs up and throw it next to each Freezard to destroy it. This is easier said than done, so don't sweat it if it takes a couple of tries to land a Bomb next to a Freezard.

Once you defeat the Freezards, another translucent platform will appear. Make a three-Link Totem, then step on the platform and it will carry you to the Triforce gateway.

ROOM 2

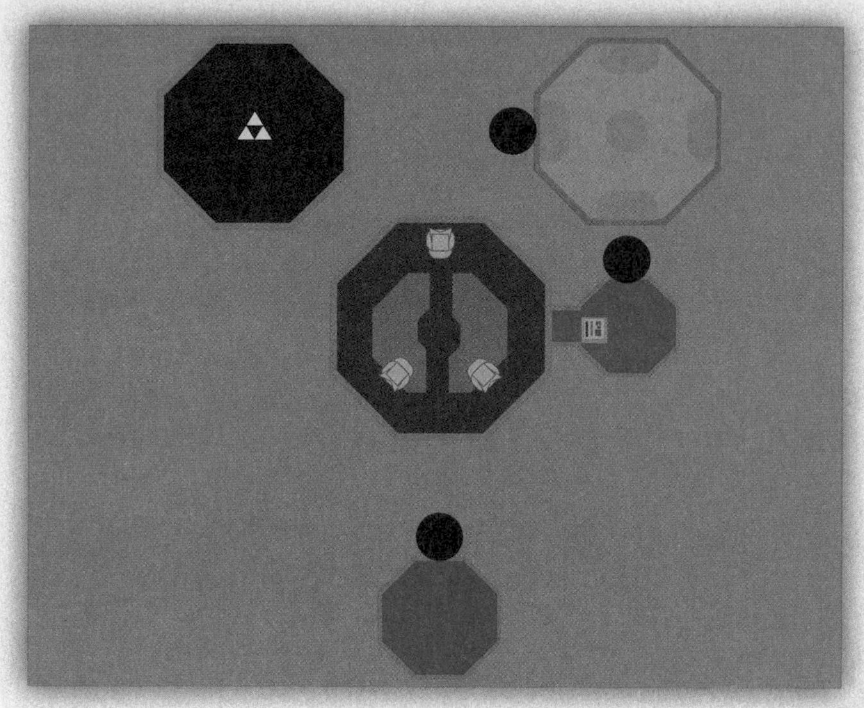

Platform One: Grab the Magic Hammer from the ring of Sub-Weapons, if you haven't already. Any other Sub-Weapons for the other Links will do, just make sure to have some sort of projectile Sub-Weapon, like the Boomerang, Bow, or Gust Jar. The Magic Hammer in the hands of a Hammerwear-wearing Link is absolutely devastating for the rest of this level. When you're ready, stand on the translucent platform with a three-Link Totem to move on.

Platform Two: As soon as you land, two Totem Armos-Riding Soldiers, two Fire Keese, and two Kodongos will appear. Smash them. Smash them all (except for the Keese)! If you're wearing the Hammerwear, the Hammer can smash the Kodongos in one hit and knock the Armos riders off of their Totem Armos. Another hit from your Hammer and the Soldiers will be dust. Now use a ranged Sub-Weapon to defeat the Fire Keese.

Once you've defeated all of the enemies, make a three-Link Totem and walk onto the translucent platform to the east.

Platform Three: You'll find four sets of the slowing, prickly Morths, three Stalfos, and a Gibdo in this room. The Hammer will take care of them all with incredible ease—just make sure not to stand still in the sand or you'll sink into it.

When you've defeated all of the enemies, make a three-Link Totem and hop onto the next translucent platform.

Platform Four: Now this platform is tricky. Well, it would be if you didn't have the Hammer. You'll face five Light Ghinis and a Sky Fire Chain Soldier, all of whom you'll have to defeat in the dark, unless you defeat the Chain Soldier first.

Move directly toward the Chain Soldier on the north side of the platform and smash it with the Hammer. As soon as it is defeated, four unlit torches on the four sides of the room will light. You'll have to use your sword to take out the Light Ghinis, but they're little more than Poes, meaning it only takes two hits to defeat them.

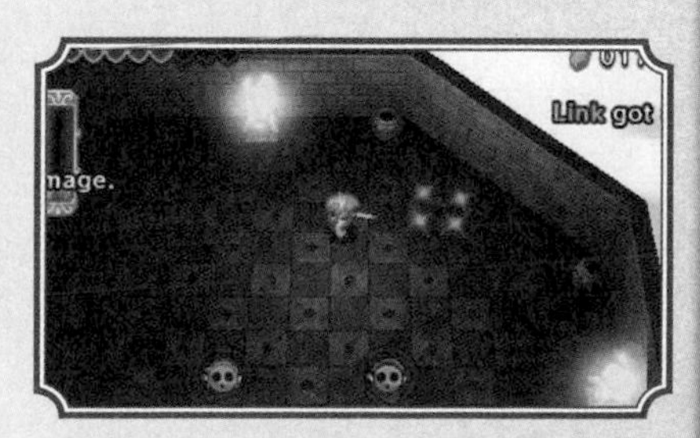

As soon as you defeat all six enemies, the Triforce gateway for this room will appear in the middle of the platform.

ROOM 3

You'll start this room on another platform with all of the Sub-Weapons. Don't bother switching them out unless you want the Links who are not using the Hammer to use something else. Once you're ready, make your way up the stairs.

As soon as all three Links enter this next area, the gates will close behind you and five Soldiers will ferry in on the north side of the platform. As the Hammer Link, wait for them to step off the ferry, then start smashing. If any Soldiers remain on the ferry, head to the south side of the platform and wait for them to drop off of it. Now go and give them a good smashing!

Once all five Soldiers have been defeated, the gates will reopen. Head up the next flight of stairs. As soon as you enter the area at the top of the stairs, five more Soldiers will ferry into the northwest corner of the platform. Again, wait for these five Soldiers to step off the ferry, then head over to them with the Hammer Link and smash them flat, same as the last set.

Now head up the northern flight of stairs. Once all three Links touch down on the platform at the end of the stairs, two Super Aeralfos will appear. The only real difference between Super Aeralfos and the Aeralfos you've fought is that these guys can use a fire attack. Other than that, they are exactly the same.

Use your Hammer as each Aeralfos swoops down at you. One direct hit with the Hammer will take them out with ease. Once both Super Aeralfos have been defeated, the northern doors will open, a Squiddy will appear, and you'll be given access to the Triforce gateway. Say your sweet, somber goodbyes to our good friend Squiddy and prepare to face the final boss!

ROOM 4

BOSS FIGHT: THE LADY

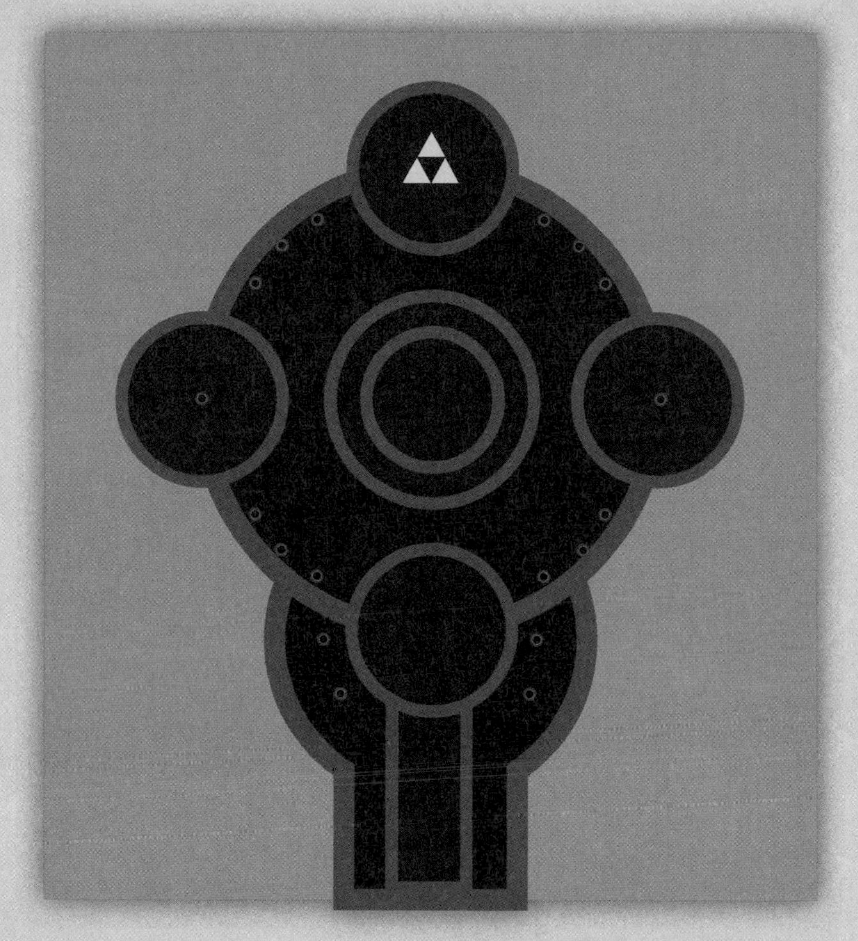

As soon as you enter this room, The Lady will appear and steal all of your Sub-Weapons. (This is why we suggested only one Link wear the Hammerwear, while the other two Links mix and match the Sword Suit and the Legendary Dress.)

Smash the pots on the sides of the hall's north end to refill your health, then have all three Links stand in the red circle. Gates will close around the Links and the red circle will lift into the air. Once you reach the top of the elevator's path, you'll begin the first phase of the fight with The Lady.

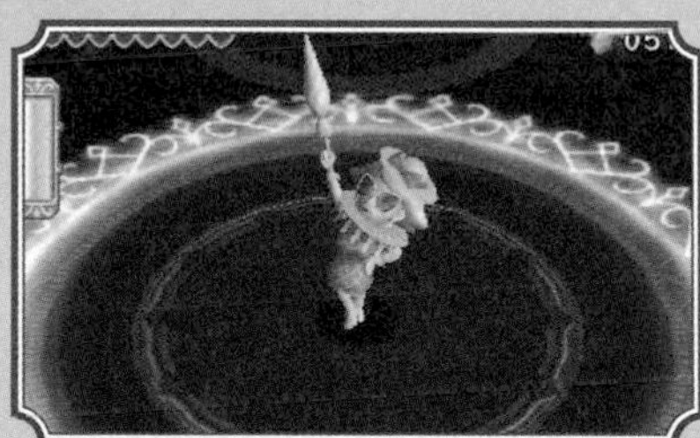

The Lady doesn't do much during this first phase of the fight. (When you look that fabulous, why would you want to fight?) She'll create a ring around her and stand on the center platform patiently. To damage her, you'll need to make a three-Link Totem, throw the top two Links over the ring, and then circle behind her with the two-Link Totem. She'll try to keep you from getting behind her and she'll also throw parasols across the room, which will damage any Link hit by one.

When you're sure you have a clear shot, throw the top Link up behind The Lady and have him strike! After a few hits, The Lady will use her parasol to shove the Link attacking her off of the platform. You'll need to throw him back over the ring, make another two-Link Totem, and attack The Lady's back once again.

After a few more hits, The Lady's platform will lower and she'll come out swinging—literally! A colored lightning bolt will begin flashing above her head and she'll start to chase whatever Link matches the bolt's color.

This is basically the Moldorm fight all over again. Lure The Lady away from the other Links, then switch to another Link and have him slash her back. (If you're playing multiplayer, just slash her back while she's chasing another Link.) She'll immediately switch her focus to the Link that did the slashing. Switch to a Link not being chased by The Lady and slash her in the back again. Repeat this process a handful of times and The Lady will transition into her next phase.

Do you remember the Phantom Ganon fights from *Ocarina of Time, Wind Waker,* and *Twilight Princess?* If not, do you remember your fight with Aghanim in *Link to the Past?* Well, this phase is those fights, but with three Links. It may not sound challenging, but things can get hectic pretty quickly, especially in multiplayer.

For those who are unfamiliar with those fights, The Lady will create a colored ball of electricity and throw it at one of your Links. The Link that matches the color of the electricity ball will need to hit the ball back at The Lady without getting hit himself.

If she throws the energy ball at a Doppel, it will often bounce into the air and change colors, giving you a chance to switch Links and hit the ball. So long as the ball bounces straight into the air, you'll almost always have time to reach it before it bounces on the ground twice and explodes. To all but guarantee that you can hit it back when it bounces, keep your Links near each other and always keep the Link you're controlling behind the other two Links. This will help to keep her from tossing the electricity ball away from you and your Doppels, disabling your ability to hit it back at her before it hits the ground.

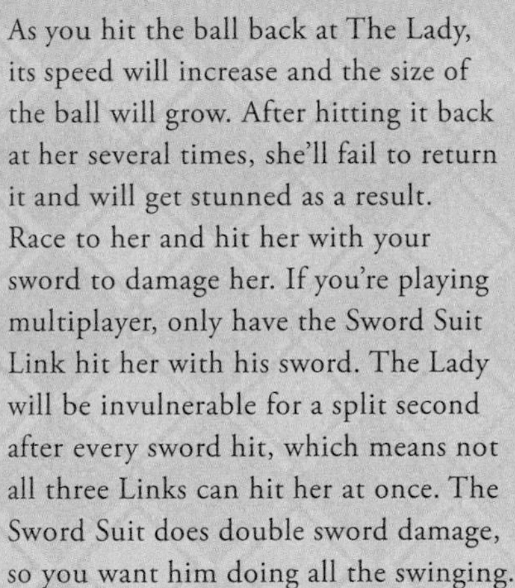

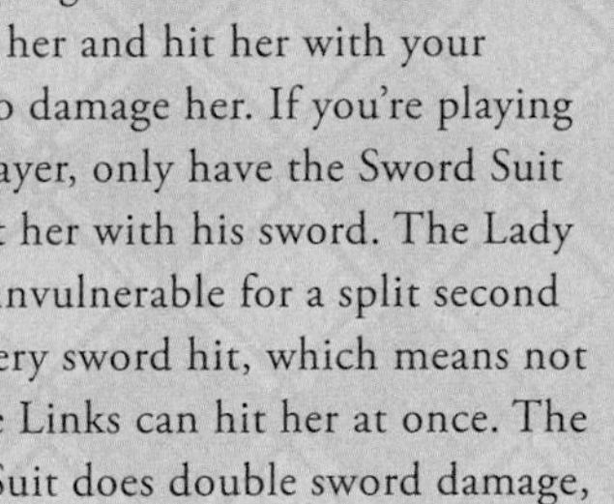

As you hit the ball back at The Lady, its speed will increase and the size of the ball will grow. After hitting it back at her several times, she'll fail to return it and will get stunned as a result. Race to her and hit her with your sword to damage her. If you're playing multiplayer, only have the Sword Suit Link hit her with his sword. The Lady will be invulnerable for a split second after every sword hit, which means not all three Links can hit her at once. The Sword Suit does double sword damage, so you want him doing all the swinging.

Repeat this one or two more times and The Lady will move into her final phase—and let us tell you, it's no joke!

The Lady will create parasol platforms of varying colors around her. Your goal is to throw your Links onto the platforms that match their colors and slash her head. The bigger platforms are closer to the ground and the smaller ones are in line with The Lady's head.

Make a Totem as soon as The Lady unfolds her parasols, then get a Link up onto one of the small parasols, or get a two-Link Totem onto the bigger parasols and slash away at her head. You will have very little time to try to get your Links up there, so keep your Links together, quickly build your Totem based on the colors of her parasols, and throw your Link up near her head.

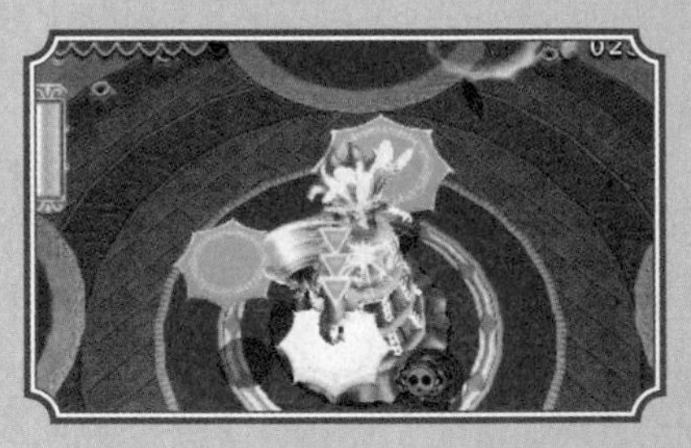

The Lady will fold some of her parasols shortly after they appear, then she'll have them spin around the room. The safest place to be is on the edges of the red circles lining the room, but you should only go there if you're feeling the heat. While she's spinning the parasols, you'll still have plenty of time to try and reach her head.

The second you see lightning bolts strike the parasols, jump back to the ground. Those bolts are indicators of even larger lightning bolts and where they're going to land. The smaller bolts can't hurt you, but the big bolts certainly can. The large bolts will also destroy all of her parasols, meaning you'll have to wait for her to pull out new ones in order to try to reach her head again.

The timing during this phase is extremely tight, so you'll have to be constantly on watch to avoid taking damage and to reach her head.

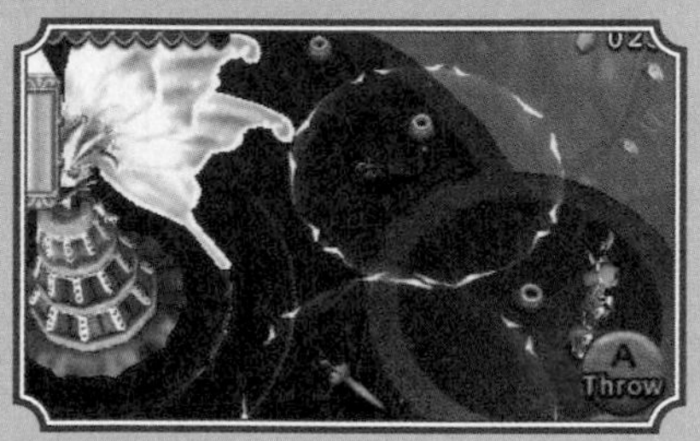

Once you've hit her head a handful of times, The Lady will move into full attack mode. She'll fold her parasols and spike them into the ground. Small lightning bolts will hit the parasols in a specific order and electric rings will come off of the parasols. These are both indicators of what order she's going to electrify the parasols and the area that the electricity can reach you in. If you're not in where any of the circles were when the big lightning strikes, you'll be completely safe.

After shocking all of the parasols, The Lady will open up several more parasol platforms for you to climb. Quickly make a Totem and throw a Link onto the smaller parasol platforms or have a two-Link Totem stand on the bigger platforms, then attack her head.

Hitting her a handful of times will make her mad once again, meaning she's going to change up her tactics one last time. The center platform will rise again, making it extra hard for you to reach her head. She'll now throw her parasol platforms onto the ground. You'll need to quickly make a three-Link Totem and stand on one of the platforms. The platform will take you near The Lady, which is your chance to have the top Link slash her head. She'll also regularly throw out another set of parasols that she'll electrify shortly after they spike into the ground.

There's a lot to pay attention to during this portion of the fight, but playing it safe is your best option. You can always stand on the edge of the red circles to avoid taking damage and collect yourself. Wait for the right time to hop onto a platform that's on the ground and don't rush! Take your time, wait for the right platforms to hop onto, then take The Lady down! It won't take but a handful of hits to end The Lady's gorgeous reign of terror once and for all!

Once the fight is finished, you'll get the final piece of the Lady's Outfit, which is necessary to break the unfashionable curse The Lady put on Princess Styla and the whole of the Hytopian kingdom. Head to Madame Couture's to create the Outfit, put it on, and then head to the throne room to break Princess Styla's curse. Now enjoy the celebration in your honor. You've certainly earned it!

The Aftermath

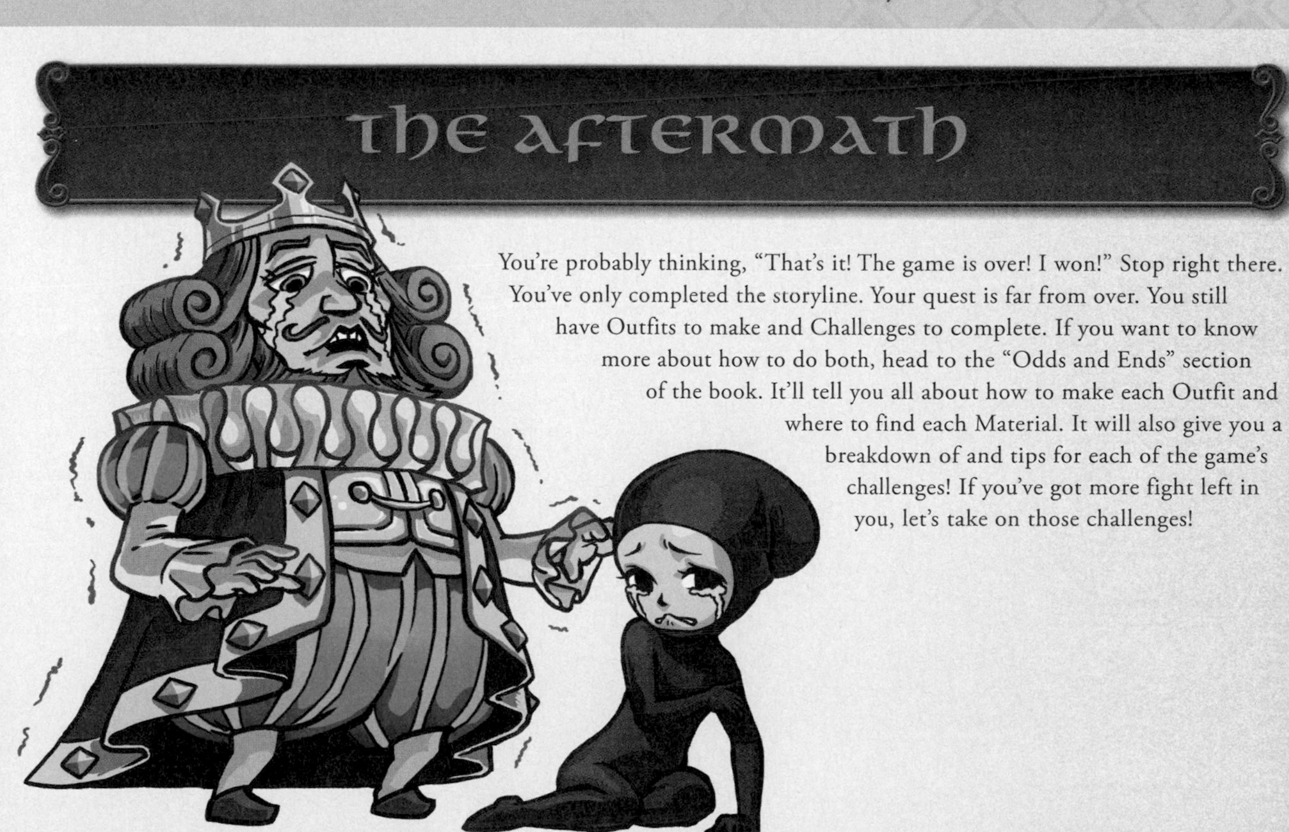

You're probably thinking, "That's it! The game is over! I won!" Stop right there. You've only completed the storyline. Your quest is far from over. You still have Outfits to make and Challenges to complete. If you want to know more about how to do both, head to the "Odds and Ends" section of the book. It'll tell you all about how to make each Outfit and where to find each Material. It will also give you a breakdown of and tips for each of the game's challenges! If you've got more fight left in you, let's take on those challenges!

Odds and Ends

This section of the guide is for just about anything we didn't cover in the walkthrough. You'll find information about each of the challenge types you'll face in the game, plus the rewards they yield. You'll find a list of all of the Materials in the game and what levels you can find them in. You'll also find a list of all the Outfits, what they do, when they're unlocked, and what Materials they require to make them. Truly this section has everything you need to get 100% completion in *Tri Force Heroes*.

Challenges

The challenges are challenging for reasons beyond puzzle solving and enemy fighting. We'll do our best to make these challenges as easy as possible, but most of what you'll have to tackle is based on your own skills, reflexes, knowledge of each level, and cunning. Most of our strategies from the walkthrough still apply here, so make sure to brush up on each level before you take on a challenge there. Getting 100% completion in this game is only for the most stalwart of heroes—no one will look down on you for not reaching this goal. If you're still not dissuaded, read on to get as much help as we are able to give you. First, here's a look at the types of challenges you will run into.

Fewer Heart Containers

Fewer Heart Containers challenges are exactly what their name suggests. Instead of having nine Heart Containers, you'll start these challenges with a mere four. To add injury to insult, these challenges, like most others, will throw more enemies your way. A lot more. You'll need to be extremely careful to complete these challenges. There is no timer in this challenge like there are in other challenges, so you can afford to crawl your way through these stages.

You can either follow the level strategies suggested in the walkthrough to pick an Outfit, or you can bring a good general Outfit, like the Sword Suit, Lucky Loungewear, or Legendary Dress. Whatever you choose, always proceed on the side of caution once the challenge begins. Things can get out of hand very, very quickly, so always be alert!

Clear Within the Time Limit

These are some of the more difficult challenges in the game. As soon as you start the level, a timer will begin ticking down. The only way to fill it up again is to pick up small and large hourglasses scattered around the level. You'll need to be quick with everything you do and you'll need to consider every way to save time to complete these stages. If you run out of time, you'll have to start the entire level over. It's a good idea to play through the levels with these challenges a couple of times before trying to tackle the challenge itself, that way you can get a refresher on the level, figure out what areas and puzzles you get stuck on, and choose an Outfit accordingly.

You'll want to pick any Outfits that make you defeat enemies quickly or help you solve puzzles faster. The last thing we can tell you about these grueling challenges is to not let the small hourglasses distract you. They only give five seconds, which isn't a lot of time. If you can't grab them on the way to your next destination, don't bother with them at all. You can very easily burn through five or more seconds going out of your way for one of these small hourglasses, meaning most of the time you'll break even or lose time. Stay focused, be quick, and don't let anything distract you! That's the only way to best these Drabland challenges.

Guard the Orb

Guard the Orb challenges require you to carry an orb to the end of each room. The orb creates a ring of light around it, which protects you from a poisonous miasma encompassing the whole level. Stand outside of the orb for too long and you'll start taking damage. There aren't too many major changes to levels that have this challenge. The way you tackle puzzles and enemies doesn't change. You just need to keep the orb around you at all times. This can be a hindrance, as it limits where you can go and since one Link must almost always have the orb in hand, you'll be down a man for just about every challenge. All of that being said, taking it slow and thinking about your surroundings before making any dramatic moves will make these challenges slow, but fairly easy.

Pop All Balloons

Pop All Balloons challenges are strange beasts. There aren't many changes to a level with one of these challenges, except that there are now several balloons. Your job is to pop them all. The number on the top of the top screen will keep you informed on how many balloons you have left. The numbers on the balloon indicate how tall your Totem will need to be to reach that balloon, but it's not as cut and dry as it might seem at first. You don't need to make a Totem that matches the number on the balloons most of the time. If you can get to a higher location, you can often just hit the balloon with your sword or shoot it with a Sub-Weapon. Another trick, which you'll need to employ for a lot of balloons that aren't numbered, is to pull out a Bomb, hold it until it's just about to blow, and then throw it right at the balloon.

A Bomb's explosion will give you some extra reach for those balloons that are just a bit too far to reach. You also don't actually need to hit balloons with a weapon of any sort—just throwing a Link at them will be enough to pop them. The real trick of these challenges comes from the hidden and hard-to-reach balloons. You'll have to get creative and think hard about your surroundings to figure out how to reach tougher balloons. Look behind structures. Look under bridges and platforms. If the room has breakable platforms, then break them and search for balloons there. Nothing is sacred when it comes to these balloons!

Clear Using Only Bombs

Despite what their name suggests, the Clear Using Only Bombs challenge doesn't actually require you to use only Bombs. This challenge will replace the Sub-Weapons for this level with Bombs, which means you'll need to solve all the puzzles with Bombs—unless, of course, you can hit something with your sword. Your sword is still completely in play, so if you can reach a switch or an enemy with your sword, do it. The real challenge comes from enemies and puzzles that originally required the use of Bows to reach them. You'll have to be creative with your Bombs by holding on to them and throwing them just before they blow to hit higher switches.

In single-player, you can also make a three-Link Totem and throw the top two Links with a Bomb in hand. They can stand by taller objects and have the Bomb explode on a higher level with no fear of them taking damage, provided you're not controlling them at that time, of course. Be clever about how you use your Bombs and solve puzzles and you'll have this challenge knocked out without much of a struggle.

Defeat All Foes Without a Sword

This challenge requires you to beat the level without using a sword. More than that, you'll have to clear each room, which is now packed with enemies, to make the Triforce gateway appear. This isn't a particularly hard challenge if you bring along the Kokiri Clothes or Big Bomb Outfit. Finding all of the enemies can be a bit of challenge, so make sure to check every corner, nook, and cranny to find all of them.

Transport the Orb Quickly

Transport the Orb Quickly challenges combine the timer of Clear Within the Time Limit challenges with the orb escorting from the Guard the Orb challenges. As terrible as that might sound, these challenges are actually more forgiving than both of their counterparts. The timer is less intense and there is no poisonous miasma to deal with. You can feel safe grabbing pretty much any hourglass you find in the level, and while you need to do everything quickly, there is room for mistakes. The best tip we can offer is that if your path to the orb pedestal and Triforce gateway are blocked (which they often will be), throw the orb up to or near a location you know you'll have to come back to. This will save you the time and effort required to pick up the orb and make a Totem to escort the orb to its pedestal. Using the Cheetah Costume will help you move faster during the level or using Outfits that help you defeat enemies as quickly as possible, such as the Sword Suit and Sword Master Suit, will help make these stages as easy as possible.

Adventure in the Dark

Adventure in the Dark challenges are exactly what their name implies. You'll have to play through the entire level, but in a level of darkness found only in the last two worlds of the game. You won't be able to see more than a foot around each Link, so taking your time is an absolute must! It's incredibly easy to walk off of a cliff or into an enemy in these challenges. To make them significantly easier, wear the Light Armor. It will create a much larger radius of light around the one wearing this Outfit. The levels with this challenge are virtually the same, so you can do a few practice runs in the No Challenge version of the level before trying to take it on with the lights out. Careful steps, an eye for detail, and exceptional patience will get you through these challenges. Don't let these challenges best you!

Clear with Halved Energy

These challenges require a good deal of patience and fortitude. Your energy bar will be halved, meaning using a Sub-Weapon and water dashing will take twice the amount of energy as they did before. You'll need to think very carefully about how you're going to solve puzzles, especially ones involving the Water Rod. You can offset this debuff by equipping the Energy Gear or Outfits specifically related to the Sub-Weapons found in the level. The Energy Gear will work for Link and the Doppels while playing in single-player, but will only work for the Link that has the Outfit equipped in multiplayer. If you want to offset the halved energy bar for everyone in multiplayer, you'll need to equip the Cheer Outfit, which will increase all three players' energy bars. You'll have to be slow and plan your moves carefully to complete these challenges, but take your time and you'll knock these out with no problems!

Evade the Wallmaster

Evade the Wallmaster challenges are pretty intense. A Wallmaster, a disembodied hand, will float over whatever Link you're currently controlling (or a random Link in multiplayer). After twenty to thirty seconds, the Wallmaster will wiggle its fingers rapidly, then swat straight down in an attempt to smash you. If it succeeds, you'll be KO'd on the spot, no matter how full your Heart Containers are. You'll need to do everything quickly while paying close attention to the Wallmaster. If you see those rapidly wiggling fingers, move! You can use the Wallmaster's swats to have it defeat enemies. You can also use it to swat nearby Bomb Flowers to have it defeat itself. The Sword Suit and Sword Master Suit will help you defeat the Wallmaster when it swats down, which will give you a bit of a breather. The Lucky Loungewear and Kinda Cursed Tights will give you a chance of avoiding death if you're unlucky enough to have the Wallmaster actually land a swat. Be smart, be careful, and you'll get through this tough challenges.

Halved Attack and Defense

As the name implies, these challenges will leave you and any of your friends with half attack damage and you'll take double damage from any attacks. While that can be a pretty rough challenge in the later levels, there are ways to easily offset these downgrades. You can wear the Sword Suit to balance your attack damage back to its normal values, or wear the Sword Master Suit to deal more than the normal values. A Legendary Dress or Lucky Loungewear can help mitigate the damage you take, somewhat neutralizing the effects of your lowered defense. For the most part, the levels are the same, but you'll likely encounter stronger enemies and more of them. Just carry on through the level as you would any other level and make sure to be more mindful of your attacks to prevent yourself from taking unintended damage. You've got this!

Don't Pop Any Balloons

These challenges are awful! Awful, we say! Balloons will be scattered all throughout the level and you can't pop a single one—not a single, solitary balloon. As if that isn't enough of a challenge, the balloons are in the worst possible places. They're practically begging to be popped. DO NOT, under any circumstances, bring Outfits that increase the size of your Sub-Weapons, or the amount of projectiles they fire! These challenges demand absolute precision. A single misfire, a sole balloon popped, and you're done. You'll lose a fairy and be forced to start the room over again, and believe us when we say it can happen much faster than you'd expect. Take as much time as absolutely necessary to avoid hitting any balloons. Think carefully about how your Sub-Weapons work. Your Boomerang always comes back to you—is it going to catch a balloon on its way back? Is that Bomb's explosion going to pop the balloon near it? You'll have to be incredibly meticulous to beat these challenges. And it doesn't stop there, friends! Fighting an enemy that throws spears, Bombs or other projectiles? What about enemies that create shockwaves, like the Stalchampion? They can pop balloons too! These are arguably the toughest challenges in the game.

Avoid the Volcanic Rocks

These challenges are pretty straightforward: Avoid volcanic rocks that are constantly falling from the sky. You've already seen these rocks while playing through world 3, Volcano. Just pay attention to the shadows on the ground to see where the rocks will land and promptly step away from them. Bringing along a Legendary Dress or Lucky Loungewear will help offset any damage you take, if you're struggling to avoid the rocks. Careful steps and an attention to detail will get you through these stages unmarred.

Only Bombs—No Swords

These challenges will replace the Sub-Weapons in a level with Bombs and remove your ability to swing your sword. Just about everything you do in levels with these challenges will require you use Bombs. You'll need to think about how to solve puzzles, how to defeat enemies, and how to complete a level using nothing but Bombs! We're being a bit more dramatic about it than these challenges deserve. They're actually quite fun, and while they require some extra thought, you shouldn't have too much trouble overcoming these new challenges. You can make them easier by bringing the Big Bomb Outfit or the Energy Gear. Bombs take an awful lot of energy to use, so bringing either Outfit will help you make the most of your exploding Sub-Weapon.

Don't Get Hit By Snowballs

These challenges are nearly identical to the Avoid the Volcanic Rocks challenges found in Volcano. Obviously, instead of fiery rocks, you have to avoid giant snowballs falling from the sky. You need only pay attention to the shadows that appear on the ground to avoid getting smashed by a snowball. You can bring the Lucky Loungewear or Legendary Dress if you want to mitigate any accidental damage. These challenges are quite simple if you pay attention and stay focused. You've got this!

Win Without Using a Sword

These are some of the easier challenges in the game, provided you have the right Outfits. To complete these challenges, you'll have to play through a whole level without a sword. You'll still have access to a Sub-Weapon, which will be more than enough to get the job done. Just put on an Outfit that works directly with a Sub-Weapon in the level you're about to do and things should go pretty smoothly. Take the time to think about how to defeat enemies with the Sub-Weapons you've been given and you'll finish these challenges in no time at all.

Don't Drop the Pot

Don't drop the pot challenges are a lot like the Transport the Orb Quickly challenges, but without the time limit. There is a bit more to it than that, however. If you drop the pot, you'll lose a fairy right then and there. This means that if the pot holder gets hit, falls off of a cliff or into a pit, falls into water, or throws the pot to the ground, there goes a fairy. Once the level begins and you pick up the pot, it has to be in someone's hands at all times. To make things even trickier, you can throw the pot to your teammates, but it's extra heavy and will fall much quicker than when you throw other Links or destructible objects. To be safe, stand right next to the person you're throwing the pot to. That will keep you from missing your target. If you're playing single-player, you can just hide the pot holder in a corner. Doppels can't take damage, so unless the pot holder is knocked off of a ledge or into lava or water, you have nothing to fear. Multiplayer is an entirely different story, but the strategies are the same. Keep your pot holder as far away from enemies as possible and get in nice and close to your teammates before transferring the pot over to them. These are hard challenges, but they are far from unbeatable.

Don't Fall at All

Don't fall at all. Don't do it. If you do, you'll end up losing a fairy immediately. As easy as it may sound to avoid falling off cliffs or platforms or into pits, it's actually much trickier than you'd think. You'll need to be on the lookout for any obnoxious enemies hanging out around moving platforms and narrow pathways—they're real killers now.

You can avoid immediately losing a fairy by wearing the Tingle Tights. They'll keep you alive after falling up to three times, so they're definitely worth wearing for these challenges. Be on your guard, look out for any would-be prankster enemies, and you'll make it through these challenges.

Avoid Falling and Quicksand

This is the Don't Fall at All challenge with an extra twist. In this particular challenge, you'll have to avoid sinking into the quicksand in addition to not falling. You can wear the Dunewalker Duds to eliminate the possibility of sinking into quicksand, but the choice is entirely up to you.

Clear Without Any Items

This is definitely one of the hardest challenges in the game, and it has very little to do with fighting the last boss. The rooms leading up to The Lady are very challenging, but if you followed our strategy and used Hammerwear plus a Hammer, you undoubtedly barreled through it. Now you'll get a real taste of what these rooms are like. Problem is, you won't have a single Sub-Weapon to help you through. This will become an exceptional burden when you reach room 3, where all of the Sky Soldiers are located. You'll have to find a way to defeat the Soldiers who have swords and shields.

The best way to tackle this challenge is to try and make the Sword Master Suit. You'll need to battle in the Coliseum and win the rare Materials in The Dunes, The Ruins, and the Sky Realm Coliseum stages. You'll need to win and get lucky enough to land each of the stages' gold Materials, but if you do, this challenge will be a lot easier. If you don't have the means to play in the Coliseum, or if it's taking longer to get the Materials than you can handle, you can also use the Sword Suit to help you.

In order to deal with the Sky Soldiers with swords and shields, you'll need to position a Link behind them. When the Soldiers get in close, switch to that Link and hit the Soldier in the back. Their attention will immediately shift to their attacker. Switch Links, so that you're behind them again, and slash them in the back. It will take several hits to defeat them, but if you keep this strategy up you should be safe from most of their attacks. You'll want to try and clear out any other Sky Soldiers in the area before taking out the Sky Soldiers with swords and shields.

If you can handle this challenge, you can handle just about anything! Now get in there and show them what you're made of!

Levels

World 1: The Woodlands

LEVEL 1: DEKU FOREST

Sub-Weapons:

 Bow

 Bow

 Bow

No-Challenge Materials:

 Blob Jelly

 Blob Jelly

 Armos Spirit

Challenge 1: Fewer Heart Containers

Materials:

 Blob Jelly

 Blob Jelly

 Tektite Shell

Challenge 2: Clear Within the Time Limit

Materials:

 Armos Spirit

 Armos Spirit

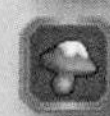 Sweet Shroom

Challenge 3: Guard the Orb

Materials:

 Tektite Shell

 Tektite Shell

 Blin Bling

LEVEL 2: BUZZ BLOB CAVE

Sub-Weapons:

 Bow

 Bow

 Bow

No-Challenge Materials:

 Blob Jelly

 Blob Jelly

 Tektite Shell

Challenge 1: Pop All Balloons

Materials:

 Armos Spirit

 Armos Spirit

 Sweet Shroom

Challenge 2: Clear Within the Time Limit

Materials:

 Tektite Shell

 Tektite Shell

 Blin Bling

Challenge 3: Clear Using Only Bombs

Materials:

 Sweet Shroom

 Sweet Shroom

 Gohma's Eye

LEVEL 3: MOBLIN BASE

Sub-Weapons:

 Bow

 Bow

 Bombs

No-Challenge Materials:

 Armos Spirit

 Armos Spirit

 Sweet Shroom

Challenge 1: Pop All Balloons

Materials:

 Tektite Shell

 Tektite Shell

 Blin Bling

Challenge 2: Defeat All Foes Without a Sword

Materials:

- Sweet Shroom
- Sweet Shroom
- Gohma's Eye

Challenge 3: Transport the Orb Quickly

Materials:

- Blin Bling
- Blin Bling
- Mystery Jade

LEVEL 4: FOREST TEMPLE

Sub-Weapons:

Bow

Bombs

Bombs

No-Challenge Materials:

- Tektite Shell
- Tektite Shell
- Blin Bling

Challenge 1: Adventure in the Dark

Materials:

- Sweet Shroom
- Sweet Shroom
- Gohma's Eye

Challenge 2: Clear Within the Time Limit

Materials:

- Blin Bling
- Blin Bling
- Mystery Jade

Challenge 3: Fewer Heart Containers

Materials:

- Gohma's Eye
- Gohma's Eye
- Mystery Jade

World 2: Riverside

LEVEL 1: SECRET FORTRESS

Sub-Weapons:

 Water Rod

 Water Rod

 Water Rod

No-Challenge Materials:

Fresh Kelp

Fresh Kelp

 Zora Scale

Challenge 1: Pop All Balloons

Materials:

Fresh Kelp

Fresh Kelp

Hytopian Silk

Challenge 2: Clear with Halved Energy

Materials:

Zora Scale

Zora Scale

Aqua Crown

Challenge 3: Evade the Wallmaster

Materials:

Hytopian Silk

Hytopian Silk

Octorok Sucker

LEVEL 2: ABYSS OF AGONY

Sub-Weapons:

 Bow

 Water Rod

 Water Rod

No-Challenge Materials:

Fresh Kelp

Fresh Kelp

Hytopian Silk

Challenge 1: Halved Attack and Defense

Materials:

Zora Scale

Zora Scale

 Aqua Crown

Challenge 2: Guard the Orb

Materials:

- Hytopian Silk
- Hytopian Silk
- Octorok Sucker

Challenge 3: Clear Within the Time Limit

Materials:

-  Aqua Crown
-  Aqua Crown
-  Fairy Dust

LEVEL 3: COVE OF TRANSITION

Sub-Weapons:

-  Gripshot
-  Gripshot
-  Gripshot

No-Challenge Materials:

-  Zora Scale
-  Zora Scale
-  Aqua Crown

Challenge 1: Halved Attack and Defense

Materials:

-  Hytopian Silk
-  Hytopian Silk
-  Octorok Sucker

Challenge 2: Evade the Wallmaster

Materials:

-  Aqua Crown
-  Aqua Crown
-  Fairy Dust

Challenge 3: Clear Within the Time Limit

Materials:

-  Octorok Sucker
-  Octorok Sucker
- 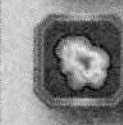 Rainbow Coral

LEVEL 4: WATER TEMPLE

Sub-Weapons:

 Water Rod

 Gripshot

 Gripshot

No-Challenge Materials:

- Hytopian Silk
- Hytopian Silk
- Octorok Sucker

Challenge 1: Fewer Heart Containers

Materials:

- Aqua Crown
- Aqua Crown
- Fairy Dust

Challenge 2: Clear with Halved Energy

Materials:

- Octorok Sucker
- Octorok Sucker
- Rainbow Coral

Challenge 3: Transport the Orb Quickly

Materials:

- Fairy Dust
- Fairy Dust
- Rainbow Coral

World 3: Volcano

LEVEL 1: BLAZING TRAIL

Sub-Weapons:

 Boomerang

 Boomerang

 Boomerang

No-Challenge Materials:

 Goron Ore

 Goron Ore

 Monster Guts

Challenge 1: Pop All Balloons

Materials:

Goron Ore

Goron Ore

Demon Fossil

Challenge 2: Evade the Wallmaster

Materials:

Monster Guts

Monster Guts

Rugged Horn

Challenge 3: Transport the Orb Quickly

Materials:

 Demon Fossil

Demon Fossil

Kodongo Tail

LEVEL 2: HINOX MINE

Sub-Weapons:

 Bow

 Boomerang

 Boomerang

No-Challenge Materials:

 Goron Ore

 Goron Ore

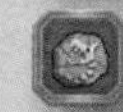 Demon Fossil

Challenge 1: Clear Within the Time Limit

Materials:

 Monster Guts

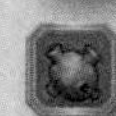 Monster Guts

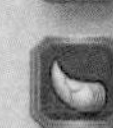 Rugged Horn

Challenge 2: Pop All Balloons

Materials:

 Demon Fossil

 Demon Fossil

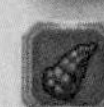 Kodongo Tail

Challenge 3: Don't Pop Any Balloons

Materials:

 Rugged Horn

 Rugged Horn

 Keese Wing

LEVEL 3: DEN OF FLAMES

Sub-Weapons:

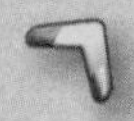 Boomerang

 Gust Jar

 Gust Jar

No-Challenge Materials:

 Monster Guts

 Monster Guts

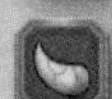 Rugged Horn

Challenge 1: Fewer Heart Containers

Materials:

 Demon Fossil

 Demon Fossil

 Kodongo Tail

Challenge 2: Avoid the Volcanic Rocks

Materials:

 Rugged Horn

 Rugged Horn

 Keese Wing

Challenge 3: Clear Within the Time Limit

Materials:

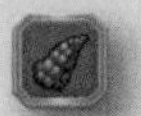 Kodongo Tail

 Kodongo Tail

 Star Fragment

LEVEL 4: FIRE TEMPLE

Sub-Weapons:

 Bow

 Boomerang

 Gust Jar

No-Challenge Materials:

 Demon Fossil

 Demon Fossil

 Kodongo Tail

Challenge 1: Clear Within the Time Limit

Materials:

 Rugged Horn

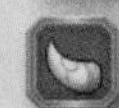 Rugged Horn

 Keese Wing

Challenge 2: Evade the Wallmaster

Materials:

- Kodongo Tail
- Kodongo Tail
- Star Fragment

Challenge 3: Only Bombs—No Swords

Materials:

- Keese Wing
- Keese Wing
- Star Fragment

World 4: Ice Cavern

LEVEL 1: FROZEN PLATEAU

Sub-Weapons:

- Fire Gloves
- Fire Gloves
- Fire Gloves

No-Challenge Materials:

- Fluffy Fuzz
- Fluffy Fuzz
- Tiny Snowflake

Challenge 1: Don't Get Hit by Snowballs

Materials:

- Fluffy Fuzz
- Fluffy Fuzz
- Serpent Fangs

Challenge 2: Pop All Balloons

Materials:

- Tiny Snowflake
- Tiny Snowflake
- Crimson Shell

Challenge 3: Guard the Orb

Materials:

- Serpent Fangs
- Serpent Fangs
- Freezard Water

LEVEL 2: SNOWBALL RAVINE

Sub-Weapons:

- Boomerang
- Fire Gloves
- Fire Gloves

No-Challenge Materials:

- Fluffy Fuzz
- Fluffy Fuzz
- Serpent Fangs

Challenge 1: Adventure in the Dark

Materials:

- Tiny Snowflake
- Tiny Snowflake
- Crimson Shell

Challenge 2: Fewer Heart Containers

Materials:

- Serpent Fangs
- Serpent Fangs
- Freezard Water

Challenge 3: Transport the Orb Quickly

Materials:

- Crimson Shell
- Crimson Shell
- Chill Stone

LEVEL 3: SILVER SHRINE

Sub-Weapons:

 Magic Hammer

 Magic Hammer

 Magic Hammer

No-Challenge Materials:

- Tiny Snowflake
- Tiny Snowflake
- Crimson Shell

Challenge 1: Win Without Using a Sword

Materials:

- Serpent Fangs
- Serpent Fangs
- Freezard Water

Challenge 2: Halved Attack and Defense

Materials:

- Crimson Shell
- Crimson Shell
- Chill Stone

Challenge 3: Evade the Wallmaster

Materials:

- Freezard Water
- Freezard Water
- Ice Rose

LEVEL 4: ICE TEMPLE

Sub-Weapons:

Fire Gloves

Magic Hammer

Magic Hammer

No-Challenge Materials:

Serpent Fangs

Serpent Fangs

Freezard Water

Challenge 1: Fewer Heart Containers

Materials:

- Crimson Shell
- Crimson Shell
- Chill Stone

Challenge 2: Don't Get Hit By Snowballs

Materials:

- Freezard Water
- Freezard Water
- Ice Rose

Challenge 3: Transport the Orb Quickly

Materials:

Chill Stone

Chill Stone

Ice Rose

World 5: Fortress

LEVEL 1: SEALED GATEWAY

Sub-Weapons:

Boomerang

Boomerang

Gust Jar

No-Challenge Materials:

Stiff Puff

Stiff Puff

Silver Thread

Challenge 1: Don't Drop the Pot

Materials:

Stiff Puff

Stiff Puff

Royal Ring

Challenge 2: Evade the Wallmaster

Materials:

Silver Thread

Silver Thread

Antique Coin

Challenge 3: Halved Attack and Defense

Materials:

Royal Ring

Royal Ring

Fancy Fabric

LEVEL 2: BOMB STORAGE

Sub-Weapons:

Bombs

Gust Jar

Gust Jar

No-Challenge Materials:

Stiff Puff

Stiff Puff

Royal Ring

Challenge 1: Win Without Using a Sword

Materials:

Silver Thread

Silver Thread

Antique Coin

Challenge 2: Transport the Orb Quickly

Materials:

- Royal Ring
- Royal Ring
- Fancy Fabric

Challenge 3: Don't Fall at All

Materials:

- Antique Coin
- Antique Coin
- Exquisite Lace

LEVEL 3: TRAINING GROUND

Sub-Weapons:

Bow

Gripshot

Gust Jar

No-Challenge Materials:

Silver Thread

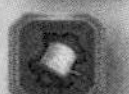
Silver Thread

Antique Coin

Challenge 1: Clear Within the Time Limit

Materials:

- Royal Ring
- Royal Ring
- Fancy Fabric

Challenge 2: Halved Attack and Defense

Materials:

- Antique Coin
- Antique Coin
- Exquisite Lace

Challenge 3: Don't Drop the Pot

Materials:

Fancy Fabric

Fancy Fabric

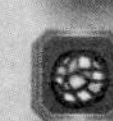
Vibrant Brooch

LEVEL 4: THE LADY'S LAIR

Sub-Weapons:

 Gripshot

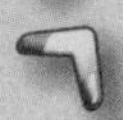 Boomerang

 Gust Jar

No-Challenge Materials:

 Royal Ring

 Royal Ring

Fancy Fabric

Challenge 1: Evade the Wallmaster

Materials:

Antique Coin

Antique Coin

Exquisite Lace

Challenge 2: Fewer Heart Containers

Materials:

Fancy Fabric

Fancy Fabric

Vibrant Brooch

Challenge 3: Only Bombs—No Swords

Materials:

Exquisite Lace

Exquisite Lace

Vibrant Brooch

World 6: The Dunes

LEVEL 1: INFINITY DUNES

Sub-Weapons:

 Water Rod

 Gust Jar

 Gust Jar

No-Challenge Materials:

 Palm Cone

 Palm Cone

 Ancient Fin

Challenge 1: Adventure in the Dark

Materials:

- Palm Cone
- Palm Cone
- Vintage Linen

Challenge 2: Guard the Orb

Materials:

- Ancient Fin
- Ancient Fin
- Gibdo Bandage

Challenge 3: Fewer Heart Containers

Materials:

- Vintage Linen
- Vintage Linen
- Stal Skull

LEVEL 2: STONE CORRIDORS

Sub-Weapons:

 Gripshot

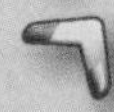 Boomerang

 Gust Jar

No-Challenge Materials:

 Palm Cone

 Palm Cone

 Vintage Linen

Challenge 1: Clear Within the Time Limit

Materials:

Ancient Fin

 Ancient Fin

 Gibdo Bandage

Challenge 2: Evade the Wallmaster

Materials:

 Vintage Linen

 Vintage Linen

 Stal Skull

Challenge 3: Don't Fall at All

Materials:

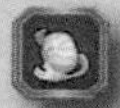 Gibdo Bandage

 Gibdo Bandage

 Sandy Ribbon

LEVEL 3: GIBDO MAUSOLEUM

Sub-Weapons:

Gripshot

 Gust Jar

 Fire Gloves

No-Challenge Materials:

Ancient Fin

 Ancient Fin

 Gibdo Bandage

Challenge 1: Clear Within the Time Limit

Materials:

Vintage Linen

Vintage Linen

Stal Skull

Challenge 2: Avoid Falling and Quicksand

Materials:

 Gibdo Bandage

 Gibdo Bandage

 Sandy Ribbon

Challenge 3: Only Bombs—No Swords

Materials:

Stal Skull

Stal Skull

Crystal Skull

LEVEL 4: DESERT TEMPLE

Sub-Weapons:

 Boomerang

 Magic Hammer

 Magic Hammer

No-Challenge Materials:

Vintage Linen

 Vintage Linen

Stal Skull

Challenge 1: Fewer Heart Containers

Materials:

Gibdo Bandage

Gibdo Bandage

 Sandy Ribbon

Challenge 2: Don't Pop Any Balloons

Materials:

- Stal Skull
- Stal Skull
- Crystal Skull

Challenge 3: Clear Within the Time Limit

Materials:

- Sandy Ribbon
- Sandy Ribbon
- Crystal Skull

World 7: The Ruins

LEVEL 1: ILLUSORY MANSION

Sub-Weapons:

- Boomerang
- Boomerang
- Boomerang

No-Challenge Materials:

- Carrumpkin
- Carrumpkin
- Mystery Extract

Challenge 1: Fewer Heart Containers

Materials:

- Carrumpkin
- Carrumpkin
- Spider Silk Lace

Challenge 2: Don't Fall at All

Materials:

- Mystery Extract
- Mystery Extract
- Poe Soul

Challenge 3: Clear Within the Time Limit

Materials:

- Spider Silk Lace
- Spider Silk Lace
- Twisted Twig

LEVEL 2: PALACE NOIR

Sub-Weapons:

 Bow

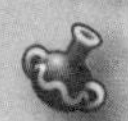 Gust Jar

 Fire Gloves

No-Challenge Materials:

- Carrumpkin
- Carrumpkin
- Spider Silk Lace

Challenge 1: Pop All Balloons

Materials:

- Mystery Extract
- Mystery Extract
- Poe Soul

Challenge 2: Halved Attack and Defense

Materials:

- Spider Silk Lace
- Spider Silk Lace
- Twisted Twig

Challenge 3: Transport the Orb Quickly

Materials:

- Poe Soul
- Poe Soul
- Lava Drop

LEVEL 3: LONE LABYRINTH

Sub-Weapons:

 Gripshot

 Gust Jar

 Fire Gloves

No-Challenge Materials:

 Mystery Extract

 Mystery Extract

 Poe Soul

Challenge 1: Don't Drop the Pot

Materials:

 Spider Silk Lace

 Spider Silk Lace

 Twisted Twig

Challenge 2: Guard the Orb

Materials:

Poe Soul

Poe Soul

Lava Drop

Challenge 3: Adventure in the Dark

Materials:

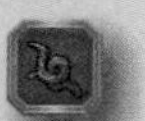 Twisted Twig

 Twisted Twig

 Sanctuary Mask

LEVEL 4: GRIM TEMPLE

Sub-Weapons:

 Gripshot

 Boomerang

 Fire Gloves

No-Challenge Materials:

 Spider Silk Lace

 Spider Silk Lace

 Twisted Twig

Challenge 1: Fewer Heart Containers

Materials:

 Poe Soul

 Poe Soul

Lava Drop

Challenge 2: Don't Fall at All

Materials:

 Twisted Twig

 Twisted Twig

 Sanctuary Mask

Challenge 3: Clear Within the Time Limit

Materials:

 Lava Drop

 Lava Drop

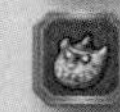 Sanctuary Mask

World 8: Sky Realm

LEVEL 1: FLOATING GARDEN

Sub-Weapons:

 Bow

 Bombs

 Gripshot

No-Challenge Materials:

- Cucco Feathers
- Cucco Feathers
- Carmine Pearl

Challenge 1: Win Without Using a Sword

Materials:

- Cucco Feathers
- Cucco Feathers
- Sky Dragon Tail

Challenge 2: Evade the Wallmaster

Materials:

 Carmine Pearl

 Carmine Pearl

 Pretty Plume

Challenge 3: Don't Fall at All

Materials:

- Sky Dragon Tail
- Sky Dragon Tail
- Mock Fairy

LEVEL 2: DECEPTION CASTLE

Sub-Weapons:

- Gripshot
- Gripshot
- Gust Jar

No-Challenge Materials:

- Cucco Feathers
- Cucco Feathers
- Sky Dragon Tail

Challenge 1: Clear Within the Time Limit

Materials:

- Carmine Pearl
- Carmine Pearl
- Pretty Plume

Challenge 2: Don't Fall at All

Materials:

- Sky Dragon Tail
- Sky Dragon Tail
- Mock Fairy

Challenge 3: Don't Pop Any Balloons

Materials:

- Pretty Plume
-  Pretty Plume
- Aurora Stone

LEVEL 3: DRAGON CITADEL

Sub-Weapons:

-  Water Rod
-  Boomerang
-  Magic Hammer

No-Challenge Materials:

-  Carmine Pearl
-  Carmine Pearl
-  Pretty Plume

Challenge 1: Avoid the Volcanic Rocks

Materials:

- Sky Dragon Tail
- Sky Dragon Tail
- Mock Fairy

Challenge 2: Halved Attack and Defense

Materials:

- Pretty Plume
- Pretty Plume
- Aurora Stone

Challenge 3: Don't Fall at All

Materials:

-  Mock Fairy
-  Mock Fairy
-  Steel Mask

LEVEL 4: SKY TEMPLE

Sub-Weapons:

All

No-Challenge Materials:

- Sky Dragon Tail
- Sky Dragon Tail
- Mock Fairy

Challenge 1: Clear Within the Time Limit

Materials:

- Pretty Plume
- Pretty Plume
- Aurora Stone

Challenge 2: Clear Without Any Items

Materials:

- Mock Fairy
- Mock Fairy
- Steel Mask

Challenge 3: Fewer Heart Containers

Materials:

- Aurora Stone
- Aurora Stone
- Steel Mask

OUTFITS

Outfits are a major part of *Tri Force Heroes*, and having the right ones for the right tasks is equally important. In order to do that you'll need to gather the proper Materials and enough Rupees to get Madame Couture to handcraft them for you.

This is My Design

The Materials are scattered around the levels and challenges in the Drablands. You'll have the chance to collect one of two possible Materials at the end of each level. You may have to try the same level multiple times to get the ones you need.

You'll find all the necessary Materials for each Outfit listed below, along with when the Outfit appears in Madame Couture's shop. Now go get yourself a new wardrobe!

Hero's Tunic

How to unlock:
Available at the start of the game.

How Many Rupees:
None

Required Materials:

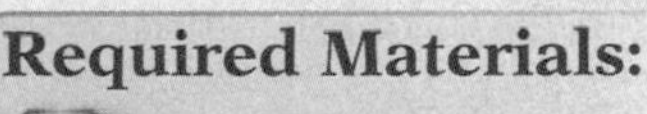

WHAT IT DOES:

They don't actually do anything, but the green tunic and tights are a staple in any potential hero's wardrobe.

Kinda Cursed Tights

How to unlock:
Available after completing world 8.

How Many Rupees:
None

Required Materials:
None

WHAT IT DOES:

This semi-cursed Outfit will have whoever's wearing it take double damage, but there is also a 50% chance that any attacks swung your way will miss entirely! Curse or blessing? You decide!

The Lady's Ensemble

How to unlock:
Available after unlocking worlds 2 through 4; you must complete the game before you can make it.

How Many Rupees:
None

Required Materials:

 Lady's Glasses

 Lady's Collar

Lady's Parasol

WHAT IT DOES:

Wearing The Lady's Ensemble will increase your Heart Containers by one for every player wearing it and you'll find Hearts with greater ease! Fabulous!

Tri Suit

How to unlock:
Available after you complete 1-1, the Deku Forest. You need to play with five different friends, then speak with the Faux-Hero to obtain the Friendly Tokens necessary for making this Outfit.

How Many Rupees:
300

Required Materials:

 Friendly Tokens x 5

WHAT IT DOES:

The abilities of this Outfit will only be activated when all three Links are wearing it. When that happens, you can expect to deal more damage, dodge 25% of attacks, and find Hearts and Rupees with greater ease!

Timeless Tunic

How to unlock:
Available after completing 1-1, the Deku Forest. You need to play with three different friends and speak with the Faux-Hero to obtain the Friendly Tokens necessary for making this Outfit.

How Many Rupees:
100

Required Materials:

 Friendly Token x 3

WHAT IT DOES:

The Timeless Tunic won't make you stronger or dodge any attacks, but it will do something so, so much cooler: It will make sound effects from the original *Legend of Zelda* as you play the game! Now you can be a true hero!

Bear Minimum

How to unlock:
Your starting Outfit.

How Many Rupees:
None

Required Materials:
None

WHAT IT DOES:

You'll start the game with this Outfit on, but believe us when we say that you're going to want to take it off as soon as possible. Wearing it will reduce your Heart Containers by one for every player wearing it and you'll also take double damage. Bear minimum indeed!

Kokiri Clothes

How to unlock:
Available at the start of the game.

How Many Rupees:
100

Required Materials:

 Blob Jelly

 Armos Spirit

WHAT IT DOES:

If you love using the Bow, this Outfit is for you! Instead of firing one shot, you'll fire three at the same time, making hitting enemies and switches a whole lot easier.

Big Bomb Outfit

How to unlock:
Available at the start of the game.

How Many Rupees:
100

Required Materials:

 Armos Spirit

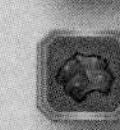 Tektite Shell

WHAT IT DOES:

The Big Bomb Outfit will turn any Bomb its wearer picks up into a giant, monster Bomb. These monster Bombs will be bigger, do double damage, and create explosions that are two to three times larger than standard Bombs. Just be careful: These Bombs make it easier to damage yourself and your friends. All in all, if you're playing a level with the Bomb Sub-Weapon or one that has a lot of Bomb Flowers, this Outfit is a must!

Legendary Dress

How to unlock:
Available at the start of the game.

How Many Rupees:
200

Required Materials:

 Tektite Shell

 Sweet Shroom

WHAT IT DOES:

This is one of the most useful Outfits in the game. Any player wearing this will have a higher chance of finding Hearts from enemies and destructible objects, like pots, grass, and rocks. There are no levels in the game where this Outfit isn't helpful. In fact, the only reason you wouldn't want to wear it is when there is an Outfit even more useful for a specific level. Make this outfit as soon as possible—you won't regret it!

Lucky Loungewear

How to unlock:
Available at the start of the game.

How Many Rupees:
200

Required Materials:

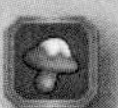 Sweet Shroom

 Blin Bling

 Gohma's Eye

WHAT IT DOES:

Any player wearing this Outfit has a 25% chance to dodge enemy attacks, perfect for accident-prone heroes! If you want to avoid attacks and make it look effortless, wear these striped PJs to your next battle!

Zora Costume

How to unlock:
Available after unlocking worlds 2 through 4.

How Many Rupees:
400

Required Materials:

 Fresh Kelp

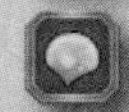 Zora Scale

WHAT IT DOES:

Water can be a real drag—always slowing you down and forcing you to swim back to shore. Well, not anymore! The Zora Costume makes being in the water not only effortless, but faster than being on land. Impress your friends as you swim around the level like Epona races around Hyrule. Wearing this in any level with large bodies of water is a near must.

Torrent Robe

How to unlock:
Available after unlocking Worlds 2 through 4.

How Many Rupees:
600

Required Materials:
 Fresh Kelp

 Hytopian Silk

 Aqua Crown

WHAT IT DOES:

Became a master of all things H_2O with the Torrent Robe. This Outfit will increase the size of your Water Rod's water platforms, making traversal so, so much easier! If there's a Water Rod in a level, you're almost always going to want to wear this ornate getup.

Jack of Hearts

How to unlock:
Available after unlocking worlds 2, 3 and 4.

How Many Rupees:
600

Required Materials:
 Hytopian Silk

 Octorok Sucker

 Fairy Dust

WHAT IT DOES:

The Jack of Hearts does one thing and one thing only: It increases your Heart Containers by one for every player wearing it. Plain and simple, cut and dry, but unquestionably useful!

Goron Garb

How to unlock:
Available after unlocking worlds 2 through 4.

How Many Rupees:
600

Required Materials:
 Goron Ore

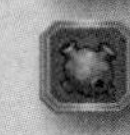 Monster Guts

WHAT IT DOES:

The Goron Garb is like the Zora Costume, but even better! You'll swim through lava like a Zora through water, but the fun doesn't stop there. Fire now no longer has any effect on you, at least while you're wearing this Outfit. Fire Keese burning you? Red Hardhat Beetles making you too afraid to swing your sword? Well, with the Goron Garb you can laugh right in their smoldering faces without fear of reproach! Any level with fire or lava is made a complete breeze with this Outfit.

Boomeranger

How to unlock:
Available after unlocking worlds 2 through 4.

How Many Rupees:
800

Required Materials:

 Goron Ore

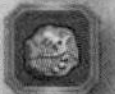 Demon Fossil

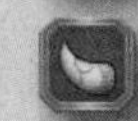 Rugged Horn

WHAT IT DOES:

The Boomeranger Outfit makes your Boomerang massive! There isn't much else to say. A massive Boomerang makes hitting enemies and grabbing teammates a whole lot easier. Simple, but effective!

Energy Gear

How to unlock:
Available after unlocking worlds 2 through 4.

How Many Rupees:
800

Required Materials:

 Monster Guts

 Demon Fossil

 Kodongo Tail

 Keese Wing

WHAT IT DOES:

This purple and yellow getup will increase your energy gauge by 50%, so you can use Sub-Weapons with little worry of running out of juice.

Cozy Parka

How to unlock:
Available after unlocking worlds 2 through 4.

How Many Rupees:
800

Required Materials:

 Fluffy Fuzz

 Serpent Fangs

WHAT IT DOES:

Slipping around on ice got you down? Tired of being frozen and left out in the cold? Then you need a Cozy Parka! With the Cozy Parka, slippery ice will be a thing of the past. Walk along frozen ice like normal solid ground and never be frozen again. Purchase yours today from Madame Couture's boutique!

Hammerwear

How to unlock:
Available after unlocking worlds 2 through 4.

How Many Rupees:
1000

Required Materials:
- Tiny Snowflake
- Crimson Shell
- Freezard Water
-  Chill Stone

WHAT IT DOES:

This familiar garb increases the radius of the Magic Hammer's shockwave, the speed at which you swing the hammer, and the amount of damage it does. If you're a fan of pounding enemies into the ground like tent poles, this is the Outfit for you.

Tingle Tights

How to unlock:
Available after unlocking worlds 2 through 4.

How Many Rupees:
1000

Required Materials:
-  Fluffy Fuzz
-  Tiny Snowflake
-  Freezard Water

WHAT IT DOES:

Tingle's an interesting fellow, as is his attire. But it would seem that it is far more than just a fascinating Outfit—his balloons actually have practical utility. While wearing the green faux-fairy's garb, you'll avoid taking damage from falling into pits and off of cliffs up to three times. Keep an eye on the number of balloons you have on your back to know just how many "free falls" you have left.

Cacto Clothes

How to unlock:
Available after unlocking worlds 2 through 4.

How Many Rupees:
1000

Required Materials:
-  Supple Leaf
-  Thornberry

WHAT IT DOES:

Attacks with thorns when foes are near. It won't hurt your friends while playing cooperatively, but while in the Coliseum, the Cacto Clothes will attack your friends with reckless abandon.

You can't earn the Materials for this Outfit anywhere else but the Coliseum, so get some friends together and do battle!

Sword Suit

How to unlock:
Available after unlocking worlds 6 and 7.

How Many Rupees:
1000

Required Materials:

- Stiff Puff
-  Silver Thread
-  Royal Ring

WHAT IT DOES:

The Sword Suit is for any heroes who love their blades above all else. If your health is full while wearing this Outfit, you will shoot out a sword beam in classic Zelda style. Now, you're probably thinking, "It's pretty hard to keep my health full, especially with two other friends! How is this suit any good?" Well, my cautious, curious friend, the Sword Suit also doubles the damage of your sword swings, making you a monster against any enemies you face in the game.

Rupee Regalia

How to unlock:
Available after unlocking world 5.

How Many Rupees:
1200

Required Materials:

- Royal Ring
- Antique Coin
- Fancy Fabric

WHAT IT DOES:

If keeping your Rupee wallet fat with currency is a struggle for you, look no further! Wearing the Rupee Regalia will cause more Rupees to drop from enemies and breakable objects, and you are more likely to find Rupees of higher values. But, that's not all! Any time Rupees appear, they'll now appear in pairs, doubling any Rupee pickups you find.

Queen of Hearts

How to unlock:
Available after unlocking world 5.

How Many Rupees:
1200

Required Materials:

-  Mystery Jade
-  Fairy Dust
-  Star Fragment
-  Exquisite Lace

WHAT IT DOES:

This lovely regalia increases your Heart Containers by three per player wearing it, making you much harder to take down in battle. Not a bad choice if you're struggling on a particularly difficult boss or level. Plus you'll look oh-so divine!

Cheetah Costume

How to unlock:
Available after unlocking world 5.

How Many Rupees:
1500

Required Materials:

 Divine Whiskers

 Beastie Patch

 Brittle Papyrus

WHAT IT DOES:

This feline ensemble won't give you nine lives, but it will turn your walking speed into running speed. Plus, it lets you talk to the cats around town! Now you can get the juiciest feline gossip and pass it around faster than anyone can keep up. Jackpot!

Dunewalker Duds

How to unlock:
Available after unlocking world 5.

How Many Rupees:
1200

Required Materials:

 Palm Cone

 Ancient Fin

 Stal Skull

WHAT IT DOES:

Like the Cozy Parka, the Dunewalker Duds turn troubling terrain into a thing of the past. If quicksand is making getting around a struggle, slap on this Outfit and you'll sink no more! Become a master of the sands with the Dunewalker Duds.

Gust Garb

How to unlock:
Available after unlocking worlds 6 and 7.

How Many Rupees:
1500

Required Materials:

 Vintage Linen

 Gibdo Bandage

 Sandy Ribbon

WHAT IT DOES:

Wearing the Gust Garb will blow your friends away—Literally! Donning this cloudy Outfit increases the distance of your Gust Jar blasts and lets you fire them faster than normal. Wear this if you're really angling to get the most out of your Gust Jar, or if you really like sending your friends flying.

Ninja Gi

How to unlock:
Available after unlocking worlds 6 and 7.

How Many Rupees:
1500

Required Materials:
- Rainbow Coral
- Ancient Fin
- Vintage Linen
- Gibdo Bandage
- Stal Skull

WHAT IT DOES:

If running is your favorite method of travel, you might want to think about wearing the Ninja Gi. Any enemy you hit with your dash attack will take triple damage, making you more than a just a stylish hero—you'll be a force of nature!

Light Armor

How to unlock:
Available after unlocking worlds 6 and 7.

How Many Rupees:
1200

Required Materials:
- Carrumpkin
- Spider Silk Lace
- Poe Soul

WHAT IT DOES:

Master all of the dark areas in the game with this outfit. While wearing the Light Armor, your visibility will increase while in dark rooms. Dahling, you're positively beaming!

Fire Blazer

How to unlock:
Available after unlocking worlds 6 and 7.

How Many Rupees:
1500

Required Materials:
- Mystery Extract
- Twisted Twig
- Lava Drop

WHAT IT DOES:

Instead of firing one measly fireball while wearing the Fire Gloves, the Fire Blazer will allow you to shoot three at a time. Muy caliente!

Serpent's Toga

How to unlock:
Available after unlocking worlds 6 and 7.

How Many Rupees:
1500

Required Materials:
- Ice Rose
- Carrumpkin
- Mystery Extract
- Poe Soul
- Twisted Twig

WHAT IT DOES:

A rolling stone gathers no moss, and a still hero takes no damage—not while wearing the Serpent's Toga anyway. Hold still with this scale suit on and you'll become a statue impervious to damage. But if you take even a single step, you'll be a mere mortal once again.

Showstopper

How to unlock:
Available after unlocking world 8.

How Many Rupees:
2000

Required Materials:
- Vibrant Brooch
- Pretty Plume
- Mock Fairy
- Aurora Stone

WHAT IT DOES:

Be a real pal when playing multiplayer and put this Outfit on! It'll draw the attention of all nearby enemies, leaving your other friends free to take them out with near zero effort. How's that for being the center of attention?

Robowear

How to unlock:
Available after unlocking world 8.

How Many Rupees:
1500

Required Materials:
- Cucco Feathers
- Carmine Pearl
- Sky Dragon Tail
- Pretty Plume

WHAT IT DOES:

Fancy yourself a cyborg, do you? Love the Gripshot, hmmm? Well then the Robowear is perfect for you! The Gripshot will fire faster, extend farther, and damage any foes it grabs. That's not all! Instead of simply stunning enemies, the Robowear makes your Gripshot pull them to you! It's the ultimate Outfit for the lazy person in us all.

Sword Master Suit

How to unlock:
Available after unlocking world 8.

How Many Rupees:
2000

Required Materials:

 Golden Insect

 Gold Dust

Fabled Butterfly

WHAT IT DOES:

You think the Sword Suit is the ultimate Outfit for cutting your foes down with your sword? Hah! You've obviously never used the Sword Master Suit. With this gold-gilded slicing 'n' dicing garb, you'll do twice as much damage with your sword than you normally would. Challenging enemies? Pushaw! Those don't exist so long as you're wearing this Outfit!

Spin Attack Attire

How to unlock:
Available after unlocking world 8.

How Many Rupees:
2000

Required Materials:

 Crystal Skull

 Sanctuary Mask

 Steel Mask

WHAT IT DOES:

Are spin attacks your favorite enemy-slashing technique? Do you want your spin attacks to be larger, stronger, and more deadly? That's good, man! That's really good! The Spin Attack Attire will both increase the radius of your spin attack and also the amount of damage you do while wearing it, so you can spin to win!

Cheer Outfit

How to unlock:
Available at the start of the game.

How Many Rupees:
100

Required Materials:

 Frilly Fabric x 3

WHAT IT DOES:

This frilly outfit inspires, energizes, and encourages your teammates, boosting their energy bars by 50%. Another team-based outfit that your friends will love you for wearing.

Dapper Spinner

How to unlock:
Available after five losses in the Daily Riches shop.

How Many Rupees:
300

Required Materials:
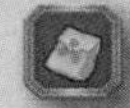
Freebie x 10

WHAT IT DOES:

Like the Spin Attack Attire, this Outfit will really get your spin game on point. Wearing the Spin Attack Attire will cause your spin attacks to do twice the amount of damage, and you'll automatically do a mini-spin attack whenever you slash your sword three times. Not bad for an Outfit that requires you to lose ten times in the Daily Riches, huh?

MATERIALS

You'll find all of the Materials in the game listed alphabetically below. We list the levels each Material can be found in by listing the world number first, then the level in that world. For example: 1-1 would be world 1 (the Woodlands) and level 1 (the Deku Forest). After that, you'll find the challenges that the Materials can be found in. No Challenge is the level without a challenge, while the other phrases are the challenge titles.

You can also earn Materials from the Daily Riches or purchase them from the Street Merchant. The Street Merchant updates his inventory daily and you can only play the Daily Riches mini-game once a day.

You can increase the Street Merchant's inventory by activating SpotPass from the Settings screen in the main menu of the game. The Street Merchant will increase his daily supply from three to five if you activate it.

If you find that you have an excess of Materials and are desperate for Rupees, you can go behind the Street Merchant's counter and talk to him directly to sell off some of your extra Materials. The amount he'll pay depends on the mood he is in. You can get a sense of his mood when you talk to him.

We suggest you check and recheck what Outfits need the Materials you have, so you don't accidentally sell off too many Materials. Trying to get them back can be a real challenge.

ANCIENT FIN

Where to find it

6-1: No Challenge, Guard the Orb

6-2: Clear Within the Time Limit

6-3: No Challenge

ANTIQUE COIN

Where to find it

5-1: Evade the Wallmaster

5-2: Win Without Using a Sword, Don't Fall at All

5-3: No Challenge, Halved Attack and Defense

5-4: Evade the Wallmaster

AQUA CROWN

Where to find it

2-1: Clear with Halved Energy

2-2: Halved Attack and Defense, Clear Within the Time Limit

2-3: No Challenge, Evade the Wallmaster

2-4: Fewer Heart Containers

ARMOS SPIRIT

Where to find it

1-1: No Challenge, Clear Within the Time Limit

1-2: Pop All Balloons

1-3: No Challenge

AURORA STONE

Where to find it

8-2: Don't Pop Any Balloons

8-3: Halved Attack and Defense

8-4: Clear Within the Time Limit, Fewer Heart Containers

BEASTIE PATCH

Where to find it

One of the prizes for winning a battle in the Ice Cavern map of the Coliseum. Can also be obtained by completing all of the Ice Cavern challenges, then speaking with King Tuft.

BLIN BLING

Where to find it

1-1: Guard the Orb

1-2: Clear Within the Time Limit

1-3: Pop All Balloons, Transport the Orb Quickly

1-4: No Challenge, Clear Within the Time Limit

BLOB JELLY

Where to find it

1-1: No Challenge, Fewer Heart Containers

1-2: No Challenge

BRITTLE PAPYRUS

Where to find it

One of the prizes for winning a battle in the Fortress map of the Coliseum. Can also be obtained by completing all of the Fortress challenges, then speaking with King Tuft.

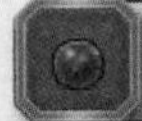

CARMINE PEARL

Where to find it

8-1: No Challenge, Evade the Wallmaster

8-2: Clear Within the Time Limit

8-3: No Challenge

CARRUMPKIN

Where to find it

7-1: No Challenge, Fewer Heart Containers

7-2: No Challenge

CHILL STONE

Where to find it

4-2: Transport the Orb Quickly

4-3: Halved Attack and Defense

4-4: Fewer Heart Containers, Transport the Orb Quickly

CRIMSON SHELL

Where to find it

4-1: Pop All Balloons

4-2: Adventure in the Dark, Transport the Orb Quickly

4-3: No Challenge, Halved Attack and Defense

4-4: Fewer Heart Containers

CRYSTAL SKULL

Where to find it

6-3: Only Bombs—No Swords

6-4: Don't Pop Any Balloons, Clear Within the Time Limit

CUCCO FEATHERS

Where to find it

8-1: No Challenge, Win Without Using a Sword

8-2: No Challenge

DEMON FOSSIL

Where to find it

3-1: Pop All Balloons, Transport the Orb Quickly

3-2: No Challenge, Pop All Balloons

3-3: Fewer Heart Containers

3-4: No Challenge

DIVINE WHISKERS

Where to find it

One of the prizes for winning a battle in the Volcano map of the Coliseum. Can also be obtained by completing all of the Volcano challenges, then speaking with King Tuft.

EXQUISITE LACE

Where to find it

5-2: Don't Fall at All

5-3: Halved Attack and Defense

5-4: Evade the Wallmaster, Only Bombs—No Swords

FABLED BUTTERFLY

Where to find it

One of the prizes for winning a battle in the Sky Realm map of the Coliseum. Can also be obtained by completing all of the Sky Realm challenges, then speaking with King Tuft.

FAIRY DUST

Where to find it

2-2: Clear Within the Time Limit

2-3: Evade the Wallmaster

2-4: Fewer Heart Containers, Transport the Orb Quickly

FANCY FABRIC

Where to find it

5-1: Halved Attack and Defense

5-2: Transport the Orb Quickly

5-3: Clear Within the Time Limit, Don't Drop the Pot

5-4: No Challenge, Fewer Heart Containers

FLUFFY FUZZ

Where to find it

4-1: No Challenge, Don't Get Hit by Snowballs

4-2: No Challenge

FREEBIE

Where to find it

Obtained from the treasure chest mini-game in town.

FREEZARD WATER

Where to find it

4-1: Guard the Orb

4-2: Fewer Heart Containers

4-3: Win Without Using a Sword, Evade the Wallmaster

4-4: No Challenge, Don't Get Hit by Snowballs

FRESH KELP

Where to find it

2-1: No Challenge, Pop All Balloons

2-2: No Challenge

FRIENDLY TOKEN

Where to find it

Obtained from the Faux-Hero in front of the castle. He'll give you one token per new player you've played with.

FRILLY FABRIC

Where to find it

Obtained from the Street Merchant. If it's not there or you've already purchased it, you'll need to wait a full day for the Street Merchant to restock his inventory.

GIBDO BANDAGE

Where to find it

6-1: Guard the Orb

6-2: Clear Within the Time Limit, Don't Fall at All

6-3: No Challenge, Avoid Falling and Quicksand

6-4: Fewer Heart Containers

GOHMA'S EYE

Where to find it

1-2: Clear Using Only Bombs

1-3: Defeat All Foes Without a Sword

1-4: Adventure in the Dark,
Fewer Heart Containers

GOLD DUST

Where to find it

One of the prizes for winning a battle in The Ruins map of the Coliseum. Can also be obtained by completing all of The Ruins challenges, then speaking with King Tuft.

GOLDEN INSECT

Where to find it

One of the prizes for winning a battle in The Dunes map of the Coliseum. Can also be obtained by completing all of The Dunes challenges, then speaking with King Tuft.

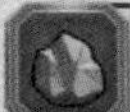

GORON ORE

Where to find it

3-1: No Challenge, Pop All Balloons

3-2: No Challenge

HYTOPIAN SILK

Where to find it

2-1: Pop All Balloons, Evade the Wallmaster

2-2: Guard the Orb

2-3: Halved Attack and Defense

2-4: No Challenge

ICE ROSE

Where to find it

4-3: Evade the Wallmaster

4-4: Don't Get Hit By Snowballs, Transport the Orb Quickly

KEESE WING

Where to find it

3-2: Don't Pop Any Balloons

3-3: Avoid the Volcanic Rocks

3-4: Clear Within the Time Limit, Only Bombs—No Swords

KODONGO TAIL

Where to find it

3-1: Transport the Orb Quickly

3-2: Pop All Balloons

3-3: Fewer Heart Containers, Clear Within the Time Limit

3-4: No Challenge, Evade the Wallmaster

LADY'S COLLAR

Where to find it

5-4: This will always appear as a second reward the first time you complete The Lady's Lair.

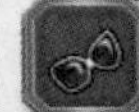

LADY'S GLASSES

Where to find it

1-4: This will always appear as a second reward the first time you complete the Forest Temple.

LADY'S PARASOL

Where to find it

8-4: This will always appear as a second reward the first time you complete the Sky Temple.

LAVA DROP

Where to find it

7-2: Transport the Orb Quickly

7-3: Guard the Orb

7-4: Fewer Heart Containers, Clear Within the Time Limit

MOCK FAIRY

Where to find it

8-1: Don't Fall at All

8-2: Don't Fall at All

8-3: Avoid the Volcanic Rocks, Don't Fall at All

8-4: No Challenge, Clear Without Any Items

MONSTER GUTS

Where to find it

3-1: No Challenge, Evade the Wallmaster

3-2: Clear Within the Time Limit

3-3: No Challenge

MYSTERY EXTRACT

Where to find it

7-1: No Challenge, Don't Fall at All

7-2: Pop All Balloons

7-3: No Challenge

MYSTERY JADE

Where to find it

1-3: Transport the Orb Quickly

1-4: Clear Within the Time Limit, Fewer Heart Containers

OCTOROK SUCKER

Where to find it

2-1: Evade the Wallmaster

2-2: Guard the Orb

2-3: Halved Attack and Defense, Clear Within the Time Limit

2-4: No Challenge, Clear with Halved Energy

PALM CONE

Where to find it

6-1: No Challenge, Adventure in the Dark

6-2: No Challenge

POE SOUL

Where to find it

7-1: Don't Fall at All

7-2: Pop All Balloons, Transport the Orb Quickly

7-3: No Challenge, Guard the Orb

7-4: Fewer Heart Containers

PRETTY PLUME

Where to find it

8-1: Evade the Wallmaster

8-2: Clear Within the Time Limit, Don't Pop Any Balloons

8-3: No Challenge, Halved Attack and Defense

8-4: Clear Within the Time Limit

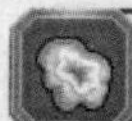

RAINBOW CORAL

Where to find it

2-3: Clear Within the Time Limit

2-4: Clear with Halved Energy, Transport the Orb Quickly

ROYAL RING

Where to find it

5-1: Don't Drop the Pot, Halved Attack and Defense

5-2: No Challenge, Transport the Orb Quickly

5-3: Clear Within the Time Limit

5-4: No Challenge

RUGGED HORN

Where to find it

3-1: Evade the Wallmaster

3-2: Clear Within the Time Limit, Don't Pop Any Balloons

3-3: No Challenge, Avoid the Volcanic Rocks

3-4: Clear Within the Time Limit

SANCTUARY MASK

Where to find it

7-3: Adventure in the Dark

7-4: Don't Fall at All, Clear Within the Time Limit

SANDY RIBBON

Where to find it

6-2: Don't Fall at All

6-3: Avoid Falling and Quicksand

6-4: Fewer Heart Containers, Clear Within the Time Limit

SERPENT FANGS

Where to find it

4-1: Don't Get Hit by Snowballs, Guard the Orb

4-2: No Challenge, Fewer Heart Containers

4-3: Win Without Using a Sword

4-4: No Challenge

SILVER THREAD

Where to find it

5-1: No Challenge, Evade the Wallmaster

5-2: Win Without Using a Sword

5-3: No Challenge

SKY DRAGON TAIL

Where to find it

8-1: Win Without Using a Sword, Don't Fall at All

8-2: No Challenge, Don't Fall at All

8-3: Avoid the Volcanic Rocks

8-4: No Challenge

SPIDER SILK LACE

Where to find it

7-1: Fewer Heart Containers, Clear Within the Time Limit

7-2: No Challenge, Halved Attack and Defense

7-3: Don't Drop the Pot

7-4: No Challenge

STAL SKULL

Where to find it

6-1: Fewer Heart Containers

6-2: Evade the Wallmaster

6-3: Clear Within the Time Limit, Only Bombs—No Swords

6-4: No Challenge, Don't Pop Any Balloons

STAR FRAGMENT

Where to find it

3-3: Clear Within the Time Limit

3-4: Evade the Wallmaster, Only Bombs—No Swords

STEEL MASK

Where to find it

8-3: Don't Fall at All

8-4: Clear Without Any Items, Fewer Heart Containers

STIFF PUFF

Where to find it

5-1: No Challenge, Don't Drop the Pot

5-2: No Challenge

SUPPLE LEAF

Where to find it

One of the prizes for winning a battle in the Woodlands map of the Coliseum. Can also be obtained by completing all of the Woodlands challenges, then speaking with King Tuft.

SWEET SHROOM

Where to find it

1-1: Clear Within the Time Limit

1-2: Pop All Balloons, Clear Using Only Bombs

1-3: No Challenge, Defeat All Foes Without a Sword

1-4: Adventure in the Dark

TEKTITE SHELL

Where to find it

1-1: Fewer Heart Containers, Guard the Orb

1-2: No Challenge, Clear Within the Time Limit

1-3: Pop All Balloons

1-4: No Challenge

THORNBERRY

Where to find it

One of the prizes for winning a battle in the Riverside map of the Coliseum. Can also be obtained by completing all of the Riverside challenges, then speaking with King Tuft.

TINY SNOWFLAKE

Where to find it

4-1: No Challenge, Pop All Balloons

4-2: Adventure in the Dark

4-3: No Challenge

TWISTED TWIG

Where to find it

7-1: Clear Within the Time Limit

7-2: Halved Attack and Defense

7-3: Don't Drop the Pot, Adventure in the Dark

7-4: No Challenge, Don't Fall at All

VIBRANT BROOCH

Where to find it

5-3: Don't Drop the Pot

5-4: Fewer Heart Containers, Only Bombs—No Swords

VINTAGE LINEN

Where to find it

6-1: Adventure in the Dark, Fewer Heart Containers

6-2: No Challenge, Evade the Wallmaster

6-3: Clear Within the Time Limit

6-4: No Challenge

ZORA SCALE

Where to find it

2-1: No Challenge, Clear with Halved Energy

2-2: Halved Attack and Defense

2-3: No Challenge

COLISEUM

If you find yourself getting worn out on all of this cooperative play, you can head to the Coliseum on the right side of the castle foyer and have yourself a brawl with one or two other players.

Each Coliseum stage reflects a world from the main story mode. You'll find Sub-Weapons that reflect the ones you'd find in those worlds, and you'll also find hazards that fit that environment.

Playing in the Coliseum is fun, but you can also get real rewards for playing in it. There are some Materials that can only be obtained one of two ways: Completing all of the challenges in a world, or by winning in the Coliseum. If you don't want to wait to complete the challenges, or if they're giving you a hard time, you can enter the Coliseum to battle friends or people on the internet for a chance at winning those rare Materials. On top of that, each fight will earn you a few Rupees. You only have a 20% chance to earn the rare Material in each stage, so make sure to play each level until you land it!

Wallmaster

If you only have one other player to fight against in the Coliseum, you'll have to tangle with a deadly, obnoxious Wallmaster. The disembodied hand will choose a victim and then float over their head. It will slap its hand down, immediately KO'ing anyone it smashes, then it will rotate to the next player.

You can get the Wallmaster off of you by jumping off of a ledge. You'll lose a Heart, but the Wallmaster's focus will shift to your opponent, giving you some breathing room. You can also use the Wallmaster to smash your opponent if you're crafty, but it's a pretty tough trick to pull off.

Make sure to take some time to play in the Coliseum, if for no other reason than to get a hold of the Materials. You'll be glad you did, we promise.

WOODLANDS

Sub-Weapons

 Bow

 Bow

 Bombs

Rare Material

 Supple Leaf 20%

RIVERSIDE

Sub-Weapons

 Water Rod

 Water Rod

 Gripshot

Rare Material

 Thornberry 20%

VOLCANO

Sub-Weapons

 Boomerang

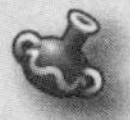 Gust Jar

Boomerang

Rare Material

 Divine Whiskers 20%

ICE CAVERN

Sub-Weapons

 Fire Gloves

 Fire Gloves

 Magic Hammer

Rare Material

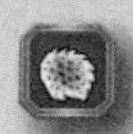 Beastie Patch 20%

FORTRESS

Sub-Weapons

 Gripshot

 Gust Jar

 Fire Gloves

Rare Material

Brittle Papyrus 20%

THE DUNES

Sub-Weapons

None

Rare Material

 Golden Insect 20%

THE RUINS

Sub-Weapons

All

Rare Material

 Gold Dust 20%

SKY REALM

Sub-Weapons

None

Rare Material

 Fabled Butterfly 20%

Written by Garitt Rocha

DK/Prima Games, a division of Penguin Random House LLC
6081 East 82nd Street, Suite #400
Indianapolis, IN 46250

Standard Edition ISBN: 978-0-7440-1668-0

Collector's Edition ISBN: 978-0-7440-1669-7

Printing Code: The rightmost double-digit number is the year of the book's printing; the rightmost single-digit number is the number of the book's printing. For example, 15-1 shows that the first printing of the book occurred in 2015.

18 17 16 15 4 3 2 1

Printed in the USA.

CREDITS

Project Manager
Jesse Anderson

Book Designer
Brent Gann

Production Designer
Justin Lucas

Production
Angela Graef

Copy Editor
Julia Mascardo

PRIMA GAMES STAFF

VP & Publisher
Mike Degler

Editorial Manager
Tim Fitzpatrick

Design and Layout Manager
Tracy Wehmeyer

Licensing
Christian Sumner
Paul Giacomotto

Marketing
Katie Hemlock

Digital Publishing
Julie Asbury
Tim Cox
Shaida Boroumand

Operations Manager
Stacey Beheler

ACKNOWLEDGMENTS

Prima Games would like to thank Pat Wells, Kanani Kemp, Emiko Ohmori, Taylor "TayTay" Stockton, Yoriko Marusich, Chiko Bird, Ali Rapp, Audrey Drake, Daniel Orihuela and Jeremy Pack for their help and support.